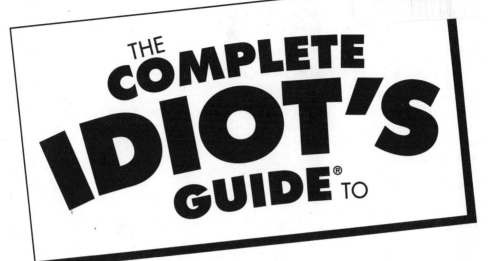

World War II

by Mitchell G. Bard, Ph.D.

alpha
books

A Division of Macmillan General Reference
A Simon & Schuster Macmillan Company
1633 Broadway, New York, NY 10019-6785

This book is dedicated to my wife and fellow idiot, Marcela Kogan, whose dedication to her work and family is an inspiration, and to my children, Ariel and Daniel, who I hope will forgive their parents for working too much.

Copyright ©1999 by Mitchell G. Bard

THE COMPLETE IDIOT'S GUIDE TO & Design is a registered trademark of Prentice-Hall, Inc.

Macmillan Publishing books may be purchased for business or sales promotional use. For information please write: Special Markets Department, Macmillan Publishing USA, 1633 Broadway, New York, NY 10019.

International Standard Book Number: 0-02862735-0
Library of Congress Catalog Card Number: 98-87597

00 99 98   8 7 6 5 4 3 2 1

Interpretation of the printing code: the rightmost number of the first series of numbers is the year of the book's printing; the rightmost number of the second series of numbers is the number of the book's printing. For example, a printing code of 98-1 shows that the first printing occurred in 1998.

Printed in the United States of America

Note: This publication contains the opinions and ideas of its author. It is intended to provide helpful and informative material on the subject matter covered. It is sold with the understanding that the author and publisher are not engaged in rendering professional services in the book. If the reader requires personal assistance or advice, a competent professional should be consulted.

The author and publisher specifically disclaim any responsibility for any liability, loss or risk, personal or otherwise, which is incurred as a consequence, directly or indirectly, of the use and application of any of the contents of this book.

Alpha Development Team

Publisher
Kathy Nebenhaus

Editorial Director
Gary M. Krebs

Managing Editor
Bob Shuman

Marketing Brand Manager
Felice Primeau

Senior Editor
Nancy Mikhail

Development Editors
Phil Kitchel
Amy Zavatto

Assistant Editor
Maureen Horn

Production Team

Production Editor
Carol Sheehan

Copy Editor
Heather Stith

Cover Designer
Mike Freeland

Illustrator
Jody P. Schaeffer

Designer
Nathan Clement

Indexer
Cheryl A. Jackson

Layout/Proofreading
Angela Calvert
Mary Hunt
Julie Trippetti

Contents at a Glance

Contents

Part 5: Let Freedom Ring   **239**

19 Invasion!   **241**

20 For You the War Is Over   **257**

21 Hitler Cheats Death   **273**

25 Liberators, Rescuers, and Avengers   335

26 Freedom's Heavy Price   351

Appendices

Foreword

I was born during World War II. I heard a lot about that war while growing up. For my generation, it was *the* war. At age 20, thanks to the draft, I was a soldier in Korea, and our sergeants who had been in World War II and Korea had no doubt which war was *the* war.

Fast-forward to 1991. NBC has me on the payroll doing color commentary for their Gulf War coverage. One of the older producers casually mentions that she came across a recently hired (right out of college) staffer who had never heard of World War II. The kid was working on the Madonna desk, so what did it matter? I was bemused.

I've been creating books and magazines on historical subjects for over 30 years, so I've kept track of reader preferences. I've seen World War II fade into that vast area of vague memories and casual indifference called "way back then." But many of the participants are still with us. And we are still suffering the effects of that war, which will continue for a while.

In fact, World War II was a series of wars, some of them still going on. Especially in Africa and Asia, armed disputes that flared up during World War II are still lingering on, the outcome still in doubt. While Germany has finally made peace with its neighbors, Japan has not. Or, rather, the Asian nations that suffered Japan's conquest still believe many issues are unresolved.

This book is something very rare: An easy read that leaves you well-informed about the war. It's a first-class treatment of the defining event of the 20th century. I once had to do a 1,000-word summary of World War II for an encyclopedia and can appreciate how hard it is to do in a few words.

The most important lesson of World War II is that something like it will happen again. Wars on the scale of World War II are nothing new. The Mongols waged a multigeneration war of conquest in the 13th century that killed a tenth of the planet's population. Several other major wars took place before World War II. No more major wars in the offing? Think again. Until the last century, no one expected the Germans to turn into world-class soldiers. Now we have many in the Islamic world urging a world-class conflict. China grows stronger, determined to make its mark in the world. Russia could revert to a military dictatorship.

Remember, the only way to stop the next world war is to understand how the last one started, was fought, and ended. Read on, and save the planet.

—Jim Dunnigan

James F. Dunnigan, author of dozens of books on military affairs and over a hundred war games, is a consultant for *NBC News* and advises governments and military organizations worldwide. His day job has nothing to do with military matters.

Introduction

World War II was the most destructive human endeavor in history. Battles were fought on every continent and involved more than 60 countries, affecting roughly three-quarters of the world's population. At least 57 million people were killed, more than half of them civilians.

Everything about the war was on a grand scale. The villains, from Adolf Hitler to Adolf Eichmann, were more evil than most. The feats of heroism of people such as Audie Murphy, Raoul Wallenberg, and the men who raised the American flag on Iwo Jima were truly extraordinary. The atrocities, from the Rape of Nanking to the Malmédy Massacre to the death camps, were more heinous than the crimes in any other wars. The destruction, from the firebombing of Dresden to the razing of Warsaw to the incineration of Hiroshima, was more devastating than in any conflict before or since.

It's no wonder that World War II is the subject of hundreds of books and movies. The fascination with the war is also reflected in the popularity of both, with several books hitting the bestseller lists and films topping the box office charts and winning Oscars. Still, a mere half century since the end of the war, the memory of the conflict is fading fast. The generation that fought for our freedom, witnessed the horrors of the Holocaust, and influenced our history will soon be gone, and we will have to rely on the evidence they left behind.

For those of us who grew up in the Vietnam era or later, it is hard to conceive of a time when Americans willingly went to war and truly believed they were fighting for democracy and against evil. Not everyone was anxious to go to war, but the majority did not try to avoid service. Some of America's peacetime heroes, such as baseball's Ted Williams and Hollywood's Jimmy Stewart, volunteered at the height of their civilian careers to be a part of the war effort.

Like every war, controversy also surrounds World War II. Historians disagree on the causes of the war. People debate whether the Holocaust could have been prevented. A national brouhaha erupted recently over an exhibition of the *Enola Gay*, the plane that dropped the atomic bomb, and whether the accompanying text should present evidence that the United States did not have to drop the bomb to defeat Japan and emphasize the destruction the bomb caused. Veterans' groups wanted more of the focus to be on the lives the bomb likely saved by quickly ending the war and the death and destruction caused by the Japanese, which prompted the use of the bomb.

The Complete Idiot's Guide to World War II will take you from the depths of the ocean in Hitler's submarine wolf packs to the skies above England, from the deserts of Egypt to the Hawaiian Islands, from the horrors of the gas chambers to the euphoria of V-E Day, and from the Manhattan Project to Operation Overlord. We'll meet the famous and infamous characters of WWII.

This book cannot possibly cover every aspect of the war, but it will give you a good summary of what happened and why. Most general histories of the war do not spend much time on the treatment of prisoners of war or the Holocaust, but separate chapters on each are included here because those subjects are crucial to understanding the impact the war had on the lives of civilians and soldiers.

Part 1, "Dark Clouds Form Over Europe," explores the causes of World War II and offers background on the men responsible for the conflict. The slow descent into war is chronicled, as is the Allies' mistaken belief that Hitler could be appeased.

Part 2, "*Blitzkrieg,*" documents how Germany quickly overran most of Europe and took control of the Atlantic with its submarine wolf packs. Only the British succeed in beating back Hitler's offensive, but only after the United States begins to provide vital supplies. Hitler's Italian ally, Benito Mussolini, meanwhile makes his own bid for a North African empire.

Part 3, "The Yanks Are Coming!," shows how the United States was shocked out of its isolationist shell by Japan's surprise attack on Pearl Harbor. Once the United States is in the war, it begins to reverse Japanese gains in the Pacific, while Hitler becomes bogged down on the eastern front by the Russian winter.

Part 4, "Allies Kick Axis," discusses the bloody combat in the Pacific, where the Japanese fought to the last man on even the smallest islands. The Soviets begin their counterattack against the German forces while the Allies drive the Axis out of North Africa.

Part 5, "Let Freedom Ring," shows how the Allies finally won the war. In Europe, a massive invasion lands at Normandy on D day, and the Western Allies and Red Army meet in Berlin. In the Pacific, the United States battles its way within bombing range of Japan and then drops the atomic bomb, which is so devastating that Japan surrenders. This section also documents the fate of many POWs.

Part 6, "The Smoke Clears, and the Reckoning Begins," gives an accounting of the material and human costs of the war. This part includes a discussion of the Holocaust and subsequent war crimes trials, as well as a look at the postwar world and the prospects for World War III.

Extras

In addition to the narrative, maps, and photographs, this book provides a number of sidebars to add some facts and trivia to the basic history.

War Lore

Some interesting aspects of the war do not always fit well into the main text and will appear in these longer sidebars. This feature will also include trivia about the war and stories that you may not have heard.

Roll Call

Statistics that do not appear in the main text will be set aside for emphasis here.

Ask the General

This feature offers some tips on how to better understand different aspects of the war.

GI Jargon

You may not be familiar with all the terms used in the book, so I've defined many of them for you right in the text. A glossary at the end of the book includes all of the words from these sidebars.

Words of War

These sidebars collect quotations from famous figures in the war.

Acknowledgments

I would like to thank Gary Krebs for giving me the opportunity to work on this project and expand my horizons from the academic to the idiotic (so to speak). I'd also like to thank Phil Kitchel for his diligence in editing the manuscript; Sue Moseson for tracking down the maps; Do You Graphics for delivering as promised on the photographs for the book; Lauren Levy for her assistance with various research tasks; production editor Carol Sheehan for putting all the elements together quickly and efficiently; copy editor Heather Stith for helping to make my prose more closely approximate the English language; and the technical editor, Williamson Murray, for making sure I got the players and the outcome of the war right.

Finally, I want to thank everyone, especially my family, for helping out when my arm was in a cast.

Part 1
Dark Clouds Form Over Europe

This section looks at the causes of World War II and the men who were most responsible for the most destructive conflict in world history. Hitler's rise to power is traced, and his decisions to annex Austria and the Sudetenland are covered. Spain breaks into civil war, while the Japanese and Italians try to build empires in Asia and Africa. The Allies appease Hitler at Munich and slowly realize their mistake. The United States, meanwhile, tries to pretend the events in Europe have nothing to do with America.

Chapter 1

Past Is Prologue

In This Chapter

➤ Learning from history

➤ The cast of characters

➤ From sea to bloody sea

➤ War gets more dangerous

➤ Humanity at its best and worst

The study of the past is often divided into ancient and modern history (beginning around the 15th century and the Reformation). If you're like me, yesterday seems like a distant memory. It is therefore not surprising that fewer and fewer people remember World War II, which has now been over for more than half a century. Yet this war was one of the most significant and cataclysmic events of world history, one whose ramifications continue to affect our lives. It is important to remember the war not just because of what it means for us today, but also because the heroes and victims of that war deserve the honor of having their sacrifices for freedom venerated.

We also need to remember the war because the witnesses who can tell us firsthand what happened and what those terrible times were like will soon all be gone. The decision-makers—Hitler, Mussolini, Tojo, Stalin, Churchill, Roosevelt, Truman—are already dead. The perpetrators, bystanders, and rescuers are aging. Old soldiers and *Holocaust* survivors still get together for reunions, but these people are among the few groups that remain united by their wartime experiences.

Those Who Repeat the Past

Another important reason to study World War II is to avoid repeating the mistakes of the past and allowing the world once again to be engulfed in war. The stakes of renewed global conflict have never been higher.

Even as late as the Second World War, the worst-case scenario (to use military parlance) was a reshuffling of political powers, shifts in borders, and great loss of life. One of the consequences of that conflict was to produce weapons so powerful that no one may be left standing at the end of a third world war.

GI Jargon

From a Greek word meaning "entire burnt offering," the term **Holocaust** refers to the Nazi policy of exterminating the Jewish people during World War II.

Even now it is difficult to fully comprehend the enormity of World War II, by far the most destructive human endeavor in history. Battles were fought on every continent and involved more than 60 countries, affecting roughly three-quarters of the world's population. The casualty figures are staggering (see Appendix A): More than 57 million people were killed, and more than half of these people were civilians. The Soviet Union alone suffered the loss of more than 30 million people. By comparison, American casualties totaled well over 300,000.

Troops advancing in France during World War I. (National Archives Still Pictures Branch)

A Different Kind of Boom

The challenges of the 1940s shaped the lives of many people, sometimes in very positive ways. War heroes such as John Kennedy and Dwight Eisenhower would go on to become presidents, celebrities such as Jimmy Stewart became unexpected war heroes, and decorated soldiers such as Audie Murphy found celebrity in Hollywood.

Society changed in fundamental ways as a result of the war. Though it would take another two decades for the liberation movement to take off, women played a vital role in the war effort, and many worked while their husbands fought. Some women participated more directly in the Women's Army Corps (WACs) and as nurses at home and abroad.

The war also helped bring the United States and the rest of the world out of the Great Depression of the '30s and stimulate an unprecedented period of economic growth. By the end, the United States was the greatest power on earth, the strongest nation that had ever existed. Returning soldiers soon made up for lost time with their families and stimulated a different kind of growth by reproducing at a rate that came to be known as the baby boom.

Words of War

"Those who cannot remember the past are condemned to repeat it."

—George Santayana

Roll Call

World War II casualties totaled more than 57 million people. More than 80 percent of this total came from four countries: the Soviet Union, China, Germany, and Poland.

Sadly, the Second World War did not turn out to be the war that ended all wars any more than the first, but it did herald a period of relative global stability that has lasted for the remainder of the century.

Black Hats, White Hats, and Stalin

World War II did not involve a lot of ambiguity. It was clear who the aggressors and victims were. Adolf Hitler was a monster. From the beginning of his political career, he spoke of his plan to exterminate the Jews. Though perhaps less obvious at first, it was soon also clear Hitler aspired to global domination. He ruled with an iron fist, using intimidation and terror to ensure loyalty. He didn't even trust his closest advisers completely. This lack of faith led him to give orders to his generals that were often disastrous. He did not tolerate opposition, however, and the military goose-stepped to the *Führer's* wishes.

Hitler's grip on Germany through terror, charisma, and the force of his will did not diminish even as the outcome of the war became clear to the German people. Hitler's influence on the world, through the cult of personality and the popularity of his racist and anti-Semitic ideology, continues to the present. Neo-Nazis are a small, but nefarious, influence in Germany and, to a lesser extent, in the United States.

Hitler's model in many ways was the Italian fascist, Benito Mussolini, a feckless individual who also ruled through the use of gangsters and thugs. Italy did not have the military or economic resources to be a dominant power, but Mussolini led Italy into campaigns in North Africa and the Mediterranean that succeeded only briefly before turning into humiliations. These misadventures inadvertently proved invaluable to the Allies, forcing Hitler to divert his scarce resources to fight on fronts that were not essential to his objectives of conquering the Soviet Union and Western Europe.

Japanese Emperor Hirohito did not serve the same wartime role as the other Axis leaders. He certainly supported the prosecution of the war, but nationalists in the government, first among them General Hideki Tojo, were the driving force behind Japanese strategy and ambition. The Japanese had their own grand ambition: to control most, if not all, of Asia and the Pacific. The Japanese, like the Germans, held a belief in their own racial superiority, which led them to massacre thousands of Chinese and Filipino civilians and abuse and murder American POWs.

Hitler dreamed of conquest for its own sake and sought to rid the world of racial impurity (notably Jews) and populate it with the Aryan race. To a lesser extent, he wanted to provide "living room" for his people. The Japanese to a larger degree needed living room beyond their small islands, and definitely required reliable sources of vital supplies. One other major difference, however, was that Germany started out with significant resources with which to build its conquering army, whereas Japan had comparatively little in the way of economic and natural resources.

Ask the General

The Nazi Party is outlawed in Germany, though politicians with Nazi sympathies have run in German elections and won significant numbers (around five percent) of votes. More alarming is the violence, particularly toward foreigners, by German extremists. The United States may have more neo-Nazis than any other country (which is still a small number), because constitutional guarantees allow neo-Nazis to organize, hold rallies, and spread propaganda. The United States is now the main source of anti-Semitic and Nazi material.

On the Allied side, the British recognized early on that they would be targets themselves of Hitler's imperial ambitions and would have to make a stand somewhere, preferably before coming directly under attack. Even the much-reviled Neville Chamberlain eventually came to the conclusion that Hitler could not be appeased.

Chamberlain's successor, Winston Churchill, became a dominant figure during the war. Though he did not interfere in the conduct of the fighting the way Hitler did, he was deeply involved in the strategy and policy. More than anything else, perhaps, Churchill provided the true stiff upper lip the country needed when the British started to quaver. His reward for successfully prosecuting the war and inspiring the nation was to be voted out of office before the postwar era began.

Long before the war began, Franklin Roosevelt was the dominant figure in American politics. He presided over a nation mired in the Depression, which responded to its victory in World War I by withdrawing again from world affairs. This isolationism contributed to the failure to stop Hitler's aggression at an early stage; Americans were simply too caught up with their own domestic troubles and were determined to stay out of other people's fights.

After the war began, Roosevelt slowly dragged his country into more open support for its Allies in Europe; however, he was still reluctant to commit the nation to fight. He was certainly under no domestic pressure to enter the war; if anything, the opposite was true. The United States might have sat out the war had Japan been content to grab a few of the Pacific islands rather than attempt to destroy the United States Navy. The attack on Pearl Harbor, however, ended all debate and prompted the greatest mobilization of men, women, and resources in history. Once awakened, the United States has since remained in the forefront of world affairs.

The last of the major players in World War II did not start out wearing either a white or black hat. Joseph Stalin was no democrat—he'd already had a bloodstained career as a communist revolutionary turned dictator. In fact, the Western powers had an interest in seeing the Soviet Union defeated in battle until it became clear that Hitler was the greater immediate danger. When the war began, Stalin conspired with Hitler to dismantle Poland and invaded Finland, actions that made him seem no less threatening than the *Führer*. Stalin became an asset to the Allies only when Hitler turned on him, and the Allies saw the Red Army as having a valuable role in at least tying down Hitler's troops, if not outright defeating them.

In the end, the Red Army did defeat the Germans on the eastern front, but it could never have done so without massive amounts of aid from Britain and the United States. Stalin, however, rarely reciprocated by cooperating logistically or sharing information. His willingness to help was restricted primarily to launching a major offensive after D day to prevent Hitler from shifting forces to reinforce the western front (and, more importantly for Stalin, to position the Red Army for the kill), and to attacking Japan after Germany surrendered.

Stalin, like Hitler, ran his country and government by means of terror and allowed no dissent. He, too, became intimately involved in the direction of military operations, though he was far more willing to listen to his military advisers. He was, however, equally willing to sack, and often execute, those whom he considered disloyal or derelict in their duty.

On May 30, 1945, a bugler blows taps at the close of the Memorial Day service at Margraten Cemetery, Netherlands, where thousands of American heroes of World War II lie. (National Archives Still Pictures Branch)

By the end of the war, Stalin's deviousness became apparent. He refused to fulfill promises regarding Polish independence and quickly annexed many of the territories the Red Army had overrun. Even the low level of cooperation that kept the Allies together in the fight against Hitler dissipated when the common enemy was gone. Within five years, the Soviet Union would replace Germany as the greatest threat to Europe and, ultimately, the world. Stalin would prove again that he was Hitler's equal in the ruthless way he dealt with his enemies.

The Front Lines

Hitler was correct in recognizing that Germany was defeated in World War I in large measure because it had strung its forces across multiple fronts that diluted their strength. He promised to focus on only one front. Events and his own myopia got in the way of the conduct of the war, however, and Hitler ended up repeating the mistake of his predecessor.

Germany began the war by rapidly overwhelming the inferior forces in Europe. Hitler's expectation was that he could then defeat Great Britain and turn his full attention to his primary target, the Soviet Union. He did not reckon the British resistance would be so fierce that he would have to abandon his hopes of forcing the British to quit. Instead of remaining focused on defeating Britain, however, he invaded Russia and left himself vulnerable to ongoing attacks from the British, who increasingly brought the war home to the German people through highly destructive bombing raids.

Hitler was further undermined by his ally, Mussolini, whose own grandiose ideas of empire led to a series of battles in North Africa and the Mediterranean. Rather than leave the Italians to their fate, Hitler felt compelled to come to their rescue and had to divert a significant portion of his resources to prevent the destruction of Mussolini's forces. In the end, after the Americans joined the fighting, helping the Italians proved impossible. It also fatally weakened Hitler's ability to overcome the tremendous human and material resources the Soviets ultimately fielded against him.

The other fronts were in Asia and the Pacific where the Americans were, for the most part, fighting alone to recover the territories the Japanese had captured almost overnight in December 1941 and early 1942. Here it was the Americans whose strength was diluted by having to also fight in Europe. Still, the superior firepower of the United States would prove decisive.

War Is Hell

It was difficult to believe that conflict could become any bloodier than the trench warfare of World War I, but war brings out a morbid form of innovation—ever more lethal means of killing the enemy. Weapons evolve from rock to arrow to sword to musket to howitzer. Soldiers progress from fighting on foot to charging on horseback to driving a tank to piloting a stealth bomber. Occasionally some good comes from the development of these weapons, perhaps the most dramatic case being the benefits associated with splitting the atom, but the cost in lives is usually high.

World War II certainly brought its share of technical innovation to the battlefield. Weapons that already existed, from guns to airplanes, were dramatically improved. The development of the atom bomb was, of course, the most significant new weapon, but there were others, such as the V-2 rockets that presaged today's ballistic missiles.

Besides making the killing business more efficient, the biggest change ushered in during the 1940s was to make the enemy anonymous. In prior wars, the combatants were face to face or close to it. This

Ask the General

Poison gas was first used in World War I to break the trench warfare stalemate. Though all the powers had chemical weapons, only Japan (in China) and Italy (in Ethiopia) used them during World War II.

began to change in World War I, when poison gas and artillery fire could kill and maim from a distance.

The separation of combat from combatants grew with the development of rockets, longer-range artillery, heavy bombers, and the growth of submarine fleets. The advancements in flight, in particular, freed soldiers—and their commanders—from the hesitancy to attack that they might show in direct combat. A bombardier sees only a distant speck where his payload will land, not the faces of the soldiers—or women and children—it might land on. Technology has advanced today to the point where war can be fought almost by remote control, with "smart bombs" and cruise missiles that can find their targets even when dropped or launched from distant bases.

Dante's Soldiers

The human mind can create ingenious tools of destruction, but it is the human heart—or perhaps the absence of one—that often leads to unspeakable crimes against humanity. Every war is marked by atrocities that go beyond even the horrors of the battlefield. World War II was exceptional in this regard. The Holocaust was, of course, the worst example of that war's crimes, but the list of atrocities against civilians and POWs is also long. Prisoners of war, for example, were murdered at Malmedy, on the Bataan Death March, and after the "Great Escape." The Nazis' euthanasia program murdered tens of thousands of the mentally ill, the disabled, and the elderly. Gays, Gypsies, and Jehovah's Witnesses were among the groups that were ground to dust by the machinery of the "Final Solution" created to exterminate the Jews.

One of the oft-noted ironies is that Germany was viewed as a particularly civilized nation. It has been said that a Nazi could send women and children to the ovens during the day and then come home to his family and read Göethe and Schiller while listening to Mozart. The Nazis used German art, music, and sport to advance their agenda. For example, the music of the rabidly anti-Semitic composer Richard Wagner was glorified, and gifted documentary filmmaker Leni Riefenstahl used her skills to deify Hitler. Riefenstahl's brilliant work of propaganda, *Triumph of the Will*, begins:

Roll Call

In 1939, the Nazis began a "euthanasia" program in which approximately 80,000 to 100,000 Germans who were disabled, mentally retarded, or insane were murdered.

September 5, 1934. Twenty years after the outbreak of the World War, 16 years after Germany's crucifixion, 19 months after the commencement of the German renaissance, Adolf Hitler flew to Nuremberg again to review a column of his faithful adherents.

The 1936 Berlin Olympic Games were used by Hitler to showcase the new Germany and demonstrate the superiority of the racially pure Aryans. That plan went awry when African-American Jesse Owens won an unprecedented four gold medals.

The Allies' Skeletons

It is easy to demonize the Axis, but it is still important to note the failings of the democracies. Although historians still debate the extent to which the Allies could have prevented the Holocaust, many of their other failures are unequivocal.

As you will see in the next chapters, countries such as France (in particular) were not much more trustworthy than Hitler when it came to fulfilling their treaty obligations. Great Britain barred the gates of Palestine to Jews fleeing the Nazis. American anti-Semitism and xenophobia played a role in the adoption of restrictive immigration quotas that severely hampered those fleeing the Nazis. Endemic racism limited the ability of African-Americans to serve their country, and those that did were usually segregated. Racism also played a role in the internment of Japanese-Americans.

After the war, U.S. officials believed it was more important to use certain Nazis as intelligence agents and sources in their evolving cold war with the Soviets than to bring them to trial. Other Allied nations, particularly in Latin America, offered safe haven to Nazis, including some of the worst war criminals (such as Adolf Eichmann, who was welcomed in Argentina). A large percentage of the Nazis found guilty of war crimes were unjustifiably spared the punishment that courts imposed.

During the war itself, the Allies were guilty of a number of atrocities, some of which went unpunished. These atrocities were *very* different, however, from the systematic genocide committed by Nazi murderers under the direction of Hitler.

True Freedom Fighters

On the other side of the ledger, many people responded to evil with great courage. Some overcame racism and defended the freedom of their oppressors, and a few risked all to save a few. Some of the stories may be familiar: Lieutenant John F. Kennedy's heroic rescue of *PT 109;* Swedish diplomat Raoul Wallenberg's determined effort to save Hungarian Jews from the Nazis by distributing protective passes; and the now-famous list of Oskar Schindler that allowed his Jewish workers to survive the war.

Other remarkable acts of courage are less widely known. For example, the distinguished service record of the Tuskegee Airmen shattered myths about black pilots; the 442nd Regimental Combat Team of Japanese-Americans became one of the most highly decorated units in U.S. military history, even as their families were being put in camps because they were "security risks," and Japan's Consul-General in Lithuania, Chiune Sugihara, defied his own government and issued thousands of lifesaving visas to Jews fleeing Hitler.

Words of War

"He negotiated the salvation of his 1,300 Jews by operating right at the heart of the system using all the tools of the devil—bribery, black marketeering, and lies."

—Thomas Keneally, author of *Schindler's List*

From Abyssinia to Zyklon

It would be easy to provide a recitation of the treaties and battles of World War II, as most history books do, but I hope to bring some of this history to life by introducing more of the human element—the good, the bad, and the ugly. This book is meant to be a general work of history and not a military history, so I will not go into great detail about the strategy and prosecution of individual battles. Others have written entire books on D day, the Battle of the Bulge, Pearl Harbor, and the rest, and I couldn't hope to cover all of the major events of the war and go into similar detail in a book of this length.

So, where do we start? Even now, more than 50 years after the war began, historians debate the causes of World War II. There is little doubt, however, that the seeds of that conflict were sown as the last great war ended. Alas, "the war to end all wars" served more as a catalyst to an even wider and bloodier conflagration. And that is where our story begins.

The Least You Need to Know

➤ World War II was the most destructive conflict in history.

➤ American society changed because of the war: women began to work, a baby boom followed the soldiers' return, and the United States became a super-power.

➤ The personalities and ideologies of Hitler, Mussolini, Hirohito, Churchill, and Roosevelt in many ways determined the conduct and outcome of the war.

➤ Hitler failed to learn from the mistakes of World War I and, instead of restricting his campaign to one front, spread his troops across Europe, the Mediterranean, North Africa, and the Soviet Union.

➤ Weapons became ever more lethal during the war, contributing to staggering military and civilian casualties.

➤ World War II reached a new level of barbarity with the massacres of civilians and soldiers and genocide.

➤ The war produced heroes on the battlefield and off.

Chapter 2

The War That Didn't End All Wars

In This Chapter

➤ Wasn't one world war enough?

➤ The Germans are bad losers

➤ A League of Nations misses its star

➤ The Great Depression's depressing consequences

➤ Gunning for a rematch

Even now, more than 50 years after the war began, historians debate the causes of World War II. Was it economics? Hitler's megalomania? Western appeasement? American isolationism? The mixture of action, reaction, and inaction in the years preceding the Second World War was much more complex than the cause of the first one, which was called the "Great War."

Despite the disagreements over the precise reasons for what might be called the "Greatest War," there's no doubt that the seeds of the Second World War were sown as the first one ended. Alas, "the war to end all wars" served as a catalyst to an even wider and bloodier conflict and is where our story begins.

Redrawing the Maps of Europe

The 20th century was just in its teens, but a lot of grown-up things were happening:

➤ The Panama Canal was completed.

➤ The unsinkable *Titanic* hit an iceberg and sank.

➤ French sculptor Auguste Rodin created *The Thinker*.

➤ Japan annexed Korea.

➤ New Mexico and Arizona became the 47th and 48th states.

➤ Albert Einstein formulated his General Theory of Relativity.

➤ Charlie Chaplin created his "Little Tramp" character.

➤ The British issued the Balfour Declaration supporting the establishment of a Jewish home in Palestine.

➤ The Chicago White Sox fixed the World Series, and Jack Dempsey became the heavyweight boxing champion.

➤ A revolution brought the end to czarist Russia.

This was also a time when a handful of nations—France, Italy, Germany, Austria-Hungary (the *Habsburg monarchy*), Russia, and Great Britain—essentially ruled the world, and their leaders were often related. Kaiser Wilhelm of Germany, for example, was the son of Victoria Adelaide Mary Louise, the eldest daughter of Queen Victoria of Great Britain, and the last Russian czar, Nicholas II, was married to the German Princess Alix of Hessen-Darmstadt.

GI Jargon

The **Habsburg monarchy** was one of the oldest and most prominent in Europe, dating back to the 13th century. The name is derived from the family castle of Habsburg, which was built in what is now Switzerland.

The populations of these and other European nations were growing, as were their economies. The powers were looking for opportunities to expand trade, particularly in places such as Africa, where colonial rivalries increased tensions among the Germans, French, and English. With nations feeling more threatened, they saw the need to expand their armies and develop more sophisticated weapons.

No nation wanted to stand alone, and therefore most nations sought out allies. Eventually, two competing alliances formed: the Triple Entente comprised of France, Great Britain, and Russia and the Triple Alliance of Austria-Hungary, Germany, and Italy. A series of crises early in the century threatened to provoke a war, but the conflicts that broke out remained regional affairs. It took a single pistol shot in 1914 to bring them all into conflict.

The Fuse Is Lit

The dominoes began to fall on June 28, 1914, when a Serbian nationalist named Gavrilo Princip assassinated the heir to the Austro-Hungarian throne, Archduke Franz Ferdinand. Backed by Germany, the Vienna government accused the Serbian government of being behind the murder. Russia mobilized its troops to defend its Serbian neighbors.

Feeling threatened by the czar's army to its east, Germany declared war on Russia and its western ally, France. When Germany suddenly attacked France through Belgium, Great Britain felt obligated to enter the war to defend its commitment to Belgian neutrality. Europe was now at war. Three years later, after Germany proposed a secret alliance with Mexico and its U-boats sank four unarmed American merchant ships, the United States entered the fray beside the other democracies and the war became a global conflict. Ultimately, 32 nations would be enmeshed in World War I, with 28 of them forming a coalition that became known as the Allies. Germany, Austria-Hungary, Turkey (the Ottoman Empire), and Bulgaria fought against them.

Battle of the Trenches

Initially, Germany hoped to quickly conquer France by marching through Belgium and outflanking the French army. When it appeared the Germans would take Paris, the French held. The Germans made a dash for the coast, hoping to capture the French ports, but they were unable to do so because of the actions of the French, British, and Belgians (who flooded the area where the Germans were advancing). At the end of 1914, the German offensive had stagnated, and Germany's opponents had failed to dislodge the Germans. Both sides then settled into stationary positions for a three-year battle from trenches.

On the eastern front, the Russians had invaded Austria and were threatening Hungary when the Austro-German armies began to drive them back. Russian losses in the battles of 1914 and 1915 were so great that the czar's forces never recovered enough to make a significant impact on the war.

Fighting spread to other fronts, including Turkey, Italy, and the Balkans. On April 6, 1917, the United States declared war on Germany after President Woodrow Wilson decided the threat to American interests had grown too serious to ignore. One of the provocations that prompted him to fight was the German decision to use submarines to attack ships bringing supplies to or from Great Britain.

War Grows More Hellish

Submarine warfare was one of the innovations that increased the level of death and destruction during World War I. Though the submarine had been used in earlier conflicts, these underwater craft did not become effective war machines until the Great War. Initially, German submarines posed a serious threat to British shipping and nearly knocked Britain out of the war, but countermeasures neutralized the danger late in the war.

Airships or zeppelins were also introduced in the war, as was aerial combat between airplanes. World War I was essentially a ground war, however, and air warfare was not a significant factor in the outcome. Because the war was fought primarily on the ground, the development of increasingly reliable and maneuverable tanks began to have an impact at the end of the war, which would presage their importance in the next world war. Other important innovations included the development and improvement of artillery, machine guns, and explosives. The most fearsome weapon of all, however, was poison gas, which was banned as a means of warfare after World War I.

It is difficult to fully capture the magnitude of the horror of the fighting and the impact of these weapons. Consider some of the numbers. More than 42 million soldiers fought on the side of the Allies against nearly 23 million from Germany, Bulgaria, the Ottoman Empire, and Austria-Hungary. More than 8 million of these troops were killed. Nearly 17 million more were wounded, taken prisoner, or missing. More than half of all the soldiers who were mobilized were casualties.

In the case of countries such as Russia, France, and Romania, the percentage of casualties exceeded 70 percent. The figures for Germany (65 percent) and Austria-Hungary (90 percent) were even higher. The United States, which didn't enter the war until 1917, sent more than 4 million men into combat; 126,000 died, and another 240,000 were injured, captured, or missing. Together casualties totaled more than 37 million. Roughly 10 million civilians also died as a direct or indirect consequence of the war. In addition to this heavy human toll, the monetary cost of the war was approximately $200 billion.

Roll Call

The British and French mobilized more than 17 million soldiers in World War I; more than half of those soldiers suffered casualties. By comparison, 8 percent of the 4.3 million American soldiers were killed, wounded, taken prisoner, or missing in action.

Winners and Losers

The British and French forces were near exhaustion, and leaders in the two countries felt they could not justify further loss of life and property. The United States was prepared to continue to fight, but the Americans had entered the war late, in 1917, and had not borne the brunt of the fighting. The British and French had sent roughly four times as many men into battle as the Americans and suffered more than 9 million casualties, compared to about 370,000 for U.S. forces.

An armistice was finally signed on November 11, 1918, 4 years, 3 months, and 14 days after the declaration of war by Austria-Hungary on Serbia on July 28, 1914. When the war ended, the global checkerboard had been rearranged. Russia was no longer a "Great Power" and the Habsburg monarchy had been dismantled, with the new nations of Yugoslavia and Czechoslovakia carved out of its remains. Poland, which had been partitioned between Russia and Prussia before the war, and overrun by Germany during the fighting, emerged as an independent state. Lithuania, which had also been occupied by Germany, also won its independence after the war. Two other nations, Latvia and Estonia, had been under the czar's control and exploited the Russian Revolution to achieve independence.

Germany remained a power even after being defeated, primarily because Britain and France decided not to destroy its army, which had been routed and was retreating. The war also introduced a new power to the scene—the only one that has grown in stature since that time—the United States.

The only other nation to emerge from the war stronger than before was Japan, which had demanded that Germany evacuate territory it held in northeastern China. When the Germans refused, Japan entered the war on the side of the Allies. During the war, Japan also exploited the chaos to extend its influence in East Asia and China.

The United States had no demands beyond Germany's acceptance of Wilson's *14 Points* and the ousting of the kaiser. The other Allies, however, wanted to reverse the territorial gains of the Germans and to ensure that the "Huns" could not renew the war. The French demanded the return of their northeastern territories; the British wanted the elimination of the German fleet. Both countries insisted on the liberation of Belgium.

The Germans were prepared to accept these terms, so it was unnecessary to continue the war. The Allies had said all along that they were not interested in destroying Germany; their goal was only to prove that aggression would not be permitted. This goal was accomplished, and an armistice was signed.

Though national rivalries remained, few people believed another European war would be fought for a generation. After all, World War I had been the bloodiest conflict ever.

GI Jargon

In a speech to Congress on January 8, 1918, President Wilson presented the **14 Points** he believed should be the basis of a peace settlement. These included: ensuring freedom of the seas, removing economic barriers to international trade, reducing arms, and recognizing the self-determination of peoples. The 14th point called for the creation of an association of nations to guarantee the independence and territorial integrity of all nations.

Ask the General

The Allies decided not to destroy the German army, thereby leaving the nucleus for it to rebuild and once again become a threat to its neighbors.

No Garden Party at Versailles

In an effort to guarantee future peace, 27 nations convened on January 18, 1919, in Versailles, France, the site of Louis XIV's grand palace. The Paris Peace Conference, as it was called, was dominated by the Big Four: President Woodrow Wilson, French Premier Georges Clemenceau, British Prime Minister David Lloyd George, and Premier Vittorio Orlando of Italy. Their aim was to impose restrictions on Germany that would reduce the chance of it again threatening its neighbors. The terms included limits on the size of the German army and navy, geographical restrictions on its military installations, and demands for large sums of money (reparations) to pay for the damage Germany caused during the war.

The "Big Four" in Paris. From left, Lloyd George, Vittorio Orlando, Georges Clemenceau, and Woodrow Wilson. (National Archives Still Pictures Branch)

The treaty signed at Versailles also resulted in a series of territorial compromises, fashioned in large part by the reluctant Wilson. To win support for his proposed League of Nations, Wilson was forced to accede to some of the victors' demands. For example, in response to French insistence that it be given control over the German-inhabited Rhineland, the United States and Britain agreed to sign a security treaty that promised they would come to France's aid if it were attacked by Germany. In return, France settled for the return of Alsace-Lorraine, the demilitarization of the Rhineland, and the placing of the Saar Valley under the League of Nations' control for 15 years.

The German people did not believe the terms of the treaty were fair, but the chastened German government had little choice but to sign the agreement. As Wilson had foreseen, the Germans felt humiliated and seethed for the next 20 years.

Needed: An International Police Officer

The Allies could do little to enforce the treaty, particularly as the years passed. Initially, they could threaten to resume the war against Germany, but this threat became increasingly impractical. No one wanted to go back to the trenches. Besides, what good would further fighting do? The ultimate result would still be an agreement that would require German cooperation.

The winners of the Great War found themselves in the peculiar position of having to support the German government to ensure that it maintained the armistice. The Germans, meanwhile, longed for the day they could reverse the outcome. The other nations of Europe understood that an unrestrained Germany would soon become the dominant power in Europe because of its superior human and natural resources. Even in defeat, Germany remained the greatest power in Europe. After all, it took almost the entire world four years to defeat its armed forces.

A World Government for an Ungovernable World

The principal instrument designed to enforce the Versailles Treaty was the League of Nations. The League had been the brainchild of President Woodrow Wilson, the scholar and former president of Princeton University turned political reformer. Wilson had offered the plan of an association of nations in 1918 as part of his 14 Points summarizing Allied war objectives. The most important part of Wilson's vision was to create an institution similar to the United Nations of today, that is, a forum where international disputes could be discussed and resolved and the membership could be collectively mobilized to keep the peace.

The covenant creating the League of Nations was incorporated into the Treaty of Versailles. As the architect of the League and the world's greatest power, the United States was expected to be the leader of the organization. This was not to be, in part because the treaty became embroiled in American domestic politics.

Words of War

"It must be a peace without victory.... Victory would mean peace forced upon the loser, a victor's terms imposed upon the vanquished. It would be accepted in humiliation, under duress, at an intolerable sacrifice and would leave a sting, a resentment, a bitter memory upon which terms of peace would rest, not permanently, but only as upon quicksand. Only a peace between equals can last."

—Woodrow Wilson addressing the U.S. Senate, January 22, 1917

Roll Call

At the end of World War I, Germany's population was 65 million; France's population was 40 million.

Woodrow Wilson reads the terms of the armistice to Congress, November 11, 1918. (National Archives Still Pictures Branch)

GI Jargon

Under the U.S. Constitution, the president has the power to negotiate treaties, but they must be submitted to the Senate for **ratification**— approval by a two-thirds vote of the members present. The Senate sometimes attaches amendments or reservations to the agreement, which must then be approved by the other signatories to the treaty.

The Senate Spurns Wilson's Baby

The commitments Wilson made for the United States in Paris had to be ratified by the U.S. Senate. Initially, *ratification* seemed assured. After all, Wilson was at the peak of his popularity and prestige when the war ended. However, a Republican majority took over Congress just before he went to the Paris peace talks, and the Republicans had little interest in cooperating with the Democratic president and vice versa.

The stage for a confrontation was set even before the Treaty of Versailles was signed. The Republicans were angry that Wilson had even gone to Europe (he was the first president ever to do so) and grew more furious when he excluded them from the U.S. peace delegation. Afterward, Republicans, particularly Conference Chairman (similar to today's Majority Leader) Henry Cabot Lodge, focused their attacks on the League of Nations.

Interestingly, critics of the League stood on opposite poles. One group believed it would be too powerful and undermine U.S. leadership, the other thought the organization would do nothing but talk and therefore be too weak to maintain peace. The principal complaint was a clause in the treaty that required all League members to preserve the territorial independence of all other members, and to take joint action against aggression. Isolationists, particularly those who became known in the debate as the *irreconcilables*, did not want any responsibility for defending Europe. Even many League supporters were unwilling to allow a nonelected body—composed primarily of non-Americans—to make foreign-policy decisions for the United States and, more specifically, to usurp Congress's constitutional power to declare war.

Senator Lodge formulated a series of amendments to the Treaty aimed at reserving U.S. freedom of action. These amendments were unacceptable to Wilson. The President, who had made a number of compromises in Paris to win European support for the League, was unwilling to accept any changes now, though such acceptance could have secured ratification. This "all or nothing" attitude, the highly partisan debate, and personal animosity between Wilson and Lodge were major factors in the defeat of the Treaty of Versailles.

GI Jargon

The **irreconcilables,** also known as "the Battalion of Death," were Senators Hiram Johnson of California and William Borah of Idaho. They were isolationists, opposed to any permanent alliances or commitments between the United States and other nations and determined to prevent any American involvement in matters beyond U.S. borders.

War Lore

The rejection of the Treaty of Versailles meant the United States remained technically at war with Germany, Hungary, and Austria until 1921, when Congress passed a resolution declaring that the war was over.

A League of Their Own

Without the United States, the League was doomed. Whether a strong, American-led League could have prevented World War II is a question that can never be answered.

As we will see, the members who did join the League were unwilling to use it to prevent aggression, and the organization's impotence ultimately contributed to Adolf Hitler's sense that he could act with impunity.

Ask the General

Permanent fortifications had played an important defensive role in World War I, and France devised a line of such fortifications to forestall another assault from Germany. The Maginot Line, named after War Minister André Maginot, extended roughly 200 miles along northeastern France from Switzerland almost to the Belgian border. It included antitank obstacles, gun emplacements, and an elaborate underground complex of railroads, hospitals, command posts, supply depots, and barracks.

The participation of the United States in World War I was crucial to the Allied victory. The American failure to continue to support its Allies in their efforts to contain Germany helped undo the result. This behavior should not have been surprising. Being far removed from Europe, Americans did not feel threatened by Germany, and they naively believed that no one else would feel threatened either.

Without the United States, Great Britain and France were the dominant powers in the League, and each had different ideas of what the organization should do. Britain hoped the League would include Germany and serve as a catalyst for reconciliation. The French still felt threatened by the Germans and wanted the League to prevent German aggression.

Even before the weakness of the League became apparent, the French began to strengthen their border defenses and to forge alliances to bolster their morale and security. In 1921, they signed a defensive alliance with Poland. This was followed by similar agreements with Czechoslovakia (1924), Romania (1926), and Yugoslavia (1927). Later, in the 1930s, the French would construct the most elaborate fortifications ever devised, the Maginot Line, to prevent the Germans from launching a frontal assault against them.

A Hindenburg Without the Hot Air

While the French prepared for possible future conflict, the Germans took a number of pacific steps in the mid '20s to normalize relations with their former rivals. First, Germany signed an agreement with the other international pariah, the Soviet Union— the first major power to do so. The economic cooperation agreement signed at Rapallo on April 16, 1922, appeared to be aimed at providing mutual assistance to the two struggling nations, but both governments had more sinister intentions. These intentions would become clear to all two decades later.

Three years later, at a conference in Locarno, Switzerland, the Germans voluntarily entered into treaties with Britain, Belgium, France, and Italy guaranteeing the existing Franco-Belgian-German borders. Germany accepted the loss of Alsace and Lorraine and agreed to keep the Rhineland demilitarized. France also won the right to defend Czechoslovakia and Poland under its existing alliances without being considered an aggressor against Germany or losing British support. Italy and Great Britain were to guarantee the agreements, but they assumed no obligations to ensure their implementation.

War Lore

The communist revolution of 1917 occurred after the Russian army's devastating losses in World War I. Vladimir Ilich Lenin and his successor, Joseph Stalin, were determined to prevent their nation from ever being threatened again. Toward that end, they concentrated on rebuilding the old Imperial Army into the powerful new Red Army. Their success helped determine the outcome of the next war and, later, provoked the Cold War.

The Locarno Treaty was a fine work of diplomacy, but it depended entirely on the good faith of the signatories, in particular Germany. The pact did usher in a brief period of optimism that peace could be maintained. Less than a year after it was signed, Germany was rewarded for its concessions with acceptance into the League of Nations. Though resentment over Versailles lingered, Germany's newly elected president, Paul von Hindenburg, believed changes could be made peacefully and remained faithful to the terms of Locarno. The German public was not anxious to return to the battlefield.

War Lore

A German blimp (also called a dirigible) was named after Hindenburg and had a bust of him on the main stairway. It was the world's first transatlantic commercial airship, but it is best known for its fiery crash-landing in New Jersey in 1937. Of the 97 people on board, 35 were killed, along with one member of the ground crew.

A Law Against War

The Americans, who otherwise showed little interest in foreign affairs in the '20s, sought to legislate war out of existence. Under public pressure, President Calvin Coolidge sent Secretary of State Frank Kellogg to negotiate an agreement with his French counterpart, Aristide Briand, that would outlaw all but "defensive wars" and encourage nations to settle international disputes by peaceful means. The Kellogg-Briand Pact (also called the Pact of Paris) was signed in 1928 and ultimately ratified by 62 nations. Practically, the agreement was worthless given the loophole that virtually any aggression could be justified as "self-defense."

War Lore

Frank Kellogg was awarded the 1929 Nobel Peace Prize. Aristide Briand already had his prize, sharing the 1926 Nobel with German Foreign Minister Gustav Stresemann for their roles in negotiating the Locarno Treaty.

Brothers, Can You Spare a Billion?

While the Europeans concentrated on borders and security, the Americans began to focus all their energy on domestic affairs. America's financial position had shifted dramatically from debtor to creditor as a consequence of the war, and the United States economy was becoming as strong as its military.

In less than a decade, the United States went from owing $4 billion to being owed $16 billion. Most of this debt was incurred by the Allies as a result of wartime loans, and the Americans were growing impatient with their failure to pay back the money.

The British and French argued that the debts should be forgiven because they had paid their share with the blood of their soldiers for almost three years prior to the United States' entrance in the war. They also resented the fact that the American economic boom was largely due to their borrowing.

Roll Call

A congressman visiting Germany during this time claimed to have paid 1,500 million marks for dinner for two and left 400 million marks for a tip.

While they tried to escape their debts to the United States, the British and French still pressed the Germans to pay $32 billion in reparations. The German refusal prompted the French to move troops into Germany's Ruhr Valley in 1923. Germany's government encouraged German workers not to cooperate with the French and printed huge amounts of money to pay them, which stimulated hyperinflation and caused the German economy to collapse.

It is difficult to conceive of the hyperinflation of that time—price increases that made the German mark virtually worthless. In 1913, the German mark was worth 2.38 dollars. By 1918, it had fallen to 7 cents, and by the middle of 1922, 1 U.S. cent would buy 100 marks. Despite the French occupation of the industrialized Ruhr, the German public blamed their predicament on the Versailles Treaty and "Jewish speculators," a preview of the scapegoating Hitler would later exploit.

Animosity also grew between the British and French, to the point where some feared the next war would be fought by the former allies. In 1924, as the arguments grew more heated and the situation more tense, American Charles Dawes negotiated a more realistic, scaled-down schedule of reparations payments. The terms were less onerous, and the Germans did make payments for the next five years. When the United States allowed private bankers to increase loans to the Germans, a circular trail of money was created, whereby Americans lent money to the Germans, who used it to pay reparations to the British and French who, in turn, repaid their loans to the United States.

The circle was broken in 1929 when the American stock market crashed, and the global economy went into a tailspin. The Germans had no chance of paying further reparations (or at least made that claim), and the Allies defaulted on their loans. The result was that the Europeans were embarrassed and embittered, and the Americans were more determined to further isolate themselves from troubles abroad.

War Lore

Finland was the only nation that did not default on its loans from the United States. It continued to make payments until its debt was paid off—in 1976!

Depressing Depression

Though the European powers had wrangled throughout the Roaring '20s, the Versailles Treaty had survived, and the League of Nations had succeeded in preventing a renewal of fighting. The Great Depression in the United States then set off a chain of events that contributed to the unraveling of the whole system of European security.

At first blush, one might have expected the opposite result from the economic hardships that arose. Though it is sometimes suggested that countries look for external enemies to distract their suffering populations in such periods, the impact of the Depression in Europe and the United States was a turning inward. Governments were cutting government expenditures and reducing wages, not building up their armies and seeking expensive military adventures.

The German government, battling inflation unsuccessfully, did make a few foreign policy overtures, first looking for an economic union with Austria and then rattling sabers along the Polish border. Neither would have improved the economy. Then the Germans refocused their anger on the conditions the Allies imposed on them at Versailles.

People Don't Kill, Guns Do

One of the Germans' main complaints concerned the restrictions the treaty had imposed on their army. In 1919, the powers had planned to begin a process of disarmament, believing that weapons were causes of war. No specifics were laid out in the Versailles Treaty, but limits on naval forces were later established at the Washington Disarmament Conference called by the United States in 1921 to 1922.

The one country left largely exempt from the new restrictions was Japan, which feared attacks from the West and insisted on reassuring concessions. This sensitivity to Japanese concerns would come back to haunt the United States 20 years later.

GI Jargon

At the close of the 19th century, U.S. Secretary of State John Hay sent a message to the great powers calling on them to respect certain Chinese rights and to permit foreign traders to engage in fair competition. In fact, Americans wanted to assure their own economic interests in China. The policy Hay advocated became known as the **Open Door Policy.**

The disarmament talks did produce two other notable agreements. The first, the Four-Power Treaty, committed the United States, the Commonwealth of Nations, France, and Japan to respect each other's possessions in the Pacific. The second, involving all the participants at the Washington conference, was the Nine-Power Treaty of 1922. This treaty guaranteed Chinese territorial integrity and a commitment to the *Open Door Policy*.

These agreements did not alleviate German discontent. A decade after Versailles, little progress had been made toward balancing the competing forces. The Germans began to insist that their rivals either reduce their armies to the German level or allow a German buildup.

In 1929, the Germans found a more sympathetic audience when a new Labor government took power in Great Britain and began preparations for a disarmament conference. By the time the conference took place in 1932, the Labor Party had been voted out of office, and the positions of both the French and Germans had hardened. The French insisted on ensuring their security, which would be impossible if Germany rearmed. The Germans were equally determined to achieve military parity with the other powers.

A Wolf at the Door

In hindsight, it is easy to question why anyone in France or Britain would have had the slightest interest in redressing the arms imbalance with Germany. But in 1932, the German economy was still in shambles. The British believed a well-armed France facing a disarmed Germany was the most likely cause of a future war.

At this point, the Treaty of Versailles and the agreements of the decade that followed became little more than interesting historical documents. The new world utopia Wilson envisioned when he formulated the League of Nations had sunk into chaos, with each nation looking desperately for ways to recover its own prosperity and seeking to take advantage of the suffering of the rest. The Western European leaders of the time were consumed with their own problems, and the United States remained in its isolationist funk. No one foresaw that a psychopath was prepared to fill the vacuum. The world's supposed powers had become as meek as sheep, and a wolf was now at their doorstep.

The Least You Need to Know

➤ World War I, the bloodiest conflict to that point in history, rearranged European boundaries, but left Germany as a major power.

➤ The Versailles Treaty was supposed to ensure future peace, but the humiliating terms imposed on Germany produced feelings of resentment that would eventually undo the settlement.

➤ President Woodrow Wilson's idea of creating an international forum for resolving disputes became a reality, but the effectiveness of the League of Nations was crippled by isolationists in the U.S. Senate who prevented the United States from becoming a member.

➤ The Great Depression had a ripple effect throughout the world, preventing Germany from paying reparations, forcing Great Britain and France to default on their debts to the United States, and sowing discontent everywhere.

➤ Germany wanted its military to be equal to that of its neighbors, but its neighbors were determined to prevent the imbalance from being redressed.

➤ By the end of the 1920s, the treaties signed after World War I had ceased to be effective, and the growing unrest offered an opportunity for a strong leader to step forward and bring order to the chaos.

Chapter 3

The Little Artist Seeks a Bigger Canvas

> **In This Chapter**
>
> ➤ Hitler's lack of talent changes history
>
> ➤ The Beer Hall *Putsch*
>
> ➤ Nazis as democrats
>
> ➤ The ruthless suppression of opposition
>
> ➤ Ideals and ideologues

Only a few men in history have had their names become synonymous with evil. In the 20th century, and for all time, Adolf Hitler has become associated with unspeakable wickedness. And to think he might never have become the scourge of the earth if he'd had enough talent to become an artist.

A few historians argue that Hitler did not have a conscious plan, that he often improvised and exploited opportunities. This argument is far too forgiving a reading of the evidence. In truth, Hitler was a unique politician, a man who said what he thought and then acted to implement his ideas. The only exceptions were when he told gullible foreign leaders that he was satisfied with his latest conquest. Otherwise, Hitler made quite clear early on his desire to purify the world, particularly by ridding it of the poisonous Jews, and then to dominate it.

Picture Imperfect

It is evidence of the incredible hold Hitler assumed over the Germans that he could promote the ideal of the blond-haired, blue-eyed, Aryan superman when he, their leader, was none of those things. The black-haired, brown-eyed Adolf Hitler was born in Braunau am Inn, Austria, on April 20, 1889.

His father, 52-year-old Alois Schickelgruber Hitler, was an Austrian customs official. His mother, Alois's third wife, was a young peasant girl named Klara Poelzl. Young Adolf resented his stern father and was relieved by his death in 1903. He was devastated, however, when his mother, whom he adored, died in 1908 of cancer.

A Portrait of the Artist

Hitler was never a good student and dropped out of school at 16. He left his home in Linz and went to Vienna hoping to become an artist. Having more confidence than talent, Hitler twice failed auditions at the Vienna Academy of Art. He spent the next five years in self-described misery, trying to sell hand-painted postcards to tourists.

During these formative years, Hitler began to develop the racist, amoral world view that would shape his political life. He was particularly influenced by two Viennese politicians, Karl Lueger and Georg von Schoenerer. Lueger was the popular socialist mayor who showed Hitler that the public would forego freedom to get economic security. Schoenerer was more interested in race than economics, blaming Jews for all of the world's evils, an argument that struck a responsive chord in young Adolf.

Years in the Service

When World War I began, Hitler avoided service in the Habsburg Empire's (Austrian) military, primarily because he would have had to fight beside "inferiors"—Jews and Slavs. Instead, he volunteered for a Bavarian (German) infantry regiment. During the war, Hitler fought with distinction and was twice decorated for bravery, but he never advanced beyond a rank equivalent to a U.S. Army private first class. He was wounded twice and spent several weeks at the end of the war recuperating from being gassed by Allied forces.

During his service, Hitler felt for the first time as though he had found a real home, a place where he made lifelong friends. He was enraged, however, by the devastating defeat and the humiliating terms imposed on Germany by the Allies at Versailles. He was convinced that the outcome was due to Marxists and Jews stabbing the Fatherland in the back.

A Nazi Is Born

It would take Hitler less than a year to find an outlet for his frustration. Hitler was assigned by the army to spy on political parties and was sent to investigate a small group of nationalists who called themselves the German Workers' Party. In 1919, Hitler joined the German Workers' Party, becoming only its seventh active member. Two years later he was chairman of what was now called the National Socialist German Workers' Party (*Nationalsozialistische Deutsche Arbeiterpartei*, or NSDAP) and became known as the *Nazi* Party.

Hitler saw the NSDAP as an instrument for gaining power and sought to give it a military caste. He created his own personal army of storm troopers, the *Sturmbabteilung* or SA. The group wore brown uniforms—the same color as the victorious British army—hence the nickname "Brownshirts." They eventually had their own marching song, which was named after the Berlin leader of the SA, Horst Wessel, who according to Nazi legend was murdered by a communist in 1930. Wessel resigned from the Nazi Party after falling in love with a prostitute; the communist who killed him happened to be the woman's pimp.

GI Jargon

The original abbreviation of National Socialist was *Nasos*. **Nazi** was a term of derision first applied to the group by journalist Konrad Heiden.

The party adopted an ancient religious emblem, the swastika, as its symbol. Its objective was to impose state control over much of society, but its greater emphasis was on a foreign policy that would bring about the creation of a greater Germany, an abrogation of Versailles, and an end to the malignant influence of the Jews. Germany, Hitler believed, was threatened by its neighbors and could never become the power it should be so long as the size of its army was restricted.

By the time he took control of the party, Hitler had already displayed his talent as an inspirational orator. Still, when he decided to make his first bid for power, he had only about 3,000 followers.

As we saw in the last chapter, the German economy was in distress in the early 1920s, and the German currency had collapsed by 1923. Hitler saw the public's discontent as his opportunity to seize power. On November 8, he led his "army" to a beer hall in Bavaria where local government leaders were holding a meeting. The Nazis quickly captured the politicians, and Hitler put himself in charge of a new national government. The group then marched on the former Bavarian War Ministry building when the police opened fire. The man beside Hitler was killed as he pulled his leader to the ground, and the Nazis all fled.

A Room with a Viewpoint

The failure of the Beer Hall *Putsch* (revolt) brought the obscure man with the funny mustache his first national publicity. Hitler was arrested and, after a 24-day trial, sentenced to five years in Landsberg Fortress. The name is misleading, because the fortress was more like one of those country club-type prisons where white-collar criminals are sometimes sent. Hitler received a steady stream of visitors and presents and was treated more like he was on a picnic than serving as an inmate.

GI Jargon

Lebensraum means "living space." Friedrich Ratzel, a German geographer and ethnologist, developed the idea, which Hitler later used to suggest Germans needed room for expansion, a convenient rationalization for his territorial ambitions.

The most important aspect of Hitler's incarceration was that it allowed him to dictate his views to his friend and cellmate, Rudolf Hess. Those views would later be published as the book *Mein Kampf* (My Struggle), a volume that remains a bible for racists, anti-Semites, and sociopaths. When it was first written, however, Hitler would not permit the book to be published in English.

In *Mein Kampf*, Hitler laid out his views on the centrality of Aryan purity to historical progress, the mortal danger posed by world Jewry and international communism, the necessity of rebuilding German power, and the importance of expanding Germany's borders to provide the living space—*Lebensraum*—the German people required. Hitler did not conceal his intentions; they were in black and white for anyone to read. The hard part, especially in the 1920s, was to take him seriously.

On December 20, 1924, Hitler was released from prison, having served only nine months. The next day, he bought himself a Mercedes.

War Lore

While in prison, Hitler envisioned the development of a "people's car," a *Volkswagen*, from the word *Volk*, meaning people or nation.

From Democrat to Dictator

The failure of the Beer Hall *Putsch* taught Hitler valuable lessons that he would use to win and hold power later. One obvious lesson was not to get into any more battles with an enemy that was larger and better armed. Hitler also decided that his best chance to gain power would be through the use of ballots rather than bullets. Hence, the would-be dictator started out as a democrat of sorts.

The Nazi Party had temporarily been banned, but as soon as the ban was lifted in 1925, Hitler began to build a constituency. The following year, he established himself as the *Führer* (leader) of the party and organized the armed and black-shirted (after the Italian fascists) SS—the *Schutzstaffeln* or protective units—to control the party.

The Allies, meanwhile, were continuing to press the German government to pay war reparations and adhere to arms limitations, stimulating a steadily rising tide of public resentment. These external pressures were partially offset, however, by an economic recovery. After the hyperinflationary period at the beginning of the decade, which

Hitler had misread as an opportunity to seize power, the German government succeeded in stabilizing the currency, and the nation's industry began to make a comeback, lowering unemployment.

Hitler at a Nazi Party rally in Nuremberg, Germany, circa 1928. (National Archives Still Pictures Branch)

America Crashes the Party

Although Germany's neighbors paid close attention to that nation's every move, Americans showed little interest in developments abroad. The Roaring '20s were in full swing, and the public was captivated by Charles Lindbergh's flight across the Atlantic, amused by Hollywood's introduction of "talkies," in a tizzy over affordable "Tin Lizzy" automobiles, awed by the already legendary exploits of Babe Ruth, and enriched by the boom on Wall Street.

Roll Call

In 1929, 1.3 million Germans were unemployed. Within three years, that figure soared to 6 million, a staggering total for a nation of 60 million people.

Ironically, those carefree, isolationist Americans unwittingly upset the global applecart and triggered a series of events that led to Hitler's ascent. When the stock market crashed on October 29, 1929, the prosperous '20s came to a thudding halt, and the most prolonged and severe depression in history quickly engulfed the United States and the rest of the world with it.

Germany was especially hard hit by the Great Depression. Industry ground to a halt, and the unemployment rolls swelled to previously unimagined levels. Once again, Hitler saw the opportunity to capitalize on the misery of the public.

A Democrat in Name Only

Rather than launch another ill-advised coup attempt, Hitler stuck to his intention to seek power by democratic means. The Nazi Party participated in the election of 1928 and won a paltry 12 seats in the *Reichstag*, Germany's parliament. The Nazis received only 810,000 votes (2.5 percent of the total).

Two years later, the impact of the Depression became more acute, and Hitler began to successfully play on the public's resentment and fear. In the 1930 election, the Nazis received well over 6 million votes—18.3 percent of the total—which was good for 107 seats. This election made the Nazis the second largest party in the *Reichstag* after the Social Democrats, who had won 143 seats. A third party, the Communists, made significant gains in that election as well and would also play a role in the unraveling of German democracy.

Though Hitler's popularity was growing, he was still largely viewed by the nation's elite as a ridiculous Austrian demagogue. Though mocked by some, Hitler built a broad base of support among the disgruntled masses and, increasingly, among influential industrialists and intellectuals. Simultaneously, he continued to expand his own private, loyal army of Blackshirts and storm troopers who engaged in frequent battles, particularly with the Communists, to control the streets. When Germans went to the polls again in 1932, few people were laughing at the frustrated artist.

Citizen Hitler

Ironically, Hitler did not even become a German citizen until February, 1932, when he decided to run for president. In the election that April, Hitler received more than 13 million votes in a runoff, short of the 19 million polled by the incumbent President Paul von Hindenburg.

A few months later, in the parliamentary election, nearly 14 million Germans (37.3 percent) cast their votes for the National Socialists, giving them 230 of the 670 seats in the *Reichstag*. The Nazis did not hold a majority; nevertheless, President Hindenburg offered to create a coalition government with them. Hitler turned him down and demanded sole power for himself. Hindenburg then dissolved the *Reichstag* and forced new elections.

The same month that Franklin Roosevelt won the first of four U.S. presidential elections, Germans again cast their ballots. The Nazis lost ground, receiving fewer than 12 million votes and 196 seats. The combined vote of the Social Democrats and Communists gave them a majority of 221 seats. The antipathy of those two parties, however, ensured that they would not cooperate. Hindenburg renewed his proposal for a coalition agreement with the Nazis, but Hitler remained unwilling to share power. The *Reichstag* had to be dissolved again.

Strange Bedfellows

Hitler felt that he could afford to be obstinate. He was now the most powerful man in Germany, the head of a party with one million members and a 400,000-man army.

The success of the Communists further strengthened Hitler's popularity because of the widespread fear and opposition to Bolshevism. Though the street fights between Hitler's SA and the Communist Red Front gave a hint of the lawless brutality the *Führer's* minions were capable of, most Germans were more afraid of a Communist revolution.

With violence in the streets, economic deprivation throughout the country, and chaos in the government, advisers to Hindenburg, including former Chancellor Franz von Papen, persuaded the president to nominate Hitler as chancellor in the hope of containing the Nazis. It was a bad idea.

Words of War

"If we have the power, we'll never give it up again unless we're carried out of our offices as corpses."

—Propaganda Minister Joseph Goebbels

The Terror Begins

Hitler became chancellor on January 30, 1933, and quickly began to consolidate his power by eliminating opponents within the Nazi Party as well as those on the outside. Hitler was given an unexpected helping hand by the "feeble-minded" Martinus van der Lubbe (a Dutch communist), who set fire to the *Reichstag* on February 27, 1933. Hitler blamed the fire on the communists, outlawed their party, and arrested their leaders.

The following month, in Germany's last free election before the war, the Nazis won only 43 percent of the vote—but majorities no longer mattered. The *Reichstag* quickly passed the Enabling Act, giving Hitler dictatorial powers. He used them to abolish trade unions, dismantle all competing parties, and complete the process of eliminating his political opponents.

Long Knives of the Gestapo

On the "night of the long knives," June 30, 1934, Hitler sent his black-shirted SS murderers to dispose of threats within the party. As many as 1,000 people were killed, including the commander of the SA, Ernst Rhöm. Rhöm helped Hitler come to power, but made the mistake of believing he could share it. Rhöm wanted to lead a revolution and turn the SA into a people's army with him at its head. His undisguised ambition antagonized the regular army, the middle class and conservative Germans Hitler was trying to woo, and two equally ambitious leaders, Göring and Himmler. No one would be allowed to rival Hitler.

GI Jargon

The Nazis identified their rule as the successor to the Holy Roman Empire and the German Empire of 1871 to 1918. They called their regime the **Third** *Reich.*

It took Hitler only a few months to destroy democracy in Germany, and no one had the moral fortitude, political power, or simple courage to try to stop him. Given the brutality with which Hermann Göring's secret state police, the *Gestapo* (*Geheime Staatspolizei*), silenced Hitler's opponents, usually through murder, it's not surprising that critics were too scared to act.

War Lore

Hermann Göring was a World War I flying ace who would become the head of Hitler's air force, the *Luftwaffe*. Göring had participated in the Beer Hall *Putsch* in 1923 and was shot in the melee. His wife spirited him out of Munich and took him to a hospital in Austria, where he became addicted to morphine. The addiction reduced his effectiveness in office over the years.

Within a year and a half of Hitler's coming to power, all state institutions were under control of the Nazi Party. In August 1934, President Hindenburg died, and Hitler assumed the role of president. He then took the title of *Führer*, the supreme leader of the *Third Reich*. At that point, as Hermann Göring said, "The law and the will of the *Führer* are one."

Marked for Persecution

When it came to eliminating enemies, the group at the top of Hitler's list was the Jews. As he had written in *Mein Kampf* and repeated throughout his political rise, Hitler believed in the superiority of the Aryan race and the importance of maintaining its purity. Although he thought other races were simply inferior, Hitler insisted the Jews were dangerous because they lived off other races and weakened them.

Now that he was firmly in command, Hitler could begin pursuing his goal of eliminating the "parasitic" Jews. The persecution began with a boycott of Jewish businesses and shops, then sporadic violence, followed by a series of decrees that stripped them of their jobs, property, and rights. The Nuremberg Racial Laws of 1935 deprived them of their citizenship. This war against the Jews will be discussed in greater detail in Chapter 24. For now, it is important to note that even while Germany was at peace and struggling to revive its economy, Hitler focused much of his attention on the persecution of the Jews.

The Jews weren't the only ones subject to Nazi persecution. The *Gestapo* and other security forces had the authority to arrest anyone. I've already mentioned a prime target was communists, but other enemies of the state and "asocials" included socialists, Jehovah's Witnesses, Gypsies (Roma), and homosexuals.

Those "criminals" who were not murdered were sent to concentration camps for an indefinite period. The first of these camps, Dachau, was opened in 1933. Before the decade was over, more than 25,000 people would be confined in concentration camps that would become more notorious in the next decade. These camps included Buchenwald, Flossenbrüg, Mauthausen, Sachsenhausen, and the women's camp at Ravensbrück.

The Master Race

Hitler was not only determined to cleanse the Aryan race, he also wanted to purify German culture. One dramatic example of this "purification" was the burning of books on May 10, 1933. That night, thousands of Germans throughout the country took books deemed "un-German" and threw them into bonfires. Works of Albert Einstein, Sigmund Freud, and other Jewish authors were burned, along with those of non-Jews such as Ernest Hemingway and Helen Keller. Even books by German authors went into the pyre, including Germany's most famous writer, Nobel Prize winner Thomas Mann. This widely publicized event provoked outrage in the United States, where *Newsweek* magazine called it a "holocaust."

The book burning was only one feature of Hitler's campaign to impose ideological conformity on his

Words of War

A century before Hitler, the German poet Heinrich Heine presciently wrote, "Where one burns books, one will, in the end, burn people."

subjects. Through a variety of institutions, children were indoctrinated with Nazi dogma. The importance of state authority was so well drilled into youngsters that some would turn in their parents to the authorities for expressing views at odds with the official Nazi political line. The Hitler Youth was created to prepare teenage boys for party membership.

Thousands of books smolder in a huge bonfire as Germans give the Nazi salute during the wave of book burnings that spread throughout Germany. (National Archives Still Pictures Branch)

Later, the Nazis would seek to create their master race through a crude form of genetic engineering. German women were encouraged to become mothers to children of soldiers going off to battle. In addition, select young women with the requisite Aryan traits were sent to Lebensborn to procreate with members of the SS. The children were cared for in maternity houses and given special benefits.

Hitler never had children and did not marry until the day before he committed suicide. In 1936, a 24-year-old photographer's assistant named Eva Braun became his mistress and remained his companion until death did them part.

Hitler Goes for the Gold

All the resources of the state were devoted to enhancing Hitler's prestige, strengthening the nation, and reinforcing Nazi ideology. The press was a vital instrument for dissemination of Nazi views, particularly the virulently anti-Semitic tabloid, *Der Sturmer*. In addition, Leni Riefenstahl, an innovative filmmaker, produced fantastic propaganda movies extolling Hitler's virtues. Huge rallies were held in Nuremberg that resembled the spectacles of ancient Rome and conveyed a sense of Hitler's power and the adoration of the German people for their *Führer*.

Perhaps Hitler's greatest propaganda triumph was staging the 1936 Olympic Games in Berlin. Hitler hoped to accomplish several goals with the Olympics: to demonstrate the rebirth of Germany, discredit reports of his anti-Semitic and totalitarian policies, and demonstrate the superiority of Aryans through their dominance of the competition.

Some Americans called for a boycott of the Games to show disapproval for Nazi policies; however, the majority argued that politics should not be allowed to interfere with the ideals of sportsmanship that the Olympics represented. (Similar arguments would be made nearly five decades later, but President Jimmy Carter ignored them and ordered a U.S. boycott of the 1980 Olympics held in Moscow to protest the Soviet invasion of Afghanistan.) In 1936, the athletes won the debate.

Germany fielded a strong Olympic team. Jews had been expelled from most German sports clubs and were banned from competition in violation of the Olympic Charter. Under pressure, the Germans ultimately allowed two Jews from mixed religious backgrounds to participate.

War Lore

Two Jews, Marty Glickman and Sam Stoller, were scheduled to run for the United States in the 400-meter relay at the Olympics; however, the president of the U.S. Olympic Committee, Avery Brundage, feared that Hitler would be even more offended by Jewish champions than a black medalist and replaced them with Jesse Owens, over Jesse's objections.

The Olympics were the grand spectacle that Hitler hoped for, but the outcome of the competition, which was beyond his control, was an embarrassment. Shattering Hitler's myth of Aryan superiority was a young black American athlete named Jesse Owens who won an unprecedented four gold medals.

War Lore

Germany did not host another Olympics until 1972. Hoping to erase the stain of Nazism and the memory of 1936, the government again staged a spectacular event. This time, it was marred by Palestinian terrorists who murdered 18 Israeli athletes. The echoes of the Holocaust reverberated again throughout the world, but even they were not powerful enough to overcome the wish to continue the Olympics. Despite calls for the Olympic Games to end, they continued after only a day's suspension.

Follow the "Leader"

Hitler had come to power largely because of the economic hardships faced by Germans. Now the *Führer* needed to solve the problem of having 6 million people out of work.

While President Roosevelt was instituting the New Deal to coax the American economy out of its depression, Hitler began to impose a "new order" that involved public works programs, such as the construction of superhighways, the imposition of wage controls, and the effective end of competition. He also set out to ensure supplies of strategic raw materials and food. A handful of banks and conglomerates came to dominate the economy. One of these businesses, I.G. Farben, owned by the Krupp family, would ultimately achieve much of its power on the backs of slave laborers taken from prisoner of war and concentration camps.

The "new order" succeeded in significantly reducing unemployment, reinvigorating the economy, and producing a reasonable standard of living. While rebuilding the economy, Hitler also began a massive rearmament program to reconstruct the German military. While the Americans and British were mired in recessions at the end of the 1930s, Germany had a labor shortage. The nation had become so strong that Hitler boasted the Third *Reich* would endure for a thousand years.

Might Makes *Reich*

Hitler needed power to achieve his global ambitions. Now that he was firmly in control of Germany, he was in position to pursue his goals of reversing Versailles, recreating the German empire, and conquering the territory needed to provide his people with "living space."

Though Germany would never become a true war economy in the way that the United States would by devoting all its resources to building up its military in the 1940s, Hitler's principal motivation was to rebuild the German armed forces and make them the most powerful in the world. He told his generals from the outset that he planned to make Germany the greatest power in Europe.

When Hitler came to power, Germany was virtually unarmed. It had no tanks, no airplanes, and no heavy weapons. Hitler's remilitarization effort began almost immediately after he assumed power and accelerated in 1935, when he used France's decision to double the length of their conscripts' service to justify the reintroduction of mandatory military service in Germany. Hitler also announced the creation of an air force in violation of the Versailles Treaty. He then offered to sign an agreement with France that would limit the size of both German and French armies. When France refused, he had the pretext to expand his force beyond the 100,000-man limitation of the treaty.

Words of War

"Germany must either be a world power or there will be no Germany."

—Hitler in *Mein Kampf*

War Lore

In the 1930s, Germany was militarily weak by any standard. Even after it began to rearm, foreign leaders did not foresee immediate danger. An article in *The Times* of London in July 1934, for example, said, "There is more reason to fear for Germany than to fear Germany." No one realized Hitler was willing to risk war even if he didn't have the resources to win, because he did not think the Western powers, especially France, would call his bluff.

In 1938, Hitler wrested control over the last important institution he needed to fulfill his goals, the military. The commander-in-chief of the army, Werner von Fritsch, had become increasingly concerned by Hitler's actions and afraid he might provoke a war. Hitler saw Fritsch and the Minister of War, General Werner von Blomberg, as obstacles to be removed because of their hesitancy and inability to see Germany's glorious future.

He got an excuse to get rid of one and manufactured a reason to excuse the other: Blomberg married a woman who turned out to have been a prostitute, and Fritsch was confronted with invented charges of homosexual behavior. With those two out of the way, Hitler created a new command in place of the War Ministry and placed himself in charge. The OKW (*Oberkommando der Wehrmacht*) became the instrument for planning Hitler's conquests. Adolf Hitler and Germany were just about ready for war.

The Least You Need to Know

➤ Born in Austria, Adolf Hitler had set out to become an artist, but his lack of talent led him ultimately into politics. His early influences were anti-Semitic, socialist politicians in Vienna.

➤ After distinguished service in the German army in World War I, Hitler joined a tiny political organization known as the German Worker's Party.

➤ Hitler was arrested after a failed coup attempt and used his time in prison to write his political manifesto, *Mein Kampf.*

➤ A central tenet of Hitler's domestic and foreign policy was the importance of racial purity. This led to his efforts to exterminate poisonous elements of society, notably the Jews.

➤ Hitler sought to reverse the terms imposed on Germany at Versailles. Toward that end, he began to rearm Germany and prepare it to conquer the territory Germans needed for "living space."

Chapter 4

The Bell Tolls for War

In This Chapter

➤ Hitler begins to revoke the Versailles Treaty by rearming

➤ The United States withdraws into an isolationist shell and refuses to intervene to influence events in Europe

➤ Mussolini's fascists set an example for Hitler in both ruthless domestic politics and aggressive foreign policy

➤ Japan joins Germany and Italy in seeking to expand its borders and power

➤ Spain dissolves into civil war and nations choose sides

The Western powers were not alarmed when Hitler came to power. As we saw in the last chapter, Germany had been disarmed, it was mired in a depression, and the new German leader was focused on consolidating his grip on power. Although anyone who read Hitler's writings or listened to his speeches had ample reason to be concerned about his plans, initially Germany was seen more as the nation being threatened than the one that posed a danger to its neighbors. To the world's lasting regret, it took everyone too long to separate perception from reality.

Meanwhile, other autocrats and aspiring dictators in Italy, Japan, and Spain were flexing their muscles and seeking to expand their own empires. It was a time for pushing boundaries, and it wasn't long before the totalitarians joined forces to advance their common agendas.

Oiling the War Machine

The first indication of future trouble was Hitler's petition to the League of Nations in May 1933 to begin rebuilding Germany's military so that it could approach parity with its neighbors. The French vetoed the idea, maintaining their long-standing position that German power must be constrained. Hitler's reaction was to withdraw from the League and announce plans to rearm without asking further permission.

When France rejected a subsequent German offer to sign an agreement in which Hitler would voluntarily limit the size of his military, the *Führer* felt justified in accelerating his remilitarization plan. He created a new air force and instituted compulsory service. To the surprise of many of Hitler's advisers, the League took no punitive action against Germany.

From Hitler's perspective, he had taken a calculated gamble that was based on his accurate reading of the French. He knew the only real threat they had was to go to war, and they weren't about to do that over the size of Germany's army. Once the army was rebuilt, they might feel compelled to fight, but, by then, Hitler figured it would be too late for the French to stop him. If France has statesmen, he said, "she will not grant us time but will jump on us."

Great Britain was equally helpless to act and made a deal with Hitler similar to the one the French rejected. In 1935, the British signed a naval pact that allowed Germany to build a fleet of ships equal in tonnage to one-third of the British fleet, and a fleet of submarines equal to 60 percent of the Royal Navy. In doing so, the British tacitly accepted the abrogation of Versailles, which had set strict limits on German naval strength and barred the construction of submarines.

Lies and Allies

The French remained concerned about Hitler's actions and sought to contain the threat by forming alliances that would form a protective ring around Germany. France already had a security pact with Poland, but this pact was largely offset by Poland's decision to sign a separate non-aggression pact with Germany in 1934. Hitler had hoped the Poles would become loyal to the *Reich* and jettison their alliance with France, but the Poles saw the new agreement as a way to gain freedom from French influence without losing the guarantee of French assistance should Germany ever become threatening.

In April 1935, France joined Britain and Italy at Stresa in northern Italy and signed an agreement to jointly oppose, "by all practicable means, any unilateral repudiation of treaties which may endanger the peace of Europe." A month later, France signed a treaty with the Soviet Union to provide mutual assistance should either nation be attacked. The Soviets signed a similar agreement two weeks later with Czechoslovakia.

Drawing a Line at the Rhine

Though none of the agreements directly threatened Germany, Hitler insisted they were provocations. He claimed the agreement with the Soviets violated the French pledge not to make war on Germany without the support of the League of Nations. With this as a pretext, Hitler ordered his troops to occupy the Rhineland on March 7, 1936, repudiating the Versailles provision to keep the region demilitarized.

Hitler had not yet created the OKW (*Oberkommando der Wehrmacht*) and taken total control of the military. One reason he eventually did so was that he viewed his generals as too timid. They demonstrated their weakness by objecting to Hitler's move into the Rhineland. The generals correctly assessed the deficiencies of the German military and the ability of the French to humiliate them—but they were wrong in their evaluation of France's willingness to act. Hitler was convinced that France would not intervene.

Words of War

"In 1933 a French premier ought to have said (and if I had been the French premier I would have said it): The new *Reich* chancellor is the man who wrote *Mein Kampf*, which says this and that. This man cannot be tolerated in our vicinity. Either he disappears or we march! But they didn't do it."

—Joseph Goebbels

The French government was receiving almost the exact opposite analysis from its military experts. The consensus was that the Germans were too strong for the French to take on by themselves. It soon became apparent they would have to do just that if they were to oppose Hitler. The Polish government essentially backed out of its treaty to help the French, and the British said they would not support any military action so long as Germany refrained from attacking France. Great Britain agreed to refer the matter to the League of Nations, but the members of the League could not even muster a condemnation of the German action.

The combination of the failure of the League and the network of alliances to stand up to Hitler unraveled the tenuous collective security arrangements built after World War I. No mechanism was left to check the appetite of an aggressor.

Americans Are Stuck in Neutral

The United States watched the ascension of Hitler and his early adventures with a measure of alarm, but the government remained fixated on domestic problems, especially the sick economy. Rather than react to Hitler's efforts to rearm and reoccupy the Rhineland with firm statements or action, the U.S. government withdrew further into its shell.

Isolationists and naive idealists dominated the debate. They blamed bankers and arms makers for

Words of War

"I have seen war.... I hate war."

—President Roosevelt's address at Chautauqua, New York, August 14, 1936.

World War I, suggesting they somehow fomented the conflict to make money. The possibility of being drawn into war by the actions of Hitler, Mussolini, or some other fascist led Congress to take steps to make U.S. involvement difficult if not impossible. Toward that end, a series of Neutrality Acts were enacted in 1935, 1936, and 1937, which imposed restrictions on the actions of the government and private Americans. These acts included bans on making loans and selling or transporting arms to belligerents.

Rather than use its newfound power to control or at least influence international events, the United States chose to abandon the field to the fascists. In reality, it was impossible to be neutral, because staying on the sidelines prevented the United States from making a distinction between the aggressors and the victims. Without American power on the side of democracy, the dictators held the advantage—and they would soon exploit it.

Moreover, the mighty American military unilaterally disarmed after World War I. Ironically, the United States voluntarily reduced the size of its army to roughly the level imposed on Germany at Versailles. As with the feckless Western European powers, Hitler saw the combined display of American military retrenchment and political neutrality as weaknesses he could capitalize on.

Roll Call

In the early 1930s, the U.S. Army had only about 130,000 soldiers, which made it the 16th largest force in the world, smaller than those of Czechoslovakia, Poland, Turkey, Spain, and Romania.

Making Fascism Fashionable

Benito Mussolini blazed the trail for Hitler by setting an authoritarian example for him in Italy. Though Hitler admired Mussolini and saw him as a key ally, the Italian's strategic bumbling would ultimately help end the German's reign of terror.

Mussolini was born in Predappio on July 29, 1883 and named after the Mexican revolutionary leader Benito Juarez. His father was a socialist blacksmith, and his mother was a teacher. When he was 17, he married Rachele Guidi, with whom he had five children. Mussolini became a schoolteacher, but he also was a socialist agitator who was arrested for criticizing Italy's war in Libya in 1911 to 1912.

GI Jargon

Fascist comes from the Italian word meaning group. The term came to be applied to right-wing advocates of totalitarianism and extreme nationalism. Fascism emphasizes the importance of the state rather than the individual, like communism, but does not call for state ownership of property.

When Mussolini got out of prison, he briefly edited the Socialist Party newspaper in Milan, but he was expelled from the party after advocating that Italy join the Allies in World War I. He then founded his own newspaper, *Il Popolo d'Italia* (The People of Italy). Unlike Hitler, Mussolini's war record was underwhelming. He was wounded by a misfired hand grenade and discharged.

The same year Hitler joined the German Worker's Party, Mussolini and other young war veterans founded the *Fascist* Party (*Fasci di Combattimento*). In a move later emulated by Hitler, Mussolini created his own black-shirted militia (really a group of thugs) to enforce party discipline and terrorize opponents. Like Hitler, he also referred to himself as "the leader," *Il Duce* in Italian. The Fascists' intentions were clear from their party slogan and the motto on their flag. The former was "Believe, obey, fight" and the latter, "The Country Is Nothing Without Conquest."

Following World War I, Italy was in chaos. Its economy was a shambles, the political parties were at loggerheads, landowners feared a peasant uprising, and industrialists worried about a Communist revolution. Mussolini stepped in to fill the vacuum, demanding in 1922 that the Fascists take over the government. To back up his demands, Mussolini prepared to march on Rome and seize power. On October 28, 1922, King Victor Emmanuel III asked Mussolini to form a government. A year later, Hitler would try unsuccessfully to emulate Mussolini. While *Il Duce* was consolidating his power, Hitler was dictating *Mein Kampf* from his jail cell.

Hitler and Mussolini in Munich, Germany, circa June 1940. (National Archives Still Pictures Branch)

Initially, Mussolini led a coalition government, but within three years, he had eliminated his opposition and turned Italy into a one-party, totalitarian state. Unlike other leaders who were turned out of office because of the worldwide depression, such as American President Herbert Hoover, Mussolini clung to power and used government intervention to prevent the collapse of the economy. He initiated a number of public works projects and began to expand and strengthen the military.

War Lore

In 1929, Mussolini ended the long-standing friction between the Catholic Church and the Italian state by signing the Lateran Treaty with the Pope, creating the independent state of Vatican City in exchange for the papacy's pledge of neutrality.

Tanks Versus Spears

Mussolini did not immediately embrace Hitler when Hitler took power. In fact, he sided early on with France and Britain, first warning Germany against hostile action in Austria in 1934 and then joining the other Western powers in the Stresa Front to protest Hitler's violations of the Versailles Treaty.

In his own act of defiance, Mussolini decided to attack Ethiopia (also known then as Abyssinia). There was no reason for Mussolini to declare war in 1935, though his stated reason was to avenge the defeat of the Italian army in 1896 at the battle of Aduwa. That battle had allowed Ethiopia to remain one of the few non-colonized nations of Africa. The fight in 1935 could hardly have been more one-sided, with Italian bombers and tanks opposed by soldiers often wielding only spears. Ethiopia, a member of the League of Nations, protested, expecting support from Britain and France.

The French were more worried about constraining Hitler and had signed a pact a few months earlier with Mussolini that concerned existing French and Italian colonies in Africa and threats to Austria. Mussolini believed that this pact meant that French Premier Pierre Laval had given him a commitment not to interfere in Ethiopia. The British were unwilling to block Italian access to the Suez Canal, which would have prevented Mussolini from importing oil and other vital supplies, because of the fear that such an act would force them into a war.

In the end it was clear to Mussolini that no action would be taken to stop him. In fact, word leaked that the powers had tried to convince Ethiopian ruler Haile Selassie to accept a deal they knew he would reject so they could charge him with the failure to resolve the crisis. Blaming the victim would become a feature of world diplomacy over the next decade. The League did condemn Mussolini's aggression, but it was unprepared to impose any severe sanctions that might deter the Italians.

On May 5, 1936, Italian troops captured the Ethiopian capital of Addis Ababa and Mussolini declared the war over. The League of Nations's response was to lift the minor sanctions it had imposed on Italy. A year later, Italy left the League.

Italy's blatant land grab alienated its erstwhile allies. When France and Britain began campaigns to build up their military forces, Mussolini was prepared to abandon them altogether and became more receptive to Hitler's entreaties. On November 1, 1936, he made a speech in which he referred to the vertical line between Rome and Berlin as "not a partition but rather an axis round which all European states animated by the will to collaboration and peace can also collaborate." From that statement came the name for the new alliance of dictators, the Axis.

War Lore

Shortly after Italy and Germany formed the Axis, Mussolini signed an agreement with Great Britain that recognized the freedom of movement for each nation in the Mediterranean. This pact became known as the Gentlemen's Agreement, a phrase that may have been first used in 1907 to describe an agreement between the United States and Japan.

The Red Sun Also Rises

While most of the world's attention focused on Europe, another expansionist power was beginning to flex its muscles in Asia. Besides the United States, Japan was the only country to emerge from World War I stronger than it had been before, and its leaders were interested in using their muscle to build their own empire.

The West European powers were as blind to the growing danger in the Far East as they were to the mounting threat just east of their borders. In 1924, Winston Churchill wrote, "I do not believe there is the slightest chance of [war with Japan] in our lifetime. The Japanese are our allies.... Japan is at the other end of the world. She cannot menace our vital security in any way.... War with Japan is not a possibility which any reasonable government need take into account." In terms of a direct confrontation with Great Britain, Churchill was correct; however, as events would later prove, the Japanese could have a profound impact on the national interests of Britain and many other nations.

When the world economy sank after the market crash, conservative elements in Japan became more powerful. They strongly believed that the Depression as well as other ills were due to the influence of the West. They particularly resented the fact that their economy became heavily dependent on the United States because it supplied most of the nation's oil.

49

Japan shared Hitler's belief in a need to expand to provide living space for its population. Unlike Germany, Japan was almost completely dependent on imports for its vital resources, such as oil, rubber, iron, and tin. Sources for these materials were in places such as Singapore, Indonesia, Malaysia, and the Philippines. The more immediate objective of Japanese rulers, however, was mainland China.

In 1931, Japan invaded Manchuria. China protested to the League of Nations, which condemned the Japanese aggression, but took no action. The United States momentarily pulled its head out of the sand and declared that it would not recognize any territorial acquisitions gained by war, but the Hoover-Stimson doctrine (named for the president and his secretary of state) was not backed by any threat of force.

Japan's response to the rebukes was to withdraw from the League and continue its operations in Manchuria, where it set up a puppet regime, and renamed the territory Manchukuo. By 1934, it was the Japanese who were issuing threats, warning that they would oppose any Western assistance given to China. They also announced that they would no longer adhere to the terms of the Washington Naval Treaty that had limited the size of their navy.

The one country that gave an indication it would not stand by while Japan conquered China was the Soviet Union, which signed a defense pact with Mongolia. This hostile alliance provoked Japan to sign its own agreement with Germany. The Anti-Comintern Pact signed in 1936 brought Japan into the Axis.

In July 1937, Japan went to war against China and within months controlled the richest portions of the country. The only real threat to their freedom of action occurred in December 1937, when the Japanese bombed and sank the American gunboat, *Panay*, in Chinese waters. Two men were killed and 30 wounded. Japan apologized, and Roosevelt let the matter pass. Had Americans not been mired in their isolationist funk, they might not have gone to war over the incident, but they certainly would have reacted more strongly. Instead, a democracy once again revealed its weakness to a dictatorship and, unwittingly, sowed the seeds for future aggression.

Ask the General

The Anti-Comintern Pact looked like a Japanese-German alliance against the Soviet Union, and the Western powers suspected that it contained secret provisions for joint action and defense. In truth the agreement only related to exchanging information to aid in the repression of the Communists. The "allies" never joined forces to fight the Soviet Union.

GI Jargon

In a two-month period from December 1937 through the beginning of February 1938, the Japanese occupiers in Nanking marched thousands of Chinese civilians into the countryside and murdered them. Japanese soldiers raped at least 20,000 Chinese women, and as many as 300,000 people were killed in one of history's worst massacres, an event known as the **Rape of Nanking.**

The day after the *Panay* incident, Japanese troops invaded China, focusing their attack on the city of Nanking. Much of the city was decimated by bombing raids. After the Japanese took over, the atrocities they committed were as heinous as those perpetrated later by the Nazis. The large-scale massacre of civilians is referred to as the *Rape of Nanking.*

What Hemingway Missed

War came closer to the homes of the Western powers when military officers led by General Francisco Franco started a rebellion in Spanish Morocco on July 17, 1936. Franco espoused fascist ideas and looked to Rome and Berlin for military assistance. Hitler and Mussolini were receptive and immediately sent weapons. The Italians were the more enthusiastic of the two supporters, sending ships, planes, and some troops to aid Franco. The general also signed agreements with his fellow fascists regarding cooperation in the future should war break out in the Mediterranean or Europe.

War Lore

The Spanish Civil War inspired two great artists to produce extraordinary works. In 1940, Ernest Hemingway wrote *For Whom The Bell Tolls*, a classic novel set in Spain during the Spanish Civil War. The book exposed the evils of fascism and reminded readers that the loss of liberty anywhere in the world endangered freedom everywhere. The book's title was taken from English poet John Donne's line, "Never send to know for whom the bell tolls; it tolls for thee." Pablo Picasso also was profoundly influenced by the Spanish Civil War and painted his masterpiece *Guernica* to memorialize the stronghold of the Republicans that was devastated by German bombs in 1937.

The liberal-left Republican government, meanwhile, received minimal assistance. The Soviet Union sent arms, but the British and French barred the shipment of any weapons to Spain. The United States, meanwhile, stuck to its policy of neutrality and imposed an arms embargo on both sides. This "evenhandedness" doomed the Republicans, because their enemies continued to be resupplied.

Franco was the effective ruler of Spain by the end of March 1939. The Spanish Civil War was even bloodier than the American one, with 1 million people, 600,000 in battle, dying during the conflict. After his victory, Franco quickly displayed the same ruthlessness as his fellow fascists, ordering the mass murder of opponents and the persecution of Catholics. For the next 36 years, Franco would rule Spain with an iron fist.

Even though the United States chose not to intervene in Spain, international instability was beginning to shake the Americans from their lethargy. They were still a long way from having any interest in risking or fighting a war, but President Roosevelt showed the first sign of impatience with aggressors after the attacks by Italy, Japan, and Franco when he spoke in Chicago on October 5, 1937:

> It seems to be unfortunately true that the epidemic of world lawlessness is spreading. When an epidemic of physical disease starts to spread, the community approves and joins in a quarantine of the patients in order to protect the health of the community against the spread of the disease.... The will for peace on the part of peace-loving nations must express itself to the end that nations that may be tempted to violate their agreements and the rights of others will desist from such a course. There must be positive endeavors to preserve peace.

Though stirring, the "Quarantine Speech" was widely attacked by isolationists who feared that the quarantine might lead to entanglements that would draw the United States into a war. Roosevelt backed off in the face of the criticism, but his speech did begin to shift the debate. The following year, the president finally won congressional approval for a billion-dollar naval construction program to begin the process of rebuilding America's weakened military.

The view from Europe was that Americans were all bluster. They had refused to join the League of Nations and then sat an ocean away criticizing their allies for the failure to halt aggression in Europe and Africa while doing nothing themselves to restrain the Axis powers. If anything, American timidity was viewed as a weakness that the fascists believed they could exploit to conquer the Old World. Now it was Hitler's turn to act.

The Least You Need to Know

➤ Hitler challenged the Allies, particularly the French, to stop his military buildup. He correctly anticipated their unwillingness to try to stop him.

➤ The League of Nations proved unwilling and unable to take effective action against treaty violations or aggressive moves by its members.

➤ Americans focused on their domestic problems, and Congress passed a series of neutrality laws aimed at preventing the United States from becoming entangled in a war in Europe.

➤ The world watches as Italy conquers Ethiopia and Japan rapes China.

➤ One of the world's worst civil wars breaks out in Spain. Italy and Germany help Franco overthrow the Republican government while the Western powers sit on their hands.

➤ Roosevelt calls for a "quarantine" to prevent the spread of aggression, but the United States is not yet ready to back its words with action.

Austria

Chapter 5

Peace in Whose Time?

In This Chapter

➤ Germany "unites" with Austria

➤ The Munich Conference fails to bring peace

➤ Jews become targets of violence

➤ Czechoslovakia ceases to exist

➤ Italy and the Soviet Union sign treaties with Hitler

➤ Poland becomes the brink for war

By the mid-1930s, Hitler was firmly in control of Germany and had begun his rearmament campaign. The European powers had stood by impotently watching events in Germany, Africa, and the Far East. Though Britain and France had begun their own military buildups, neither was looking for a fight. Quite the opposite was the case. The United States and its leaders were happy to be thousands of miles from the turmoil. The day was fast approaching, however, when none of these powers could avoid facing the Axis menace.

The *Anschluss* Was No *Sound of Music*

Austria had struggled with internal divisions since the end of World War I, conflicts exacerbated by the onset of the worldwide depression. The political divide was primarily between left-wing socialists, who were particularly strong in Vienna, and conservatives from much of the rest of the country, who were represented by the Christian Social Party that dominated the government. The equation was further destabilized by the National Socialist Party, which grew more popular after Hitler ascended to power and lent support from Berlin.

To quell the discontent and political opposition, Austrian Chancellor Engelbert Dollfuss dissolved parliament in 1933 and sent the army out to murder the leftist opposition. In a move that recalled the Beer Hall *Putsch*, the Austrian Nazis sought to take advantage of the nation's divisions and staged a coup in July 1934, in which Dollfuss was assassinated. The Nazis were quickly arrested and order restored under the new chancellor, Kurt von Schuschnigg.

At this point, Mussolini had not yet thrown his lot in with Hitler and remained committed to Austria's independence; Mussolini even went so far as to move troops near the Austrian border. Italy's posture led Hitler to resist the temptation to support the Nazis' attempt to seize power.

After Mussolini joined Hitler to form the Axis, the Austrian guarantee dissolved. Later, excited by the news that he would not face any Italian opposition, Hitler said, "Tell Mussolini I will never forget this…. Never, never, never, whatever happens…. If he should ever need any help or be in any danger, he can be convinced that I shall stick to him …." This was a promise Hitler actually kept.

One Happy German Family

Six million Germans lived in Austria, and Hitler believed they should be under his rule. The Versailles Treaty barred Austria and Germany from uniting, but this provision was just one more that Hitler hoped to nullify.

Initially, the *Führer* was content to influence Austrian policy from afar. The Germans ratcheted up the pressure on Austrian Chancellor Schuschnigg. On July 11, 1936, he signed a gentlemen's agreement acknowledging Austria as a German state in exchange for Hitler's recognition of the "full sovereignty" of Austria. Privately, Hitler was already planning to expand the *Reich* and would soon fire his war minister, Werner von Blomberg, for protesting that the French were too strong for Germany to risk military adventures.

By the beginning of 1938, Hitler had forced Schuschnigg to appoint Nazis to key positions in his government. Talk began of an *Anschluss*, a political union of the two nations, but Schuschnigg still hoped to preserve his nation's independence and called for a vote in 1938 to determine the future disposition of the country. He also refused to appoint a Nazi in his place as chancellor. At that point, Hitler would no longer brook any opposition; he demanded, and received, Schuschnigg's resignation.

Hitler told one of his Nazi allies, Austrian Minister of Interior Arthur Seyss-Inquart, to declare himself head of a provisional government and ask for German assistance. Everything went as Hitler wanted, and on March 12, 1938, German troops easily overran the country. Originally, the plan was to simply set up a puppet government in Vienna, but Hitler spontaneously decided to incorporate Austria in the Third *Reich*. The Germans now referred to the region as *Ostmark* (Eastern March).

German police enter Imst as Austria becomes German, March 1938. (National Archives Still Pictures Branch)

War Lore

Millions have learned about the *Anschluss* from the Rodgers and Hammerstein play and film *The Sound of Music,* based on the real-life family of Baron Georg von Trapp, who married his children's governess, Maria Augusta Kutschera, in 1927. Von Trapp, a widower, had seven children before marrying Maria, with whom he had three more. The family began singing together in the mid-1930s and toured Europe in 1937. After the *Anschluss,* the family escaped through the Alps and moved to the United States, settling in Stowe, Vermont, where they opened a hotel that is still owned by the family (their Web site is http://www.trappfamily.com/index.htm). The baron died in 1947, and Maria died in 1987 at the age of 82.

Freud Takes His Couch to the United States

It did not take long for Hitler to demonstrate that the future for occupied peoples would not be a good one, particularly if they were Jewish. The Austrian people had, by and large, welcomed the Germans, and they were disturbingly receptive to the anti-Semitic measures of the Nazis. By September 1939, thousands of Jewish businesses had been closed, and apartments and other property had been confiscated. An estimated 75 percent of the Jewish population, which numbered 185,000, had left Austria.

One of the Jews who escaped was Sigmund Freud. President Roosevelt and, oddly enough, Mussolini paid a ransom to get permission for Freud to leave. The famous psychologist was already in his 80s and suffering from cancer, but he was persuaded by his friends to flee after he signed a statement attesting to being treated well. "I can heartily recommend the *Gestapo* to anyone," he wrote sarcastically. His four sisters did not leave and were later killed in the concentration camps. Freud died in London in 1939.

"I Have No More Territorial Demands"

It did not take a diplomatic genius or military strategist to figure out that Czechoslovakia would be next on the wolf's plate. Like Austria, Czechoslovakia had a large German minority (3 million), and Hitler's propaganda machine claimed these people were being persecuted in the Sudetenland region. Czechoslovakia would also provide Germany with more "living space" and vital resources such as coal and gold.

The Czechs Stand Alone

The Czechs had a large army, but no one believed it could resist the Germans. The Soviet Union could defend the Czechs, but only if given permission to send their troops through Romania or Poland, something neither country was prepared to do. The Poles further complicated efforts to stop Hitler by declaring they would abrogate their alliance with France if the French came to the Czech's defense. (Poland was not prepared to fight Germany, particularly over Czechoslovakia, and feared Soviet intervention.)

In May 1938, the Czechs began to mobilize their reserves. Hitler, remember, faced resistance from his generals, so it is conceivable that a tough response from the powers might have encouraged them to try to overthrow the *Führer*. The French and British both warned the Germans not to attack Czechoslovakia, but Hitler was convinced they would not intervene, and his opponents in the German military did not feel they had the backing needed to stage a coup.

The Czechs were bluntly told not to expect help from France. British Prime Minister Neville Chamberlain made his views clear in a radio address to the British people in which he said, "How horrible, fantastic, incredible it is that we should be digging trenches and trying on gas masks here because of a quarrel in a faraway country between people of whom we know nothing!"

War Lore

British Prime Minister Neville Chamberlain was 69 years old and had never been in an airplane before when he decided to fly to Germany to discuss with Hitler a resolution to the building tensions in Czechoslovakia. He asked Hitler if he would be satisfied if he were given control of the Sudetenland. When Hitler said he would be, Chamberlain said he would get the Czechs and the French to accept this solution. The British prime minister, whose name would come to represent naivete in foreign affairs, believed Hitler was "a man who could be relied upon when he had given his word."

The Czechs were already more scared of the Soviets than the Germans, so they could not look to the east for help either. Faced with few options, Czech President Eduard Benes reluctantly concluded that he would have to accept the loss of the Sudetenland to have any hope of saving the rest of the country.

Hitler became more bellicose, however, and warned he would take the Sudetenland by force if the issue was not resolved within a few days. To avert bloodshed, Chamberlain succeeded in enlisting Mussolini's aid to convene a conference of the four European powers. Hitler accepted, joining Chamberlain, Mussolini, and French Premier Edouard Daladier in Munich from September 29 to 30, 1938. No one from Czechoslovakia was invited to participate.

"Peace For Our Time"

Hitler was perfectly reasonable, especially when the other leaders acknowledged that 3 million Germans should not be under Czech rule. Ceded control of the Sudetenland, Hitler could reassuringly declare, "I have no more territorial demands to make in Europe." Though the United States did not participate in the conference, Americans supported the sellout of their fellow democracy.

For the moment, the Munich conference seemed a great triumph. The French and British leaders returned to their homes and received tumultuous welcomes. Chamberlain declared, "I believe that it is peace for our time."

In hindsight, Munich has become a symbol of naivete in dealing with despots, but to give some perspective, it is important to realize the only alternative to negotiation was war. Chamberlain and the rest of the democratic leaders hoped to find an agreement that would satisfy Hitler's ambitions and avoid a broader conflict. Simultaneously, they hoped to deter his aggression without provoking it. The lesson, which few leaders have assimilated in the succeeding 60 years, is that tyrants cannot be pacified.

Words of War

"[Munich turned out to be] surrender on the installment plan. It was like giving a cannibal a finger in the hope of saving an arm."

—Thomas Bailey and David Kennedy

The results of Munich should have surprised no one, given the precedents set since Versailles. No leader had stood up for the enforcement of the old peace terms to stop Germany's military buildup, her reoccupation of the Rhineland, or the *Anschluss* in Austria. Ironically, Hitler did not view Munich as a triumph. He considered it a colossal mistake on his part that cheated him out of a war he wanted.

Hitler must have felt that he had completely fooled his foreign rivals. Within weeks after agreeing to the compromise at Munich, he was already telling his generals to plan for the liquidation of what remained of independent Czechoslovakia.

This Sudeten woman (circa 1938) is unable to conceal her misery as she dutifully salutes the triumphant Hitler. (National Archives Still Pictures Branch)

No sooner was one crisis resolved when Hitler began to publicly provoke another. This time it was with Poland. In a message to the Polish government, the *Führer* demanded changes in the terms set out at Versailles regarding the Free City of Danzig. President Wilson had forced Germany to give up territory in Poland, but he insisted on keeping Danzig in limbo because of its overwhelming German population. Under the compromise he fashioned, the city's internal affairs were internationally supervised, but because the city was democratic, the Germans had effective control. Poland was given authority, however, over Danzig's foreign policy. Now Hitler wanted guarantees regarding a corridor through Poland that would connect Germany and Danzig.

The Night of the Broken Glass

Germany's neighbors were already nervous, and the powers skeptical of Hitler's trustworthiness, when the Nazis launched their most brutal and openly violent attack on the Jews. The pretext, and it was only that, was the assassination in Paris of a German official by a 17-year-old Jew named Herschel Grynszpan, whose parents were deported from Germany but were not allowed to return to their native Poland. Grynszpan had wanted to kill the German ambassador to avenge the mistreatment of his family. Ernst von Rath, the official sent to deal with him after he asked for a visa and who he killed, was, ironically, being investigated by the *Gestapo* for not being anti-Semitic.

GI Jargon

A **pogrom** is an organized massacre of helpless people.

Though the Germans suggested the violence that followed was a spontaneous reaction to news of the murder, the truth was that the Germans had planned a *pogrom*. On the night of November 9, 1938, the head of the *Gestapo* sent a message to all police units informing them that attacks would soon begin against the Jews and that no one should interfere.

During the next two days, rampaging mobs throughout Germany and the newly acquired territories of Austria and Sudetenland freely attacked Jews in the street, in their homes, and at their places of work and worship. At least 96 Jews were killed and hundreds more injured. More than 1,000 synagogues were burned. Thousands of Jewish businesses, cemeteries, and schools were vandalized, and 30,000 Jews were arrested and sent to concentration camps.

GI Jargon

Kristallnacht, "The Night of Broken Glass," refers to the windows and store fronts shattered when the Nazis attacked Jews throughout Germany, Austria, and Sudetenland. *Kristallnacht* also represented the destruction of Jewish life under the Nazis—thousands saw it as a message to flee before it was too late. Millions more did not read the message correctly.

Afterward, the Jews had to clean up the mess from what came to be called *Kristallnacht.* Not only were they denied compensation, but a fine of $400 million was imposed on the Jewish community. Within a few weeks, Jews could no longer attend schools, they were barred from most public places, and their remaining businesses were confiscated. It was the last incident of street violence against the Jews.

Czech Mate

The powers continued to ignore Hitler's persecution of the Jews, confirming his view that no one cared a whit about the Jews. The weakness of the British and French was further exemplified by their ongoing efforts to negotiate new agreements, such as the one guaranteeing the Franco-German border signed in December 1938.

Less than six months after Munich, Hitler sent Austrian Nazis to Slovakia to demand that they declare their independence and ask for German protection. At almost the same time, the Czech president, Emil Hacha, came to see Hitler and was told he must essentially surrender or face an invasion. Hacha agreed to allow Germany to be his nation's "protector." On March 16, 1939, German troops took control, and Czechoslovakia ceased to exist. For the second time in a year, Hitler had conquered a neighbor without his army having to fire a shot.

The Fate of Czechoslovakia. (UPI/Corbis-Bettmann)

The British and French seemed shocked that Hitler had so quickly repudiated his Munich declarations, but they remained unwilling to act, in part because of the fig leaf of Hacha's "invitation" seeking German intervention. Still, Chamberlain, who had rationalized the sellout of the Sudetenland on the basis of the German majority living there, now stood by while Hitler became the ruler over 10 million people who were not German.

America's behavior was certainly no better than that of its European allies. Roosevelt took no action to back up his call for a "quarantine," which ran into a buzz saw of domestic opposition. The president also began to campaign for the repeal of the neutrality laws, but he was again met with fierce opposition from the isolationists. Roosevelt's reaction to Hitler's latest display of belligerence was to try to persuade him to sign a 10-year non-aggression pact with 31 countries; he succeeded only in convincing Hitler of the unlikelihood of U.S. intervention to stop his grand design. Hitler viewed U.S. neutrality as a sign of American incompetence and consequently gave little thought to preparing for conflict with their armed forces.

The German people were not thrilled with their leader's expansionist policy, but Hitler was not particularly concerned with public opinion. He was less interested now in persuasion and therefore did not spend as much time making demagogic speeches. Instead, he focused his attention on his war plans, spent most of his time at army headquarters, and forced adherence through terror.

Poles Apart

Events were quickly spiraling toward another, broader confrontation. Six days after occupying Prague, the Germans seized Memel, a predominantly German area that had become part of Lithuania after World War I. (After annexing Memel, Hitler visited the town. It was one of his few known trips on a ship, and he is said to have gotten seasick.) Shortly after that, Hitler annulled his 1934 nonaggression treaty with Poland.

As German rhetoric concerning grievances with Poland heated up, the British and French, over Polish objections, began to discuss a possible alliance with the Soviet Union. As early as March 1939, Stalin had shown an interest in making a deal. The diplomatic maneuvering was intense and delicate, with both sides hoping to minimize the risk of fighting and maximize their freedom of action. The French and British were reluctant to cooperate with Stalin, and many in both countries hoped the Nazis and Communists might destroy each other. They also feared the opposite result: that a strictly European war would decimate the powers and leave the Soviet Union to dominate the Continent.

The Poles, meanwhile, had their own suspicions about Stalin's intentions and refused to allow Soviet troops to cross their territory to attack Germany.

Words of War

"I saw my enemies at Munich, and they are worms."

—Adolf Hitler

From their perspective, this was no better than permitting Hitler to march through Poland to invade Russia.

War Lore

Stalin's real name was Joseph Vissarionovich Djugashvili. He was born on Dec. 21, 1879. When the Russian Social Democratic party split into Mensheviks and Bolsheviks, Djugashvili aligned himself with V.I. Lenin's Bolsheviks. While becoming an influential member of Lenin's inner circle, Djugashvili became the first editor of the party newspaper, *Pravda*. In 1913, he began using the pseudonym Stalin, which means "man of steel." He was exiled to Siberia by the czarist government, but he returned after the March Revolution had over-thrown the czar and eventually became a key party leader. After Lenin's death in 1924, Stalin used his position to outmaneuver his rivals and institute absolute control over the Soviet Union.

Entangling Alliances

While continuing their negotiations with the Soviets, the British and French announced they would defend Switzerland, Belgium, and the Netherlands against a German attack. Several days later, on March 31, 1938, the British extended their defense umbrella to include Poland. When Mussolini suddenly invaded Albania on April 7, France and England agreed to defend Greece and Romania as well.

Mussolini then cemented his alliance with Hitler by signing the Pact of Steel, in which both leaders promised to go to war together. By doing so, *Il Duce* also hoped to gain influence with Hitler and jointly plan their future conquests.

The Japanese, on the other hand, were reluctant to take part in a war that might be fought with the British and French and potentially bring in the Americans. Their main concern was the Soviet Union, and they preferred an alliance against Stalin. Germany, however, wanted to ally with the Soviet Union. Hitler feared that a German-Japanese alliance against the Soviets would prompt them to ally with the Western European powers.

Even as he was making increasingly bellicose threats against Poland, Hitler made conciliatory gestures toward the Europeans. He told Switzerland, the Netherlands, Belgium, and Luxembourg he would recognize their neutrality—so long as they didn't join an alliance against him. He even offered to sign an agreement with Great Britain.

The British response was to introduce the first peacetime conscription law in preparation for the likelihood of war.

Poland lacked natural barriers to invasion and was therefore even more difficult to defend than Czechoslovakia. Moreover, Hitler didn't think the British were serious about defending Poland. If they weren't prepared to fight over Czechoslovakia, why would they aid a country in which they had even less interest? Hitler wanted to fight—he had told his generals to begin planning an attack in early April—but he was afraid the British might pressure the Poles to accept his demands, as they had the Czechs, to avert war.

Totalitarians Unite!

The Germans desperately wanted to avoid a two-front war, so Hitler entered negotiations with the Soviets even as talks continued between Stalin and the British and French. The Soviets, who wanted no trouble from Germany, saw no contradiction in dealing virtually evenhandedly with dictators and democrats.

In this case the democrats had little to offer Stalin. They wanted his help without offering anything in return. Hitler, however, decided to make short-run concessions to his fellow autocrat with an eye toward the confrontation he planned in the future. In August 1939, German Foreign Minister Joachim von Ribbentrop held several meetings with his Soviet counterpart, Vyacheslav Molotov, before reaching an agreement on August 23.

The public version of the treaty outlined what amounted to a non-aggression pact; that is, both countries agreed not to go to war or join an alliance against each other. The secret provisions were the crucial determinants for Stalin, because they represented a division of spoils in which Hitler agreed to recognize a Soviet sphere of influence and held out the likelihood of a partition of Poland. More specifically, the agreement allowed the Soviets to impose treaties on Estonia, Latvia, and Lithuania, which put them under Moscow's thumb. Hitler also gave Stalin a green light to do as he wished in Finland. In addition, Germany sent the Russians naval blueprints, torpedoes, mines, and airplane engines.

The United States had received information about the Nazi-Soviet negotiations from an informer in the German embassy in Moscow. Still, the agreement surprised everyone, including the Japanese, who had expected to ally with Germany *against*

Ask the General

Hitler believed that allying with Russia would discourage British intervention. Instead, it promised to provoke a response from both England and France if Germany moved against Poland. Hitler would be unable to dispose of Russia, as he had planned, before confronting with Britain and France. Germany was now fated to fight the multifront war that had been its undoing in World War I.

Russia. The pact's benefit to Germany was a supply of vital materials such as oil, cotton, iron ore, and manganese. As you will see in Chapter 10, Stalin kept up the flow of these goods up to the moment German troops began to cross into Russia.

Hitler's ultimate plan was to destroy the Soviet Union to capture the living space his people needed. To get there, he had to go through Poland. Because of England's pledge to defend Poland, Hitler would have to defeat the French and British before he could continue east, and he could not risk a rearguard action from the Poles. Strategy dictated that he eliminate the Polish obstacle quickly. However, when the French reacted to the Nazi-Soviet pact by reasserting their guarantee for Poland, the British signed a formal alliance with the Poles, and Mussolini said Italy would not participate in the fighting, Hitler decided to postpone the invasion of Poland.

It Must Be War

Once again, the logic that came out of World War I, that territory should be divided along demographic lines, emerged as a factor in judging Hitler's claims. As was the case in Austria, the Sudetenland, and Memel, Germans made up a sizable proportion of the population in Danzig, so there were precedents for his demands. However, the Polish government would not bend to Hitler's will. The ambassador in Berlin agreed to negotiate, but the *Führer* refused to meet with him because he did not have the authority to make any decisions without consulting with his government first.

Ask the General

Poland made a vital contribution to the Allied war effort. In July 1939, Polish code-breakers gave the British and French reproductions of the German Enigma machine used for encoding radio messages. British cryptographers spent months deciphering the codes and eventually intercepted messages sent by the Germans, particularly by their air force during the blitz. The code word *Ultra* designated information derived from German secret messages.

On August 30, 1939, the Poles mobilized their armed forces. Though German propaganda sought to portray this mobilization as a prelude to an attack by Poland, the Poles otherwise avoided any provocations that might be used as a pretext for a German attack. The Polish strategy was also a deliberate attempt to play for sympathy should war come, so they couldn't be blamed for the outbreak.

Hitler wasn't concerned with appearances. His goal for the invasion he planned was not the installation of a puppet regime. He sought nothing less than the destruction of the Polish people. He warned, "I shall strike like lightning with the full force of a mechanized army, of which the Poles have no conception."

On August 31, Germans wearing Polish uniforms attacked a German radio station at Gleiwitz. Even before he gave a speech in which he blamed Polish soldiers for the mission, Hitler's troops had launched their invasion. Britain and France demanded that Germany withdraw. When Hitler refused, they declared war. No one knew it yet, but World War II had begun.

The Least You Need to Know

➤ Hitler united the German people by taking over Austria in an *Anschluss* that was popular with most Austrians, but foreshadowed future aggression.

➤ The democracies forced Czechoslovakia to give Germany the Sudetenland in the vain hope of appeasing Hitler.

➤ *Kristallnacht*, a night in which hundreds of Jews were killed and injured in violent attacks by German mobs, signaled the end of Jewish life under Hitler.

➤ After promising he had no further territorial ambitions, Hitler wasted little time before conquering the rest of Czechoslovakia.

➤ Mussolini signed the Pact of Steel with Hitler, creating the alliance that would go to war against the rest of Europe.

➤ England and France wooed the Soviets, but Stalin chose to align with Hitler in an agreement that allowed him to expand the Soviet empire in exchange for providing vital resources to Germany.

➤ Hitler prepared to unleash a *Blitzkrieg* against Poland.

Part 2
Blitzkrieg

The war begins in earnest with the German invasion of Poland. What will turn out to be a brief alliance between Germany and the Soviet Union keeps the Russians from intervening in Poland while allowing the Red Army to roll over Finland. Britain and France declare war and find themselves unable to stop Hitler's blitzkrieg across Western Europe. Many Allied troops are saved for future combat by evacuating from Dunkirk, but the Germans overrun France.

The Germans also wreak havoc at sea, where their U-boats hunt Allied shipping in wolf packs. Britain comes under air attack as Germany stages the blitz on London. The British repel the attacks sufficiently to discourage Hitler from invading Britain. The United States, meanwhile, becomes the arsenal of democracy, doing whatever it can to aid its allies short of joining the war.

Italy's advances in North Africa are reversed by the British, and Hitler feels obligated to save Mussolini's troops. This diversion will have a great impact on the invasion Hitler launches against the Soviet Union.

Chapter 6

Goose-Stepping Across Europe

> ## In This Chapter
>
> ➤ Germany's lightning attack overwhelms Poland
>
> ➤ Britain and France declare war on Germany
>
> ➤ Securing the flow of vital resources
>
> ➤ The Soviets attack Finland
>
> ➤ The Allies debate how to respond to Hitler and Stalin
>
> ➤ The Katyn Massacre and the building of Auschwitz

For 20 years, Europe had feared a rejuvenated Germany. The safeguards that were put in place at Versailles and in subsequent treaties proved to offer no safety at all. Germany had been allowed to rebuild its military and overrun two nations without firing a shot. Poland represented a brink, at least for two of the three Western powers. The United States would remain on the sidelines for two long years, watching as Europe became consumed by war.

The Nazis Roll Over the Poles

The Poles had a choice of strategies as the likelihood of war increased. Instead of concentrating their forces in one area where they could try to hold out until the Allies arrived, the Poles chose to spread themselves thinly to defend virtually the entire country. What's more, though the Polish army numbered around 1 million men, its weapons were mostly from World War I. The air force had only a few hundred modern planes; the navy had only four destroyers, five submarines, and a handful of small ships. Given these resources, military strategy probably made no difference in the outcome.

On the morning of September 1, 1939, shortly after the fake Polish raid on the German radio station, the German *Luftwaffe* attacked and, within three days, destroyed the Polish air force. The Germans quickly cut the lines of communication, and the Poles were unable to complete their mobilization. The *Luftwaffe* bombed rail lines, munitions dumps, and caused panic everywhere. This onslaught from the air was followed by an equally quick and brutal land invasion by infantry backed by artillery and tanks. In some cases, the Poles met this massive force with horse cavalry.

Britain Mounts a Confetti Campaign

On Sunday morning, September 3, the British announced they were at war with Germany. Chamberlain had come to realize that "the essential preliminary to any settlement of European problems was the destruction of Hitlerism." He would not be satisfied with rolling German gains back; it would be necessary to replace Hitler, who had finally used up the last ounce of trust he had among the gullible Allies.

The night Britain declared war, she launched her first attack on Germany, dropping 13 tons of leaflets that said:

> *Your rulers have condemned you to the massacres, miseries, and privations of a war they cannot ever hope to win.*

While Great Britain was dropping confetti on Germany, the Nazis were shooting at the British. That same night, a German submarine torpedoed and sank the passenger liner *Athenia*, killing 112 people, including 28 Americans.

The murder of Americans could have been a provocation, but the United States almost immediately announced it would remain neutral. The American people were solidly behind the Allies and were virulently anti-Nazi, but they remained unwilling to fight a foe thousands of miles away. They were also confident that the British and French could stop Hitler.

Roosevelt believed war was necessary and was willing to do as much as possible to aid the effort—short of joining it. He campaigned for abrogating, or at least revising, the neutrality laws. He won support for a new Neutrality Act, which at least allowed the United States to sell war materials to the Allies. The catch was that the French and British would have to pay cash for the goods and then transport them in their own ships.

The new cash-and-carry law enacted on November 4 was by no means neutral: It benefited only the Allies, perhaps none more than the United States. The restrictions cleverly allowed the United States to avoid providing the kinds of loans that provoked so much hostility after World War I when repayment was demanded. By forcing the recipients to transport the weapons, U.S. ships were

Words of War

"Force is the only language they understand, like bullies."

—Franklin Roosevelt, of Hitler and Mussolini

kept out of danger. Finally, the cash payments for much-needed supplies helped the U.S. economy rebound.

A Merciless Victor

Britain's declaration of war came too late for the Poles. The Germans had already cut off Poland's outlet to the sea and were advancing on Warsaw. It took only three weeks to crush Polish resistance. The quick, devastating, and decisive German operation was labeled a *Blitzkrieg*—a "lightning war"—by Western newspapermen.

The Nazis did have help. The Soviets resisted Hitler's entreaties to join the fighting until September 17. Then Stalin's troops invaded, cutting off the Poles' escape route to the east and capturing more than 200,000 prisoners. Soviet Foreign Minister Molotov declared that Poland ceased to exist, and as agreed in the Soviet-Nazi pact, the Russians seized the eastern part of the country. The Poles holding out in Warsaw asked for a truce, but Hitler was determined to bomb them into submission. Finally, on September 27, the 140,000 Polish troops surrendered.

War Without Rules

Besides the lightning thrust of the German army, what made the attack on Poland different was the widespread atrocities committed against prisoners of war and civilians. In early October, Hitler decided to annex part of Poland and to establish what amounted to a colony in the rest. The Nazis' legal adviser, Hans Frank, was chosen as the governor-general of the new government based in Cracow. He quickly instituted a range of laws to show the Poles who were members of the "master race" and who were the inferiors. The apartheid-like rules included serving Germans first in shops, requiring Poles to stay off the pavement when Germans were passing, and barring Poles from speaking to German women.

From the outset, Polish soldiers taken prisoner were often summarily executed. Some were killed in the most brutal fashion, such as being confined in a building that was burned down with them inside. The massacre of civilians started slowly and escalated as the war went on, but Hitler had stated his intent long before the *Blitzkrieg*. On January 30, 1939, he warned that if war broke out, "the consequence will not be the Bolshevization of the earth and thereby the victory of the Jews, but the annihilation of the Jewish race in Europe."

Roll Call

When the fighting ended, the Germans had lost 14,000 men. Roughly 60,000 Polish soldiers and 25,000 civilians were killed. Nearly 700,000 Polish soldiers had been taken prisoner by the Germans, and another 217,000 had been taken prisoner by the Russians.

War Lore

The district controlled by Hans Frank was called the Gau of the Vandals, named after the Germanic tribe that ruled part of North Africa in the 4th and 5th centuries. The group's name comes from the time they dominated the western Mediterranean and sacked Rome. The Vandals, ironically, persecuted Orthodox Christians. By 534, the Vandal empire had been destroyed. The word *vandal* is derived from this group's reputation for plundering and inspiring fear in its victims.

The beginning of the war marked an escalation in Hitler's campaign to destroy the Jews. Many were expelled from their homes and barred from their jobs. All Jewish males between the ages of 14 and 60 were assigned to government labor details, and dozens of slave labor camps were built.

This was a turning point for those who foresaw the danger and hoped to escape. The more Germany expanded, the less opportunity anyone had to leave. The borders were gradually sealed, and restrictions were placed on movement and communication. Meanwhile, the other nations of the world erected their own obstacles, in the form of quotas and other immigration barriers, to prevent most people hoping to flee Hitler from finding refuge. The reasons for doing so were a combination of anti-Semitism, xenophobia, and concern for the domestic economy.

The Germans also changed the rules that had governed international relations for the first half of the 20th century relating to the drawing of boundaries. Borders were typically based in large measure on the population in a particular area. The basis, for example, of German claims to Danzig, Austria, and the Sudetenland was that these areas were predominantly German. After the Nazi *Blitzkrieg*, the new model was for the conqueror to determine boundaries without regard to demography and to expel or exterminate unwanted groups.

Spy Versus Spy

The Allies had no illusions that Hitler's appetite for conquest had been sated. They learned that Hitler was planning to attack France, Holland, and Belgium on November 12. One source of the information was General Hans Oster, the number two person in the intelligence branch headed by Admiral Wilhelm Canaris. A second mole on Canaris's staff, Paul Thmmel, also passed on Hitler's war plans.

The British did hold out some hope for Germans to put an end to Hitler's regime themselves. On November 8, Hitler went to Munich to celebrate the 16th anniversary of the Beer Hall *Putsch*, but left the hall earlier than expected. Eight minutes later, a bomb exploded near where he'd been standing, killing seven people. Hitler viewed his good fortune as further evidence that it was his destiny to fulfill his ambition.

The same month, the British government authorized its agents to contact Nazi opposition figures in the Netherlands. It turned out the SS had set up the British and kidnapped their agents. The Venlo Incident (named after the Dutch town where the fiasco occurred) was a watershed because the British would never again believe a coup could be provoked to defeat Hitler.

Interested Spectators

All the nations of Europe had some interest in what the Germans were up to, but some played greater roles at this time than others. One key nation was Romania, which provided Germany with much of its oil. Securing these supplies would be a concern of Hitler's throughout the war. The British knew this and tried unsuccessfully to sabotage the oil fields. The Romanians, meanwhile, also had to contend with other neighbors that coveted their territory, notably the Soviet Union, Hungary, and Bulgaria. Early on, Romania stayed on the tightrope that kept it out of the war. This position would not be sustainable in the long run.

Sweden performed a similar balancing act. The Swedes also had critical resources Hitler needed, in this case high-grade iron ore and ball bearings. The quality of the ore made German steel production more efficient, and the willingness of the Swedes to deliver the material eased the logistical burden on the Nazis. The Germans might have simply seized the iron, but they feared the Swedes would sabotage the mines. At the beginning of the war, at least, the two nations had a mutually beneficial trade relationship, with the Germans getting the material they desperately needed and the Swedes gaining substantial profits.

The British and Americans believed that cutting off the Swedish pipeline, along with the Soviet oil deliveries, could cripple the Nazi war machine. The Allies had little success, however, in convincing the Swedes to change their policy. Much later in the war, in 1943, the Allies reached a trade agreement with Sweden: The United States and England agreed to increase exports to Sweden in exchange for the reduction in iron ore and ball bearing exports, the prohibition of German use of Swedish territory to transport goods and troops, and the cessation of Swedish naval escorts for German ships in the Baltic. When the outcome of the war became clear, Sweden felt confident it could stop trading with Germany with impunity and finally did so in November 1944.

Another interested party was Spain. Hitler very much wanted Franco's support for his war effort, but the *Generalissimo* wanted to focus his attention on rebuilding the nation after its three-year civil war. Many Spaniards were not happy with the Nazi-Soviet pact and were also concerned about the supply of vital goods, which came primarily from Germany's opponents. Still, the Nazis did use Spain as a base from which to spy on the

Allies and were allowed to use Spanish harbors to repair and refuel their submarines. Private Spanish merchants also provided Germany vital commodities smuggled from Latin America and Africa, such as platinum and industrial diamonds.

Slovakia, meanwhile, was not neutral. It behaved as a loyal subject of Germany and joined the fight against Poland. Its reward was a slice of Poland. Germany also allowed the Slovaks some freedom and treated their leaders with a modicum of respect. Hitler hoped that Slovakia would serve as an example to other nations of how to behave properly and the rewards that accompanied such cooperation.

The Winter of Stalin's Discontent

When Stalin agreed to his pact with Hitler, he saw it as a means to expand the Soviet empire. His first move was to demand basing rights for his troops in Estonia, Latvia, and Lithuania. Several months later, he annexed those countries. His next target was Finland, a small nation that would prove more difficult to impose his will upon.

Stalin did not like the fact that the Finnish border ran dangerously close to the Soviet Baltic ports and the city of Leningrad. Finland had gained its independence during the Russian Revolution after being a part of Russia for more than 100 years. In October 1940, Stalin demanded that Finland give back territory leading to Leningrad and grant the Soviet navy basing rights at its ports.

The Finns were not impressed by Stalin's generous offer and declined the invitation. On November 30, Stalin responded to this stubbornness by sending 30 divisions into Finland, a number that eventually grew to a total of 1 million men fighting a Finnish army of 175,000. Roughly a thousand Soviet aircraft were opposed by 150 obsolete Finnish planes. In one of its last futile acts, the League of Nations expelled the Soviets for their aggression. Like its other feeble efforts to sanction dictators, this one had no impact.

The Finns staged a courageous defense of their homeland. Despite their small number, they were often able to outmaneuver the Soviets because of their superior training, intimate knowledge of their surroundings, and efficient use of their meager resources (to make *Molotov cocktails* for instance). For example, the Finnish soldiers could better negotiate the forest paths in deep snow using skis.

The United States was sympathetic to Finland's plight, but was not about to abandon its neutrality. Congress agreed to provide $30 million to allow Finland to buy nonmilitary supplies, but that was the extent of the United States's contribution to the Finns' defense.

GI Jargon

The Finnish soldiers effectively used a new type of weapon against the Soviet tanks: a bottle filled with gasoline that had a rag stuffed inside that could be lit. The lit bottles were then thrown like grenades. These bombs became known as **Molotov cocktails** in honor of the Soviet foreign minister.

The British and French were prepared to go further. In early December, they finally made a tangible contribution to the war effort by sending large quantities of arms to Finland, everything from planes to grenades to ammunition. Volunteers from both nations also went to Helsinki to join the fighting Finns.

It would still be another two months before Chamberlain would declare, "Finland must not be allowed to disappear off the map." Both he and his French counterpart agreed to send troops to stop the German advance. The British planned to send theirs via Narvik, Norway, with the intention of also cutting off Swedish iron ore supplies to Germany. By this time, however, the Finns had reached the point of exhaustion and had no reserves to throw into the fight; the Soviets meanwhile had a seemingly inexhaustible supply of reinforcements.

Words of War

"The Soviet Union, as everybody who has the courage to face the fact knows, is run by a dictatorship as absolute as any other dictatorship in the world."

—President Roosevelt, speaking to the American Youth Congress, February 10, 1940

Hitler watched events in Scandinavia unfold and kept his eye on his long-range goals of fighting a one-front war first with the west and then turning east to take on the Soviets. In the short run, the *Führer* wanted to keep Stalin happy and neutral. In February, as the war in Finland reached its climax, Hitler negotiated a new deal with Stalin whereby the Soviets would supply Germany with agricultural products and oil in exchange for arms and plans and prototypes of new ships, planes, tanks, and bombs.

On March 15, 1940, the Finnish parliament accepted the peace terms sought by the Soviets. Finland kept its independence, but the Soviet border had been extended to create greater defensive depth. By the end, Soviet dead numbered 200,000, compared to 25,000 for the Finns.

War Lore

Stalin seriously miscalculated Finnish resistance. He thought the Red Army would make quick work of the tiny Finnish army. Instead, his poorly trained troops, ill-equipped for winter combat, faced a determined force that held out against superior numbers for three months. Hitler would make a similar error in judgment when he attacked the Soviet Union the following year. Stalin also learned later that by making enemies of the Finns, he had placed the Soviet territories he had set out to protect in greater danger.

The British plan to land troops in the Norwegian port of Narvik was shelved with the end of the "Winter War" in Finland because it was too late to save the Finns from defeat. Moreover, England's War Cabinet decided that interfering with Swedish iron ore exports would be counterproductive. Though Churchill objected, the view that dominated the debate was that the operation would only anger the Norwegians and Swedes and provoke them to join Hitler. The only real "military" action the British continued against Germany was the dropping of millions of leaflets.

War Lore

Historian Martin Gilbert writes that a popular joke "told of an airman who was rebuked for dropping a whole bundle of leaflets still tied up in its brick-like packet: 'Good God, you might have killed someone!'"

Massacre in the Forest

Having achieved his goal of securing his northern border, Stalin again became concerned with his western frontier. During the fighting in Poland, thousands of soldiers were captured by the Red Army. Many Poles surrendered to the Soviets to avoid falling into German hands. Stalin ordered 15,000 Polish officers imprisoned in special camps at Koziels, Ostaszkow, and Starobielsk. He feared these men might form the nucleus for a movement to resist the Communist takeover of Poland in the future.

In April 1940, Stalin ordered 5,000 Polish officers taken into the Katyn forest. They were marched into the woods, still wearing their uniforms, many with their hands tied behind their backs, and shot in the back of the neck. Thousands were buried in mass graves, which were not discovered for three years. The Soviets kept this crime a secret. Not until 1989 were Communist documents released documenting the fact that the Soviet NKVD (the secret police force that later became the KGB) carried out the Katyn Massacre.

The Germans had their own ideas about what to do with the Poles. Around the time Stalin was issuing his order, the head of the German Concentration Camp Inspectorate, Richard Gluecks, told the head of the SS, Heinrich Himmler, that he had found an ideal site for a new camp where the Poles could be imprisoned. It was an old cavalry barracks just outside the Polish town of Oswiecim. The Germans called the place Auschwitz.

The Least You Need to Know

➤ Germany introduced the *Blitzkrieg* method of warfare: a quick thrust by an overwhelming force against an unsuspecting enemy. It was first employed against Poland.

➤ The invasion of Poland provoked Great Britain and France to declare war, starting what became World War II.

➤ Hitler continued his campaign to annihilate the Jews with atrocities in Poland.

➤ Sweden and Romania had vital resources Germany needed; Spain was strategically located and provided logistical support to the Nazis.

➤ Stalin hoped to expand his empire and secure his northern border by attacking Finland. Though he ultimately succeeded, his troops performed surprisingly poorly against determined defenders.

➤ The United States remained neutral even as war broke out in Europe.

➤ The Soviets massacred thousands of Poles in the Katyn forest while the Germans prepared for even larger-scale murders by building a new concentration camp in Auschwitz.

Chapter 7

The Not So Phony War

> ## In This Chapter
>
> ➤ German submarines begin the war in the Atlantic
>
> ➤ Denmark is defeated
>
> ➤ Allies and Germans have first clashes in Norway
>
> ➤ Hitler invades the Low Countries
>
> ➤ Thousands of Allied troops are saved at Dunkirk
>
> ➤ France is defeated
>
> ➤ Italy looks for French spoils

The war between Russia and Finland was a sideshow that was only tangentially related to what became the world war. The Russians had attacked to protect their own interests rather than to expand their empire.

Meanwhile, Hitler had remained fairly quiet since the end of his Polish campaign. He was planning his next move and continuing to build up his forces. As you learned in the previous chapter, Hitler was very concerned about securing his supplies of Sweden's iron ore. He also wanted to protect Germany's access to food provided by Norway and Denmark. These would be his next targets.

While Hitler schemed, the Allies prepared for war as well. For six months, an uneasy calm prevailed in European capitals—other than Helsinki, which was under siege. This period is referred to as the *Sitzkrieg* (sit-down war) or Phony War. Outside Finland, things may have been quiet on land, but they were becoming literally explosive at sea.

The U-boats

The Germans realized early on that they were at a serious naval disadvantage to the British and French. They were also inferior to the Americans, but did not yet give them much thought. To compensate for deficiencies in their surface fleet, the Germans focused their naval efforts on submarine warfare, which allowed them to wreak havoc on their enemies' military and commercial shipping.

Hitler did not distinguish between military and civilian targets. In October 1939, he specifically ordered submarine attacks on passenger ships that traveled in convoys or sailed without lights.

Hunting in Packs

At the beginning of the war, the Germans had 57 submarines or *U-boats*. This fleet would eventually grow to a menacing 300 ships. The commander of the U-boats was Karl Dönitz, a World War I submarine captain.

Surface ships usually were faster than submerged submarines, so the U-boats often missed the chance to sink their targets. When the ships traveled alone, the submarine captains could usually just wait for the next target to come along. The British Royal Navy, in particular, realized that sending merchant ships together with naval escorts in convoys reduced the probability of any one ship being sunk. If the U-boat missed the group, it might have to wait some time for another convoy.

GI Jargon

A German submarine was also known as a **U-boat**, short for the German *Unterseeboot.*

Admiral Dönitz devised a strategy to overcome the speed disadvantage. He figured out that groups of submarines could remain on the surface, where their speed matched that of the other ships, and identify approaching convoys. A coordinated attack by the group of submarines could then overwhelm the escorts and sink several ships at a time. These submarine groups, which became active in 1941, became known as "wolf packs."

Magnetic Mines

Along with the strategic advance, the Germans also made a technological break-through that aided their naval warfare capability. In November 1939, the Germans deployed mines that were detonated by the magnetism of any iron-hulled ship that passed over them. The magnetic mines did not distinguish between enemy ships and those of neutrals or Germany's friends, so Italian and Swedish ships were among those sunk.

The Allies got a break when an unexploded German mine was found in the mud. It was analyzed, and the British quickly figured out a way to demagnetize ships, making them less susceptible to this type of mine. Churchill did not want the Germans to know the secret had been discovered, so he ordered that ships lost to conventional mines should be said to have gone down because of a magnetic mine.

The Doomed Danes

The British also had some success in the burgeoning war at sea. In December 1939, for example, British warships put the German battleship *Graf Spee* out of commission after it had harassed merchant shipping in the South Atlantic. A few months later, near Norway, the British captured a German supply ship carrying 300 British merchant seamen who were taken prisoner earlier by the *Graf Spee*. These losses helped convince Hitler of the need to take over Norway to keep the British out of the sea lanes. The *Führer* saw Denmark as a stepping stone to that goal.

Denmark had no inkling of Hitler's malevolent intentions, and no real army to defend itself in any event. Consequently, Hitler made short work of the Danes, invading on April 9, 1940, and forcing the nation's surrender the same day with the threat of bombing Copenhagen.

The Allies Start to Fight

Hitler had received intelligence indicating that the British planned to move troops to Norway. He hoped to use this movement of troops as a pretext for his own invasion. When the British canceled their operation, Hitler was unsure of whether to act, but finally was persuaded that a confrontation would likely occur in Norway eventually and he was better off striking first.

The French had decided to mine Norwegian waters and land troops at four ports, including Narvik. However, by the time the mine-laying operation began, the Germans were already on the march.

Roll Call

The British had the largest merchant fleet in the world, with 3,000 ocean-going vessels and another 1,000 coastal ships. These ships were manned by 160,000 sailors. The merchant ships were protected by 220 naval ships.

Ask the General

Grand Admiral Erich Raeder, head of the German navy, believed the lack of adequate bases was a major factor in the Germans' defeat in World War I. He thought the navy could launch more effective attacks on Britain from Norwegian bases. The chief of the German army, Franz Halder, opposed Raeder's plan. Halder thought Germany should protect Norway's neutrality, ensuring it would remain open for shipping Swedish iron ore through the port city of Narvik. England's naval success helped sway Hitler to Raeder's point of view.

The Germans also planned to land at the ports targeted by the French, but they added several other cities to their list to put themselves in position to quickly crush any Norwegian resistance. The task was made more difficult by the geography involved, because the cities the Germans planned to assault were far apart and far from German bases.

On April 9, 1940, the attack began. Though surprised, the tiny Norwegian army of 15,000 men held off their enemies long enough to allow King Haakon VII and his family to escape to London. The Norwegians were quickly overwhelmed, but they refused to surrender.

The British, meanwhile, sank 10 destroyers that had brought troops to Narvik—half the total in the German navy—and two other German cruisers were sunk in other battles. By the end of the fighting, the German navy had been largely devastated, having only four destroyers and three cruisers left from its surface fleet.

Initially, the Germans landed unopposed at Narvik; the commander of the local garrison was a supporter of former Norwegian Foreign Minister *Vidkun Quisling*, who had told him not to resist. Later, Norwegian troops backed by a total of nearly 25,000 British and French troops retook Narvik and threw the invaders back.

After the German offensive in Belgium and the Netherlands, the Allies decided their troops should be pulled out of Norway. This left the Norwegians practically defenseless; the native troops soon were overrun, and the Germans regained the advantage.

GI Jargon

Before invading Norway, Hitler conferred with the leader of the Norwegian Nazi Party, **Vidkun Quisling**, who encouraged the Germans to attack quickly and provided intelligence to aid in the Nazi takeover. When the fighting ended, Quisling was made the head of a puppet government. His treasonous behavior made his name synonymous with the word traitor. Fifteen days after taking over Norway, Hitler replaced Quisling with a German Nazi Party official.

On June 9, Norway agreed to an armistice. Hitler ultimately stationed 300,000 men in the country to guarantee Germany's security in the north and the protection of its iron ore shipments from Sweden.

The wars in Scandinavia had a profound impact on the British and French, proving that neither the Germans nor the Soviets could be trusted. The Germans were now seemingly determined to conquer Europe. The failure of the French and British to prevent the victories of the dictators also caused growing disenchantment with the political leaders in both nations.

The naked aggression against the peaceful Scandinavian nations raised the level of concern in the United States, but didn't yet shake it from its self-imposed isolation. The American government looked for ways to bolster other potential targets of Hitler's ambitions, notably Greenland, which was under Danish sovereignty, and Iceland, which had close ties to Denmark. The United States later negotiated the right to build airfields and other facilities to defend Greenland. The British occupied Iceland for a time and were later replaced by American troops to allow the British forces there to fight elsewhere.

Hitler Takes the Low Road

On January 10, 1940, Hitler met with his military commanders and told them the attack on the West would begin in one week. He had already deployed 2 million troops along the frontiers of Belgium, the Netherlands, Luxembourg, and France and had laid out his strategic plan in detail. Shortly before the scheduled date of attack, a German plane crash-landed in Belgium. One of the passengers, Major Helmut Reinberger, was caught by Belgian soldiers as he was burning the plans for the *Luftwaffe*'s attack on Belgium.

Despite the security breach, Hitler was determined to go forward with his attack on the *Low Countries*, but the weather dealt him a setback. Forecasts indicated it would not be possible to launch the air attacks needed to support the next *Blitzkrieg*, so Hitler postponed the assault. When it became clear the weather would not improve in the coming days, he decided to put the operation off until spring.

Misreading the Numbers

Even after being tipped off about the German plan, the Allies' rearmament effort had not made much progress and was not sufficiently accelerated. The French still felt relatively secure behind their Maginot Line, the neutrals were confident that their neutrality would protect them, and the British were geographically far enough from Germany to ensure no attack against them was imminent.

The Allies also had the military advantage, at least on paper, with the British, Belgian, Dutch, and French armies totaling 4 million men, compared to roughly 3 million for the German army. The Allies had a small advantage in the number of tanks and a nearly equal number of fighter planes (though the Germans had nearly twice as many total aircraft as Britain and France).

On the other side of the ledger, the British had few trained reserve troops and not a single battle-ready armored division. The French army had been considered the strongest in the world, but it also

Ask the General

The plane crash in Belgium prompted Hitler to issue an order: "No one—no agency, no officer—is permitted to learn more about a matter that is to be kept secret than he absolutely needs to know for official purposes." Today, the universal policy of governments is to provide information on defense and intelligence operations on a "need to know" basis.

GI Jargon

The **Low Countries** are Belgium, Luxembourg, and the Netherlands. The term refers to their location near sea level on the North Sea.

had weak reserves and the overall armed forces were of uneven strength, and their better weapons were inefficiently distributed. The Allies were at an even greater disadvantage in military strategy, because they did not yet understand how to create concentrated tank divisions that could mount coordinated attacks with the air force.

The Germans, by contrast, were well-equipped and even better organized into armored, infantry, and motorized divisions. Whatever they lacked in numbers, the Germans expected to make up for with superior tactics, particularly lightning thrusts made by *panzer* (tank) divisions backed by the *Luftwaffe*, which were aimed at catching enemies by surprise and crushing them before they had time to mobilize and counterattack. (The tank-infantry formations used by the Germans served as a model throughout the war and are still used today.)

The Dike Breaks

On May 10, 1940, Hitler launched a massive attack on Belgium and the Netherlands with 136 divisions. The *Luftwaffe* then sent 2,500 planes in waves against both countries, as well as targets in France and Luxembourg. Paratroopers landed in the Hague, Leiden, and Rotterdam.

Words of War

At five o'clock the morning of May 13, King George VI was awakened at Buckingham Palace and told that Dutch Queen Wilhelmina wished to speak to him. "I did not believe him," wrote the king in his diary, "but went to the telephone and it was her. She begged me to send aircraft for the defense of Holland. I passed this message on to everyone concerned and went back to bed." The king commented: "It is not often that one is rung up at that hour, and especially by a queen. But in these days anything may happen, and far worse things too."

—from Martin Gilbert, *The Second World War*

Up until the surprise attack, the Belgians naively believed that Hitler still might respect their neutrality and had, therefore, earlier refused to allow the British and French to deploy troops on their territory or to coordinate defense planning with them. Now that Belgians were under attack, they had to wait for the Allies to move their troops into position.

The new outbreak of fighting provoked a crisis in Britain, where Neville Chamberlain had hoped to form a coalition government to deal with the emergency. Chamberlain's policies were already in disrepute, and he now lost his remaining support and resigned. As Britain's equivalent to secretary of the navy, Winston Churchill also bore some responsibility for the failure to stop the aggressors. Still, Churchill was the one person under whom all the parties agreed to serve, so he became prime minister and defense minister on May 10, 1940. Chamberlain remained in Churchill's cabinet as lord president of the council until October 1940, when illness forced his resignation. He died shortly thereafter.

The French already had a new government. In March, before the Norwegian campaign began, Edouard Daladier's government fell and was replaced by the more conservative Paul Reynaud. Daladier would later be arrested by the Vichy government and sent to prison in Germany. He returned to France after the war and once again became a major figure in his party.

Speaking of political leaders, it was particularly ironic that the ex-kaiser of Germany, Wilhelm II, was living in the Netherlands at the time of the invasion. He had been there since his exile in 1918 and refused Churchill's offer of safe haven in England. Instead, he stayed put in Doorn, his place of exile, which was soon captured. The troops that were reenacting the attack the kaiser had launched 25 years earlier were now guarding him. He died the following year still in exile in the Netherlands.

The Dominoes Fall

The Dutch army of 400,000 men was unable to hold out long. The country had stayed out of World War I and hadn't participated in any war since 1830. The only real hope was that the network of waterways would delay the Germans, but the *Luftwaffe* was not impeded by land or water barriers and bombed the Dutch into submission while paratroopers seized key bridges. The backbreaker was a merciless attack on Rotterdam that flattened the city and killed thousands of civilians. Queen Wilhelmina, afraid of being captured and held hostage, hoped to flee to another part of the Dutch empire, but she had to be evacuated by a British destroyer to London. Shortly thereafter, on May 14, the Dutch commander surrendered. It had taken Hitler only four days to conquer the Netherlands.

The Belgians put up stiffer resistance, but the Germans still were advancing even more quickly than they'd anticipated. Hitler became nervous at their success and was tempted to stop, but did not. The army overran Brussels, the fifth capital to be conquered in nine months, and moved onward, taking Antwerp, Belgium's main port, on May 18. King Albert was urged to follow the example of the Netherlands's queen and go into exile, but he insisted on remaining in the country and was taken prisoner for the duration of the war. After liberation, he would be deposed by his own people.

"Conquer We Must"

Even though German troops remained far from British shores, Churchill foresaw the danger that was coming. He ordered barbed-wire road blocks and other enhanced security measures around Downing Street and Whitehall to protect the seats of government. Speaking to the British people for the first time as prime minister, he said the French and British were fighting together to "rescue not only Europe but mankind from the foulest and most soul-destroying tyranny which has ever darkened and stained the pages of history." He said the conquered peoples of Czechoslovakia, Poland, Norway, Denmark, the Netherlands, and Belgium would face "the long night of barbarism...unless we conquer, as conquer we must; as conquer we shall." Even today, long after the war, Churchill's wartime speeches stir the soul, and it is easy to see how his grit and courage rallied the British people in their darkest hours.

Words of War

"I have nothing to offer but blood, toil, tears, and sweat. We have before us an ordeal of the most grievous kind. We have before us many, many months of struggle and suffering. You ask, what is our policy? I will say. It is to wage war, by sea, land, and air, with all our might and with all the strength that God can give us; to wage war against a monstrous tyranny never surpassed in the dark, lamentable catalogue of human crime. That is our policy."

—Winston Churchill speaking to Parliament May 13, 1940

Words of War

"The war is beginning as badly as it could. Therefore it must go on. For this the world is wide. If I live, I will fight wherever I must as long as I must until the enemy is defeated and the national stain is washed clean."

—Charles de Gaulle

Churchill also sent a message to Roosevelt saying that he expected that England would be attacked. The American response was to allow the British to purchase large numbers of fighter planes and to assure them of a continuing supply as new aircraft came off the assembly lines. It would be some time, however, before Britain could benefit from this agreement.

The French, meanwhile, committed a series of strategic blunders that would soon have dire consequences. In particular, the French commander, General Maurice Gustave Gamelin, deployed half his force to defend the Maginot Line and rushed his main reserve force to the Netherlands leaving none to defend France should the Germans break through the Maginot. The Belgians had complicated the French situation by their insistence on neutrality, which left their mutual border—which extended roughly 250 miles—largely undefended. Hitler had planned all along to outflank the Maginot Line by exploiting this weakness.

The French Are Fried

On May 10, Hitler unleashed the *Blitzkrieg* on France, attacking through the wooded Ardennes. Launching the assault there was a combination of good planning and good luck. The Germans had correctly calculated that this point of attack would allow them to outflank the Maginot Line. What they had not counted on was that the French troops they would have to face were composed largely of newly mobilized reservists and were the weakest of the French divisions. The bulk of French troops, including many of their best-trained soldiers, were hunkered down in their Maginot bunkers and unable to re-deploy to face threats that did not come directly at them.

One of the men who were valiantly trying to counterattack was a relatively unknown French soldier named Charles de Gaulle. During the span of the war, he would become the nation's greatest patriot and future leader.

It took only five days before the French were demoralized. Prime Minister Reynaud called Churchill and stunned him with the news that the road to Paris was already open and that the battle was lost. The following day, Churchill flew to Paris to meet with Reynaud and Gamelin. During their talks, Churchill was again shocked to learn that the French had no strategic reserve. Churchill could do little to bolster the crumbling French defense beyond offering to send more fighters.

Even this gesture was futile. The capture of airfields closer to the French border allowed the *Luftwaffe* to dominate the air. Though the United States rushed airplanes to France, and the British Royal Air Force sent 350 aircraft, the Germans still enjoyed a more than two-to-one advantage in fighters and bombers.

Even as the situation in France grew bleaker, the Allied armies fought on in Belgium. A British counterattack helped frighten Hitler into calling a temporary halt to the advance of the *panzers*. The Germans had suffered heavy tank losses, and Hitler feared the remaining tanks would get bogged down in the soggy lowlands and canal areas of Belgium. Hitler and his commanders agreed the *panzers* had outrun their own infantry and should wait for that shield to catch up.

Meanwhile, Reynaud recalled two World War I heroes, Philippe Pétain and Maxime Weygand, in the hope of lifting the nation's morale and turning the tide of the war. Shortly thereafter, he decided to replace Gamelin with Weygand as commander in chief. Weygand immediately tried to compensate for the lack of reserves. His strategy was to create a new line of defense running from the Channel coast to the Maginot Line at Montmedy. Along the new Weygand Line were villages and woods where French outposts, referred to as "hedgehogs," were assigned the task of stopping, or at least slowing down, the *panzer* advance.

Miracle at Dunkirk

The brief respite from the *Blitzkrieg* allowed the British and French to withdraw. On May 20, the British government had decided to plan Operation Dynamo to evacuate some of its troops from Belgium. The hope was that the bulk of the British Expeditionary Force (BEF) could still join the French First Army in defense of the Weygand Line. The British learned from documents they captured, however, that the Germans were preparing a trap that would have cut off the Allied troops. At the same time, the avenues of retreat were disappearing, so the British commander, Lord Gort, decided to abandon the plan to move south and defend the evacuation route instead.

When Hitler rescinded his stop order, British ships had already begun to arrive to take French and British soldiers back to England. The action wasn't a complete surprise to Hitler, who had been told by Göring that an evacuation could be prevented. The *Luftwaffe* did stage constant bombing raids on Dunkirk, the site of embarkation, but failed to slow or prevent the operation. One reason was Göring's decision to attack five different ports rather than Dunkirk alone. Another explanation was the effective covering operation of the Royal Air Force.

Initially, the British had hoped to have two days to carry out the evacuation and save perhaps 45,000 men. The German time-out bought extra time. Still, what the British planned as a limited withdrawal became a mass evacuation after the Belgian army surrendered on May 28. Belgium had resisted for 18 days, the longest any country had held out against the Germans.

War Lore

The two-day halt Hitler called made little difference in the short-run campaign to conquer the Low Countries and France. Churchill said at the time that "wars are not won by evacuations." Still, the halt may have affected the outcome of the war because it ultimately allowed the Allies to save a significant proportion of their forces through the evacuation at Dunkirk. These troops would return to the fight later. Had Hitler stayed on the offensive, these troops probably would have been destroyed or captured.

Between May 26 and June 4, 1940, nearly 340,000 Allied soldiers were evacuated from Dunkirk. Of these, more than 100,000 were French, who quickly re-crossed the channel to rejoin the fight in France. More than 800 vessels—from destroyers to fishing boats to private yachts—from Belgium, France, the Netherlands, and Great Britain carried out the ferry operation under almost constant attack. In nine days of bombing, the *Luftwaffe* damaged many vessels, but succeeded in sinking only eight destroyers. The RAF, meanwhile, shot down 176 German aircraft while losing 106.

Those Left Behind

As successful as the Dunkirk evacuation was, and as big a boost as it gave British morale, it was not without its downside. More than 30,000 British soldiers did not escape and were taken prisoner. In addition, most of the BEF's weapons had to be left behind, allowing the Nazis to capture a treasure trove of thousands of guns and vehicles, hundreds of tanks, and millions of tons of ammunition.

War Lore

One of the private yachts that evacuated soldiers from Dunkirk was owned by a retired naval commander, C. H. Lightoller, the senior surviving officer of the *Titanic*. His son was one of the first pilots killed in action in September 1939.

After the evacuation from Dunkirk, the main concern of the British was whether Hitler intended to make them his next target. According to secret communications intercepted by British intelligence, the Germans planned to finish off France. The British people were still understandably fearful of Hitler's next move. Churchill sought to reassure them, telling the nation:

> We shall fight on the beaches, we shall fight on the landing grounds, we shall fight in the fields and in the streets, we shall fight in the hills; we shall never surrender, and even if, which I do not for a moment believe, this island or a large part of it were subjugated and starving, then our Empire beyond the seas, armed and guarded by the British Fleet, would carry on the struggle, until, in God's good time, the New World, with all its power and might, steps forth to the rescue and the liberation of the Old.

As the decrypted messages indicated, however, the fate of Britain was not immediately at stake. The future of France was, and it did not look very promising.

About the time the last of the Allied troops had arrived safely in England, the Germans renewed their offensive in the south. Though many of the outmanned and outgunned soldiers in the "hedgehogs" fought valiantly, they could not halt the German onslaught. The Weygand Line was broken and the last hope for France vanished.

Churchill tried to convince Reynaud to fight on. He told him the United States had pledged to provide huge amounts of arms. Reynaud asked Churchill to send more planes, but the British prime minister said he could do no more. Even though a German attack did not appear imminent, Churchill did not believe he could risk losing aircraft he would need, sooner rather than later, to defend Great Britain. "If we cast away our defense, the war would be lost," Churchill told his cabinet, "even if the front in France were stabilized, since Germany would be free to turn her air force against this country and would have us at her mercy."

General de Gaulle was promoted to undersecretary of war in early June and immediately tried to overcome the increasingly defeatist attitude of the military and political elite. He suggested to Churchill that France and Britain form a union in an effort to strengthen his nation's resolve. Churchill did offer the proposal, but it was rejected by the Reynaud government, which, even as it was about to fall, was worried about "British domination."

A Stab in the Back

Despite the Pact of Steel and his close relationship to Hitler, Mussolini had stayed out of the war. When France was on the verge of defeat, however, he decided to take advantage of his neighbor's weakness and grab what spoils he could. On June 10, Italy invaded France and declared war on Britain.

The British and French anticipated the Italian move, thanks to their intelligence services, and almost immediately bombed targets in Italy and the Italian colonies in Africa. The Italians bombed British targets in Malta, Aden, and Port Sudan.

In a foreshadowing of the American response to Pearl Harbor, the British reacted to Mussolini's actions by interning all Italians between the ages of 16 and 70 who had lived in England for less than 20 years. As it turned out, this number was relatively small, about 4,000, similar to the number of American citizens who would be interned by the Nazis (see Chapter 24).

Words of War

"On this tenth day of June 1940, the hand that held the dagger has struck it into the back of its neighbor."

—Franklin Roosevelt

The Italians' initial thrust into France was a debacle, with French forces inflicting 5,000 casualties while losing only eight of their own soldiers. Mussolini then had to ask for German help. The territorial gains Italy ultimately made at the end of the campaign were primarily due to Hitler's insistence that France sign an armistice with Mussolini before the agreement with Germany took effect.

The Arc de Defeat

The same day Mussolini declared war, Marshal Pétain urged the French government to surrender. In the hope of sparing its capital from destruction, the government declared Paris an open city, and Reynaud withdrew to Tours. There he met with Churchill, who again encouraged the French to fight on, and suggested that Reynaud make an urgent plea to Roosevelt for help. Reynaud agreed and asked Roosevelt to declare war if he could and, if not, send every other possible type of assistance.

By the time Roosevelt replied, Reynaud had retreated further, to Bordeaux. The United States, Roosevelt said, would redouble its efforts to furnish war material to the Allied forces, but would not declare war. On June 14, about the time Reynaud received Roosevelt's message, the Germans captured Paris. The army marched down the Champs Élysées and festooned the Arc de Triomphe with a giant Nazi flag.

The war was not yet over. The Maginot Line, strangely enough, remained largely intact. It was not until a few days later that German troops reached the Swiss border and cut off a half million French soldiers in their fortresses. Still, only one section of blockhouses was ever captured in a German attack.

Pétain contacted the Germans to arrange for the surrender. Hitler agreed to receive a French delegation, which was taken to Compiegne on June 21 and invited into a train car to sign the armistice agreement. In a calculated bit of theater, Hitler had ordered that the final capitulation occur in the same coach that the Germans had signed the armistice of 1918.

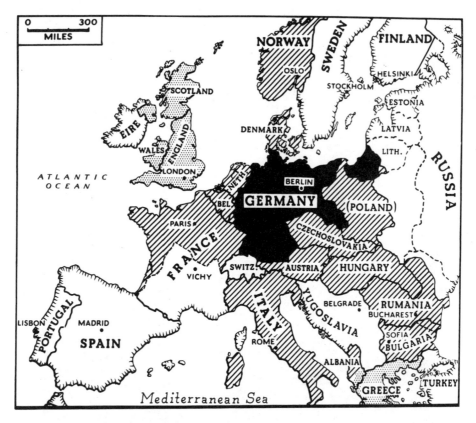

The Fall of Western Europe. (AP/Wide World Photos)

Hitler was not content with the French surrender: He wanted to humiliate the nation as he felt his homeland had been after World War I. According to the agreement, the French would establish a government in Vichy and retain control over their colonies in Africa and Asia. The Germans would occupy northern France. Italy would rule southeastern France. The French army would be reduced to 100,000 men, the navy demilitarized, and the prisoners of war held by Germany. The decision not to take over the entire French empire was designed not to provoke further resistance.

The financial terms were far less generous. Hitler imposed a fine of $120 million for the trouble the French caused and charged them for the cost of the occupation. These sums far exceeded Germany's World War I reparations.

Roll Call

The war for France lasted 42 days. German casualties totaled at least 27,000 dead. The number of French dead exceeded 100,000; another 200,000 were wounded, and 1.5 million were taken prisoner. The Dutch lost 2,900 men, the Belgians 7,500, and the British 3,500.

Hitler in Paris, June 23, 1940. (National Archives Still Pictures Branch)

While Pétain established a new collaborationist government in Vichy, General De Gaulle fled to London. He would not accept defeat and called on the people of France to resist the Nazi occupation. The Vichy government tried and sentenced him to death in absentia, but de Gaulle would live for another 30 years, first establishing himself as the leader of the Free French and then helping to liberate his country.

The Least You Need to Know

➤ Germany perfected the use of U-boat wolf packs to wreak havoc on Allied shipping.

➤ Hitler overran Denmark in one day.

➤ Quisling betrayed his country, and the Allies' first military confrontations with German troops couldn't prevent the fall of Norway.

➤ The *Blitzkrieg* met opposition, but not enough to prevent the Germans from conquering Belgium, the Netherlands, and Luxembourg.

➤ Nearly 340,000 Allied soldiers were evacuated from Dunkirk. By saving them from certain death or capture, the British maintained a fighting force that later contributed to the Allied victory.

➤ Churchill foresaw having to defend Great Britain and was forced to hold back aid to France. The United States increased its supply of military equipment, but remained unwilling to enter the war.

➤ Paris fell to the Germans, and a collaborationist government was established in Vichy. General de Gaulle fled France and became a leader of the resistance.

➤ After France was defeated, Italy attacked in hopes of grabbing some of its territory. The battles didn't go well for the Italians, but Hitler forced France to make concessions to Mussolini to get an armistice with Germany.

Chapter 8

Puttin' on the Brits

In This Chapter

➤ America increases aid to the Brits

➤ German U-boats wreak havoc on Allied shipping

➤ Hitler plunders his conquests

➤ Britain is attacked in the air and at sea

➤ The Axis expands

➤ The United States rebuilds its military

Two decades were spent creating mechanisms to prevent war and, specifically, to restrain Germany. All proved worthless. It took Hitler less than a year to conquer most of Europe. Although some people may have had illusions about his intentions before, none now doubted his ambition to rule the world.

The British could have made a more determined effort to help defend France, but Churchill correctly calculated this would probably be futile. He understood that Hitler was gunning for his island next and that the British would need more than a stiff upper lip to keep from joining the ranks of the vanquished.

America Takes a First Step

The prospect of a British defeat shook Americans out of their lethargy. Finally, they realized that their security was also threatened with democracy on life support and all of Europe on the verge of becoming slaves to Hitler. Roosevelt responded to the emergency by persuading Congress to significantly strengthen the United States's armed forces and to institute the first peacetime draft (in September 1940). Roosevelt used loopholes in the neutrality laws to send surplus weapons to Great Britain. Warplanes were also being shipped nearly as fast as they were built.

Isolationists remained determined to keep the United States out of the war, suggesting that the United States should only fight if directly threatened. One of the leaders of the movement was Charles Lindbergh, the aviator who'd won lasting fame for being the first person to fly solo across the Atlantic. However, events in Europe had stimulated a counterweight to the isolationists. These "interventionists" insisted the United States must defend democracy. "Britain is fighting our fight" was the cry of those who argued for more direct involvement. Others were less anxious for the United States to join the fighting and hoped to contain the conflict in Europe, but they believed the United States should do everything short of sending troops to help its allies.

Roll Call

Congress appropriated $37 billion for one of the greatest arms buildups in history. That sum exceeded the total cost of fighting World War I.

In September 1940, Roosevelt took unilateral action to aid the British, refusing even to involve Congress. He decided to transfer 50 aging World War I destroyers to Britain in exchange for basing rights in eight different strategic locations. Though the executive action prompted howls of protest from the isolationist lobby, the move was supported by the majority of the public.

Wolves at Sea

While the war raging on land altered boundaries, governments, alliances, and the fate of peoples across Europe, other battles were being fought at sea. While Hitler was trying to knock out his weaker opponents in Europe, he was conducting the war in the Atlantic to deliver body blows to soften his stronger rivals.

Words of War

"The only thing that ever really frightened me during the war was the U-boat peril.... It did not take the form of flaring battles and glittering achievements, it manifested itself through statistics, diagrams, and curves unknown to the nation, incomprehensible to the public."

—Winston Churchill

The German U-boats ruled the waves early in the fighting. Though Admiral Dönitz started out with only 57 U-boats, he wreaked havoc on Allied shipping. Initially, Dönitz had to operate far from the British sea lanes because Hitler was reluctant to violate the neutrality of the nations along the coast. After Germany conquered France, however, the German navy gained access to the French Atlantic ports, and the wolves were able to prowl the route to western and southern Africa. By March 1943, the U-boat fleet consisted of 400 submarines. When the war in the Atlantic ended, the Germans had sunk 2,452 merchant ships and 175 warships, preventing millions of tons of material from reaching the Allies and killing thousands of sailors.

Though the U-boats were extremely effective weapons, Hitler still anticipated the need for a strong surface fleet to project German power across the Atlantic, particularly against the United States. Thus, even after conquering most of Europe, he continued the shipbuilding program he would need for future campaigns.

Still Some Fight in the French

When Charles de Gaulle fled France, he did not have the prestige of men such as World War I heroes Philippe Pétain and Maxime Weygand. He could not set up a government in exile as leaders of Poland, Norway, the Netherlands, Belgium, and Czechoslovakia did. "The cause of France is not lost," he said in a broadcast from London. "The very factors that brought about our defeat may one day lead us to victory. For France is not alone! She is not alone! Behind her is a vast empire, and she can make common cause with the British Empire, which commands the seas and is continuing the struggle." Few people responded initially to de Gaulle's plea. Over the next two years, his patriotism, charisma, and leadership gradually rallied French citizens and colonists throughout the former empire to resist Hitler.

De Gaulle's Free French were based in Fort Lamy, the capital of Chad, and joined the British in fighting to keep north and west Africa out of German and Italian hands. As historian Gerhard Weinberg observed, "it was a long road from Fort Lamy, Douala, Brazzaville, and Libreville to Paris; but then, one had to start somewhere."

Words of War

"Today we are crushed by the sheer weight of the mechanized forces hurled against us, but we can still look to a future in which even greater mechanized forces will bring us victory. Therein lies the destiny of the world."

—Charles de Gaulle

The Last Neutrals

Hitler had rampaged through Europe, but left both Sweden and Switzerland alone. He knew neither nation could mount any serious military opposition, yet he decided not to attack them. Why?

Actually, Hitler had planned to invade Switzerland and divide the country with Mussolini. Before doing so, however, he became distracted by other military endeavors. Throughout the war, Switzerland remained afraid to provoke Hitler lest he change his mind.

Sweden was the other neutral country in constant peril. As noted earlier, Germany was heavily dependent on the Swedes for vital resources, and Hitler was tempted to seize the country to ensure the supplies. Once Germany controlled both Denmark and Norway, the Swedes had little choice but to accede to Hitler's wishes. Until the tide of the war shifted, the survival instincts of Sweden's leaders convinced them to go along to get along with Hitler.

The Scourge of the East

While Hitler was showing restraint, Stalin was ravaging Eastern Europe. In June, the Soviets took over Lithuania, Latvia, and Estonia. Perhaps it should have been obvious that the two empire-building dictators would clash as their forces overwhelmed all the buffer states. Hitler met with his military commanders the same day Stalin formally annexed the three nations to instruct them to plan for an attack on Russia. For the time being, however, the two powers remained faithful to their mutual cooperation agreement.

Germany's Art Thieves

In June 1940, Hitler ordered that all French art objects be confiscated for "safekeeping." Later, Alfred Rosenberg, one of the Nazi Party's theoreticians and later minister of the conquered territories, created a special group to transport valuable works of art to Germany from the occupied territories. The Nazis plundered the cultural icons of every nation, stealing thousands of paintings, pieces of jewelry, furniture, coins, and sculptures from museums and private collections.

According to a document found in the U.S. National Archives, the director of the Metropolitan Museum of Art estimated in 1945 that art stolen by the Nazis was worth more than $2.5 billion, a total greater than the value of all art in the United States at that time. Some of the loot was stored away for the *Reich*'s use after the war, a portion was displayed in Berlin, and a great deal went into the private collections of high-ranking Nazis.

War Lore

In France alone, it is estimated that the Nazis seized 100,000 works by artists such as Rembrandt, Monet, Cézanne, and Rubens. Fewer than half of these works were returned after the war. In 1998, Holocaust survivors and their heirs began to press claims that their artworks were hanging in museums, such as the Seattle Art Museum and the Boston Museum of Fine Art, as well as others around the world. Under pressure to restore artworks to their rightful owners, the Association of Art Museum Directors, which includes the heads of the 170 largest museums in North America, agreed to research the ownership history of their holdings.

Far more ominous than what the Nazis were doing with objects were their plans for French Jews. In September 1940, Jews were forced to carry special identity cards. Business owners had to put up posters in their windows saying the shops were Jewish. Later Jews would have their property confiscated, and thousands would be deported to concentration camps.

The Battle of Britain

On June 18, 1940, Churchill told the House of Commons, "The Battle of France is over. I expect that the Battle of Britain is about to begin." The night before British bombers had attacked German factories in the Ruhr. As Churchill expected, it was now England's turn to learn about terror from the skies.

Words of War

French Jews were required to register with the police and list their homes, nationality, and profession. Henri Bergson wrote on his form:

Academic. Philosopher. Nobel Prize winner. Jew.

Hitler wanted to invade Britain and had the forces to subdue it as he had Germany's other victims, if he could get his troops across the Channel. Germany had no amphibious landing craft or any of the components the Allies would later use for their own crossing; nevertheless, Hitler believed Britain could be conquered if the RAF (Royal Air Force) was destroyed, or at least neutralized. He sent the *Luftwaffe* to accomplish that goal in early July. The attacks intensified after the Germans established bases in France and the Low Countries. For nearly five months, the *Luftwaffe* bombed ports, shipping, airfields, factories, and cities.

British intelligence greatly overestimated the strength of the German air force until deciphering the *Luftwaffe's* messages. Still, the true size of the force was about 1,300 bombers, more than double the number of fighters available to the RAF, and 900 fighters. As the Americans would do when they entered the war, the British people were asked to contribute whatever scraps of aluminum they had to be turned into aircraft. Britain's economy then went into overdrive to produce all the materials needed for war.

Hitler's strategic plan to attack Britain, code-named "Sea Lion," met with what was turning out to be typical reluctance from his generals. The military men did not believe they had the naval forces necessary to mount a land campaign (and were correct). Generals Raeder and Göring, representing the navy and the air force, were even more dismayed by Hitler's expressed intention (with the support of the army generals) to fight the Soviets and create the very two-front war that Hitler himself viewed as a cause of Germany's downfall in the last war. Even before the failure of the air war was obvious, however, Hitler postponed the invasion of Britain.

The Allies Turn on Each Other

Part of the German navy's difficulty had to do with the battle going on at sea. When it became clear France was about to fall, Churchill had sought to convince the French to either sail their fleet to England or, at least, to neutral waters to keep it out of German hands. Before the fighting ended, the French were prepared to go along with Churchill; however, when the armistice was signed, they were afraid to violate the agreement and upset Hitler.

The British could not allow Germany to incorporate the French ships into its navy and launched an operation to eliminate the threat. "Operation Catapult" was aimed, ideally, at seizing the French ships. This was done in several cases, mainly where the French ships were in British ports. The main exception was at the French naval base at Mers-el-Kebir, which had the largest number of ships in one place. When the French refused to accept any of the choices they were offered to ensure the Germans couldn't get the ships, the British attacked, sinking several battleships and killing more than 1,000 Frenchmen.

Churchill was unrepentant. It was true the British had fought beside the French just a few weeks before, but it was also the case that at a crucial moment when British security was at stake, the French chose to side with their conquerors rather than their allies.

The *Blitz*

Hitler's efforts to soften up the British for an invasion began in mid-July 1940 and essentially ended at the end of October. The first wave of German attacks were aimed at British ports and shipping. The *Luftwaffe* inflicted devastating losses on the RAF, downing 450 RAF planes (roughly 70 percent of the British air force) in the first month of fighting.

The next stage in the air assault, Operation Eagle, began August 13, 1940, with a series of aerial engagements and attacks on RAF airfields and British aircraft factories. British fighters now began inflicting serious damage on the Germans. In one attack, the *Luftwaffe* lost 144 of its 1,000 attacking planes, but the British lost only 18. The *Luftwaffe* was reporting very different results and thereby misleading the Berlin commanders, who believed British defenses had been broken and began in early September to order large-scale attacks on inland cities.

The British didn't sit back and take a beating, though. They took the fight to the Germans, bombing military targets around Berlin starting at the end of August. The Germans responded in kind on September 7, 1940, when 300 German bombers accompanied by 600 fighters attacked London. Shifting from targeting air bases, the *Luftwaffe* began to bomb residential areas and to cause mounting tension in the British capital.

Once the Germans had set the precedent of indiscriminately bombing civilian population centers, the British resolved to repay them with almost nightly attacks on Berlin. The damage was light, but the psychological impact of bringing the war into the German capital was powerful.

War Lore

Ireland remained more neutral than perhaps any other country in the war. The Irish Republican Army (IRA) and others adopted the attitude that the enemy of my enemy is my friend; that is, a German victory over Britain might end the division of their island. They apparently gave little thought to the possibility that the German conquest of Ireland might have far worse results than the British control over the north. The British hinted at negotiating an end to the partition of the country if Ireland became its ally, but Irish leader Eamon de Valera demurred. It was not until the *Luftwaffe* bombed Belfast in 1941 that he would provide any support for the Allies, and, even then, he kept Ireland out of the fighting.

People are evacuated from opposite University College Hospital, London, where an unexploded 2,500 pound German bomb was found buried. (National Archives Still Pictures Branch)

The London Blitz consisted of more than 70 attacks and continued until May 1941. Terrified Londoners were forced to sleep in shelters; some retreated to the underground subway stations. Nearly half a million children were sent for safekeeping to homes outside London. The danger was real. In just one week in mid-October, for example, more than 1,300 Londoners were killed in German attacks.

Despite the RAF's disadvantage in numbers, it had the tactical advantage, attacking the German fighters and bombers before they could reach England's shores or driving them back once they reached British air space. When the raids on London began, the concentrations of German bombers became easier targets. The RAF was inflicting such heavy losses on the *Luftwaffe* that Hitler cut back on the number of daylight raids and ordered nighttime raids, which were more terrifying for the civilians being bombed, but less accurate and effective militarily.

Though Hitler would continue to attack Britain for another seven months, the Battle of Britain was essentially over by the end of October. The RAF had lost nearly 800 fighters, but the *Luftwaffe* had lost nearly 1,400 aircraft. Most important, the British had staved off an invasion. The magnitude of the sacrifice and the threat that had been repulsed prompted Churchill to declare: "Never in the field of human conflict was so much owed by so many to so few."

In addition to the courage of the 2,500 young pilots, the British benefited significantly from a new invention that aided their efforts: radar. Ironically, the technology was based in part on work done by a German physicist and an engineer in the 1880s, but it was turned into a practical device in the 1930s by British physicist Sir Robert Watson-Watt. By the start of the war, the British had a chain of radar stations in operation that allowed them to detect incoming German aircraft.

For all Churchill's brave talk, the threat of Britain's defeat had been real. Before the Battle of Britain had begun, he had prepared for this contingency by shipping all the nation's gold, foreign exchange reserves, and negotiable foreign securities to Canada.

Words of War

Even as Britain was absorbing the ferocity of the German blitz, Churchill sought to reassure the French of British conviction. On October 21, 1940, he told them:

"Good night, then: sleep to gather strength for the morning. For the morning will come. Brightly will it shine on the brave and true, kindly on all who suffer for the cause, glorious upon the tombs of heroes. Thus will shine the dawn."

Hitler Declares Victory

Despite having to abandon his plan to invade England, Hitler told Mussolini, "The war is won." He was convinced the British could not hold up under the relentless attacks of the *Luftwaffe*. Even after the Battle of Britain was essentially over, the Germans continued to inflict severe damage on England. In one of the worst raids on November 14, 1940, bombers destroyed more than two dozen factories in Coventry and set fire to the city center, destroying or damaging 80 percent of the city's 75,000 buildings and killing more than 500 people.

Hitler was not going to wait for England's collapse to pursue his other military objectives. On October 7, 1940, his troops entered Romania. A couple of weeks earlier, he had signed a new tripartite pact with Italy and Japan in which the wider Axis agreed to come to each others' aid in the event they were attacked. Hitler had hoped to draw Franco into an alliance as well, offering him Gibraltar in exchange for permission to attack British troops on the island via Spain. Franco, however, wanted more from Hitler than Hitler was prepared to offer.

Both Italy and Japan had their own aggressive intentions. At the end of October, Mussolini sent his troops into Greece. The Japanese, meanwhile, were pressuring Hitler's friends in Vichy to give up France's military bases in Indochina.

Both Japan and Italy were affected by a British attack on the Italian fleet in the port of Taranto. The Italians were affected directly because three of their battleships were sunk and several other vessels damaged, and the Japanese were affected indirectly through what they learned about the use of aerial torpedoes to carry out the attack. Admiral Isoruku Yamamoto, the commander of the Japanese fleet, saw the British raid as a model for what could be done to the American navy at Pearl Harbor. The U. S. Secretary of the Navy, Frank Knox, read events the same way and warned that "precautionary measures be taken immediately to protect Pearl Harbor against surprise attack in the event that war should break out between the United States and Japan."

An Arsenal for Democracy

After the U. S. draft was instituted in September, the first day for Americans to register for service was October 16, 1940. More than 16 million signed up that day. Roosevelt, meanwhile, was campaigning for reelection and insisting that America would stay out of the fighting:

> And while I am talking to you mothers and fathers, I give you one more assurance. I have said before, but I shall say it again: Your boys are not going to be sent into any foreign wars.

Even as he was making these public pronouncements, Roosevelt was admitting privately that "the time may be coming when the Germans and the Japs[sic] will do some fool thing that would put us in. That's the only real danger of our getting in ...."

Hitler's aggression may have also played a role in Roosevelt's decision to run for an unprecedented third term. He had been reluctant to run again, but, after German troops swept through Europe, he was encouraged to stay on to steward the nation through the increasingly bleak future. To further prepare the nation, he created what Gerhard Weinberg calls the closest thing to a coalition government in U.S. history by bringing in Republicans to head the War Department (Henry Stimson), the Navy (Frank Knox), and special assignments (William Donovan).

While preaching nonintervention, Roosevelt pressed for strengthening all the services, a need that was clear when you consider the United States had only about 150 fighters and 50 bombers, a 10th of the number in the *Luftwaffe*, when Hitler began his march through Western Europe. America unwittingly provoked the Japanese by its military buildup. After Congress voted to create a "two-ocean navy" in July 1940, the Japanese began to realize they would be hopelessly outgunned if they sat back and waited for the United States to complete its shipbuilding program.

The American military buildup was not just for the sake of the United States, it was for Britain and all democracies. On December 29, 1940, the president told the American people during his fireside chat:

> *The people of Europe who are defending themselves do not ask us to do their fighting. They ask us for the implements of war, the planes, the tanks, the guns, the freighters, which will enable them to fight for their liberty and for our security. We must be the great arsenal of democracy.*

The Least You Need to Know

➤ Hitler's U-boats attempted to strangle the British by cutting off their supplies.

➤ The Germans were not satisfied with conquest; they also looted the cultural treasures of their victims.

➤ In preparation for an invasion, Hitler launched a massive bombing campaign against England, but the RAF shot down so many German planes in the Battle of Britain that Hitler cancelled his plans.

➤ Britain brought the war home to the Germans by bombing Berlin as both nations became indiscriminate in their attacks.

➤ Italy, Japan, and the Soviet Union continued to expand their empires without opposition.

➤ A successful British attack on the Italian fleet provided a model for the Japanese raid on Pearl Harbor.

➤ The United States began a massive rearming campaign and began to ship large amounts of weapons to Britain.

Chapter 9

America Inches Closer to the Spreading War

In This Chapter

➤ America rearms with a vengeance

➤ Britain gets a new Lend-Lease on life

➤ Greece and Yugoslavia are blitzed

➤ Germany drops in on Crete

➤ Africa becomes a new battleground

By the second half of 1940, Germany controlled all of the European continent directly or by intimidation. The British had staved off an invasion, but remained under siege from the air and sea, with little doubt that Hitler had not given up his goal of incorporating the British Empire into the German sphere of influence.

Hitler also had succeeded in arousing American anger, and though Roosevelt remained unwilling to send Americans into combat, he would do everything else in his power to aid the Allies. He had not yet anticipated that another Axis power would leave him no alternative but to fight. The plans of Hitler, Churchill, and Roosevelt were all complicated by Mussolini's dreams of empire, which ensnared the combatants in far-flung battles across North Africa and in the Mediterranean.

The Giant Awakens

Though given some warning by his diplomats in Washington, Hitler never grasped the war-making capability of the United States. U.S. resources dwarfed those of Germany and Japan combined. Although Roosevelt remained adamant about staying out of the

Words of War

"Democracy alone, of all forms of government, enlists the full force of men's enlightened will.... It is the most humane, the most advanced, and, in the end, the most unconquerable of all forms of human society. The democratic aspiration is no mere recent phase of human history. It is human history.... We...would rather die on our feet than live on our knees."

—Franklin Roosevelt, Third Inaugural, January 20, 1941

war, he began to rearm. He doubled the size of his first love, the navy, allocated funds to create an air force with nearly 8,000 combat aircraft, and increased troop strength from 200,000 to 1 million. Those numbers only grew larger as the war dragged on. By 1944, the tank force had surged from 346 to 17,565, and the number of aircraft grew from 2,141 to an astonishing 96,318. At that time, the United States was responsible for the production of 40 percent of the world's arms.

The military buildup helped lift the United States out of the Depression, which had left 9 million people unemployed in 1939. Nearly 19 million people went to work during the course of the war, more than half of whom were women (more on that later in Chapter 14).

The United States was not out to prove that "might makes right" so much as right sometimes requires might. Roosevelt held the United States out as not only the arsenal of democracy but its guiding light as well. On January 6, 1941, he laid out *his* vision of a new world order based on four essential freedoms:

The first is freedom of speech and expression, everywhere in the world.

The second is freedom of every person to worship God in his own way, everywhere in the world.

The third is freedom from want—which, translated into world terms, means economic understanding, which will secure to every nation a healthy peacetime life for its inhabitants everywhere in the world.

The fourth is freedom from fear, which translated into world terms means a worldwide reduction of armaments to such a point and in such a thorough fashion that no nation will be in a position to commit an act of physical aggression against any neighbor, anywhere in the world.

War Is as Easy as ABC

The United States and Britain shared these objectives and met at the end of January 1941, to discuss how they could be pursued in light of the Axis threats. The ABC talks, the code name for American-British Conversations, brought senior military officials together to plan a coordinated strategy for defeating Germany should the United States enter the war. They agreed to create joint planning staffs in both Washington and London. The Americans also committed the nation to defeating Germany first even if the United States found itself at war with Japan.

Arms on the Installment Plan

Britain was a great industrial power in 1940 and, like the United States, its productivity was enviable. For example, tank output increased from fewer than 1,000 in 1939 to nearly nine times that figure by 1942. Similarly, fewer than 800 bombers were produced when the war began, but the number increased tenfold by 1943. Some of the British arms were first-rate, such as the Spitfire fighter, but others were inferior. For example, British tanks were so ineffective that the army ultimately relied almost completely on American Sherman tanks.

Although the British people were making enormous sacrifices, and their American friends were providing massive amounts of aid, the British economy was shattered by the expense of arms. By 1941, the government could no longer pay for U.S. arms. Roosevelt wanted to help, but could not do so politically without the British making an effort to pay what they could. The British did just that, which allowed the president to ask Congress for aid under a new program called Lend-Lease.

Congress heatedly debated the measure, not coincidentally numbered House Resolution 1776 and titled "An Act Further to Promote the Defense of the United States." Roosevelt had waited until after the election to bring up the matter, and then argued that it was the way to keep the United States out of the war. Under the program, the recipients of the arms could return them after the war. Roosevelt used the analogy of someone lending a hose to a neighbor whose house was on fire, expecting that it will be returned when the fire is out. Opponents, particularly the isolationists, took issue with this analogy. As Senator Robert Taft from Ohio put it, lending arms is like lending chewing gum: you don't want it back.

Ultimately, the measure passed with overwhelming majorities on March 11, 1941. This, Roosevelt said, was "The end of compromise with tyranny." By the end of the month, the first allocation, $7 billion, was approved. That year, approximately 12 percent of Britain's military equipment came from the

Words of War

"I say that the delivery of needed supplies to Britain is imperative. I say that this can be done; it must be done; and it will be done.... The only thing we have to fear is fear itself."

—Franklin Roosevelt, fireside chat, May 27, 1941

Ask the General

Hitler made no bones about his plans to exterminate the Jews, nor did he leave any doubt as to the brutality he planned to employ against the Russians when he issued the Commissar Decree in May 1941. The order called for the murder of anyone captured wearing the Soviet insignia of the hammer, red stars, and sickle. Thousands of Russians were subsequently killed.

United States. By the end of the war, the percentage was nearly 30. Throughout the war, the British obtained roughly 30 percent of their food from the United States as well.

Just as the Americans were cementing their commitment to aid the British war effort, Hitler revealed to his senior officers his plan to invade the Soviet Union on June 22. A few more conquests remained, however, before he launched what he believed would be the decisive blow in the east.

Hitler Won't Take "No" for an Answer

To prepare the diplomatic ground for the assault, Hitler succeeded over the next several months in cajoling Hungary, Romania, and Bulgaria to join the Tripartite Pact and become members of the Axis. Yugoslavia resisted, but it soon learned the price of saying no to Hitler.

After receiving essentially worthless assurances that Yugoslav territory would not be used for military actions, Prince Paul agreed to join the pact on March 25. The following evening a group of Serb officers staged a coup, forced the prince to resign as regent, and denounced the treaty with Germany. Yugoslavia hoped to get help from Russia, but Stalin offered no guarantees, so the country was on its own when Hitler made clear his intention to attack. Despite having, in theory, a million-man army, Yugoslavia had little chance of defending its 1,700 mile border with virtually no modern weapons.

On April 6, the Germans launched yet another devastating *Blitzkrieg*. The *Luftwaffe* bombed Belgrade, killing more than 17,000 people—the largest single-day death toll to that point in the war—and wiping out the Yugoslav communication center. On April 10, troops from the country's Croat minority mutinied, causing two Yugoslav armies to disintegrate. By April 14, Yugoslavia was prepared to surrender and signed an armistice agreement three days later. By the end, nearly 70 percent of the Yugoslav army had been captured, but only 151 Germans were dead.

To aid the German onslaught in Yugoslavia, Hitler convinced both Hungary and Bulgaria to join him, with the promise of spoils from the fighting. Germany claimed portions of the north and gave the Italians a piece of the northwest and the coast, Hungary received a share in the northeast, and Bulgaria a chunk in the south. A new regime in Croatia was then installed as Hitler's puppet. The divisions and rivalries created by this dissection of Yugoslavia, combined with existing historic ones, helped perpetuate a conflict that continues to this day.

Mussolini's Greek Misadventure

Mussolini wanted to be a big shot and resented Hitler grabbing all the glory of conquest. This was one reason he decided to attack Greece in October 1940. Hitler reluctantly endorsed Mussolini's decision because *Il Duce* thought he'd walk over the Greeks. Because Greece was Britain's last remaining European ally, Hitler also figured it would put an additional strain on British resources.

The Italians had numerical superiority over the Greeks, but their unenthusiastic troops were met by soldiers determined to defend their homeland. Hitler miscalculated the Italians' ineptitude, so when the Greeks began to push back Mussolini's forces and the British sent troops to back them, the *Führer* realized the campaign could backfire. He feared his enemies might establish air bases from which to attack his oil resources in Romania and to threaten Germany's sources of other vital resources such as tin, copper, and bauxite. Now, instead of maintaining the offensive against England, he was forced to send troops to fight the British on another front.

Greek forces were spread out thinly and left the Yugoslav border lightly defended. This border is where the Germans focused their April 6 attack, along with a strike force from Bulgaria. British forces aiding the Greeks were quickly forced to retreat toward Mount Olympus while the Greek army tried unsuccessfully to withdraw from Albania. Ultimately, the British were forced to evacuate, but not before suffering 12,000 casualties. By the end of April, Greece was in Nazi hands at a cost of 1,100 German dead.

What distinguished the German conquest of Greece from all others in the war was the Germans' behavior during and after the fighting. In other countries, the Germans committed unspeakable atrocities against soldiers and civilians alike, but Hitler had personally ordered the Greeks to be treated differently. Unlike the racist view he held toward most other non-Aryan peoples, he re-spected the Greeks. In a display of that respect, the Greek officers were allowed to keep their swords when they surrendered. Then again, within nine months hundreds of thousands of Greeks were starving to death.

Ask the General

The Greek commander, General Alexandros Papagos, ignored British advice and insisted on a suicidal deployment of troops along the border with Bulgaria, near Mount Olympus, and facing the Italians in Albania. He failed to anticipate the German *Blitzkrieg* against Yugoslavia, which allowed Hitler's troops to outflank his defenses. Like other commanders, Papagos made the mistake of trying to defend every-thing and ended up with nothing.

Stalin Protects His Back

While Germany completed its conquest of two more countries, the United States and the Soviet Union took defensive measures in preparation for the likelihood of fighting their own battles with Hitler. In April, Roosevelt sent troops to the Danish colony of Greenland and extended the area of U.S. naval operations in the Atlantic.

Stalin, meanwhile, was increasingly nervous about Hitler's intentions and decided to protect his back by signing a neutrality treaty with Japan. Both nations hoped the agreement would allow them to focus all their attention on one front and not have to worry about each other.

Mercury Conquers Crete

Hitler also continued to prepare for a confrontation with the Soviets. In addition to the danger British bases in Greece could pose to his invasion plans, Hitler feared enemy outposts in other areas of the Mediterranean, notably Malta and Crete. Both islands gave the British bases from which to threaten Germany's vital resources and supply routes to North Africa.

Hitler struck against Malta first, launching air strikes on British bases in January 1941. For once, however, he was denied a quick victory. Fighting went on there for two years, but Hitler did succeed in neutralizing the British threat from the island for the next several months.

By launching Operation Mercury, the invasion of Crete, Hitler also hoped to secure the southern flank of Eastern Europe in preparation for his campaign in Russia. On May 20, German paratroopers were dropped onto the island, where they met fierce opposition by Greek, British, and New Zealand troops who knew the attack was coming, thanks to the deciphering of German messages.

Though the paratroopers initially suffered heavy casualties, the tide of battle turned when German forces secured an airfield to fly in reinforcements and offer a base to the *Luftwaffe*. Afterward, the resistance crumbled. By the end of the month, the Allies were again forced to evacuate, this time suffering roughly 20,000 casualties compared to 4,000 dead for the Germans. In contrast to the gentlemanly treatment of the Greeks, the Germans adopted a scorched earth policy in Crete, destroying almost everything in their path and murdering Cretan civilians.

Despite taking the island, Hitler saw the battle as a fiasco and lost faith in the paratroopers under General Kurt Student. He refused to use them against Malta, which allowed Allied forces to hold out as long as they did, and he never ordered another major airborne attack for the remainder of the war. Of course, Hitler didn't know that the paratroopers had failed in part because the Germans lost the element of surprise after the British intercepted their plans.

The Atlantic Is Not the Pacific

The one bright spot for the British in early spring was that the Royal Navy attacked and disabled Germany's prize battleship, the *Bismarck*, in the Atlantic on May 27, 1941. A total of 2,300 German sailors drowned.

On the other side of the ledger, Admiral Dönitz's U-boat fleet continued to devastate British shipping. In the first half of 1941, the wolf packs sank more ships than the British built. The British caught a break when they were able to decipher the German Enigma naval codes used from July to December of 1941. That information allowed them to route convoys around U-boat concentrations. The sinkings dropped from close to 400,000 tons per month in May and June to less than 100,000 tons per month for most of the rest of the year.

In April, the United States attacked a submarine that had sunk a Dutch freighter, its first hostile act against Germany. The nation moved another step closer to war when it began to escort British freighters. Opponents of Lend-Lease had argued the United States might be "convoyed into war," but Roosevelt decided in July 1941 that it made no sense to lend Britain arms that would end up at the bottom of the sea because of the German submarine attacks.

Churchill interpreted Roosevelt's willingness to protect his convoys as a sign the president hoped the Germans would provoke the United States to enter the war, but Hitler had ordered his U-boat commanders not to attack any American ships. It was inevitable, however, that U.S. ships would be in danger once the convoys began. On September 4, the United States destroyer *Greer* was attacked by a German submarine off Iceland. The ship reached port safely, but Roosevelt warned that Axis ships entering those waters would do so at their own peril.

Words of War

"The Royal Navy lived on rum and the American Navy on whiskey, but the Italians stuck to port."

—World War II joke

A German U-boat in heavy seas. (National Archives Still Pictures Branch)

Two days later, an American merchant ship on its way to Egypt was sunk by the *Luftwaffe* in the Red Sea. The following month on October 31, a U-boat sank the destroyer *Reuben James* in the Atlantic, killing 115 men. Roosevelt still would not go to war; contrary to the views of some, including Churchill, the president was not looking for a pretext to join the fighting. Congress certainly didn't clamor for revenge, so it is unlikely Roosevelt could have gotten support for declaring war even if he wanted to. It had become clear that it would not be easy to provoke the Americans to fight.

Italy's Brief Empire

When World War II began, the focus was naturally on Europe. After the fall of France, however, Mussolini's aggressive actions in Africa drew the British into fighting on a new front. The Allied cause was further complicated after the fall of France by the decisions of the leaders in French North Africa to side with the Vichy government.

Hitler had not initially planned to fight in Africa, but after Mussolini started his campaign, the opportunity arose to create a vast empire throughout Africa that would include both the French and British colonies. Still, the German entrance into the fighting in Africa was prompted by the need to avert yet another Italian debacle.

The fighting began in June 1940, and over the next several months, British and Italian troops clashed in Libya and Egypt, with Italy capturing British Somaliland and making incursions into Kenya. The British, under the command of General Archibald Wavell, launched an offensive in December 1940 against the Italian front line in Egypt. What had been planned as a brief battle to throw back the Italians went so well that the decision was made to continue the advance. Over the next several weeks, Wavell's forces steadily made their way across the coasts of Egypt and northern Libya, taking tens of thousands of Italians prisoner along the way. By early February 1941, the British, whose forces numbered only about 30,000 men, had advanced more than 500 miles and captured 130,000 prisoners while losing only 500 men.

In February, General Alan Cunningham began a new British offensive from East Africa, attacking Eritrea and British Somaliland from Kenya. Major Orde Wingate led a force from Sudan against Italian troops in Ethiopia. After the British drove the Italians out of Ethiopia, Haile Selassie, who'd fled after the Italian conquest in 1936, was returned to power.

One secret for the success of the attacks mounted by Wavell and Wingate was an advantage the Italians knew nothing about. By the end of 1940, the British had broken all of the Italian codes and knew the movement and strength of the Italian divisions. The British had the

Roll Call

In roughly the first 10 months of fighting in Africa, British casualties numbered fewer than 1,200; however, nearly 75,000 accidents and illnesses were recorded, including 10,000 cases of malaria and another 10,000 instances of dysentery, which caused approximately 750 deaths.

opportunity to destroy the remaining Axis forces in North Africa, but, at the height of the campaign, the Greeks, who had refused help earlier, requested assistance to prepare for an anticipated German attack. Given the small force in Africa, the British had to choose between ignoring the Greeks and continuing their advance or sending troops to help Athens and abandoning the offensive in Africa. As discussed earlier in the chapter, the choice was to help the Greeks, though, unfortunately, it made no difference in the outcome.

While British troops were being sent to try to rescue the Greeks, Hitler's forces were in Africa to bail out the Italians. Mussolini had gone to visit Hitler seeking help around the time the British offensive began in eastern Africa. The *Führer* agreed to send General Erwin Rommel to stop the British offensive.

Enter the Desert Fox

Rommel arrived in Tripoli on February 12, 1941, and, after a few weeks of light skirmishes, led his Afrika Korps on the attack. By early April, the weakened British forces had begun to suffer losses. The Germans began to win back the territory in Libya that the British had so easily won only a few weeks earlier. Wavell recognized Rommel was likely to be targeting the Suez Canal and began to reinforce his forces and fortify their positions near the Egyptian border. He also had to reduce the number of troops he planned to send to fight in Greece. Rommel, meanwhile, was hindered by Hitler's planning for the invasion of Russia, which prevented additional divisions from being sent to Africa.

Rommel's spectacular advance across the desert hit quicksand in Tobruk, where the British successfully repulsed his repeated thrusts throughout April. Wavell launched Operation Battleaxe in June in an effort to dislodge Rommel from Tobruk, but the attack failed, and the British were forced to withdraw. Wavell was subsequently relieved of command and replaced by General Claude J. E. Auchinleck.

The British had greater success in the Middle East, however, where a combined force of British and Free French troops attacked Vichy-backed garrisons in Syria and Lebanon. Though it would take several weeks, the British succeeded in securing control of these territories. By later occupying Iran, in addition to most of the other countries in the region, the British virtually ensured that the Germans could not threaten their interests in the Middle East.

For the rest of the spring and summer, both sides in Africa were hindered by events elsewhere and a stalemate ensued. Although Africa became a sideshow, the main event was shaping up in Eastern Europe, where the most ruthless dictator of the century would finally meet his match.

War Lore

During the fighting in Lebanon, a 26-year-old Jewish volunteer from Palestine was wounded and lost an eye. He would later become the most famous person in the world to wear an eye patch: Moshe Dayan. Less well-known, but also playing a key role in Palestinian politics, was the former Mufti of Jerusalem, Haj Amin al-Husayni. In addition to inciting violence against Jews in Palestine, Husayni curried favor with Hitler in hopes of winning support for the Arab cause. Hitler did nothing to aid the Arabs directly and, through his genocidal policies, may have done more than anyone to influence the establishment of Israel.

The Least You Need to Know

➤ The United States began an unprecedented military buildup in 1941 that dwarfed the production of its enemies.

➤ Britain and the United States began to plan for future joint action, and the Americans offered massive aid to the British through the new Lend-Lease program.

➤ Hitler convinced Romania and Bulgaria to join the Axis, but when Yugoslavia balked, he overran the country.

➤ Mussolini sought to build an empire in North Africa and the Mediterranean, but his troops were outfought, and Hitler had to send German forces to rescue them, capturing Greece in the process, but bogging down in North Africa.

➤ The United States and Germany had their first clashes at sea, but Roosevelt was unwilling to go to war even after a U-boat sank an American destroyer.

Chapter 10

Adolf Turns on Joe

In This Chapter

➤ Germany rejects alliance with Russia

➤ Roosevelt extends Lend-Lease to Stalin

➤ Hitler orders the invasion of Russia

➤ Japan prepares for war

➤ The Atlantic Charter is signed

➤ The Red Army turns the tables

In 1941, the United States had begun to pour weapons into Great Britain; however, this action could not prevent British defeats in Greece and Crete. After the British army had some initial successes in driving the Italians out of Africa, the introduction of Rommel's Afrika Korps stymied their advance and placed British interests in the region at risk. Although German troops found themselves fighting in far-flung places they never expected, Africa and the Mediterranean, Hitler never lost sight of his goal of creating living space for his people, which still meant the conquest of Russia.

Shifting Alliances

The first signs of tension in the Soviet-German relationship appeared in November 1940, when Soviet Foreign Minister Molotov met with Hitler in Berlin. Molotov wanted to obtain guarantees that Germany would remain faithful to its treaty obligations. He also made a number of demands with regard to expanding the Soviet sphere of influence, particularly in the Balkans. Hitler tried to soothe Molotov's fears, but made clear he would not sanction a Soviet move to annex Finland or any other aggressive moves in Europe.

Molotov continued his negotiations with German Foreign Minister Joachim von Ribbentrop, who talked as if the war with Britain were already won. About that time, British bombers flew over Berlin and forced the diplomats to retreat to Ribbentrop's air-raid shelter. Ribbentrop still insisted the British were beaten and that Russia should join the Axis so it could reap the spoils when their empire was carved up. Molotov responded, "If that is so, why are we sitting in this air-raid shelter? And whose bombs are those that are falling so close that their explosions are heard even here?"

The following month, Hitler issued a directive outlining the planned (since July 1940) attack on Russia, Operation *Barbarossa*. In the first phase of the attack, the German army was to engage the main Soviet force as close to the Russian border as possible and destroy it before the Red Army could withdraw to the vast interior and establish a defensive position. The second phase aimed at establishing a front along the north-south line running from the Volga River to Archangel. German forces were to be divided into three strike forces, one which would attack north, in the direction of Leningrad, a second in the south would move against Kiev, and the center force would be directed toward Smolensk, with Moscow as its ultimate target.

The army and the air force enthusiastically supported Hitler's decision to invade the Soviet Union. Few people dared challenge the *Führer*'s judgment, but Admiral Erich Raeder, the navy commander-in-chief, warned Hitler that it was a mistake to take on the Russians before finishing off the British. Raeder offered Hitler several alternative plans, but could not dissuade him from his dreams of colonizing Russia and seizing its resources. Even as Hitler was planning his campaign to destroy the Soviet Union, he entered into a new agreement with Molotov on January 10, 1941, in which the Soviets offered economic concessions to the Germans. It was all more ironic because Hitler had refused to respond to the Soviet request to join the Tripartite Pact.

GI Jargon

The invasion of Russia was originally called Operation Fritz. Hitler changed the name to **Barbarossa,** after Frederick Barbarossa, the Holy Roman Emperor who had set out to conquer the Holy Land in 1190.

Although his generals knew war with Russia would require an all-out effort, Hitler was still unprepared to place the German economy on a wartime footing. Unlike the Allies, for example, he did not want to put women to work, reduce the production of civilian goods, or impose rationing. So even as Great Britain and the United States were shifting more and more of their resources to war production, Germany continued to operate as though it were business as usual.

Mindless Bolsheviks

One of Hitler's main problems in dealing with the Soviet Union was his lack of respect for the Red Army. In large part, this attitude was based on his prejudices. He believed that Bolshevism was a part of the disease spread by the Jews, and that the Soviet Union was a breeding ground for the bacteria, despite the fact that Stalin was also an anti-Semite.

Hitler's attitude toward the Red Army was also based on the reality of its performance against the tiny Finnish army in 1939 and 1940. The *Führer* was convinced that the "inferior" Slavic population could not resist his Aryan onslaught. Many of his commanders shared this view, including Army Chief of Staff General Franz Halder, who called the Red Army "leaderless" and the Russian soldiers "mindless." Even Raeder, who had expressed doubts about Operation Barbarossa, thought it would take less than three months to subdue the Russians.

Words of War

"Russia is never as strong as she looks. Russia is never as weak as she looks."

—Old saying

The Russians were in fact good fighters, particularly when defending their homeland; however, Stalin had weakened their capabilities through the constant purge of his real and imagined enemies. The other consequence of Stalin's rule by terror was to ensure he had total control over the Red Army.

Regardless of the low opinion Hitler had of Russian war-making capabilities, he was still determined to wage a racial, ideological war against them. He distinguished this from the "conventional" war against the French in which the rules of war applied. With regard to the fight against Russia, Hitler said, "We have a war of annihilation on our hands." Even before going to war, he issued the Commissar Decree, ordering the murder of Russians wearing the Communist insignia.

Roll Call

For an example of the extent of Stalin's purges, by the fall of 1938, he had ordered the execution of three of the five Red Army marshals, 13 out of 15 army commanders, 110 out of 195 divisional commanders, and 186 out of 406 brigadiers.

Stalin Tries to Buy Time

Hitler tried to disguise his intentions by launching a series of bombing raids on England in May. On the 10th, nearly 1,500 civilians were killed (the most ever in a single raid), the Houses of Parliament were badly damaged, and the debating chamber of the House of Commons was completely destroyed. Only three days earlier, Churchill had told the House of Commons, "I feel that we are fighting for life and survive from day to day and hour to hour."

War Lore

In one of the most bizarre episodes of the war, Hitler's deputy and confidant, Rudolf Hess (the man to whom Hitler had dictated *Mein Kampf*), flew across the North Sea and parachuted into Scotland on May 10, 1941, to negotiate a peace agreement. Hitler had known nothing about Hess's intention and was furious for months after he found out. The British, meanwhile, didn't know what to make of Hess, but concluded he was mentally unbalanced. This was also the line put out by the Nazis, who said Hess had suffered a hallucination. Hess was kept as a POW and then given a life sentence at the Nuremberg War Crimes Trials.

Hitler's original plan called for the invasion of Russia to begin on May 15, but logistical problems and the need to rescue Mussolini's forces in Africa and the Mediterranean forced a postponement. When the *Blitzkrieg* finally came, the Russian people were surprised; however, Stalin had ample warning of the German attack.

Roll Call

Up until the invasion of Russia, the German death toll had been low, given the number of battles that had been fought. By June 1941, after 21 months of fighting, Germany had lost 17,000 men in Poland, 3,600 in Scandinavia, 45,000 in France and the Low Countries, 151 in Yugoslavia, and approximately 5,000 in Greece and Crete. About 200,000 German soldiers had been wounded. The toll would grow dramatically in the next 21 months.

A variety of intelligence sources relayed information to Stalin that an invasion was imminent. Richard Sorge, his spy in Tokyo, who had access to the German ambassador's messages, sent word of the date of the invasion. Both the British and Americans passed on a variety of warnings and details about German troop movements. However, Stalin could not be persuaded that Hitler would turn on him and did not want to provide an excuse for him to do so. He continued to ship strategic materials as agreed in his economic treaty with Germany up until the moment *Wehrmacht* troops crossed into Russia.

Meanwhile, the United States took a few steps to ratchet up the pressure on the Axis. In June, Roosevelt froze all German and Italian economic assets in the United States and, at Churchill's suggestion, sent troops to Iceland, another of Denmark's possessions that had been left to the British to defend.

By the time Hitler was ready to order his latest *Blitzkrieg*, he was on one of history's greatest military winning streaks—undefeated in almost two years of fighting. The

Nazi swastika flew over the capitals of Athens, Belgrade, Brussels, Copenhagen, The Hague, Oslo, Paris, and Warsaw. He now had his sights set on Moscow. Within six months, his troops would get close enough to see the city, but they would never enter it. Like Napoleon before him, Hitler's dreams of world conquest would ultimately be shattered by the Russian bear and its greatest ally: winter.

Moving on East

At 4:15 a.m. on June 22, 1941, the *Luftwaffe* began to bomb Soviet naval and air bases, destroying roughly one-quarter of the Russian air force. Before the Russians had time to react, the German army began its three-pronged attack across the nearly thousand-mile front. Within a week, Hitler's allies had also declared war, leaving the Soviet Union alone to fight Germany, Romania, Italy, Finland, Hungary, and Albania.

No one knew it yet, but this titanic struggle between Adolf and Joe would become the key to the outcome of the entire war. For the next four years, most of the fighting would be on the eastern front, and more people would die in those battles than in all the others combined.

America Arms the Commies

The Russians were aided by Roosevelt's decision to provide them with equipment according to the terms of Lend-Lease. Americans were not anxious to help the Soviets. The majority were fiercely anti-Communist and feared that providing equipment and arms to the Russians would reduce the amount available to the British. On the other hand, the public was equally if not more opposed to the Nazis and wanted to see them defeated. In retrospect, critics argued this aid should have been conditioned on Soviet behavior and commitments. Stalin, however, was unwilling to bargain, and the Allies made no great effort to extort concessions from him.

Roll Call

Germany attacked Russia with more than 3 million soldiers. They had more than 3,000 tanks, 2,500 aircraft, 7,000 artillery pieces, 600,000 motor vehicles, and 625,000 horses. The Romanian army contributed 250,000 men and the Finns 500,000. Initially, the Soviets had 2,500,000 men and another 2,200,000 in reserve to defend Moscow and other key cities. The Red Army had more tanks and planes than their enemies, but with the exception of many of the tanks, the equipment was obsolete or inferior.

Roll Call

From March 1941 until October 1945, the United States provided the Russians with 15,000 aircraft, 7,000 tanks, 350,000 tons of explosives, 51,000 jeeps, 375,000 trucks, 2,000 locomotives, 11,000 rail wagons, 3 million tons of gasoline, and 15 million pairs of boots. Britain contributed another 5,000 tanks and 7,000 aircraft.

The War Is Won

"[The] Russians lost this war in the first eight days," Hitler exulted. In the opening weeks of the invasion, Hitler appeared justified in believing this. German Army Group North quickly overran Lithuania and took control of most of Latvia; German Army Group Center captured the Polish territories annexed by the Soviets in 1939; and Army Group South drove into the agricultural and industrial heartland of the Ukraine. The Germans succeeded in capturing hundreds of thousands of Russian soldiers but failed to encircle the main Red Army concentrations to prevent their falling back into the Russian interior. The Russians were resisting with fierce determination and inflicting heavy casualties on their attackers.

On July 12, 1941, Britain signed a mutual assistance pact with the Soviet Union in which both agreed not to negotiate a separate peace with Germany. At the same time, Britain launched a series of bombing raids on the German cities of Hanover, Hamburg, Frankfurt, Mannheim, and Berlin. "We have thrown upon Germany about half the tonnage of bombs thrown by the Germans upon our cities during the whole course of the war," said Churchill. "But this is only a beginning."

Meanwhile, Army Group Center continued to push its advance, and within six weeks was within 220 miles of Moscow. The northern and southern advances, however, had stalled. Ignoring the advice of his generals, Hitler now ordered Army Group Center to break off its attack and send tanks to assist in the advances on Leningrad and Kiev.

The Russians were preparing for the worst. To protect some of their great works of art from damage and theft by the Germans, the treasures of the Hermitage Museum were moved out of range of Hitler's attacking forces.

The determination of the Russians to defend their homes was further reinforced by the atrocities being committed by the Germans. Prisoners of war were being mistreated or slaughtered, captured civilians were being murdered, and cities under siege were being starved. The Russians recognized this war would be to the death and fought with a sense of desperation none of Hitler's other victims completely felt.

The Allies were also taking note of how the Germans were prosecuting the war against Russia. In a national

Ask the General

On July 14, 1941, the Soviets introduced a new weapon, the Katyusha, which could fire 320 rockets in 25 seconds. Today, more than 50 years later, the Katyusha remains an effective weapon.

Ask the General

In their search for allies, the Russians agreed to recognize the Polish government-in-exile operating in London. They renounced the Soviet-German treaties of 1939 and consented to release all Polish prisoners to join a new Polish Army. Stalin's failure to keep his end of this seemingly minor bargain would play a significant role in splitting the Allies before the war was over.

broadcast on August 25, Churchill announced, "Scores of thousands, literally scores of thousands, of executions in cold blood are being perpetrated by the German police-troops upon the Russian patriots who defend their native soil. Since the Mongol invasions of Europe in the 16th century, there has never been methodical, merciless butchery on such a scale, or approaching such a scale."

Japan Threatens the West

The prospect of Allied intervention in Russia was reduced by the emerging danger in the Far East, where Japan's moves were becoming more ominous. In 1940, Japan had signed the Tripartite Pact, pledging support to Germany in the event it was attacked. Similarly, Germany agreed to come to Japan's aid should it be the victim of aggression. The expectation was that Japan would back Germany if Russia invaded, and the Germans would fight with Japan if it were attacked by the United States. When Japan signed a neutrality agreement with Russia in April 1941, it opted out of a future conflict beside Germany with Russia.

The Japanese made another strategic decision that spring when they shifted from concentrating on war against China to preparing for conflict with the West. The first move was to occupy southern Indochina, which was a more logical base for assaulting British, Dutch, and American bases than Chinese targets. Roosevelt tried to discourage the Japanese from taking this action by offering them economic inducements; however, they were determined and moved 125,000 troops into the country. Japan then took over Cam Ranh naval base, placing troops within 800 miles of the Philippine capital of Manila and the British base in Singapore.

By this time, the United States had already broken the Japanese diplomatic codes, so their actions did not come as a surprise. The president responded by freezing Japanese assets in the United States and imposing an oil embargo. The British followed suit. With little more than the stroke of a pen, the Western powers had denied Japan 90 percent of its oil imports and cut off three-quarters of its foreign trade.

U.S. policymakers began to plan for the possibility of the Japanese attack, which was expected to be directed at American bases in the Philippines. The United States had adopted the Tydings-McDuffie Act in 1934 (which was to make the Philippines independent in 1946), so little had been done to fortify the American position there. Military planners did not believe it was possible to defend the Philippines; nevertheless, on July 26, 1941, General Douglas MacArthur was assigned to quickly build up forces on the island.

The United States was unaware that the Japanese had made up their minds to attack. Roosevelt *did* know that if America went to war, the fight would not be limited to the Pacific. British intelligence intercepted a message from the Japanese Ambassador in Berlin reporting that Hitler had promised to declare war on the United States if Japan fought the United States.

The Atlantic Charter

Though Roosevelt was very popular, his foreign policy was under constant attack. In August 1941, his proposal to extend the term of draftees passed the House of Representatives by only one vote, and this was at a time when American forces were still seriously undermanned. Secretary of War Henry Stimson compared them to the combined force of the Belgian and Dutch armies that Hitler defeated.

On August 9, 1941, Roosevelt met Churchill for four days of talks aboard the *USS Augusta* off Newfoundland. At the end they agreed on eight principles that would inform their policies on war and peace:

➤ Renunciation of territorial aggression

➤ Opposition to territorial changes without consent of the peoples concerned

➤ Support for the right of people to choose their own government

➤ Access to raw materials for all nations

➤ Support of efforts to improve the economic condition of people throughout the world

➤ Freedom from fear and want

➤ Freedom of the seas

➤ Disarmament of aggressors

Ask the General

Finland was one of the war's biggest losers. Forced to make territorial concessions to Russia in 1940, the Finns sided with Germany and retook the territory they'd lost the year before, but little else. Their actions prompted Britain to declare war against them. At the end of 1941, the Soviets agreed to the pre-1939 border if the Finns made peace. They rejected the offer and later suffered the consequences of siding with the loser.

The Atlantic Charter, as the document came to be known, echoed Wilson's 14 Points and offered an ideal vision of the postwar world.

The two world leaders also renewed their commitment to providing aid to the Soviets, with the United States subsequently granting Russia $1 billion of Lend-Lease credit. Stalin was not satisfied, however, because he wanted the Allies to open a second front to divert German power from its eastern offensive. Despite his persistent appeals to this effect, it would be three years before that front would be opened.

The Sixth Man

Back at the front, German Army Group North was encountering a series of man-made and natural obstacles to its objective of taking Leningrad. The main natural barrier was Lake Ladoga, which prevented the city from being encircled from the north. Finnish troops had moved toward the Lake, but were unable to link up with the Germans. After recapturing the territory they were forced to give up in the war with Russia the year before, the Finns' offensives bogged down. Meanwhile, the Russian-made impediments—barbed wire, anti-tank ditches, and a series of other defensive barricades—slowed the German's assault. Stalin was also going on the offensive, ordering the first air strike by the Soviet Air Force on Berlin in early August.

In early September 1941, Army Group Center was preparing for an assault on Moscow. Meanwhile, the army groups in the north and south were threatening the two largest cities in the Soviet Union after Moscow: Kiev and Leningrad. Overcoming desperate fighting by the Red Army, German troops encircled large concentrations of Russian soldiers in the Ukraine, taking more than 660,000 prisoners, the largest mass capture in military history. On September 19, the Germans captured Kiev.

In the north, the seige on Leningrad was being tightened. The day the German forces entered Kiev, Leningrad suffered the worst bombardment of the war. The Germans had 30 Soviet divisions trapped in Leningrad, but the Soviets gained a reprieve when Hitler ordered most of the air support and several divisions to join the fight for Moscow. Before throwing the full weight of the newly fortified Army Group Center against the Russian capital, he hoped to quickly complete the capture of Kharkov on the way to conquering the Crimea.

As the Germans moved forward, Soviet prisoners were sent west to POW and sometimes concentration camps. They may have been the lucky ones; many prisoners were executed on the spot. The rest marched for miles through rain and snow with little or nothing to eat. Those who could not keep up were shot. As explained in Chapter 20, the Germans had little interest in protecting their prisoners or adhering to the *Geneva Convention*, particularly when it came to Soviet POWs. The biggest concern most German officers had about the murder of POWs was that there were sometimes witnesses.

Even with the successes on the battlefield, the German high command began to more realistically assess the campaign. After three months of fighting, the Germans had lost 86,000 men, more than in all the previous campaigns combined. General Alfred Jodl, the army commander-in-chief, observed that the Soviets were unlikely to collapse anytime soon. In addition, weather began to influence the fighting. Russia had always counted on its climate, particularly its harsh winters, to wear down invaders. Of course, both sides faced the

GI Jargon

The **Geneva Convention** is a series of international agreements aimed at ensuring the humane treatment of prisoners, civilians, and wounded soldiers in war. Sixteen countries agreed in the first convention to respect the neutrality of civilians and of medical personnel and hospital ships identified with the Red Cross insignia and to treat the war wounded humanely. This agreement was signed in Geneva, Switzerland, in August 1864. Subsequent conventions added additional guidelines for behavior during wartime. Hitler routinely violated the conventions.

same conditions, but the Russians were better prepared mentally, physically, and in terms of equipment than their adversaries in the past.

German troops in Russia. (National Archives Still Pictures Branch)

Hitler and his generals had expected to complete their conquest of the Soviet Union long before the weather would become an issue, so their forces were not equipped for winter fighting. Hitler blamed Mussolini's Greek misadventure for throwing off his timetable and forcing the invasion to start a month late. Even before the onset of winter, the weather began to have an impact. With fall came rain, and the roads that had allowed the rapid advance of Hitler's *panzers* were reduced to mud. All three army groups came to a near halt.

A new factor in the war also began to come to the fore in September 1941—resistance. The Russians were just beginning to harass German troops behind the lines. Elsewhere, handfuls of partisans were becoming a growing nuisance and were ruthlessly suppressed by the Nazis. The largest resistance group, 70,000 Yugoslavians who rallied behind Josip Broz (better known as Tito), captured the town of Uzice in September and held it for two months. For much of the rest of the war, Hitler would have to devote resources to trying to stop Tito and the other partisans in German-occupied territories.

Russians Dream of a White Christmas

As winter approached, Russian troop strength had been reduced to 800,000 men, a total of 90 divisions, and 364 aircraft. Hitler had 80 divisions backed by 1,400 aircraft in Army Group Center alone. The Germans were only 65 miles from the capital and occupied 600,000 square miles of the Soviet Union.

On October 15, Molotov advised the British and American embassies to prepare to evacuate Moscow and move to Kuibyshev on the Volga. The equipment from local industries, especially arms makers, was also transferred out of Moscow. The city became gripped by panic, and thousands of Muscovites fled the city.

Stalin called on Marshall Georgi Zhukov to try to save the day. During the summer, Stalin had fired Zhukov as chief of staff, but he had brought him back to lead the defense of Leningrad, which he did successfully. Now he would have to rally the troops and civilians in the capital. Zhukov recruited one-quarter of a million people—two-thirds of whom were women—to dig anti-tank ditches outside the city. The bridges approaching Moscow were all mined and would be demolished if the Germans threatened the city. He also brought in his top commanders to organize the defense of Moscow. Russian peasants between the German army and the capital burned everything in the Germans' path as they beat a hasty retreat.

About the only good news for Stalin came from his agent in Tokyo, Richard Sorge, who informed him that the Japanese had no immediate plans to attack Russia. An element of disaster was also associated with this news, however: Sorge was arrested by the Japanese on October 18 along with 35 members of his espionage ring, shutting off one of the Russians' most valuable sources of intelligence.

After capturing most of the Crimea and a large portion of the Ukraine, including the city of Kharkov (which would change hands several times), Army Group South seized Rostov at the mouth of the Don River. It appeared Hitler would achieve his goal of seizing the Caucasus oil fields. As the weather worsened, the Germans began to lose momentum, and Russian counterattacks began to drive them back. In a crucial battle in late November, the Red Army repelled the Germans from Rostov and effectively ended the threat to the Soviet Union's oil supplies for the immediate future.

With the full force of winter approaching, the Germans had to decide whether to settle into their positions and reinforce them in the hope of mounting new offensives in the spring or try one

Ask the General

Had Japan chosen to fight Russia instead of the United States, at least initially, the outcome of the battle on the eastern front, and perhaps the entire war, might have been different. By draining Soviet resources, the Japanese would have prevented Stalin from reinforcing his beleaguered troops, particularly in Moscow. If Hitler had captured Moscow in the fall of 1941, the direction of the war would have changed completely.

last time to overrun Moscow. In the meantime, German forces were further drained by the need to send aircraft to Africa to help Rommel stave off a new British offensive.

So Close, Yet So Far

Hitler and his generals decided to go for Moscow, with *panzer* groups striking from the north and south. In the last two weeks of November, the two forces inched closer to their objective. The *panzers* in the north got within 21 miles of the city when "General Winter" again came to Russia's rescue.

Because the German army had planned to win the war before winter, it had not equipped the German troops with cold-weather gear, nor was their equipment adapted for the severe climate. With temperatures of 60 degrees below zero, the Germans were literally frozen in place. To prevent frostbite, Hitler attempted to get fur coats from German women to make winter boots. (The Red Army already had boots designed for the extreme cold and would later receive millions of additional pairs from the United States.) To give some indication of how cold it was, sentries who fell asleep at their post were found frozen to death. German soldiers had to light fires under their tanks for hours to warm up their engines enough to operate. The *Wehrmacht* recorded 100,000 cases of frostbite, 2,000 of which required amputations.

The Red Army, on the other hand, was used to the conditions and mounted a devastating counterattack. Thanks to information provided by the spy Sorge, Stalin knew he could afford to withdraw forces from Siberia. This withdrawal allowed him to reinforce the Moscow troops with 10 divisions, supported by 1,000 tanks and an equal number of aircraft. Zhukov now had the resources to repel the Germans and threaten *them* with destruction.

Words of War

"In Hitler's launching of the Nazi campaign on Russia, we can already see, after less than six months of fighting, that he has made one of the outstanding blunders in history."

—Winston Churchill before the House of Commons, December 11, 1941

Hitler refused to allow his generals to retreat and lost confidence in them. Throughout December he fired his top commanders, culminating with the dismissal of the army commander-in-chief, General Walter Brauchitsch. Instead of choosing a replacement, Hitler assumed direct command of the army.

On December 5, Britain further complicated Hitler's life by declaring war on his allies in Finland, Hungary, and Romania. Australia, South Africa, Canada, and New Zealand also declared war on the Axis.

By December, Soviet casualties already exceeded 4 million, but Hitler did not realize the strength left in the Red Army. In less than six days, the Russians recaptured 400 hundred towns and villages. Barbarossa had failed, but Hitler refused to consider a change of strategy even as the Red Army began to drive back his troops. By the end of 1941, Army Group Center, which had gotten tantalizingly close to Moscow, was on the verge of being encircled by the rejuvenated Russian troops. For the next year, the situation would only get worse—for both sides.

The Least You Need to Know

➤ Hitler rejected the Soviet Union's request to join the Tripartite Pact and planned an invasion of the Soviet Union.

➤ The United States granted huge amounts of aid to Russia under the Lend-Lease program.

➤ Stalin was given intelligence by the Allies and his own spy that Germany planned to attack, but he chose not to believe it.

➤ On June 22, Operation Barbarossa began, and the German army's rapid advance fooled Hitler into thinking the war was quickly won, but Soviet defense and counterattacks ended this illusion.

➤ Japan signed a treaty with the Soviet Union, ensuring that it would not join Germany's campaign. This allowed the Japanese to begin preparations for a war against the West.

➤ Churchill and Roosevelt signed the Atlantic Charter, laying out eight principles to guide the post-war world.

➤ German troops came within sight of Moscow before being turned away. Winter arrived, and it was clear Barbarossa had failed.

Part 3
The Yanks Are Coming!

After sticking their heads in the sand for the first two years of the war, Americans are forced to join in the fighting by the Japanese attack on Pearl Harbor. The early action is dominated by the Japanese, who take over most of the Pacific. The United States counterattacks and wins a series of naval battles, culminating in the decisive victory at Midway.

Once the United States enters the war, the country is galvanized and shifts quickly to a war footing. Women are employed in large numbers for the first time. Hollywood does its part as major film stars join the armed forces, starlets entertain the troops, and studios produce training and propaganda films. To its shame, the United States also interns Japanese-Americans. Despite the mistreatment of Japanese-Americans and blacks, both groups are represented in the armed forces and serve with distinction.

Meanwhile, Germany discovers why the Russian winter stopped Napoleon and other would-be conquerors.

Chapter 11

The Day of Infamy Arrives

In This Chapter

➤ Japan looks to seize the resources it needs

➤ The Allies are caught unprepared

➤ The U.S. Navy is knocked down, but not out, at Pearl Harbor

➤ America finally goes to war

➤ A Japanese-style *Blitzkrieg* creates a new empire

In retrospect, it is difficult to believe that the United States was not fighting by mid-1941. Germany had overrun most of Europe; the United States's closest allies, the British, had been fighting for their lives; and battles raged in the Mediterranean, Africa, and the Soviet Union. Roosevelt kept his promise to do everything short of going to war to help the United States's allies, in the face of stiff opposition from the still strong isolationists in Congress. He even resisted declaring war after the Germans attacked and sank U.S. ships.

Even threatening acts by the Japanese were not sufficient to convince the president of the necessity to fight. Ironically, the sanctions he imposed to discourage Japanese aggression had the opposite effect and ultimately led to the United States's entrance in the war.

Grabbing Supplies to Meet Demand

The Japanese had done little to hide their intentions throughout the 1930s. Beginning with their seizure of Manchuria in 1931, the Japanese had made steady gains toward creating an Asian empire. Ten years later, the Japanese had moved into Indochina and set their sights on expanding their conquests to the Pacific.

The Japanese believed it was a necessity to move beyond their shores. The swelling population on the relatively small islands, which lacked most of the resources needed to feed the population and expand its economy, forced them to take over nations that could guarantee their supplies—or so went the argument. The reaction of the United States and her allies to Japanese aggression—imposing sanctions that denied them the materials needed to make war—forced them to decide whether to abandon their dreams of conquest or launch new attacks to secure their vital resources elsewhere.

Roll Call

In 1940, Japan imported approximately 60 percent of its aluminum, 85 percent of its iron ore, 40 percent of its steel, and 60 percent of its copper. Virtually all of its oil, nickel, and rubber were imported.

Though the decision to go to war against the United States may not have been made until 1941, Japan had begun preparing for such a conflict years earlier by launching a massive shipbuilding campaign aimed at gaining naval superiority over the U.S. fleet. This campaign was, in part, a reaction to the Washington Naval Treaty of 1922, which had imposed limits on the size of the Japanese navy. By trying to ensure the relative numerical inferiority of the Japanese, the British and Americans had bruised the Japanese psyche and provoked the kind of resentment that Versailles had in the Germans. Because the treaty limited the size of Japan's navy to 60 percent of that of the United States, the Japanese focused their shipbuilding efforts on faster and more powerful warships.

No Surprise from Japan

When Japan signed the Tripartite Pact in September 1940, it became inevitable that Japan would become a combatant at some point and would have Hitler's backing (a fact confirmed by British intelligence, which had intercepted a message regarding the *Führer*'s commitment to join Japan in battle). The Japanese further strengthened their hand by signing a neutrality treaty with the Soviets in April 1941, which enabled both countries to focus on their principal enemies without worrying about an attack from the rear.

The extreme nationalists in the Japanese government, Minister of War Hidaeki Tojo in particular, lobbied for going to war with the United States sooner rather than later so the Americans would not have time to build up their still-weak forces. However, not everyone in Japan was itching for a fight. Japan's ambassador to the United States, Nomura Kichisaburo, favored peace and negotiated with his counterparts in the U.S. government throughout 1941; he even had a meeting with the secretary of state the day of the attack on Pearl Harbor.

Unfortunately, the ambassador was not in the decision-making loop in Tokyo, and the anti-Western hardliners there could not accept American demands that Japan withdraw from China, even when offered trade concessions. Tojo, who became prime minister in October, would offer only a withdrawal of the troops recently inserted into Indochina in exchange for a million tons of aviation fuel and assurances of peace in the Pacific, a proposal he knew would be rejected.

U.S. Secretary of State Cordell Hull did reject the Japanese proposal and reiterated American demands regarding withdrawal from China. Japan believed the United States was trying to impose a humiliating diplomatic defeat on the nation and that it did not respect the Japanese empire and its military power. This feeling of insult further fueled Japan's inclination to go to war.

Empire Versus Empire

As stated in Chapter 10, because Roosevelt recognized the growing danger and anticipated an attack on the Philippines, on July 26, 1941, he ordered General MacArthur to mobilize troops on the islands to prepare for their defense. By December, the American-led force had reached 130,000 men, the largest force available in the region. Together, the Allies could muster only about 350,000 ground troops, fewer than 100 warships, and 1,000 aircraft, scattered throughout the Pacific. The Japanese military had 2,400,000 men and another 3,000,000 in reserves, supported by 7,500 aircraft and more than 200 warships.

The Americans were not the only ones threatened by the Japanese in the Pacific; British and Dutch colonies were also in danger. Hitler tried to persuade the Japanese to attack the British in Singapore and went so far as to provide Tokyo with intelligence that the British could not send significant naval resources to defend against an attack there.

The Japanese plan was, in fact, to quickly seize the Philippines and Malaya as a springboard to the Dutch East Indies. After capturing Burma, the Marshall and Gilbert Islands, Thailand, Borneo, Java, and other key islands and territories in Asia and the Pacific, Japan would have the vital resources it needed and, the military believed, a secure perimeter to defend the new empire.

This bold plan depended on surprise and the ability to mount a series of almost simultaneous operations across a wide area. Unlike the German *Blitzkriegs*, which featured overwhelming force concentrated in a single assault, the risky scattering of Japan's forces was a calculated gamble based on an

Ask the General

American defense planners did not have the means to defend the Philippines or other islands in the Pacific; nevertheless, they put great faith in a new weapon, the B-17 Flying Fortress. This four-engine bomber was expected to discourage a Japanese attack and give the U.S. Air Force the potential to bomb Japan. This view was partly based on the belief that air power had become the preeminent tool of war. The illusory nature of this belief would soon be apparent in the Pacific, though it would persist among military planners in the European theater.

accurate reading of Allied strength in the Pacific. Success depended, however, on delivering a knockout blow to the Americans.

On November 3, a top-secret order was issued from Tokyo: Pearl Harbor was to be attacked in 34 days. Twenty-one days later, U.S. Navy commanders in the Pacific were warned a surprise attack might soon be launched in any direction. The message specifically mentioned the Philippines and Guam, but not Pearl Harbor.

On November 27, Roosevelt had become convinced there would be war with Japan, but he did not want to be the one to start the fight. The War Department telegraphed General MacArthur in the Philippines, "Hostile action possible at any moment.... If hostilities cannot be avoided...United States desires that Japan commit the first overt act."

Black Sunday

Tojo knew there was one major obstacle to overcome if Japan's dreams of conquest were to succeed in the long-term: the United States Pacific fleet. On December 7, 1941, most of that fleet—more than 75 battleships, destroyers, cruisers, and submarines—was anchored at Pearl Harbor on the Hawaiian island of Oahu, having moved a year and a half earlier from its former base in San Diego, California.

A Japanese task force commanded by Vice Admiral Chuichi Nagumo, consisting of six carriers, two battleships, three cruisers, and several other ships had left the Kuril Islands on November 26. On December 6, U.S. intelligence intercepted a secret message sent using the Japanese "Magic" code. American cryptographers had already broken the code, so it was not long before the translator discovered the message was sent from Tokyo to Japan's Consul-General in Honolulu asking for information about ship movements and berthing positions at Pearl Harbor. Sounding suspicious, the translator gave the message to the department head who said he'd get back to her on Monday, December 8.

War Lore

"Tora, Tora, Tora." Captain Mitsuo Fuchida sent this message to the Japanese fleet after flying over Oahu to indicate the Americans had been caught by surprise. Nearly 20 years later, Fuchida became a U.S. citizen and died in the United States in 1976. These code words were also used as the title of a 1970 movie about Pearl Harbor.

On December 7, Private Joseph Lockard, a radar operator at a relatively new station on Oahu, looked at his screen and could not believe what he saw. It was the largest concentration of aircraft he'd ever detected and was only 130 miles away. When he called a superior officer, who thought it might be a group of B-17 bombers expected in California, he was told not to worry about it.

Just before 8:00 a.m., 366 Japanese fighters and bombers attacked the port and airfields. About an hour later, a second wave of 168 planes completed the assault on "Battleship Row." Thanks to Japanese intelligence, the attackers knew where each vessel was anchored. The entire attack had taken approximately 1 hour and 15 minutes.

When the smoke cleared, 4 battleships were blown up or sunk (*Arizona, California, West Virginia, Oklahoma*), 4 other battleships were damaged (*Nevada, Pennsylvania, Tennessee,* and *Maryland*), 11 other ships were sunk or seriously damaged, 188 aircraft were destroyed on the ground, and 159 aircraft were damaged (they'd been parked wingtip to wingtip to prevent sabotage). Casualties totaled approximately 2,403 dead, including 68 civilians, and more than 1,100 wounded. Nearly half the dead (1,177) were aboard the battleship *Arizona,* which exploded and sank with 1,102 men trapped inside.

The USS Arizona *burning after the Japanese attack on Pearl Harbor, December 7, 1941. (National Archives Still Pictures Branch)*

War Lore

A memorial to commemorate the men of the *Arizona* was dedicated in 1962. The 184-foot long, white concrete structure spanning the wreck was designed by Alfred Preis and was built directly over what remains of the ship. The bodies of the men who were trapped inside were never removed. The names of all those killed on the *Arizona* are engraved on a marble wall. Contrary to popular belief, the *Arizona* is no longer in commission. As a special tribute to the ship and its crew, the U.S. Navy allows the United States flag to fly from the flagpole attached to the severed mainmast of the battleship.

Several Internet sites are devoted to the *Arizona:*

The National Park Service (which operates the Memorial) pages at http://www.nps.gov/ usar/ and http://www.nps.gov/crweb1/history/maritime/nhl/arizona.htm

The University of Arizona's site at http://www.library.arizona.edu/images/USS_Arizona/ USS_Arizona.shtml

Don Schaaf's "Pearl Harbor Remembered" site at http://www.execpc.com/~dschaaf/ mainmenu.html

The Arizona Memorial Museum Association page at http://members.aol.com/azmemph/

On the Japanese side, losses totaled 29 aircraft and 5 midget submarines. None of their carriers or warships were sunk. One Japanese soldier was taken prisoner, and approximately 129 soldiers died in the attack.

The following day, Roosevelt asked Congress to declare war on Japan. In one of the most famous speeches in history, he said:

> *Yesterday, December 7, 1941—a date which will live in infamy—the United States of America was suddenly and deliberately attacked by naval and air forces of the Empire of Japan.... No matter how long it may take us to overcome this premeditated invasion, the American people, in their righteous might, will win through to absolute victory.*

Congress voted to declare war on Japan with only one dissenting vote, Montana Republican Jeanette Rankin. In 1917, Rankin had been the first woman elected to the House of Representatives. She served two nonconsecutive terms (1917 to 1919 and 1940 to 1942) that coincided with the two world wars and was the only House member to vote against the United States's participation in both.

Pres. Franklin D. Roosevelt signing the declaration of war against Japan, December 8, 1941. (National Archives Still Pictures Branch)

Maybe Yamamoto Wasn't So Smart

The attack on Hawaii was brilliantly conceived by the commander of the Japanese fleet, Admiral Isoroku Yamamoto. Though it was a stunning success, the course of the war would later turn in large part because of what the attack failed to accomplish. The Japanese knew the flaws in the operation, but did not comprehend how serious their consequences would be.

First, the attack failed to destroy America's aircraft carriers. The *Saratoga* was being repaired, and the *Lexington* and *Enterprise* were on their way to Wake and Midway Islands. The Japanese knew the carriers had left Pearl Harbor, but they went ahead with the attack anyway. In fact, war games the previous summer had simulated the sinking of the *Yorktown*, which they knew had sailed to the Atlantic several months earlier.

Second, by choosing Sunday to launch the raid, they correctly guessed the state of alert at the bases would be lower, but didn't think as much about the fact that most officers and many sailors would be on shore and would therefore survive to fight later.

Ask the General

One of the cruisers that survived the Pearl Harbor raid was the *Phoenix.* More than 40 years later, sailing for the Argentine navy under the name *General Belgrano,* she was sunk by a British submarine in the South Atlantic.

Third, the Japanese did not blow up the oil tanks at Pearl Harbor. Had they done so, they would have made it even more difficult for the fleet to recover.

Fourth, because Pearl Harbor is relatively shallow, many ships did not completely sink. Those that were grounded and not too seriously damaged could be repaired and sent into battle.

Finally, Japan's greatest mistake was the failure to anticipate the reaction of the American public to a direct attack on the United States. Had Japan simply grabbed the territories it wanted in the Pacific, it is unlikely that the American people would have been willing to go to war over distant islands they'd never heard of. It is conceivable that a negotiated settlement could have then been reached whereby Japan could have retained some or all of its conquests. Not so after Pearl Harbor.

Perhaps Tojo and the other Japanese militarists were misled by the American reaction to Germany's provocations and the isolationists' success in keeping the United States out of the war in Europe. Of course, there was no comparison between the sinking of a ship on the high seas and a massive air and sea attack against the homeland. The Germans may have pulled a few of the eagle's feathers, but the Japanese tried to cut off its wing. Once the Americans were in the fight, Japan had little hope of winning the war.

War Lore

Roosevelt appointed a commission to investigate the Pearl Harbor disaster. The commission concluded that Navy commander, Rear Admiral Husband Kimmel and his Army counterpart, Major General Walter Short, had made "errors of judgment" and been derelict in their duty. The conclusion was controversial, and a congressional committee revisited the issue in November 1945. Kimmel and Short were again blamed, but the criticism was not as harsh, and neither one was accused of derelictions of duty. Both officers retired with their reputations ruined.

Island Paradises No More

Pearl Harbor was not the only target on December 7. That day the Japanese fleet also attacked Wake Island and the Philippines. Only 524 Americans were on Wake to defend the island, but they put up fierce resistance, killing more than 5,000 Japanese soldiers and sinking two destroyers. The Japanese returned about two weeks later with reinforcements—and two light aircraft carriers—overwhelmed the Americans, and captured the island.

When the war began, MacArthur had not made much progress in building up the defenses on the Philippines. He planned to make his primary stand on the largest island, Luzon, where the Americans would try to hold off the Japanese as long as possible before falling back to the Bataan Peninsula. The hope was that the U.S. Navy would come to the rescue before it was too late.

The Japanese encountered little resistance when they began their attack on Luzon, knocking out the American airfields and destroying the naval base at Cavite. The 16 surviving American bombers, which had been counted upon to deter the Japanese, had to be flown to Australia to prevent them from being destroyed.

MacArthur had originally hoped to stop the Japanese on the beaches before they could gain a foothold; however, he did not have the forces to implement the strategy. Instead, he was unable to prevent the Japanese from landing more than 43,000 men and roughly 100 tanks on Luzon. In short order, the Americans were forced to retreat to Bataan. Unfortunately, they did not have adequate time to stockpile food, munitions, and medical supplies.

Not everything went so well for the Japanese. On the island of Guam, only 430 U.S. Marines and sailors defended the island against an invasion force of 5,400 Japanese troops. The Americans held out for nine hours before surrendering.

On December 8, the Japanese attacked Hong Kong. Within 10 days, the British, Canadian, and Indian defenders had given up. Also on the 8th, Japanese forces from their bases in French Indochina took control of Thailand, advanced into Burma, and attacked Malaya.

Unlike most of the places under Japanese assault, the defenders of Malaya had the numerical advantage, in this case two-to-one, but the British still were unable to stop the invaders. The British sent the battleship *Prince of Wales* and battlecruiser *Repulse* to challenge the Japanese, but both were sunk by Japanese planes early in the campaign. The losses stunned the British, who now had no naval

Words of War

"This is no time to speak of the hopes of the future, or the broader world which lies beyond our struggles and our victory. We have to win that world for our children. We have to win it by our sacrifices. We have not won it yet. The crisis is upon us."

—Churchill speaking to the Canadian Senate and House of Commons, December 30, 1941 resources to speak of in the Pacific theater. When Churchill heard the news, he said, "In all the war, I never received a more direct shock."

In their own version of the *Blitzkrieg* across Southeast Asia and the Pacific, the Japanese mounted one more invasion before the end of 1941. On December 15, the victim was Borneo, which was coveted for its oil. The island was divided between the Dutch and British, but neither was in a position to mount a strong defense, given the need both had to protect their other possessions in the region. Though the defenders from both nations tried to destroy the oil installations before they retreated, neither succeeded in putting them out of commission.

Germany Jumps In

The Japanese did not tell Hitler that they planned to attack Pearl Harbor, but when the *Führer* heard about the raid, he was thrilled. "Now it is impossible for us to lose the war," he exulted. "We now have an ally who has never been vanquished in 3,000 years." Although the Tripartite Pact called for Germany to defend Japan if it were attacked by the United States—not the other way around—Hitler made the biggest mistake of his life and declared war on the United States on December 11.

War Lore

After the sneak attack at Pearl Harbor, fears for Roosevelt's safety prompted the Secret Service to look for a bulletproof car for the president. Mike Wright relates that government regulations prohibited spending more than $750 to buy a car, so the only one they could find was a limousine seized from Al Capone by the Treasury Department after he was arrested for tax evasion. "I hope Mr. Capone won't mind," Roosevelt said when he learned of the previous owner. Later, Wright says, Ford agreed to build a special limo for the president and lease it to the government for $500 a year.

As 1941 came to an end, the Japanese had the Allies on the run. Pearl Harbor was in ruins; Hong Kong, Wake Island, and Guam had fallen; and Japan was on the march in Malaya, Borneo, and the Philippines. Until the United States could rebuild its naval strength, the situation in the Pacific would only get worse.

The Least You Need to Know

➤ Japan's dependence on others for vital resources encouraged its leaders to consider conquering lands that had what it needed.

➤ The West had plenty of warning that Japan was looking to expand, beginning with its conquests in China in the 1930s.

➤ Britain's focus on the war in Europe precluded sending resources to defending its possessions in Asia; the United States had not completed its buildup yet and was too weak to deter the Japanese.

➤ The United States was surprised by the Japanese attack on Pearl Harbor, but flaws in the raid assured that the Pacific fleet would have an opportunity for revenge.

➤ Pearl Harbor ended the debate about isolationism and united the American people behind the war effort.

➤ In less than a month, the Japanese succeeded in conquering much of the Pacific and Southeast Asia and achieving their war objectives.

➤ Hitler leaped at the opportunity to declare war on the United States to back his ally Japan—and thereby sowed the seeds of his undoing.

War in the Pacific

After resisting for two years all provocations and entreaties to enter the war, the United States found itself not only fighting a war, but *losing*. The attack on Pearl Harbor did have one positive effect: It unified the nation behind the armed forces in the quest to not only seek revenge but destroy the menaces in Europe and the Far East.

Although the United States had at least one strong ally fighting beside it in Europe, the United States was essentially on its own in the war with Japan. As the new year began, the prospects for victory seemed dim. The United States suffered many more terrible defeats. It took several months before the United States reached the turning point that altered the momentum in the Pacific.

America's U-boats

Now that the United States was fighting, it held nothing back. For example, U.S. submarines were ordered to sink just about anything that floated, whereas in the past

Ask the General

The attack on the United States further globalized the war. Most of Latin America declared war on the Axis. They also severed diplomatic relations with the Axis, with the exception of Chile, which did not do so until 1943, and Argentina, which waited until 1944. Besides diplomatic support, however, none of these nations could provide much help to the Allied cause.

they were largely restricted to attacking warships. At the beginning of World War II, a lot of the world's attention was focused on the German U-boat fleet; in 1942, America submarines would begin to have an impact on war as well.

At the outset, the United States had only 28 submarines, but these subs slowly began to ruin Japanese shipping. Over the next three and a half years, U.S. submarines succeeded in reducing Japanese shipping from nearly 7 million tons to less than 2 million tons at the end of the war. This undersea campaign helped cause crippling shortages of raw materials, such as aviation fuel needed for pilot training. Initially, however, the American submarines had a major problem: Their torpedoes were defective! Some did work, but it took nearly two years to develop reliable torpedoes.

At the beginning of 1942, a Japanese submarine made the biggest splash. On February 23, it shelled the California coast, the first foreign attack on the American mainland since the war of 1812.

Britain's Humiliation

Singapore was a symbol of British strength in the Far East. This city was the obvious prize sought by Japan when it invaded Malaya at the end of the year. Despite this, the British made little effort to prepare for the coming onslaught. When it did come, on February 8, the Japanese were able to quickly overrun the city. On February 15, the British commander, General Arthur Percival, surrendered. A total of 130,000 soldiers were captured by a force half the size. This defeat was considered the greatest disaster in British military history, and it resulted, in part, because the troops were badly trained, poorly positioned, and inadequately armed. The British had also seriously underestimated their enemy.

The news of the capitulation in Malaya was a terrible blow to the morale of the British people. As he did so often, Churchill tried to rally the nation, telling his people "to display the calm and poise, combined with grim determination, which not so long ago brought us out of the very jaws of death." He reminded them that they were no longer fighting alone: "We are in the midst of a great company. Three-quarters of the human race are now moving with us. The whole future of mankind may depend upon our action and upon our conduct.... We have not failed. We shall not fail now. Let us move forward steadfastly together into the storm and through the storm."

I Shall Return!

Malaya was not the only country to fall before the Japanese. By March 1942, they had either conquered, or were on the verge of conquering, New Guinea, the Mariana and

Caroline Islands, the Admiralty Islands, the Bismarck Archipelago, the Gilbert Islands, Burma, the Solomon Islands, and Borneo, among others. For the United States, however, the most important battle was still being fought for the Philippines.

By the end of December, the Americans were in full retreat. They had declared Manila, the capital, an open city in the hope of sparing it destruction; the Japanese bombed it anyway. Most of the 80,000 troops, 15,000 of whom were Americans, had retreated to the Bataan Peninsula. The situation was further complicated by more than 26,000 civilian refugees who needed to share the scarce food supplies.

In late January and early February, ferocious battles were fought, with the Americans succeeding in repulsing the Japanese thrusts. The food shortages and poor sanitation began to take their toll on the Americans, however, as hundreds began to contract malaria, dysentery, and beriberi. Disease was to be an impartial enemy of all the forces in the Pacific theater.

By mid-March, the troops were allowed only one-third rations and would soon be too weak to fight off the Japanese. With the fall of the Philippines now a foregone conclusion, Roosevelt ordered MacArthur on March 11 to move to Australia, where he was named commander of the Allied forces in the Southwest Pacific. MacArthur knew that he was leaving his troops behind to face almost certain death or capture. When he arrived in Australia, he uttered the immortal words, "I shall return." Less than a month later, the troops on Bataan surrendered.

War Lore

In 1863, during the Battle of Chattanooga in the Civil War, 18-year-old Arthur MacArthur picked up his unit's flag from a fallen comrade and carried it onward to the Union Army's objective. He was awarded the Congressional Medal of Honor. In 1903, Arthur's son Douglas (1880–1964) graduated first in his class at West Point. He later distinguished himself in World War I; afterward, he was appointed the youngest superintendent in the history of West Point. In 1928, he was the head of the U.S. Olympic Committee. He became Army chief of staff in 1930, but was criticized for implementing President Hoover's order to expel the Bonus Army from Washington during the Depression. During World War II, he won the Medal of Honor. He directed the Allied occupation of Japan after the war. Later, he was the commander of U.N. forces in the Korean War, but he disagreed with his superiors on strategy and was fired by President Truman for insubordination.

The Bataan Death March

The fight for the Philippines was still not over, because about 2,000 men had succeeded in reaching the fortified island of Corregidor. The contingent withstood nearly a month of Japanese bombardment before being forced to surrender on May 6. The Japanese, who believed in fighting to the death, had no respect for the Americans who had given up. Many prisoners were executed immediately; others were humiliated and tortured. Hundreds of Filipino prisoners had their hands bound with telephone wire and were then beheaded or stabbed with bayonets. The majority were taken on a 65-mile march that came to be known as the Bataan Death March. The already starved prisoners were given no food or water.

The surrender of American troops at Corregidor, May 1942. (National Archives Still Pictures Branch)

More than 5,000 Americans were killed on the march. The 9,300 who survived (along with approximately 45,000 Filipinos) were imprisoned at Camp O'Donnell, where hundreds more prisoners died each day. The most common methods of execution were beheading and bayoneting.

The brutality of the Japanese rivaled that of the Germans. The Japanese murdered their enemies, but they did not do it in the scientific, systematic way the Nazis devised for the "Final Solution," nor did they murder their captives as part of a campaign of genocide. There was, however, an element of racism in their behavior, because they believed that other races were inferior.

In less than five months of fighting, the Japanese had proven as successful in war as the Germans, expanding their empire into China, Southeast Asia, the East Indies, and the Philippines. They had also inflicted humiliating defeats on two empires the Germans had already wounded—the British and Dutch—and on the United States. Things were looking bad on all fronts for the Allies.

Doolittle's Raiders

In March, the United States started preparing to go on the offensive. In addition to MacArthur being given command of the Southwest Pacific, Admiral Chester Nimitz was appointed commander of the Pacific Ocean Area. Because of confusing and sometimes overlapping mandates, many of the battles were fought between the commanders over strategy.

Marines and sailors would do much of the fighting in the Pacific, but the United States's first offensive operation would not be mounted on land or sea, but in the air. Roosevelt wanted to strike back after Pearl Harbor, so the decision was made to try to bring the war home to the people of Japan by bombing its cities, the way the British had done to the Germans during and after the Battle of Britain. It was also designed to lift the morale of Americans. Launching an air raid from the United States against Japan, however, was logistically far more difficult than initiating one from London against Berlin.

The man chosen to plan and lead the attack was Colonel James Doolittle. To reach the mainland, his planes would have to be launched from an aircraft carrier as close to Japan as possible, but beyond the range of Japanese land-based planes. On April 18, 16 B-25 bombers took off from the *Hornet* and flew more than 800 miles across the Pacific to bomb oil and navy installations in Tokyo, Kobe, Yokohama, Nagoya, and Yokosuka.

Before Doolittle's pilots took off, they knew they could not return to the carrier, because the bombers couldn't land on it (and didn't have enough fuel to fly that far anyway). The plan was to fly to a base in China, but the plan was complicated further when enemy ships were detected by the *Hornet's* companion carrier, the *Enterprise*. Fearing that the element of surprise would be lost, the decision was made to launch the bombers, even though they were 650 miles from Tokyo, 150 miles farther away than planned. Now the pilots would have to crash-land as close to the Chinese airfields as they could get.

War Lore

James Doolittle (1896–1993) was a flight instructor in World War I. After the war, he took charge of experimental flying in the army air corps (the predecessor of the air force). In 1922, he was the first pilot to fly across the country in less than 24 hours. Before the Second World War, he was managing Shell Oil's aviation department, but he was recalled to help convert the process of building civilian automobiles to building military aircraft. In 1942, he was given command of the force assigned to bomb Tokyo, an operation that earned him the Congressional Medal of Honor. Later, he was sent to Africa to command the air force there and then to England to command the Eighth Air Force in its campaign against the *Luftwaffe* and German industry before ending up back in the Pacific at Okinawa. When he retired from the military, he returned to work for Shell.

The raid was a success, but hardly flawless. Most of the planes flew off course and missed their targets. Doolittle's payload was intended for an armory, but it destroyed the city's largest hospital instead. Another pilot had to drop his bombs in the ocean. One plane aborted the mission immediately when pilot Edward York realized he didn't have enough fuel to reach his target. York's plane crashed in the Soviet Union, where he expected to be helped, but was instead imprisoned for several months. Two other bombers crashed on Japanese territory, and eight members of the crews were captured, three of whom were executed; the rest were held prisoner for more than three years.

However, Doolittle's raiders did boost the morale of the American public. They also sent a powerful message to the Japanese public, which had been told it was immune from attack. The daring operation also became the subject of a 1944 movie starring Van Johnson and Spencer Tracy and based on the book *Thirty Seconds Over Tokyo*, written by Ted Lawson, who lost a leg when he crash-landed in China.

Corralled in the Coral Sea

The fighting returned to the ocean in early May when U.S. intelligence learned that a Japanese and amphibious force was sailing through the Coral Sea to occupy Port Moresby in New Guinea. The Americans decided to stop them.

On May 7, an American naval carrier task force attacked and sank a Japanese escort carrier. The following day, aircraft from both Japanese and American carriers were launched in what was to be the first carrier versus carrier battle in history. The ships did not exchange fire; however, Japanese planes damaged both American carriers.

The *Yorktown* was later repaired, but the *Lexington* had to be scuttled. One Japanese carrier, the *Shoho,* was also sunk.

The Battle of the Coral Sea lasted two days, with the United States losing 81 aircraft and the Japanese 105. More important, the Japanese were forced to abandon their attack, the first time in the war they were beaten. Up to this point, the Japanese had believed they were invincible and superior to the decadent Westerners.

Midway Tips the Balance

Both the Doolittle raid and the Battle of the Coral Sea had an impact on what was to be the pivotal battle of the Pacific war. The Japanese believed Doolittle's bombers had been launched from the small atoll known as Midway (named because it is in the center of the Pacific) and that the island would have to be taken to eliminate the threat of future attacks on the homeland. Admiral Yamamoto also believed, this time correctly, that the Americans would fight for the island, provoking what he hoped to be the decisive victory over the U.S. Navy. For this battle, Yamamoto organized a fleet comprised of 5 carriers, 11 battleships, and 5,000 troops. Submarines were deployed to hunt for the Americans.

Yamamoto was wrong about something else as well. He thought both U.S. carriers had been put out of action in the Coral Sea. The United States then would have only two left and, he believed, neither was in a position to defend Midway. Unfortunately for Yamamoto, the Americans knew his intentions from the messages they had intercepted and had moved the carriers *Enterprise* and *Hornet* on a course for Midway. The *Yorktown* rushed back from the South Pacific, and repairs, which were expected to take 90 days, were finished in 45 hours, and it immediately sailed for a rendezvous with the other carriers defending Midway. The good news for the United States was that the Japanese carriers outnumbered the Americans by only five-to-three instead of five-to-two; the bad news was that the Japanese advantage in aircraft was 272-to-180.

On June 4, the Japanese First Air Fleet, the one that attacked Pearl Harbor and was still commanded by Admiral Nagumo, launched air raids on Midway, inflicting serious damage without losing a single plane. Meanwhile, a spotter detected American ships, including a carrier, which turned out to be the *Yorktown*. The Japanese were unaware, however, that the other two carriers were also present.

The Americans' initial sorties were ineffective. Out of 41 torpedo planes, all but six were shot down. A second group of torpedo bombers was launched from the *Enterprise* and *Hornet*. They arrived over the Japanese fleet shortly after Nagumo's second wave of planes had returned to refuel and rearm. The Japanese Zeros (the best fighter plane in the

Words of War

"Hit hard, hit fast, hit often."

—Admiral William Halsey's formula for waging war

navy) patrolling the skies overhead engaged the Americans and shot down most of the planes before they could threaten the fleet.

Nagumo thought he was out of danger, but another group of torpedo bombers from the *Yorktown* followed the trails of smoke to the Japanese carriers. Again, the defenders won the air battle, shooting down 7 of the 12 American planes. None of the Japanese ships had suffered any damage.

Nagumo prepared to go on the offensive. Aircraft on all his carriers were being fueled and armed to seek out what he now believed were disarmed carriers and destroy them. He did not expect the arrival of a group of dive-bombers from the *Enterprise*, which had flown off course and found the Japanese ships almost by accident.

At 10:25 a.m. on June 4, 37 dive-bombers attacked the denuded Japanese fleet. A bomb set the carrier *Akagi* on fire. Then four bombs ignited the fuel on the *Kaga*. By 10:30, a third carrier, the *Sorya*, was crippled and later sunk by a submarine. Yet another carrier, the *Hiryu*, was hidden by an air squad and was able to attack and badly damage the *Yorktown*. The *Hiryu* was sunk later in the day.

Navy fighters during the attack on the Japanese fleet off Midway, June 4–6, 1942. A burning Japanese ship is visible in the center of the photo. (National Archives Still Pictures Branch)

It took a total of five minutes to change the course of the entire war and achieve what may have been the most decisive victory in the history of naval warfare. The Japanese fleet Nagumo had led against Pearl Harbor had been almost completely destroyed. Not only had it lost four carriers, but also 3,500 men and nearly 300 planes and their irreplaceable aircrews.

The U.S. lost a destroyer, 150 aircraft, and 307 men. Though the Americans would lose the badly damaged *Yorktown* two days later (to a submarine), thereby balancing the number of carriers both sides had deployed in the Pacific, the advantage now clearly shifted to the Americans, whose greater resources would allow them to recoup. During the course of the war, Japan was able to send a total of 14 carriers of all types to sea, compared to 104 for the United States.

The Japanese tried to hide the disaster from the public and their German allies, but there was no escaping the fact that their empire had reached its limit, and they would now have to fight to the death to keep any of it. In retrospect, we can see how Midway altered the course of the war, but the immediate impact was less obvious, and three years of fighting remained.

Ask the General

The same week the battle was fought over Midway, the Japanese invaded and occupied two American islands in the Aleutians near Alaska, Kiska and Attu. To give you a sense of the anxiety of the time, some Americans feared the northwest United States would be invaded from these distant islands, and U.S. forces were diverted to deal with the "threat." American troops reclaimed Attu after a three-week battle in May 1943. The Japanese withdrew from Kiska in August before the Americans arrived on that island.

America Takes Offense

The next major battle in the Pacific involved the first American offensive designed to retake a key base of Japanese operations. In July 1942, the Japanese had begun to build an airfield on Guadalcanal and were preparing to use the island as a staging ground for future operations.

Guadalcanal is approximately 90 miles long and 25 miles wide. The island is dominated by mountains and dormant volcanoes that reach up to 8,000 feet. The oppressive heat is a breeding ground for mosquitoes carrying malaria and other diseases. The island is ringed by coral reefs, with only a portion of the north central coast clear enough for landings. The terrain favored the defenders.

The United States sent two task forces, which included the carriers *Saratoga, Wasp,* and *Enterprise,* to seize the island. On August 7, the 1st Marine Division landed on the offshore islands of Tulagi, Gavutu, and Tanambogo and quickly overwhelmed the 2,000 Japanese defenders. Another 16,000 troops landed on Guadalcanal.

The appearance of the marines set off alarm bells in Tokyo, which recognized that their defensive perimeter depended on holding the island. "Success or failure in recapturing Guadalcanal is the fork in the road which leads to victory for them or for us," a captured Japanese high command document revealed. The Japanese immediately began sending reinforcements.

War Lore

The commander of the land-based planes in the attack on Guadalcanal was Admiral John S. McCain. McCain's father was also an admiral, but the best-known McCain may be his son John. A third-generation navy man, John McCain became an aviator and spent 22 years in the service. In 1967, he was shot down over Hanoi and was a prisoner of war in Vietnam for five and a half years (1967–73). He received numerous awards, including the Silver Star, Bronze Star, Legion of Merit, Purple Heart, and the Distinguished Flying Cross, before retiring as a captain in 1981. In 1982, McCain went into politics, serving two terms in the House of Representatives as a Republican representative from Arizona. He has represented that state in the Senate since 1986.

Over the next several weeks, five separate sea battles would be fought in the campaign. The first, on August 8, occurred after the Japanese surprised the Allied fleet and sank three U.S. cruisers and one Australian cruiser, killing more than a thousand men. The Americans were having more success on the ground, advancing quickly and capturing an airfield, which was later named Henderson Field in honor of one of the U.S. Marine Corps pilots who died at Midway.

On August 24, 1942, in the Battle of the Eastern Solomons, the Americans also got the better of their enemies, intercepting ships carrying reinforcements and sinking a Japanese carrier, cruiser, and destroyer. The *Enterprise* was damaged, and the Americans lost 20 aircraft; the Japanese lost 60 aircraft.

The setback did not stop the Japanese from landing reinforcements. Approximately 6,000 Japanese soldiers reached Guadalcanal in the next month. The Americans also sent in more marines. Both sides, but especially the Japanese, needed the troops. After the first month of fighting, the Americans had already lost 1,600 men, and the Japanese had lost 9,000. The marines also learned a lesson they would see repeated throughout the war: The Japanese fought to the death. Those who survived the fighting killed themselves to avoid capture.

Fighting continued throughout the summer, but escalated in October when the Japanese made a last-ditch effort to retake Henderson Field. They were unsuccessful and forced to retreat.

The U.S. Navy had equal success repulsing Japanese ships bringing reinforcements, but not all of the engagements were great victories for the Americans. One of the most serious clashes took place on October 26 in the Battle of Santa Cruz, when the Japanese sent in 4 carriers, 4 battleships, 9 cruisers, 28 destroyers, and a number of other ships to face a much smaller American force consisting of 2 carriers, 1 battleship, 6 cruisers, and 14 destroyers. In one day, the Japanese sank the carrier *Hornet* and a destroyer and damaged a battleship, cruiser, and destroyer, as well as the carrier *Enterprise*. The Americans also lost 74 planes. Three Japanese carriers were damaged and most of their planes shot down, but it was the Americans who were forced to retreat this time.

Words of War

"I have never heard or read of this kind of fighting.... These people refuse to surrender. The wounded will wait till men come up to examine them and blow up themselves and the other fellow with a hand grenade."

—Major General Alexander Vandergrift, writing to the Marine Commandant

The five Sullivan brothers, all of whom were lost in the sinking of the USS Juneau, *November 13, 1942. (National Archives Still Pictures Branch)*

War Lore

George, Francis, Joseph, Madison, and Albert Sullivan enlisted in the Navy after a friend was killed on the *Arizona* at Pearl Harbor. The brothers insisted on sticking together and were allowed to serve together aboard the *USS Juneau*. The ship was torpedoed during the Battle of Guadalcanal, and all five were killed. In 1943, the boys' mother christened a new destroyer named in their honor, the *USS The Sullivans.* The ship was decommissioned in 1965 and is moored at the Naval Servicemen's Park in Buffalo, New York (the web address is http://www.spear.navy.mil/ships/ddg68/). A film about the brothers, *The Fighting Sullivans,* was released in 1944.

Roll Call

When the fighting on Guadalcanal ended on February 9, 1943, the Americans had suffered 1,600 dead and 4,245 wounded, with the marines taking most of the casualties. The Japanese dead totaled nearly 15,000, with another 9,000 succumbing to disease and 1,000 taken prisoner. The Japanese tried at the end to pull a Dunkirk maneuver and evacuate their troops, but only 13,000 soldiers made it off the island.

This battle was followed by the Battle of Guadalcanal from November 12 to 15, during which 17 different Japanese ships of different types were sunk and another 9 damaged, and the Americans lost 9 vessels and had 8 damaged. At the end of the month, the Battle of Tassafaronga was fought in which the Japanese came out ahead in terms of damage, but were still forced to turn back without putting their troops and cargo ashore.

While the Japanese troops on the island were being worn down by the constant pressure of the American offensive and the lack of food and supplies, the U.S. forces grew stronger. By the end of 1942, the United States had effectively won Guadalcanal, though the Japanese held out for almost two more months.

At Guadalcanal the Japanese learned they were not invincible and that they had been wrong to think the Americans would not care about distant lands in which they had no particular strategic interest. The Americans gained confidence that they could win this war, but they also discovered that their enemies did not fight by the rules they were used to, and that victory would only come at a very high cost.

The Least You Need to Know

➤ The United States began to use its submarine fleet to disrupt Japanese shipping.

➤ Britain's main colonial base in the Far East, Singapore, fell to the Japanese in what was considered that nation's greatest military disaster.

➤ The Japanese swept through the Pacific and drove the United States out of the Philippines.

➤ Americans learned what it meant to be prisoners of the Japanese on the horrific death march on Bataan.

➤ Doolittle's daring raid on Tokyo lifted American spirits and imposed the reality of war for the first time on the Japanese public.

➤ In five minutes, U.S. bombers destroyed most of the fleet that attacked Pearl Harbor in the battle of Midway. The victory marked the turning point in the war in the Pacific.

➤ The United States ended 1942 on the offensive, wearing down the Japanese defenders on Guadalcanal and beginning a steady march toward Japan.

Chapter 13

We're Coming for You, Adolf

In This Chapter

➤ Roosevelt and Churchill decide war priorities

➤ The U-boats are neutralized

➤ British bombers target German towns

➤ The White Rose blooms

➤ Stalingrad is saved

➤ Rommel takes a licking

➤ America goes to war in Europe

The attack on Pearl Harbor focused American attention on the Pacific, but the war in Europe continued to rage. To recap, by the beginning of 1942, Germany controlled all of part of Austria, the Sudetenland, Poland, Belgium, Luxembourg, Yugoslavia, Poland, Norway, Denmark, the Netherlands, Greece, France, Bohemia, Moravia, and Serbia, and had puppets in Finland, Romania, Bulgaria, Croatia, Hungary, and Slovakia. Though their offensives had stalled, the Germans also remained in control of a large swath of the Soviet Union.

Fighting also continued in Africa and the Mediterranean, where the Italians were being disabused of their dreams of empire. Soon they would also have to fight the Americans, a frightening prospect for an army that already had its hands full with the British.

Huns First, Japs Later

In December 1941, Churchill had gone to Washington for the three-week Arcadia Conference to discuss common war aims. The two sides almost immediately disagreed. The Americans, not surprisingly, wanted to build up the Allied forces in the Pacific, but they were not certain that either Britain or Russia could survive without immediate American intervention. Because the Americans were confident they could hold off the Japanese, they agreed to try to knock out the Germans first and then concentrate Allied power on Japan. The idea would be to mount a sustained air campaign against Germany, help the Soviets repel the Germans, and land troops in North Africa. Afterward, the Allies would initiate a large-scale land offensive against Germany from either the English Channel or the Mediterranean.

Disagreements arose, however, over strategy. The British preference was to build on the limited success they'd had in the Mediterranean to pressure Hitler from the south, but the Americans preferred to attack the Germans through France. This would remain a point of contention for many months. In the meantime, a structure was needed to plan the details of the Allied strategy. A Combined Chiefs of Staff was therefore created, consisting of the top military officials in each nation. The British already had a body of chiefs, but the United States did not. From then on, the American military officers responsible for interservice coordination and policy for their branch became known as the Joint Chiefs of Staff.

On January 1, 1942, Britain and the United States were joined by the Soviet Union, France, China, and 21 other countries in signing the Declaration by the United Nations in Washington. This accord called on the parties to use their resources to defeat the Axis, to refuse to make a separate peace with their enemies, and to subscribe to the principles in the Atlantic Charter.

Words of War

"Never before have we had so little time in which to do so much."

—Franklin Roosevelt, fireside chat, February 23, 1942

The following day, Churchill and Roosevelt met and decided the United States should launch a massive arms-building program. The two leaders significantly raised the benchmarks of an earlier agreement to 45,000 planes and tanks and 500,000 machine guns by the end of 1943. Even larger increases were planned for other military supplies.

The military began working on plans for the invasion of Europe. In March, the Allies agreed to install 1 million American troops in England to prepare for the confrontation with Germany. The project was code named Bolero.

War Lore

On January 17, 1942, Churchill was returning from the United States when his plane veered off course and came within range of German anti-aircraft guns in France. Before encountering any enemy fire, the pilot realized his mistake and headed back toward England, where British radar operators interpreted the incoming blip as a German bomber. Six Royal Air Force fighters were sent up to meet the threat, but failed to find the approaching plane. Churchill landed safely.

Slaves of the *Reich*

Hitler was not sitting on his hands while the Allies planned his demise. Germany was beginning to feel the strain of war. Losses at the fronts, and through the Allied blockade, were beginning to affect the *Wehrmacht*'s fighting ability. Hitler no longer had the luxury of maintaining the standard of living of the average German. War production had to increase, and Hitler ordered his armaments minister, Fritz Todt, and Todt's successor, Albert Speer, to make it happen.

Although Hitler embarked on a desperate effort to mobilize the resources of Germany and the territories he controlled, he remained convinced that the superior quality of Germany's weapons would make up for any differences in quantity. This conviction proved to be true, however, in the case of only a handful of weapons, and not those that decided battles, such as aircraft, tanks, and electronics.

Hitler had another production-related problem: a shortage of workers. With the country fully mobilized and Hitler unwilling to employ large numbers of women, he was forced to look elsewhere for laborers. The solution was to import workers from the occupied territories and to employ slave laborers from the concentration camps. The largest

Words of War

"Books cannot be killed by fire. People die, but books never die. No man and no force can abolish memory.... In this war, we know, books are weapons."

—Franklin Roosevelt to the American Booksellers Association, April 23, 1942, nine years after the Nazi book burnings

source of workers came from the east. Beginning in 1942, millions of Soviet POWs and Russian civilians, mostly from the Ukraine, were put to work for the *Reich*.

Thousands of Jews were also among the slave laborers, but Hitler remained more interested in killing them. On January 20, 1942, the Wannsee Conference laid out the "Final Solution" to the Jewish problem (see Chapter 24).

No Let-Up in the Atlantic

A new war was in full swing in the Pacific, but the old one in the Atlantic had not subsided. And it wasn't only the Atlantic: German U-boats also patrolled the Gulf of Mexico. In the first quarter of 1942, more than a million tons of goods were sunk by these submarines. The German wolf packs also began to attack Latin American shipping (with the exception of Argentina, which Hitler hoped to keep out of the war) and provoked Mexico (in May) and Brazil (in August) to declare war.

Early on, Admiral Dönitz had claimed he could strangle Britain if he had 300 submarines. By the time Germany had that many, in July 1942, the opportunity had been missed. The U-boats continued to send millions of tons of shipping to the bottom of the sea, and to sink ships faster than England could build them, but foreign shipping replaced much of this, and with the entrance of the United States into the war, its substantial shipbuilding resources were now available to the Allies. The United States would also soon send dozens of its own submarines into the fray.

Still, in November 1942, the Allies suffered their greatest losses of the war, 860,000 tons of goods. Part of the success the U-boats enjoyed was due to changes in the German enigma code machines, which prevented the Allies from intercepting their messages. It was also a result of the Germans' own success in breaking Royal Navy codes. The Allies regained the advantage the following spring when the new enigma codes were broken.

GI Jargon

In the summer of 1942, the Allies began using direction finders that allowed them to locate submarines by their radio transmissions. The High-Frequency Direction Finders (HF/DF) were nicknamed **Huff-Duff.**

Another factor in the battle for the Atlantic was the development, primarily by the British, of more sophisticated radar and antisubmarine countermeasures. The use of *Huff-Duff* in particular befuddled the Germans for the remainder of the war and played an important role in the Allies' victory at sea.

Unlike their Japanese allies, the Germans had no surface fleet to speak of. The few ships they had were assigned to protect their shipping lanes in Scandinavia. One of them, the battleship *Tirpitz*, was a target of the British, who feared it might be used against them in the Atlantic. To forestall that possibility, British commandos staged a daring raid on March 28 on the French port of St. Nazaire and disabled the only dock on the Atlantic coast that could handle the *Tirpitz*.

Another British commando operation at the end of December resulted in the sinking of five German merchant ships in Norway. Hitler was now being attacked from different directions and felt the need to fortify his empire from the border of Norway and Finland to the border between France and Spain, creating what he hoped would be "Fortress Europe."

Bombs Away

Submarines were silent killers prowling the seas, taking direct aim at their prey. Bombers were thunderous merchants of death that dropped their deadly cargo unmercifully and with far less precision. The air war had started off in as gentlemanly a fashion as one could expect, with Hitler ordering that attacks be confined to military targets. A German bomber accidentally bombed east London in 1940, provoking the British to strike Berlin. This gave Hitler the pretext for abandoning all restraints on the *Luftwaffe*.

The blitz on London caused devastating damage. The British attacks were not comparable. By the end of 1941, Churchill concluded that the German people must learn what it means to be at war. In early 1942, a new generation of higher performance bombers, the Lancasters, allowed the British to mount a series of devastating attacks aimed at setting German industrial towns on fire.

After the British raids on Lübeck and Rostock, the *Luftwaffe* responded with a series of attacks beginning April 23 on Bath, Norwich, York, Canterbury, and Exeter. The Baedeker Raids, as they were called (after a series of travel guides), caused irreparable damage to landmarks in these historic towns and killed nearly 1,000 civilians in just five days.

The Germans and British seemed equally convinced that it was necessary to inflict the maximum terror on the enemy population to bring their governments to heel. Minister of Propaganda Goebbels said Hitler agreed with him that "cultural centers, health resorts, and civilian centers must be attacked now. There is no other way of bringing the English to their senses. They belong to a class of human beings with whom you can talk only after you have first knocked out their teeth."

Words of War

"This war no longer bears the characteristics of former inter-European conflicts. It is one of those elemental conflicts which usher in a new millennium and which shake the world once in a thousand years."

—Hitler speaking to the *Reichstag*, April 26, 1942

Words of War

"Cologne was an advance payment on the vengeance that must and shall be taken on Hitler's Germany for the millions of Jews they have killed. So the Jewish population of tortured Europe considered Cologne its personal act of vengeance."

—Emanuel Ringelblum, historian trapped in the Warsaw Ghetto

In the race to see who would end up toothless, the British dealt the next devastating blow. On May 30, the largest aerial armada ever organized—1,046 bombers—left British bases and flew over Cologne, dropping nearly 1,500 tons of bombs on the city in 90 minutes. Operation Millennium killed 476 Germans, and the property losses were staggering. Approximately 45,000 people lost their homes, 250 factories were destroyed, and roughly 600 acres of the city were burned. Operation Millennium was a mere prelude to the destruction that would come from the skies in the next three years.

Throughout the war, Hitler supported research on secret weapons that he was convinced would guarantee victory for Germany. Nothing came from the program until June 13, when scientists at Peenemünde, on the Baltic, tested the first rocket, known eventually as the V-2 (A-4 to the Germans). The rocket was designed to fly up to 200 miles and alter the balance of power with England permanently. That day, however, the test was a failure.

The White Rose

Little internal opposition had ever developed to threaten Hitler. Despite the length of the war, the privations it caused, and, more recently, the deadly Allied bombings, most Germans still were very supportive of Hitler. When they did have complaints, they tended to direct them at the Nazi Party rather than the *Führer*. Even on the brink of defeat, Hitler did not lose his hold on the public. When even modest opposition arose, it was usually ruthlessly suppressed, which is why the creation of The White Rose was so unusual.

One day in 1942, copies of a leaflet entitled "The White Rose" suddenly appeared at the University of Munich. The leaflet spoke about the evils of the Nazi regime and the need to revolt. This leaflet was the first time that internal dissent had surfaced in Germany. Other leaflets soon appeared, and copies turned up in people's mailboxes. Students distributed them at other universities and began to use graffiti to express their opposition to Hitler.

The group that came to be known as The White Rose was started by two young Germans who, like others their age, had served in the Hitler Youth. Hans and Sophie Scholl were different, however, because their father was convinced Hitler was leading the country to ruin. The children came to realize their father was right and recruited like-minded friends Christoph Probst, Alexander Schmorell, Willi Graf, and their psychology and philosophy professor Kurt Huber to join them in producing anti-Nazi leaflets.

On February 18, 1943, Hans and Sophie were caught leaving pamphlets at the University of Munich and were arrested, as was Probst. A few days later they were tried for treason, convicted, and executed. The same fate awaited Schmorell, Graf, and Kurt Huber. Others involved were either executed or sent to concentration camps. The White Rose had shown that dissent was possible, and that opponents to Hitler existed, but the risks of coming forward were so great that this movement became well-known for its uniqueness.

Russia's Cold Winter

As well as the obvious direct impact of killing and terrorizing people and causing tremendous damage, the British air attack had an indirect impact on the German advance in Russia. The bombing campaign over the next several months forced Hitler to divert precious aircraft to defense and retaliatory attacks against Britain. Thus, in the space of about a year between the summer of 1942 and spring of 1943, the percentage of the *Luftwaffe*'s fighters on the eastern front dropped from 43 to 27.

In addition, both the German and Soviet armies were recuperating from the winter. The Soviets were mobilizing men in an effort to raise their troop strength to 9 million. The factories they had moved out of harm's way were cranking out 4,500 tanks, 3,000 aircraft, and 14,000 guns. By midyear, the Soviets would grow even stronger due to supplies from the British and Americans. Among the vital contributions to the Red Army were 4,400 tanks and 3,100 aircraft.

The Germans did their part to harden the resistance of their enemies by their treatment of Soviet prisoners. By February 1942, 2.8 million of the 3.9 million POWs were dead. Hundreds of thousands were executed; most of the rest died because of the hellish conditions in which they were transported and incarcerated. The situation was so bad that German officers petitioned Hitler to revoke his Commissar Decree so the Russians would not fight with such desperate resolve.

One other result of the German conduct of the war was to provoke resistance from the people in the areas they'd overrun. By the end of 1942, roughly 200,000 *partisans* were engaged in efforts to interfere with German operations.

Though the Germans did not suffer in the same way as the Russians, their dead, which by the end of April numbered more than one million, could tell no difference. Evidence of Germany's desperation to make up for its losses can be seen in Hitler's willingness for the first time to accept women into the military to serve in administrative and clerical positions so the men could be sent east.

GI Jargon

Partisans are irregular troops engaged in guerilla warfare, often behind enemy lines. During World War II, the term was applied to resistance fighters in Nazi-occupied countries.

Ask the General

Hitler and Stalin had many similarities. Neither man ever visited the battlefront during World War II, both were indifferent to casualties, and both exercised direct control over their armed forces. Stalin, however, may have been more willing to listen to proven military advisers, whereas even the greatest German heroes were cast aside by Hitler when they displeased or failed him. Whatever defeats the *Wehrmacht* suffered were inevitably the fault of someone else.

Hitler planned to launch a summer offensive in 1942 with the goal, yet again, of capturing the oil and other resources of the Caucasus. He believed Stalin would pull out all the stops to prevent the loss of his oil supplies, allowing the Germans to win the decisive victory of the campaign. Stalin, meanwhile, expected Hitler to attack in the direction of Moscow and mistakenly concentrated his forces there.

Also, by spring, Hitler had purged his military command and taken direct control of operations on the front. In July, he moved his headquarters from Rastenburg to Vinnitsa in the Ukraine to be closer—albeit still 400 miles away—to the front.

Before advancing, however, the Germans were thrown on the defensive again in mid-January when Hitler ordered the first large-scale withdrawal of the war in response to the defeats suffered during the winter, thereby allowing Army Group Center to retreat to a line 85 miles from Moscow. The Germans were able to hold their position until early spring, when the rains turned the battlefield into a bog that forced both armies to a virtual standstill.

Stalin was not content to wait for Hitler to strike. He ordered an attack in May 1942 on Kharkov in the southwest, but the Russians encountered surprisingly strong German resistance and were forced to retreat. Within two weeks, the assault had turned into a debacle as the Germans encircled the Russian army and took more than a quarter of a million prisoners.

Shortly thereafter the Germans began their summer offensive. After an eight-month siege, Sevastopol was overrun on July 1. The victory was costly, with the loss of perhaps 100,000 German troops. Still, they moved on toward the oil fields in Maikop and Grozny, reaching the latter in August only to discover the Russians had destroyed the oil fields. Hitler then set his sights on Stalingrad.

Stalin issued orders that no one retreat from Stalingrad and sent troops to reinforce the city's defenders. In addition to its strategic location, the city had some sentimental value to Stalin—to the extent one can call the dictator sentimental. The city was named after him and had been the place in 1918 where he had led a group of dissidents who defied Trotsky.

Over the next several months, the German army laid siege to Stalingrad. At the end of August, a bombing raid destroyed a large part of the city. Afterward, however, the Germans found themselves getting bogged down in the rugged country area where most of the city's factories were located. Fierce battles were waged over every inch of the city. Soldiers engaged in hand-to-hand combat in the cellars, staircases, and hallways of houses. The *Luftwaffe* was flying thousands of sorties, and the

Roll Call

While Hitler believed he was winning a war of attrition with the Soviets, it became increasingly obvious that the opposite was true. In September, he learned that the Soviet Union still had more than 4 million soldiers, with more available for conscription, compared to roughly 3 million in the *Wehrmacht*.

artillery barrage against the Russian defenders was unceasing. In early November, the German army finally succeeded in reaching the Volga to completely encircle the city.

On November 19, 1942, just after Hitler was forced to send a large contingent of men and supplies to North Africa, Zhukov led a counterattack, Operation Uranus, against the German and Romanian forces besieging Stalingrad. Within a few days, the situation had been reversed, and the Axis forces were surrounded. As he had done earlier, Hitler denied his commanders' requests to retreat, placing hundreds of thousands of men in imminent danger of capture or death.

The year ended as it had begun, with the Germans again on the defensive and one of their main armies encircled and in danger of being destroyed. The dreams of a quick victory in Operation Barbarossa were long gone. In 1942, the Germans had failed to make any progress toward defeating the Soviet Union and had suffered tremendous losses with little gain.

The Soviets also had calamitous casualties, but they were proving to be far more resilient and tenacious than Hitler expected. The German threat against Russia's major cities had dissipated, and it would not be long before the term *eastern front* would take on a new meaning: the line of defense against the Red Army.

Words of War

"Never contradict the Führer. Never remind him that once he may have thought differently of something. Never report casualties to him—you have to spare the nerves of the man."

—Advice from Hitler's deputy, Wilhelm Keitel, to General Kurt Zeitzler after Hitler chose him as army chief of staff

"If a man starts a war, he must have the nerve to bear the consequences."

—Zeitzler's reply

Rommel's Wild Ride

At the end of 1941, Hitler had transferred forces from the eastern front to reinforce Rommel in Africa. German and Italian submarines, meanwhile, had inflicted serious damage to the Royal Navy, including sinking the aircraft carrier *Ark Royal*.

On November 18, 1941, General Auchinleck (commander of the British army in North Africa) launched Operation Crusader in an effort to succeed where his predecessor had failed in dislodging Rommel from Tobruk and, ultimately, Libya. It took three weeks, but the British forced Rommel to withdraw to El Agheila, the place where he had started his advance eight months before. Rommel counterattacked on January 21, 1942, and quickly took Benghazi and much of the territory he'd lost, but the advance stalled, and an uneasy lull prevailed until May. The two-month battle had already cost 38,000 German and Italian lives, and 18,000 British lives.

In late May, Rommel again attacked and gained the advantage, pushing the British back near Alamein and retaking Tobruk. In less than a month of fighting, and with his forces outnumbered nearly two to one, he captured 30,000 men and tons of valuable equipment, gasoline, and food. Churchill considered the defeat a disgrace, almost on a par with the loss of Singapore in February.

The news reached Churchill while he was in Washington lobbying Roosevelt to take part in an operation in North Africa. Though some of the president's advisers, particularly his chief of staff George Marshall, wanted to invade France, Churchill argued it would not be possible in 1942. The debate continued in London between Churchill and Marshall. Ultimately, the British desire for an African campaign won the day, and plans were made for Operation Torch. Churchill had also accomplished one other important goal in his initial meeting with the president: The United States promised to ship new Sherman tanks to the British troops in Egypt.

While the Allies planned their operation, Rommel began his own, a drive to seize Egypt. With Crete as a base of supplies, the Afrika Korps rolled across the desert and into Egypt, just 60 miles from the key port city of Alexandria.

Auchinleck managed to stop Rommel at El Alamein, but he was already preparing options for an evacuation should the Germans reach the Suez Canal. Auchinleck was then replaced as Middle East commander-in-chief by General Harold Alexander, who had overseen the evacuation from Dunkirk. The principal army command was handed over to General Bernard Law "Monty" Montgomery.

General Bernard L. Montgomery watches his tanks move up, North Africa, November, 1942. (National Archives Still Pictures Branch)

Rommel, recently appointed field marshal by Hitler, made one last effort to push through the British defense on August 30. Unbeknownst to him, however, British intelligence knew he was coming, and information about his supply ships allowed the Royal Navy to sink three fuel ships. The shortage of fuel, combined with Montgomery's staunch defense, stopped the Afrika Korps. The British continued to hold the line against Rommel's repeated thrusts until September 3, when he was forced to withdraw. He would never reach Alexandria or the Suez Canal.

Montgomery was not finished with Rommel. On October 23, 1942, he went on the offensive to chase Rommel out of Africa, starting with an attack on El Alamein. Rommel was in Germany at that moment on sick leave. His replacement, General Georg Stumme, died of a heart attack, however, and the Desert Fox, as Rommel was called, returned to the battlefield on the 25th.

The British force consisted of 150,000 men, including New Zealanders, South Africans, and Australians, and was supported by 700 aircraft and 1,000 tanks. In the seesaw battle that followed, both sides suffered heavy losses, but the British emerged victorious, forcing Rommel into what would be a 2,000-mile retreat on November 5. The British would continue their march across North Africa, reaching Tripoli by the end of January 1943. By that time, the Italians' African empire was gone.

Torching the Germans

Three days after Rommel withdrew, Operation Torch began with the landing of 107,000 Allied troops on the beaches of Algeria, Morocco, and Tunisia, the largest amphibious invasion force in history. The Americans were now in the fight for Europe.

It took the Allies only three days to capture Vichy-controlled Algeria and Morocco. The French high commissioner in North Africa, Admiral Jean Francois Darlan (who coincidentally was in Algiers to visit his fatally-ill son), switched sides and joined who he now believed would be the victors in the war. He tried to get the commander of the French fleet at Toulon to hand his ships over to the Allied forces in Africa. Partly to forestall that possibility, the Germans moved to occupy all of France on November 11, but the crews scuttled almost all of the 58 warships before the Nazis could grab them (three submarines joined the Allies in Algiers and a fourth was captured by the Germans).

Though a temporary benefit to the Allies, the association with Darlan after his sudden conversion was not popular. The willingness to cooperate with an Axis collaborator suggested the Allies were prepared to place expediency over principle. This would become even more evident toward the end

Words of War

"No bastard ever won a war by dying for his country. He won it by making the other poor dumb bastard die for his country."

—General George Patton, speaking to his troops in North Africa, 1942 of the war when the Allies helped Nazis escape whom they thought could be useful to the cause of confronting the Soviet Union (see Chapter 25).

Vichy loyalists opened the Tunisian ports and airfields to the Axis, which poured in reinforcements to stop the Allied advance. Over the next few months, roughly 30,000 Italians and 150,000 Germans, along with huge quantities of material and aircraft, were deployed in Tunisia. The British, American, and Free-French troops did capture half the country, but they could not reach the capital of Tunis. Part of the problem for the Allies was the fact that more North Africans remained loyal to Vichy than they expected. A major consequence of the failure to quickly overrun Tunisia was to force the postponement of the cross-Channel attack. Military planners now concluded it would be impossible to mount an operation before 1944 and that 1943 would have to be devoted to a Mediterranean campaign. On the other hand, the U.S. Army learned crucial lessons about the Germans and how they fought in an arena where they could bring little of their military power to bear.

There was better news for the Allies when the British succeeded in breaking through German defenses to relieve the siege on Malta in late November. This battle had been such a high priority for Churchill that he had convinced Roosevelt to send the American carrier *Wasp* to participate in the defense of the island. Once the siege was broken, the Allies were able to use Malta as a key base of operations, which helped them gain control of the Mediterranean.

Just as the war had begun to turn in the Pacific, so had the Allies' fortunes changed in Europe. The United States was in the war, and the dictators—other than Stalin—who had enjoyed so many quick victories with little opposition, now found themselves in a fight for their lives. Still, with all the setbacks, 1942 ended with Germany still occupying 14 European nations and the Baltic states of Lithuania, Estonia, and Latvia. The war was far from over.

Ask the General

Marshal Pétain tried to disavow Darlan, but Hitler knew better. The admiral had betrayed his country first and then his puppet-masters. Pétain may have deluded himself that he had some power, but he was a figurehead. To the extent any Vichy official had power, Pierre Laval was now in charge. Pétain was convicted of treason in 1945 and sentenced to death; the sentence was commuted by Charles de Gaulle to life imprisonment.

The Least You Need to Know

➤ In January 1942, Roosevelt and Churchill decided the top priority of the war would be to defeat Germany and then combine forces against Japan.

➤ Early on, the German U-boats wreaked havoc on Allied shipping; however, by the spring of 1943, new antisubmarine technology helped to significantly reduce the threat.

➤ Massive British air raids on German cities caused such severe damage and killed so many people that the German population began to feel the terror Londoners experienced during the *Blitz*.

➤ For the first time, organized public dissent emerged when a group of students began to denounce the Nazi regime. The White Rose, as the group was called, was quickly crushed.

➤ Germany's hopes of defeating Russia were dashed, and the counteroffensive began to push Hitler's forces west.

➤ Rommel's initial success in Africa was reversed, and he was forced to retreat, ending his threat to Egypt and the Middle East.

➤ America joined the war in Europe, landing troops in North Africa as part of Operation Torch. The Allies were unable to defeat Italian, German, and Vichy French troops and were forced to postpone the invasion of Europe.

America at War

After years of isolationism and a justifiable obsession with an economy in the throes of history's worst depression, the United States entered the war with a vengeance—in more ways than one. Almost overnight, the American people became united behind the war effort and everything it entailed, from enlisting in the service to sacrificing luxuries to working to produce the tools of war. Other nations might match the United States's commitment, but none could duplicate its output. The all-around performance of the American people in the three years the country was at war has never been equaled before or since.

The War Machine Revs Up

To fight a world war, the United States needed to mobilize all its material and human resources and do so quickly. Though the United States had certainly followed events in Europe and Asia with great interest and had provided various types of assistance, there was not really a gradual buildup toward war. In retrospect, one can see events moving in that direction, but at the time, the American people were still looking for any excuse to stay out of the fighting and may have continued to stay out of the fighting had the Japanese been content with the conquest of distant islands. Then everything changed.

One day the nation was at peace, mired in depression, and split over the question of foreign intervention. The next, the United States was at war. Economic growth accelerated, and the public united behind the war effort. A War Production Board was established to assign priorities for the production of civilian and military goods. For example, automobiles were considered nonessential, so a suspension was ordered in their production. The output dictated by the board's needs was truly awesome: 300,000 aircraft, 86,000 tanks, 76,000 ships, 2.6 million machine guns, and 40 billion bullets.

In 1942 alone, military orders totaled $100 billion. By war's end, that figure would increase to $330 billion. To pay the bill, the government raised taxes; in some cases, the maximum reached 90 percent. In addition, the government had to borrow heavily from the U.S. Treasury, raising the national debt from $49 billion in 1941 to $259 billion in 1945. Part of the cost was offset by the tremendous economic expansion that saw the nation's gross domestic product more than double.

War Lore

Henry John Kaiser (1882–1967) was one of the civilian heroes of the war. After a career in highway construction, Kaiser began to build dams and bridges in the 1930s, including the Hoover Dam in Colorado, the San Francisco-Oakland Bay Bridge, and the Grand Coulee Dam in Oregon. During World War II, he pioneered the mass production of prefabricated cargo vessels and became known as Sir Launchalot. Altogether, his shipyards built 1,460 vessels. After the war, Kaiser Industries grew to include steel, cement, and aluminum plants. Kaiser also founded a car company that failed, but he may be best known today for the Kaiser-Permanente health maintenance organization he created in 1945.

The rapid expansion of the economy also had the negative effect of causing the prices of goods to rise. To control inflation, the Office of Price Administration (OPA) was created to regulate wages and prices. In 1942, prices were frozen on most food items, and ceilings were placed on wages.

The wage controls angered the labor unions, which at that time remained powerful forces in American society, with a membership of 13 million workers. After a rash of strikes threatened war production, Congress passed in June 1943 the Smith-Connally Anti-Strike Act allowing the government to seize and operate vital industries crippled by work stoppages. Strikes against government-operated businesses were criminalized. Because of the commitment of the overwhelming majority of workers to the war efforts, the law was rarely applied. Two exceptions involved the seizure of coal mines and railroads. On the other side of the ledger, millions of workers found new jobs, and people flocked to cities such as Detroit, Seattle, Baton Rouge, and Los Angeles, where war industries were located.

While producing as much as possible, the public was also asked, and in some cases required, to conserve as much as possible. Meat, sugar, butter, and other staples were rationed. Families were given ration books that determined how much of each item a person could buy. Violations of the rules were punishable by up to 10 years in prison and a $10,000 fine.

The government also imposed a national speed limit and gasoline rationing to conserve rubber. Different stickers determined how much gas you were allowed. The average person was entitled to four gallons per week. People who needed their cars for work were given more. No limit was placed on fuel bought by people providing essential services, such as doctors. A large black market grew with stolen and counterfeited ration cards, stamps, and gasoline stickers readily available to those willing to pay and risk arrest. Still, for the most part, the ration system did work.

Words of War

"To American production, without which this war would [be] lost."

—Stalin toasting the Americans at the 1943 Tehran Conference

Women Go to Work

One of the keys to America's wartime production was the contribution of female workers. Prior to the war, only about one-fourth of women worked outside the home. As the work force was depleted by men going to war, the government mounted a publicity campaign to encourage women to get jobs. "Rosie the Riveter" was created to show women that it was not unfeminine to work and that they could make an important contribution to the war effort. In addition to "Rosie," the government put out posters showing things such as a woman with a wrench in her hand and a combat soldier in the background with the caption: "'The girl he left behind' is still behind him. She's a WOW (Woman Ordinance Worker)."

Women responded. More than 6 million, half of whom had never earned money before, joined the workforce. Even during the war, however, most women by far chose to remain homemakers; by 1944, though, the percentage of females in the labor force had jumped to 36 percent. So many of these new working women were mothers of small children whose husbands were in the military that the government set up 3,000 day-care centers.

Ruby Reed and Merle Judd of Grumman Aircraft Engine Corporation. (National Archives Still Pictures Branch)

War Lore

The most famous real-life "Rosie the Riveter" was Rose Will Monroe, who was a riveter at the Ford Willow Run Aircraft Factory in Ypsilanti, Michigan, where bombers were built. Monroe was the model for the most famous poster, showing a woman wearing a polka-dot bandanna on her head, with her sleeves rolled up, flexing her muscles, and the caption, "We Can Do It!" Unlike most of the "Rosies," Rose kept working after the war. An even more famous Monroe worked in an aircraft factory in Bakersfield, California, during the war, though she went by a different name then. Norma Jean Baker worked at the same factory as her then husband James Dougherty. An Army photographer spotted her and asked her to pose for posters for the troops. That led to a modeling career, a whole new life, and a new name: Marilyn Monroe.

Once women had the chance to work, the overwhelming majority (80 percent in a Labor Department survey) wanted to stay on the job. However, most women lost their jobs when the men returned and the work of war was finished, yet the idea of working women had come of age, and the next generation would begin the long, difficult, and still uncompleted climb toward equality in the workplace.

Hollywood Commandos

The Nazis had proven that motion pictures could be a valuable propaganda device. Films such as *The Eternal Jew* and *Triumph of the Will* helped reinforce Hitler's messages regarding the evils of Jews and glory of the *Reich*.

America, the birthplace of movies, was slower to recognize the propaganda value of film, initially seeing the medium as a training tool. In 1942, General Hap Arnold asked Jack Warner, who along with his three brothers had founded the Warner Brothers studio, to help the war effort. Warner agreed and was made a lieutenant colonel and put in charge of the newly formed Army Air Force First Motion Picture Unit.

Warner's group produced films on everything from mundane training to resistance after capture to lessons on the prevention of venereal diseases. By combining education with entertainment, the films effectively made their points. To give an idea of the caliber of people making movies for the War Department, two of the directors were Frank Capra and John Huston.

War Lore

Jimmy Stewart (1908–97) won the Academy Award for the *Philadelphia Story* the year before the war broke out. He was later drafted, but he was too thin for the Army. Already a pilot, he joined the Air Force and flew 25 missions in a B-17 named *Four Yanks and a Jerk* with the 445th Bombardment Group. He won the Distinguished Flying Cross and retired as a brigadier general in the reserves. After the war, he resumed his acting career, but remained in the Air Force reserves. In 1985, he received a special Academy Award for lifetime achievement and the Medal of Freedom, America's highest civilian honor. In addition to his many film roles, Stewart was a poet whose book of verse made the bestseller list in 1989. He died in 1997 at the age of 89 and was eulogized as an authentic American hero and one of the country's most beloved actors.

Perhaps the most famous and inspiring movie was a simple 20-minute recruiting film for the Air Force. The star was someone with more than a passing familiarity with both acting and flying, James Stewart. Stewart was furious when he was recalled from Europe to do a film. He had, after all, quit acting to fight for his country. When Stewart found out the purpose of the film, however, he was happy to cooperate. The movie combined appeals to patriotism and the sense of adventure associated with flying so effectively that 150,000 new volunteers were traced directly to the film.

The Actors Fight for Real

In addition to Stewart, a long list of actors fought in the war, including Clark Gable (photographer), Paul Newman (radioman and gunner), Kirk Douglas (communications officer), Rex Harrison (radar operator for the British), Mel Brooks (combat engineer), and Ed McMahon (marine fighter pilot). Several were decorated, including the following:

➤ Henry Fonda won a Bronze Star in the Pacific.

➤ Walter Matthau was awarded six battle stars while serving on a B-17.

➤ David Niven fought with his British countrymen, participated in D day, and was awarded the U.S. Legion of Merit.

➤ Christopher Lee, a pilot in the Royal Air Force, won a number of awards.

GI Jargon

USO is the acronym for the United Service Organizations, which was created in 1941 to provide a variety of services to American soldiers, such as recreation centers, care packages, and celebrity shows. There are approximately 175 USO centers around the world, staffed mainly by volunteers, meeting the educational, social, and religious needs of American military personnel. Between 1941 and 1947, more than 7,000 "soldiers in greasepaint" performed 428,521 USO shows. The USO is on the Internet at http://www.uso.org/.

Some of America's greatest movie heroes were rejected by the military for a variety of health-related reasons, including John Wayne, Marlon Brando, Errol Flynn, Frank Sinatra, and Gary Cooper.

One actor got his start because of his war service. Twenty year-old Lieutenant Audie Murphy was America's most honored soldier, the winner of 24 decorations including the Congressional Medal of Honor for single-handedly killing 50 Germans. After the war, he played himself in the 1955 film *To Hell and Back*. He had roles in several other films, including *The Red Badge of Courage*, but he never became a star. He was killed in 1971 in a plane crash at the age of 46.

Celebrities Find a New Spotlight

Although many famous people risked their lives and careers to defend the nation, others used their talent to serve in other ways. Some did so without even trying, notably beautiful actresses such as Betty Grable and Rita Hayworth, whose "pinups" were carried by GIs everywhere.

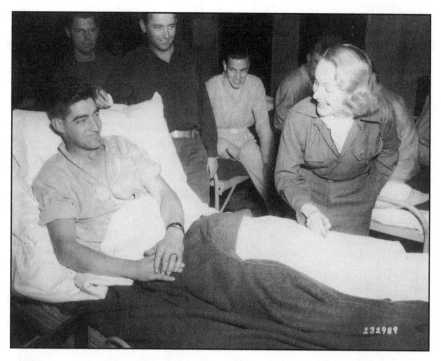

Marlene Dietrich autographs the cast on the leg of Earl E. McFarland of Cavider, Texas, at a hospital in Belgium, where she was entertaining the GIs, November 24, 1944. (National Archives Still Pictures Branch)

It was also during World War II that an actor/comedian named Leslie Townes Hope, better known as Bob Hope, assembled a group of celebrities to entertain the American troops under the auspices of the *USO*. Over the next half-century Hope would become one of the most famous men in the world and entertain millions of American GIs in every war they fought.

Glenn Miller joined the Air Force and entertained the troops with his orchestra. On December 15, 1944, en route to Paris to plan the band's next performance, his plane was lost. The 1954 film *The Glenn Miller Story*, makes his role as conductor seem heroic, as in the scene where he keeps the orchestra playing while the troops take cover during an air raid, winning a standing ovation for this act of bravery. The star of the film? Jimmy Stewart, of course.

Words of War

"Really the writer doesn't want success…. He knows he has a short span of life, that the day will come when he must pass through the wall of oblivion, and he wants to leave a scratch on that wall—Kilroy was here!—that somebody a hundred, or a thousand years later will see."

—William Faulkner

Perhaps the oddest American participant in the war was Kilroy. Everywhere you found GIs, you could find the message "Kilroy was here" written somewhere nearby. No one knew who he was or whether he existed. He was fictitious, but it's unclear where Kilroy originated.

Athletes Play on a Different Field

In addition to stars of the silver screen, sports heroes also enlisted, including future baseball Hall of Famers: Brooklyn Dodgers shortstop Pee Wee Reese, New York Yankee catcher Yogi Berra and outfielder Joe DiMaggio (who never made it to the front), Cleveland Indians pitcher Bob Feller, and Detroit Tigers first baseman Hank Greenberg. Greenberg was the first baseball star to enlist and the only Jew in the major leagues at the time.

War Lore

The player whose career is generally thought to have suffered most because of the war was Boston Red Sox outfielder Ted Williams, who became a marine fighter pilot. One of the greatest players ever, Williams missed playing three years when he was at the top of his game. In 1941, he won the American League batting championship with an average of .406, a figure that has not been topped since, and won the Triple Crown (leading the league in average, home runs, and runs batted in) in 1942 and 1947. He is 10th on the all-time home-run list with 521 and might well have broken many major-league records had the war not interrupted. Williams also fought in Korea.

War Is Good Politics

The careers of many U.S. politicians, including every president from Eisenhower to Bush, were heavily influenced by the war:

➤ Dwight Eisenhower won the presidency on the strength of his wartime reputation.

➤ John Kennedy became a hero in the Pacific.

➤ Lyndon Johnson was already a congressman when he joined the Navy. Roosevelt later ordered the eight Congressmen in the service to return to Washington; four resigned so they wouldn't have to. Johnson went back to Congress without serving in combat.

➤ Richard Nixon was in the navy and served in the Pacific.

➤ Gerald Ford served on a carrier.

➤ Jimmy Carter was still a student at the U.S. Naval Academy.

➤ Ronald Reagan was rejected for service because of poor eyesight, but he contributed to Jack Warner's film unit by acting in training and recruiting films.

➤ George Bush was the Navy's youngest pilot. In September 1944, his plane was shot down during an attack on Iwo Jima. The three-man crew bailed out, but only Bush survived. A submarine spotted him floating in his life raft and rescued him. He was later awarded the Distinguished Flying Cross.

➤ Bill Clinton was born a year after the war ended.

Three longtime senators were seriously wounded in the war and, like the other politicians, made good political use of their injuries and war records. One was Bob Dole, whose right arm was shattered and upper body wounded by shrapnel trying to help a buddy while fighting in Italy. He lost almost half his weight and nearly died. He went on to represent Kansas and become a leading figure in the Republican Party.

A second was Strom Thurmond, who today is 96 and the oldest man to ever serve in the Senate. A few days after Pearl Harbor, when he was 39, almost too old to enlist, Thurmond joined the army. He was wounded at Normandy and won a Purple Heart, Bronze Star, and the Legion of Merit. The third was Daniel Inouye, who served in the Japanese-American regiment discussed later in this chapter.

All the News That's Censored to Fit

For those of us who grew up with today's freewheeling press and remember the coverage of blood and gore from Vietnam, it's difficult to conceive of the sanitized version of the news Americans received during World War II. The government hired veteran newsman Byron Price to be the director of censorship. He was given the authority to withhold information and determine what could be reported, though much of the censorship was self-imposed by a then-cooperative press corps.

Perhaps the most dramatic example of the impact of censorship was that pictures of dead Americans could not be shown to the public. This remained true until at least mid-1943. Today, before every military conflict or potential war, analysts ask how the public will respond to seeing Americans coming home in body bags. It was never an issue in World War II because the press wasn't allowed to show them.

Another area of censorship that I'll talk more about in Chapter 20 was the half-truths and lies disseminated regarding the treatment of American prisoners of war. The government was afraid that morale would suffer and families would be upset if it revealed that POWs were being mistreated and killed.

This is not to say Americans were denied information about the fighting. Roughly 800 correspondents, including 24 women, served during the war, fewer than cover a major sporting event today. At least 38 were killed. One, the Associated Press's Joseph Morton, was executed at Mauthausen while covering an *OSS* operation, probably the only American journalist killed in a concentration camp.

Out of a group that included Walter Cronkite, William Shirer, and Eric Sevareid, two war correspondents stood out for their reporting. One was Ernie Pyle, whose columns about life with the front-line soldiers were published in hundreds of newspapers. He said that he wrote "from the worm's-eye point of view" and was beloved by combat soldiers because he brought their daily struggles to life for the folks back home. After following the campaign in Europe, he went to the Pacific and landed on Iwo Jima and Okinawa with the marines. On April 4, 1945, Pyle was shot by snipers on the island of Ie Shima and there was laid to rest.

GI Jargon

The **OSS,** Office of Strategic Services, was the forerunner of the Central Intelligence Agency. It was established on June 13, 1942, to collect and analyze information for the Joint Chiefs of Staff and was run by William Donovan. One of its principal activities was to conduct secret missions behind enemy lines.

A last column was found in Pyle's pocket. It talked about how easy it was to forget the dead. "But there are many of the living who have had burned into their brains forever the unnatural sight of cold men scattered over the hillsides and in the ditches along the high rows of hedge throughout the world. Dead men by mass production—in one country after another—month after month and year after year. Dead men in winter and dead men in summer. Dead men in such familiar promiscuity that they become monotonous. Dead men in such monstrous infinity that you come almost to hate them."

Americans got to know Pyle through his words, but they became familiar with Edward R. Murrow from his voice over the radio. Murrow, whose name is still revered in the profession, brought the war home in a way no one else could. As Archibald MacLeish said, "You burned the city of London in our houses, and we felt the flames that burned it. You laid the dead of London at our doors, and we knew that the dead were our dead."

The power of Murrow's imagery was nowhere more apparent than when he entered Buchenwald after the camp was liberated:

There surged around me an evil-smelling stink, men and boys reached out to touch me. They were in rags and the remnants of uniforms. Death already had marked many of them, but they were smiling with their eyes. I looked out over the mass of men to the green fields beyond, where well-fed Germans were plowing....

[I] asked to see one of the barracks. It happened to be occupied by Czechoslovaks. When I entered, men crowded around, tried to lift me to their shoulders. They were too weak. Many of them could not get out of bed. I was told that this building had once stabled 80 horses. There were 1,200 men in it, five to a bunk. The stink was beyond all description.

As we walked out into the courtyard, a man fell dead. Two others, they must have been over 60, were crawling toward the latrine. I saw it, but will not describe it.

In another part of the camp they showed me the children, hundreds of them. Some were only 6 years old. One rolled up his sleeves, showed me his number. It was tattooed on his arm. B-6030, it was. The others showed me their numbers. They will carry them till they die. An elderly man standing beside me said: "The children—enemies of the state!" I could see their ribs through their thin shirts....

We proceeded to the small courtyard. The wall adjoined what had been a stable or garage. We entered. It was floored with concrete. There were two rows of bodies stacked up like cordwood. They were thin and very white. Some of the bodies were terribly bruised; though there seemed to be little flesh to bruise. Some had been shot through the head, but they bled but little.

I arrived at the conclusion that all that was mortal of more than 500 men and boys lay there in two neat piles. There was a German trailer, which must have contained another 50, but it wasn't possible to count them ....

But the manner of death seemed unimportant. Murder had been done at Buchenwald. God alone knows how many men and boys have died there during the last 12 years. Thursday, I was told that there were more than 20,000 in the camp. There had been as many as 60,000. Where are they now?

I pray you to believe what I have said about Buchenwald. I reported what I saw and heard, but only part of it. For most of it, I have no words. If I have offended you by this rather mild account of Buchenwald, I'm not in the least sorry....

America Interns Its Own

Perhaps America's most shameful episode in the war was the decision by Roosevelt to intern citizens of Japanese descent after Pearl Harbor. The rationale for the action was the fear that some Japanese-Americans might be spies or saboteurs, and it was impossible to distinguish them from loyal citizens. Initially, many Japanese-American leaders were arrested. On February 19, 1942, Roosevelt signed an order allowing military officials to exclude anyone they wanted to from military areas.

Adopting the kind of racial selection process employed by Hitler, the government ordered the removal from the West Coast of anyone with at least one-sixteenth Japanese blood. The U.S. Army then forced Japanese-Americans in California, parts

Words of War

"How could such a tragedy have occurred in a democratic society that prides itself on individual rights and freedoms?... I have brooded about this whole episode on and off for the past three decades...."

—Milton S. Eisenhower, director of the War Relocation Authority of Oregon and Washington, and southern Arizona to move to 16 makeshift detention areas (often at fairgrounds, racetracks, and other large open structures).

A few weeks later they were sent to relocation centers surrounded by barbed wire in isolated areas of states such as Utah, Arizona, Wyoming, and Arkansas. Each camp held between 8,000 and 20,000 men, women, and children in military-style barracks. The largest was in Owens Valley, California. A total of 110,000 Japanese-Americans, two-thirds of whom were American-born, were ultimately interned.

These young evacuees of Japanese ancestry are awaiting their turn for baggage inspection upon arrival at this assembly center in Turlock, California, May 2, 1942. (National Archives Still Pictures Branch)

Two Japanese-Americans, Gordon Hirabayashi and Toyosaburo Korematsu, challenged different elements of the internment order in the courts. Both cases went to the Supreme Court, which decided the threat of espionage or sabotage in an area threatened by Japanese attack justified the suspension of the rights of the Japanese-Americans. Only 10 people were convicted of spying for Japan during the war, all of whom were Caucasian. After decades of debate, Congress enacted, and President Ronald Reagan signed, the Civil Liberties Act of 1988, which offered Japanese-Americans an apology and a payment of $20,000 for each surviving internee.

The Great Patriotic War

One other aspect of the war that is difficult to comprehend in the post-Vietnam era is the tremendous spirit of patriotism in the country and the willingness of men to risk their lives to fight in far-off lands to defend freedom. Although Russians labeled World War II "The Great Patriotic War," that name was no less true for the Americans.

To join the military, you had to be 17 years old, at least five feet tall, and 105 pounds. Calvin Graham managed to sneak into the Navy when he was only 12 and won a Bronze Star and Purple Heart before the Navy realized he was underage and sent him home. When he was the legal age, he re-enlisted. Other boys, though none so young, also managed to sneak into the military before they were eligible.

Of course, not everyone was anxious to fight. In the first few years of the draft, married men were exempt, so many rushed to get married, especially if they had already been in a relationship. After Pearl Harbor, however, the draft board became suspicious of "quickie" marriages. Fathers were also spared service until the end of 1943, when the need for manpower outweighed the desire to keep families together.

War Lore

The U.S. Army executed 96 soldiers in the European theater for crimes. On January 31, 1945, Pvt. Eddie Slovik was shot for desertion, the first American executed for the crime since the Civil War and the only one to suffer this punishment during World War II. Slovik and the others were originally buried individually near the site of their executions, but their remains were later transferred to a special "dishonored" plot adjacent to the U.S. World War I cemetery at Oise-Aisne, France. Public visitation to this plot is not encouraged.

Two groups of Americans that wanted to fight, women and blacks, spent nearly as much time fighting their own government as they did the enemies.

WACs, WASPs, and WAVES

At the outset of the war, women served in the military only as nurses. They were under military rule, but they enjoyed none of the advantages of higher pay, rank, or benefits. When the war started, and women began agitating for a role in the war, the War Department looked for a way to keep them at arm's length. The solution was to create the Women's Army Auxiliary Corps (WAACs), which initially had only 727 members.

183

When the women continued to complain that they were not only being shunted aside but given lower pay and benefits than the men, General George Marshall finally stepped in. "I want a women's corps right away, and I don't want any excuses," he ordered. The Women's Army Corps (WACs) was then established under the leadership of Colonel Oveta Culp Hobby. Before taking command, Hobby, the wife of the former governor of Texas, had been the chief of the Women's Interest Section in the Public Relations Bureau of the War Department.

Women also had a series of groups in the Air Force, which ultimately became the Women's Air Force Service Pilots (WASPs). The Navy had the Women Accepted for Voluntary Service (WAVES), and the Coast Guard employed the SPARs (from the motto, *Semper Paratus*, always ready). Though they didn't get a special force with a clever name, nearly 20,000 women also served in the marines.

Only a tiny percentage of the 216,000 women in these forces, perhaps a total of 10,000, were allowed to serve overseas. The 669th Headquarters Platoon was the Army's first experiment with a female unit in the field. Assigned to Lieutenant General Mark Clark's Fifth Army, the women traveled throughout Italy performing mostly clerical tasks in the group headquarters.

Only the most qualified women got these "plum" positions, which took them everywhere from the Pacific to Europe to Africa, but the jobs were almost always clerical. Those stateside performed a broader array of tasks, from clerical and administrative to weather forecasters, cryptographers, radio operators, parachute riggers, aerial-photograph analysts, and control-tower operators.

Words of War

"During the time I have had WACs under my command, they have met every test and task assigned to them ...their contributions in efficiency, skill, spirit, and determination are immeasurable."

—General Eisenhower speaking in 1945 about the five women who'd served on his staff throughout most of the war

A tremendous surge of public hostility toward the WAACs emerged in 1943 as soldiers began to complain about real and imagined problems with the women. Reports were circulated of large numbers of pregnant WAACs, as were nasty rumors about the loose morals of the female soldiers. The WAACs survived and were merged into the WACs in July 1943. Women were given the choice of joining the Army or going back to civilian life, and one-fourth chose the second option.

After the war, Colonel Hobby received the Distinguished Service Medal and 62 WACs received the Legion of Merit for exceptionally meritorious conduct in the performance of duty. A total of 657 women received medals and citations. When the war ended, all but about 10,000 WACs returned to their homes. Despite political opposition, the Congress voted in 1948 to make the WACs a permanent part of the army. In 1978, women were allowed to join the regular army, and it was no longer necessary to have a separate corps.

Segregation in the Army

In 1941, only 4,000 blacks were in the military, only a dozen of whom were officers. They were drafted, but generally not assigned to combat, and confined to segregated units. Even their blood banks were segregated. There were voices in the government who urged integration, such as Judge William Hastie, Roosevelt's adviser on Negro affairs, but the military objected.

The 93rd Infantry Division, reactivated in May 15, 1942, was the first all-black division to be formed during World War II. Second Lieutenant Arthur Bates waits for zero hour to give the command to attack, Fort Huachuca, Arizona, 1942. (National Archives Still Pictures Branch)

Like women soldiers, black soldiers were often assigned menial or administrative duties as orderlies, drivers, construction workers, and cargo handlers. Black soldiers were not sent to the front until late in the war, after heavy casualties had forced their use. More than a million black men and women served in the armed forces by the end of the war.

The Negro Seabees, members of Naval Construction Battalions, are trained in landing tactics as well as in general military drill, circa 1942. (National Archives Still Pictures Branch)

World heavyweight boxing champion Joe Louis was at Fort Riley, Kansas, where he met a future sports legend, Jackie Robinson. Robinson had already had a dazzling track, football, and baseball career in college, but he had not yet made history with the Brooklyn Dodgers. Even before breaking the color barrier in baseball, he had to break another after being turned down for officer training school. After Louis intervened on his behalf, Robinson got into the program. He landed back at Fort Riley as a morale officer. While riding on a bus at Fort Hood, Texas, Robinson was told to move to the back and reputedly threatened the driver. He was brought before an army court-martial and acquitted. He received an honorable discharge as a first lieutenant in 1944. Louis, meanwhile, fought more than 100 exhibition matches during the war.

The black women who served in World War II also were segregated. Even among the WAACs, the 40 black women in the officer training school were kept in a separate platoon and were not allowed to use many of the base facilities. When they became officers, the black women were assigned to all-black units.

Black women were not given an overseas assignment until February 1945. Then 800 women were stationed first in Birmingham, England, and later Paris. Their job was to help ensure that mail reached American servicemen in the European theater.

War Lore

Although Hitler's theory of Aryan superiority was shattered at the 1936 Berlin Olympics by the heroics of Jesse Owens, he did win a propaganda victory when German heavyweight boxer Max Schmeling knocked out the world champion, Joe Louis, in a non-title bout. It was the only time Louis was ever knocked out. Their 1938 rematch was billed as a battle of Nazism versus democracy. This time, Louis won in the first round. Schmeling, interestingly enough, never joined the Nazi Party, despite Hitler portraying him as the Aryan archetype. He later was a paratrooper and fought in Crete.

The Tuskegee Airmen

In 1925, the Army War College conducted a study that found blacks could never be pilots because they lacked intelligence and were too cowardly in combat. Yancy Williams, a Howard University student, sued the government to be allowed to become an aviation cadet. "Can you imagine," Lieutenant Colonel Herbert Carter said, "with the war clouds as heavy as they were over Europe, a citizen of the United States would have to sue his government to be accepted to train so he could fly and fight and die for his country?"

The Air Force subsequently agreed in November 1941 to set up a pilot training center for blacks in Alabama's Tuskegee Institute. The original instructors were white, but they didn't treat their cadets any differently than they would white trainees. The cadets ran into trouble, however, when they left the base, so they spent almost all of their time at the Institute. The Tuskegee Airmen, or Black Eagles as some called them, graduated on March 7, 1942, but initially were not allowed to leave Alabama. Finally, more than a year later, in May 1943, they were sent to North Africa under the command of Lieutenant Colonel Benjamin Davis, Jr. Davis had been only the third black man to graduate from West Point. Two years earlier, his father had been promoted to general.

Words of War

"We proved that the antidote to racism is excellence in performance."

—Tuskegee Airmen Lieutenant Colonel Herbert Carter

Three other all-black squadrons were later added to the original 99th Fighter Squadron to create the 332nd Fighter Group of the 15th Air Force. Operating mostly in Italy, the Tuskegee Airmen shot down 251 enemy planes and logged more than 15,000 sorties. None of the bombers they escorted was ever shot down. The Germans called them *Schwartze Vogelmenschen*, the Black Birdmen.

Officer returns salute as he passes the cadets lined up during review in Tuskegee Field, Alabama. (National Archives Still Pictures Branch)

About 1,000 men trained at Tuskegee; 445 were sent overseas for combat duty. The 332nd lost 66 men and had 33 taken prisoner. Among the 850 awards the group won were 150 Distinguished Flying Crosses, 8 Purple Hearts, 14 Bronze Stars, and 744 Air Medals. Ben Davis, Jr. went on to become the first black air force general. Another airman, General Chappie James, became America's first black four-star general in 1975.

Japanese-American GIs

It is important to mention one other group of American soldiers, the Japanese-Americans. Even while their families and friends were being sent to internment camps, thousands of Japanese-Americans volunteered to fight. Initially, Japanese-Americans were not allowed to enlist, but a battalion from Hawaii was allowed to go to Europe in 1943. The following year, that group became part of the 442nd Regimental Combat Team, one of the most highly decorated units in the war, which consisted entirely of Japanese-Americans.

In October 1944, the unit was sent to extricate a group of soldiers surrounded by Germans in southern France. It was so cold, soldiers would shoot at the enemy and then put their wet gloves on the hot barrel to keep warm. The rescue operation succeeded in saving 211 men from the so-called Lost Battalion. The cost was dear, however, with the 442nd suffering 800 casualties. One infantryman who lost an arm was Daniel Inouye, who has served as a Democratic senator from Hawaii since 1962. The 442nd earned more than 18,000 medals for valor and nearly 10,000 Purple Hearts.

War Lore

The Hasbro Toy company announced plans in 1998 to sell a Japanese-American as part of its GI Joe collection. The doll will be an action figure honoring the 442nd Regimental Combat Team. In 1997, Hasbro introduced a black GI Joe figure honoring the Tuskegee Airmen.

The Least You Need to Know

➤ The U.S. economy mobilized for war and produced astounding amounts of material. The cost was high, and the public learned to live with wage and price controls and the rationing of goods.

➤ Millions of American women went to work for the first time and decided they liked it. Most lost their jobs after the war, but the stigma against women working had broken down. Women also overcame great resistance to form their own military units, which were largely restricted to clerical tasks. Only a small percentage of women were assigned overseas.

➤ Six of the next eight presidents fought in the war, and many other future politicians served with distinction.

➤ Censorship limited the information available to the public, but war correspondents such as Ernie Pyle and Edward R. Murrow brought the horrors and triumphs of war home.

➤ Fears about security prompted the suspension of rights of Japanese-Americans and their forced relocation to internment camps. Japanese-American soldiers still fought with distinction despite this mistreatment at home. One Japanese-American unit was the most decorated in the war.

➤ Reflecting the racism of the time, blacks were largely kept in segregated military units. After being threatened with a lawsuit, the government allowed a group of blacks to become pilots. The Tuskegee Airmen had extraordinary war records.

Part 4
Allies Kick Axis

U.S. forces roll back Japanese gains in the Pacific, retaking island after island, but only after the defenders fight to the last man and inflict high casualties on the Americans. The introduction of the kamikaze adds a new and terrifying dimension to the war in the Pacific.

The Allies drive the Axis out of North Africa, capture Sicily, and begin to move into Italy. In Europe, the Allies temporarily knock out Hitler's secret rocket program and inflict heavy casualties and damage on German cities in bombing raids.

On the eastern front, the Soviets have taken Germany's best punch and begin their counterattack. The "Big Three" meet and discuss how they will defeat Germany and Japan.

Chapter 15

The Axis Goes in Reverse

In This Chapter

➤ Roosevelt and Churchill call for unconditional surrender

➤ The Battle of the Atlantic is won

➤ The cost in lives grows as America's Pacific fleet rolls back Japan's gains

➤ Britain and the United States begin their combined bombing campaign against Germany

➤ Hitler's rockets go boom

By the beginning of 1943, the United States was fully mobilized and fighting in two theaters, the Pacific and North Africa. For the combatants in Europe, the war was entering its fourth year. The toll had been heavy for all, and it was far from over.

The Allied forces were clearly making headway, throwing back the Japanese in the Pacific and the Germans in North Africa. The Soviets had effectively ended the German threat to their major cities. Still, Germany occupied a huge area of the Soviet Union and had not lost any ground in Europe; Rommel's forces had been beaten back in North Africa, but were not yet defeated; and Japan controlled China, the Philippines, French Indochina, British Burma and Malaya, and the Dutch East Indies.

Envisioning Victory

On January 14, 1943, Churchill and Roosevelt met in Casablanca (no, not in Rick's place) in newly liberated French Morocco and began to lay out the broad strategy that would determine the future conduct of the war. On the 24th, Roosevelt announced that peace could only be achieved when Germany, Italy, and Japan were no longer able to make war. This announcement meant the destruction of their armies and the unconditional surrender of their governments.

The announcement ensured the Allies were working from the same playbook. The Casablanca decision also was meant to reassure the Soviet Union of the British and American commitment in order to discourage Stalin from considering a separate peace with Hitler. Some critics have suggested the insistence on unconditional surrender gave the Germans and Japanese an incentive to fight to the death rather than seek a peace that might have left them with some gains from their years of sacrifice. It's impossible to prove either way, though there's no evidence this policy prolonged or shortened the war.

The British were insistent on the point because of their prior experience with Hitler. Germany could not be trusted so long as he remained in power. The American motivation was both political and historical. Roosevelt knew that Woodrow Wilson's decision to accept an armistice had been viewed domestically as a sign of weakness, and that the Democratic Party had suffered in the next election as a result. The president also knew that the Germans maintained they had been "stabbed in the back" rather than defeated on the battlefield in World War I, and he wanted there to be no doubt this time around.

The other important decision made in Casablanca was to postpone the planned cross-Channel invasion. The military planners of both the United States and Britain concluded they would not have the men and supplies and equipment they needed in place before the summer of 1944. This conclusion was a great disappointment to Churchill and Roosevelt, who recognized that this decision meant the war would drag on for at least two more years. The "Big Two" also knew this would complicate relations with Stalin, who'd been agitating for a second front to relieve him. Churchill and Roosevelt tried to reassure their erstwhile ally by pledging to provide him equipment, escalate the air war against Germany, and mount the invasion as soon as it was possible.

Two days later, as if to impress upon the Germans their seriousness, the Americans launched their first bombing raid against the warehouses and factories at Wilhelmshaven. Three bombers were shot down, as were 22 German planes.

Voyage to the Bottom of the Sea

The Casablanca Conference also decided the highest priority should be assigned to ending the U-boat threat, which was still sinking ships faster than the Allies could build them (this trend was finally reversed in February). The U-boats also threatened the ability of the Americans to move the men and material to Europe they would need for the assault on Germany.

War Lore

One idea for overcoming the submarine threat was to build a cargo plane that could carry supplies and soldiers across the ocean. The Hughes (after its builder, Howard Hughes) Flying Boat, or "Spruce Goose" as it became popularly known, was the largest plane ever built, with eight huge Pratt & Whitney engines and a wood (mostly birch, not spruce) air frame. Its wingspan was just under 320 feet, the fuselage was 219 feet long, and the plane weighed approximately 400,000 pounds. It was designed to fly at 200 miles per hour with a range of approximately 3,000 miles.

The government eventually decided to drop the project, but Hughes was determined to finish it. On November 2, 1947, Hughes himself was at the controls for its first and only flight. It reached a top speed of 80 miles per hour and flew 70 feet above the water. It never flew again, but some of the design features helped pave the way for building the jumbo jets of the future. The current owner of the plane, Evergreen International Aviation, plans to display the plane at its headquarters in McMinnville, Oregon.

One practical decision was to put the German submarine construction yards at the top of the list of targets for future bombing raids. Over the course of the next year, despite thousands of sorties, the Allies inflicted little damage on the U-boat fleet from the air.

By March 1943, nearly 400 U-boats were patrolling the seas and that month sank 120 ships. Within two months, however, the Allies had neutralized the threat. Greater success was achieved through the use of convoys, particularly after the introduction of Huff-Duff on all escorts.

By May, the Allies were sinking a U-boat a day, sending some of the Germans' most experienced and successful commanders to the bottom of the sea. On May 6 alone, a wolf pack of more than 30 submarines attacked a convoy, and Germany suffered the devastating loss of four U-boats. Shortly thereafter, two submarines collided and sank, and in an attack on the next convoy, two more U-boats went down, one of which had Admiral Dönitz's son on board. By the end of the month, Dönitz was forced to admit the Battle of the Atlantic had been lost and redirected his fleet from the North Atlantic to safer waters in the South Atlantic.

The U-boat war was not over. The submarines continued to harass Allied shipping, but far less effectively. In 1945, the Germans launched a new submarine that used a "schnorkel" that allowed it to stay under water longer and to operate at a higher speed when submerged. Unfortunately for the Germans, the new technology was introduced too late in the war to make a difference. It did, however, herald the development of today's nuclear submarines.

Roll Call

When the Battle of the Atlantic (September 1939 to May 1943) ended, Germany's U-boats had sunk nearly 2,500 merchant ships and 175 warships. Out of 830 submarines that put out to sea, 696 were lost. A total of 40,900 sailors had manned these ships; 25,870 were killed, and 5,000 were taken prisoner. The casualty rate was 75 percent (63 percent died), making the German submarine corps by far the most dangerous place to serve in World War II.

Words of War

"It is fatal to enter any war without the will to win it."

—Douglas MacArthur

Better to Give Than Receive

Apparently, the Japanese paid little attention to events in the Atlantic, because they failed to learn from the mistakes and corrections made by the Allies. In the Pacific, the American submarines endangered shipping and threatened to strangle Japan and the outlying islands it had conquered. Despite this, the Japanese neglected to construct enough ships to offset their losses or to develop antisubmarine tactics that might have protected their existing fleet.

As I mentioned in Chapter 12, the first U.S. subs went to sea with defective torpedoes. When this problem was fixed, the "kill rate" went up dramatically. For example, in October 1942, American submarines sank a total of 100,000 tons of Japanese shipping for the first time. In 1943, the monthly average exceeded this figure and, by the following year, the monthly average was more than 200,000 tons.

The Japanese did have a submarine fleet of their own, but it did not cause anywhere near the damage the German U-boats did in the Atlantic. In one incident, in May 1943, a Japanese submarine sank an American hospital ship, killing 268. The war was going badly for the Japanese on land as well. At the end of January, American troops retook Papua at a cost of 12,000 Japanese and 850 Americans.

As I noted in Chapter 12, the Americans had effectively won the battle for Guadalcanal. At the end of January and early February, the defenders retreated to a neighboring island and began to evacuate, leaving the marines in control by the middle of the month. The Japanese had fought bravely, but they had little chance against the overwhelming firepower of the Americans, which killed more than 20,000 Japanese soldiers; the Americans lost just over 1,000 soldiers.

While fighting continued on the various fronts, American military leaders were having their own battles over divisions of responsibilities and the allocation of resources. In 1943, 460,000 troops were in the Pacific compared to 380,000 in Europe. More troops were needed in Europe for the Allies to threaten Hitler. The commanders in the Pacific, however, also wanted more troops to sustain their advance toward Japan.

In April, the Pacific command was slightly reshuffled with Admiral Chester Nimitz placed in charge of the entire theater and responsibility for the Southwest Pacific given to General Douglas MacArthur and the South Pacific to Admiral William Halsey. They agreed the next major operation, code-named Operation Cartwheel, would be a pincer movement in which MacArthur and Halsey would attempt to encircle the Japanese stronghold of Rabaul on the island of New Britain, the largest in the Bismarck Archipelago. For the next several months, the two commanders would lead offensives on the islands leading to New Britain.

Also in April, American intelligence intercepted news that Yamamoto planned to visit his airmen at a base in Bougainville to encourage them in efforts to attack Guadalcanal. Nimitz decided to try to kill him and sent a squadron of fighters to ambush him on April 18. The admiral's plane was shot down, and he was killed (his successor later died in an airplane accident). The loss of Japan's top military strategist was a serious blow to the country's morale and operational capability.

On May 12, 1943, the Americans attacked the Aleutian island of Attu, which was occupied by a garrison of 2,500 Japanese soldiers. The garrison held on for three weeks against the 11,000 American soldiers, but it was eventually decimated. The other Aleutian island held by the Japanese, Kiska, was abandoned by the time U.S. troops arrived in mid-August.

War Lore

Despite American successes in the central Pacific, the Japanese succeeded in raising doubts in the minds of Filipinos about the prospects for a U.S. attack to retake the island. A decision was made to use a submarine to smuggle "Victory Packages" into the Philippines to lift their spirits. Each package was wrapped in the American and Philippine flags and contained cigarettes, gum, pencils, and, most important, MacArthur's signature above the words "I shall return."

They Sank My Boat

One of the Navy's most famous commanders also made his mark that August. Lieutenant John Kennedy commanded a patrol boat used for torpedo shipping, the *PT 109*, which was trying to intercept Japanese ships in the Ferguson and Blackett Straits near the islands of Gizo, Kolumbangara, and Vella-Lavella. About 2:00 a.m. on August 2, 1943, the PT boat was struck by a Japanese destroyer and cut in two. Kennedy was thrown into the cockpit, injuring his already bad back. Four other members of the crew were hanging onto the section of the ship with Kennedy. Six other survivors were in the water; one was severely burned, and the other had hurt his leg. Two men were dead.

Kennedy swam out to rescue the two injured men. It took him two hours to get them back to the piece of the ship still afloat. It became clear that it would soon sink, and the survivors decided to swim to a barely visible island that turned out to be three miles away. It took five hours for them to get there. Kennedy had given the burned man his life jacket and towed him the entire distance with the jacket's strap in his teeth.

Unfortunately, the island had no food or water. Kennedy decided to swim through the Ferguson Passage in hopes of spotting another PT boat. He didn't see one, nor did a crewmate who also swam out in search of help. The men then decided to swim to a larger island. Kennedy again towed the injured man.

On Nauru Island, they found coconuts to eat and also a handful of natives. Kennedy carved a message in a coconut that said:

> NAURO ISL
> COMMANDER...NATIVE KNOWS
> POS'IT...HE CAN PILOT...11 ALIVE
> NEED SMALL BOAT...KENNEDY

He gave it to the native and told him to take it to Rendova where the Americans had a PT base. The message worked and the group was rescued. Kennedy was awarded the Navy and Marine Corps Medal for gallantry in action and a Purple Heart for his injuries. Kennedy briefly commanded another PT boat but was eventually sent stateside because of his back injury, a recurrent problem that would plague him for the rest of his life. While he was recuperating, he wrote the Pulitzer Prize-winning book, *Profiles in Courage*.

After Kennedy was elected president, one of the prize possessions he kept at the White House was the coconut he'd written on. The movie *PT 109*, starring Cliff Robertson (who was rejected for service because of his eyesight), dramatized Kennedy's wartime experience. It was released in 1963, the year Kennedy was assassinated.

Words of War

"It was involuntary. They sank my boat."

—John Kennedy's answer when asked how he became a hero

The Blood-Soaked Island of Tarawa

War isn't just hell; it's bloody hell. For all the successful offensives the Allies were launching, thousands of young men were dying. As Ernie Pyle wrote, it was too easy to forget or to become calloused. All the horrors of the war were brought home with a vengeance, however, during the battle for the island of Tarawa in November 1943.

Sign on Tarawa illustrates marine humor and possible lack of optimism as to the duration of the war, June 1944. (National Archives Still Pictures Branch)

Five thousand Japanese soldiers defended the eight-square-mile atoll against an equal number of Americans. The battle lasted for just over three days. At the end, only 17 Japanese were left alive. The United States had suffered 3,000 casualties, 1,000 of whom were dead. For the first time, the censors allowed the press to publish the horrifying pictures of the corpses.

Words of War

"The American people have had every reason to know that this is a tough and destructive war. On my trip abroad, I talked with many military men who had faced our enemies in the field. These hardheaded realists testify to the strength and skill and resourcefulness of the enemy generals and men whom we must beat before final victory is won. The war is now reaching the stage where we shall all have to look forward to large casualty lists—dead, wounded, and missing. War entails just that. There is no easy road to victory. And the end is not yet in sight."

—Franklin Roosevelt, fireside chat, Christmas Eve, 1943

The disastrous battle led marine commanders to alter their tactics and build special amphibious vehicles that could be used to coordinate air and sea support for their landings. They also recreated the Tarawa defenses and used them to train troops for future missions.

The battle had an even greater psychological impact. It demonstrated to the United States that Japan could be defeated only at a great cost. If this is what it took to overcome a small force on a tiny island, what would be required to invade Japan itself? It was a question that would ultimately be a major consideration in the debate over the use of the atomic bomb.

With the victory on Tarawa, the battle in the central Pacific came to an end, almost two years to the day from the attack on Pearl Harbor. The United States had unquestionably turned the tables on the Japanese and were steadily advancing toward the Emperor's home. The fighting had been savage, with the Japanese suffering enormous losses of men and material. Comparatively speaking, American losses were light. The United States also gained valuable lessons that would be useful in the continuing offensive in the Pacific and the planned invasion of Europe. Still, it would be another year and a half before the Japanese could be forced to surrender. Thousands more lives would have to be lost first.

War Hits Home in Germany

By 1943, Japanese civilians had only one brief, direct experience of the war when Doolittle's raiders bombed Tokyo. In contrast, the German people had been under bombardment for nearly three years. The attacks only got worse for them in the last half of the war. The mounting losses of men and machinery also began to take their toll by 1943. More and more families were directly touched by the deaths in the fighting, and the words "eastern front" had acquired a frightening meaning akin to "cannon fodder."

As mentioned before, Hitler had resisted the idea of fully mobilizing the nation for war. He had hoped to maintain the quality of life at a high enough level to discourage discontent and allowed his people the highest rations in Europe. This level of rations was maintained even as pressure grew for more war material.

A handful of voices were raised in opposition to Hitler; some opposed him because of the atrocities being committed against the Jews and others, but these people were either not taken seriously or never marshaled enough support to create an opposition movement to challenge Hitler. When an opposing voice was raised beyond a whisper, the speaker was usually murdered or sent to a concentration camp to suffer a slow death.

The adoration of Hitler was such that even critics often tried to attribute whatever problems Germany had to the Nazi Party rather than its leader. But the two were indivisible, and the Nazi Party only grew in strength under the aggressive leadership of Martin Bormann as the war ground on.

A kind of shadow government—though still tightly controlled by Hitler—also evolved as the SS under Heinrich Himmler expanded its bloodstained influence in Germany and the occupied territories. The SS operated a police state within the country and was a law unto itself outside it. As the overseer of the concentration camp system, the SS built its own industrial power base. The military division of the SS, the *Waffen SS*, also began to take on a more influential and corrosive role in the German military, imposing its doctrines of racial purity and disregard for the rules of war on those who were recruited from the regular army.

Ask the General

Evidence of dissent in the army was most apparent in March when two officers gave a third unsuspecting officer accompanying Hitler on a flight to his headquarters in Rastenburg a package containing a bomb. The bomb was supposed to explode in the air, and then a group of co-conspirators in Berlin was to seize the government. Hitler's plane landed without incident. When the parcel was retrieved, the officers who'd put the bomb together discovered it had a defective detonator.

Making Hamburger of Hamburg

For the German people, the physical danger and psychological stress of living in a war zone grew larger in 1943 as Britain and the United States began to combine their air power to destroy Germany's war-making capability and terrorize its population. The United States and Britain agreed during the Casablanca Conference in January 1943 to combine forces to bomb German submarine construction yards, aircraft manufacturers, railways, oil refineries, and other military installations. The two countries disagreed on tactics, however, and ultimately divided responsibilities so the RAF could continue its existing campaign of bombing cities and the Americans could attack precise military targets.

In March, the British began what was to be a three-month "Battle of the Ruhr" in which 18,000 sorties were flown over the German industrial center, destroying, among other things, dams that supplied much of Germany's hydroelectric power. In July, the RAF attacked the city of Hamburg over the course of four nights, damaging approximately 80 percent of the city's buildings and killing approximately 40,000 people, including thousands of women and children. Succeeding attacks on smaller cities also resulted in tremendous death and destruction. In Hamburg's case, the city was able to quickly rebound, at least in terms of its industry, and increase its production beyond the levels that prevailed before the attack.

Göring and the rest of the *Luftwaffe* leadership realized that Germany could not continue to withstand such attacks. They were determined to seek new weapons and alternative tactics to counter the Allied bombers. Hitler was resistant, however, because he was confident as ever that Germany was winning the war and the Fatherland was not in danger.

The first American raid, in August 1943, was on the ball-bearing plant at Schweinfurt. The raid was a fiasco. The 229 B-17s flew during daylight across parts of France and Germany without any fighter escort and ran into a withering defensive line of fighters, which shot down 36 bombers. The Germans downed another 24 bombers in an attack on Regensburg, and a total of 100 others were heavily damaged in the two attacks.

Words of War

"The enemy is still proud and powerful. He is hard to get at. He still possesses enormous armies, vast resources, and invaluable strategic territories.... No one can tell what new complications and perils might arise in four or five more years of war. And it is in the dragging-out of the war at enormous expense, until the democracies are tired or bored or split, that the main hopes of Germany and Japan must reside."

—Churchill speaking to a joint session of Congress, May 19, 1943

Afterward, the Air Force decided the bombers could not fly unescorted. At that time, they did not have a fighter with the range to accompany the B-17s into Germany, so the immediate attack plans had to be scrapped. It was a tough pill for the airmen to swallow, because they'd come to believe "the bomber will always get through." The loss of 600 men in two days, however, had sobered them.

A week later, however, the RAF was back, this time attacking Berlin itself. The August 23, 1943, raid killed more than 800 people; the British lost 298 men and had another 117 taken prisoner. The RAF was not discouraged, however, and continued its attacks. On November 22, another massive raid was conducted against Berlin, infuriating Hitler because of the damage caused to several government buildings, including his chancellery (he was in Rastenburg at the time) and the special train he traveled in (ironically called *Amerika*). More than 1,700 people were killed. The RAF returned the following night, and their bombs killed another 1,300 people and again caused widespread destruction, including to the home of Joseph Goebbels. The British did not get off easily; in two nights, they lost nearly 300 men.

Knocking Out Peenemünde's Rockets

Throughout the war, Hitler expected to have secret weapons that would give Germany a decisive advantage in the war. At one point, he had considered the use of poison gas, and Germany had developed and stockpiled a new nerve gas. When he was told the Allies could retaliate with their own gas warfare, he shelved the plan until a way to protect German citizens could be developed. That never happened.

A more successful program was the development of rockets. The *Vergeltungswaffe* (retaliation bombs), more commonly known as the V-1, was an unmanned airplane that carried a large warhead. A second, more sophisticated rocket, the V-2, was also in development. This predecessor of the intercontinental ballistic missile was designed to fly 200 miles and carry a one-ton warhead. Hitler wanted to use both weapons to terrorize London.

The British had heard rumors about a German rocket program, but they didn't have details or proof. On March 22, 1943, two German generals captured in Tunisia had a discussion in which one mentioned an apparent delay in the rocket program and a visit to the experimental rocket site. The British, who bugged the generals' room and overheard their conversation, were now convinced the rumors were true.

Over the next few months, British intelligence gathered more information on the rocket program and discovered it was headquartered at the Baltic island of Peenemünde. They probably did not know that the previous October a successful test launch of the V-2 had stimulated a drive to mass-produce the missiles.

Churchill ordered a raid aimed at destroying the facility and killing the people who knew how to build the new weapons. On August 17, 594 British aircraft attacked the island, dropping bombs that did substantial damage and killed 130 people involved in the missile program, including the designer of the rocket's propulsion system. Another casualty was the chief of the German Air Staff, General Hans Jeschonnek, who was responsible for the defense of Germany. He committed suicide.

War Lore

Even after the Peenemünde raid, the Germans managed to test another rocket. On August 22, a rocket with a dummy warhead that was supposed to land in the sea crashed instead on a Danish island, where it was retrieved by the naval officer in charge of the island. According to Martin Gilbert, Lieutenant-Commander Hasager Christiansen took pictures of the rocket and succeeded in passing them to the British. He was subsequently arrested by the Germans and tortured. Members of the Danish resistance spirited him out of the hospital where he'd been sent and helped him escape to Sweden. Britain awarded him the Distinguished Service Cross.

The raid set back the production of the rocket by two months and forced the Germans to transfer the project to an underground factory at Nordhausen. It is difficult to assess how big a difference the raid made on the war, but the first of the pilotless bombs did not land in Britain until the following June.

At the end of the war, German scientists were also working on an even more powerful rocket, which was meant to be the first intercontinental ballistic missile to reach the United States from Europe. This weapon could have brought the war home to the Americans on the East Coast the way the V-1 and V-2 did to the British. Fortunately, the research was not completed before Germany surrendered.

D Day Is Set

In the middle of the bombing campaign, Churchill and Roosevelt met again in the United States to work out a coordinated strategy. The May meeting, called the Trident talks, produced agreement on the Allies' priorities. First, they would invade Sicily and then Italy and, finally, on May 1, 1944, cross the Channel to attack Germany. A date was now fixed for the showdown with Hitler, but it was still a year away.

The Least You Need to Know

➤ At the Casablanca Conference in January, Roosevelt and Churchill decided on the Allies' war aims and emphasized the Axis must unconditionally surrender.

➤ After the German U-boats had dominated the Atlantic for roughly three years, the Allies developed tactics and technology that all but ended the threats of submarines to their shipping.

➤ The Americans continued to advance toward Japan in the Pacific, but the death toll was steep.

➤ The United States and Britain split responsibilities for the strategic bombing campaign against Germany, with the Americans engaging in relatively unsuccessful precision attacks on military targets and the British executing very damaging raids on cities.

➤ Hitler's great hope for salvation was his secret weapons program, but it was set back when the British bombed its base at Peenemünde.

Taking the War to Hitler

When the British convinced the United States to launch Operation Torch, their expectation was that the operation would not meet too much resistance. They hoped to quickly overrun the troops in North Africa and set the stage for the planned cross-Channel invasion. All went according to the schedule in Morocco and Algeria, but Allied troops became seriously bogged down in Tunisia, where the Vichy loyalists allowed the Germans to bring in reinforcements.

By the end of 1942, it was clear to the Allies that the invasion would have to be delayed at least until 1944 and perhaps even longer. The good news was that the Americans were getting their baptism by fire, learning as they went how to fight the Germans. In the shorter run, the benefit was that the Allies forced Hitler to siphon off troops and aircraft he desperately needed on the eastern front and thereby helped Stalin.

Ask the General

The one Vichy leader who switched to the Allied side, Jean-Louis-Xavier-François Darlan, caused great embarrassment. The idea of close cooperation with a former collaborator was anathema to many people. The problem went away in late December when a young Frenchman assassinated Darlan.

Words of War

"One of the bravest men I ever saw was a fellow on top of a telegraph pole in the midst of a furious fire fight in Tunisia. I stopped and asked what the hell he was doing up there.... He answered, 'Fixing the wire, Sir.' I asked, 'Don't those planes strafing the road bother you?' And he answered, 'No, Sir, but you sure as hell do!' Now that was a real man. A real soldier. There was a man who devoted all he had to his duty, no matter how seemingly insignificant his duty might appear at the time, no matter how great the odds."

—George Patton's speech to the Third Army, June 5, 1944

The Torch Is Passed

One of the decisions Churchill and Roosevelt made at Casablanca in January 1943 was to invade Sicily by the end of July and use the island as a stepping-stone to try to knock Italy out of the war altogether. The Americans were again reluctant; they saw the plan as another distraction from the prime directive of confronting Hitler. The British argued that the campaign would allow the Allies to control the Mediterranean, threaten Germany's southern flank from France and the Balkans, and possibly drive Mussolini from power. The British strategy would also free up a number of merchant vessels by opening up the Mediterranean to Allied shipping. The British argument won the day, but first North Africa had to be pacified.

The original plan had been for the Allies to quickly take Tunis and then drive into Libya and destroy Rommel's forces as they retreated from Montgomery's oncoming troops. German-Italian resistance made this plan impossible. Moreover, the rainy season made new offensives impossible and led to a revised plan, whereby Allied forces would be built up for the spring and then they would try to destroy the newly arrived German troops, finish off what remained of the Italians, and finally destroy Rommel's Afrika Korps.

In February 1943, the Axis launched a brief offensive in the hope of breaking through and getting behind the British troops. After an initial advance, the armies were forced back to their original position. The Americans performed badly and suffered 2,000 casualties in the fighting, prompting a decision to change commanders. General George Patton and General Omar Bradley now joined the fighting and would play key roles throughout the remainder of the war.

The British saw the Americans' poor performance in their first test against Rommel as evidence that their commanders were not very good and the troops were inadequately trained. This condescending view would be a source of friction between Montgomery and his American counterparts throughout the rest of the war.

War Lore

George Patton, Jr. (1885–1945), was one of America's best and most controversial generals, known for the ivory-handled pistols he wore. A graduate of West Point, Patton ran a tank-training school and commanded a tank brigade in France during World War I. Patton was a key commander in North Africa, Sicily, and the drive on Berlin after Normandy. A longtime friend of Eisenhower, he complicated the Supreme Commander's life by his comments to the press and the famous "slapping incident." Visiting a military hospital in Sicily, Patton slapped a combat-exhausted soldier and called him a coward. Eisenhower forced him to publicly apologize, but Patton's reputation was tarnished. In 1945, he was killed in a car accident. George C. Scott immortalized the general with his Oscar-winning performance in the 1970 film *Patton.*

Loaded with urgent war supplies, an Air Transport Command plane flies over the pyramids in Egypt in 1943. (National Archives Still Pictures Branch)

By the beginning of May, the Allied forces had been reinforced, and Montgomery's troops, which had stayed on the attack since the victory at El Alamein, had swept through Libya and linked up with the American and British forces in Tunisia. On May 7, after heavy fighting, the Allies captured Tunis and the port of Bizerta.

Roll Call

Roughly 370,000 soldiers were taken prisoner in Tunisia, the largest number the Allies captured in the war. Approximately one-third of the POWs were Germans. In three years of fighting in Africa, nearly 1 million Axis soldiers were killed or captured.

The remaining Axis troops withdrew to the tip of Tunisia with the intention of evacuating. The *Luftwaffe*, confronted by an overwhelming force of 4,500 Allied aircraft, flew its planes to Sicily, leaving the Allies with supremacy in the skies. On May 9, 1943, the Allies caught up to their retreating enemies and accepted their surrender. Only 800 soldiers, including Rommel, escaped.

Rommel had made his reputation in the North African desert, becoming the "Desert Fox," but he was undone by the Allies' superior military intelligence and firepower. The defeat in North Africa, however, did not diminish his reputation or his effectiveness in later battles with the Allies.

Fallout from the Fox's Fall

Even after being driven from Africa, Hitler remained confident of Germany's ultimate victory. He rationalized the defeat as the result of Italian incompetence. The Italians, he believed, had been poorly armed, trained, and led, and were reluctant to fight, but the Germans' best commander, Rommel, had also been bested. Hitler was correct, at least in the short run, in not believing the North Africa campaign would affect his empire. He had intervened there primarily to help his old friend Mussolini, the one who had really been committed to domination in Africa.

The war in North Africa had been a complete disaster for Italy. Mussolini had repeatedly asked Hitler to make peace with Russia so the Axis could concentrate its firepower on Africa and the Middle East. Now all of Italy's possessions and conquests were lost. With the defeat of Italian forces at Stalingrad, Italy had lost the bulk of its army. Disaffection with Mussolini had grown to the point where plots were being hatched to stage a coup.

Hitler could see his friend's position inside and outside Italy weakening. The danger of the Allies defeating Mussolini and threatening Germany from Italy had to be taken seriously. On May 18, he secretly gave orders to prepare for the invasion of Italy and put Rommel in charge of what he code-named Operation Alaric.

Another consequence of the fighting in North Africa was to unify the French resistance behind the French Committee of National Liberation under Charles de Gaulle and General Henri Honore Giraud. The committee was then recognized by the United States, Britain, and the Soviet Union as the legitimate government of France.

War Lore

When Germany invaded France in 1940, General Giraud was captured. He escaped in 1942 and became commander of the Free French Forces fighting with the Allies in North Africa. After Admiral Darlan was assassinated, Giraud also became French high commissioner in Africa. Eventually, conflict with de Gaulle would lead him to resign as co-president of the French Committee of National Liberation. He later also gave up his military post. After the liberation of France, he served briefly in the Provisional Assembly.

The Man Who Never Was

In May 1943, the Allies met again in Washington for the Trident Conference. It was at this meeting that they fixed May 1, 1944, as the day of the cross-Channel attack. In the meantime, the United States planned to move approximately 1,300,000 troops to Britain. For the moment, the war aim was to attack Sicily and neutralize or eliminate Mussolini's remaining troops.

In preparation for the invasion of Sicily, the Allies had mounted a deception campaign to confuse the Axis and encourage them to spread their troops to different locations. A British submarine put a dead body ashore on the coast of Spain. On it were documents suggesting that the buildup against Sicily was just a ruse to hide the Allies' intention to attack Greece. The documents even mentioned a code name for the operation, Husky, which was the real code name for the Sicily invasion.

Franco's people passed the information on to the Germans, who bought the whole story, as the Allies learned from reading their coded Enigma messages. German troops were diverted to Greece, and Rommel was sent to organize the defense. The "Man Who Never Was" had made his contribution to the war effort.

Sicily Is Rubbed Out

In June, the Allies made short work of the island of Pantelleria, and the 15,000-man Italian garrison surrendered. It was now time to move onto Sicily. The combined British and American forces were now under the supreme command of General Dwight D. Eisenhower with land troops directed by General Harold Alexander. The two main forces were the U.S. Seventh Army commanded by Patton and the British Eighth Army under Montgomery.

Roughly 140,000 men landed on the Sicilian beaches on July 10. They were opposed by 350,000 Axis defenders, 80 percent of whom were Italians. The Allies' objective was to destroy or at least trap the enemy forces and prevent them from escaping across the Strait of Messina to Italy.

Patton's troops sliced through the Axis defenses, but Montgomery's army initially became bogged down. After about six weeks of fierce fighting between the Axis and Allied forces, the two Allied generals linked up in Messina, and the remaining Axis defenders surrendered. The Allies failed in their primary objective, however, because 100,000 enemy soldiers escaped to Italy and the fighting had cost the Allies nearly 20,000 casualties.

War Lore

Summary executions were commonplace when Axis troops captured prisoners. The Allies, by contrast, treated their prisoners according to the Geneva Convention. Still, the Allies did sometimes mistreat POWs. In July 1943, American soldiers shot 48 POWs who were captured in Sicily. When Bradley told Patton about the incident, Patton said the Americans should claim the prisoners were trying to escape or were snipers. Bradley refused to play along and had the men court-martialed. Sergeant Horace West was found guilty and sentenced to life imprisonment; Captain John Compton was found not guilty. The disparity in the treatment of the enlisted man and the officer provoked an outcry that resulted in West's release after a year. Compton was killed in combat.

Operation Husky was not a total failure. The Germans were forced to end all their offensive operations on the eastern front and transfer large numbers of troops and quantities of material to the Mediterranean. Though not exactly the second front Stalin had hoped for—that would have to wait until Operation Overlord—the consequences were still to his benefit.

Benito Is Finito

Even before the fighting ended in Sicily, Mussolini was arrested by the police after his own Fascist Grand Council turned on him. He was replaced on July 25 by Pietro Badoglio. King Victor Emmanuel III took command of the military. In a matter of days, Mussolini's 21 years of autocratic rule came to an end. He was then taken from Rome and imprisoned on the island of Ponza.

Hoping to quickly capitalize on the events in Italy, the Allies relayed secret messages to the new leaders through diplomatic channels to see whether an armistice could be arranged. The Italians were amenable, but they initially balked at the demand for unconditional surrender. When the Allies threatened an invasion with severe consequences, Badoglio agreed to cease fighting and signed a secret armistice on September 3, 1943.

Ike Takes Command

Just as the Italians were dropping out of the war, the combined chiefs of staff were meeting in Quebec to once again discuss joint strategy for the final conflict with Germany. As before, divisions were sharp. The Americans continued to insist on a specific date for an all-out assault on the Germans; the British preferred to build on their success in the Mediterranean and further weaken the *Wehrmacht* before committing to the cross-Channel operation. The two allies compromised and kept the May 1, 1944, target date, but they left open the possibility of a change.

> **Words of War**
>
> "The massed, angered forces of common humanity are on the march. They are going forward—on the Russian front, in the vast Pacific area, and into Europe—converging upon their ultimate objectives: Berlin and Tokyo. I think the first crack in the Axis has come. The criminal, corrupt Fascist regime in Italy is going to pieces."
>
> —Roosevelt, fireside chat, July 28, 1943

Operation Overlord was to be the top priority; however, the Americans did agree to a second, diversionary invasion in southern France to satisfy the British. A British general was originally going to be in charge of planning and implementing both invasions; however, when it became clear the United States would provide the bulk of the manpower, the British deferred to Roosevelt, who chose Dwight Eisenhower. Eisenhower didn't formally begin his new assignment until January 16, 1944. The command was then renamed the Supreme Headquarters, Allied Expeditionary Force (SHAEF).

During the Quebec meetings, another interesting subject came up: the capture of Berlin. Roosevelt and Churchill were confident of winning the war, and the president had already begun to think about what would happen next. He realized, even in 1943, that the Soviets might cause new problems for Britain and the United States and suggested to Churchill that their forces be prepared to reach Berlin at the same time as the Russians. At that moment, both armies were approximately 1,000 miles from their objective.

War Lore

At the beginning of the war, Dwight Eisenhower (1890–1969) was hardly a household name. Once, visiting the White House, he was listed in the appointment book as Lieutenant Colonel Eisenhaur. "Ike" never wanted to be a soldier. He couldn't afford college, but he learned that West Point offered a free education to those who received congressional appointments. He got in, but he did not distinguish himself, finishing 61st out of 164 in his class. During World War I, he trained soldiers for the tank corps in the United States and received the Distinguished Service Medal for his contribution. After Pearl Harbor, Chief of Staff George Marshall appointed him head of the War Plans Division. By June 1942, Eisenhower had been promoted to lieutenant general and put in command of the European theater. He did not go into combat until November 1943, during Operation Torch. His troops were initially routed, but he rallied them and eventually succeeded in helping to lead the Allies to their North African victory.

General Dwight D. Eisenhower, Supreme Allied Commander, at his headquarters in the European theater of operations. He wears the five-star cluster of the newly created rank of General of the Army, February 1, 1945. (National Archives Still Pictures Branch)

No Roman Holiday, Yet

Plans for the grand finale were being made, but the middle acts were not yet complete. By the time the armistice was signed with Italy, Allied troops were ready to land on the mainland to drive out the German forces in the north and center of the country. Montgomery's troops landed at the toe of the boot (the southern tip of Italy) and planned to march north to meet up with Clark's Fifth Army, which was landing at Salerno, 180 miles north of Montgomery's troops. After the Italians signed the armistice, the Allies moved swiftly through the southern part of the country, capturing most of their objectives in the first six weeks. Offshore, they also took the Italian island of Sardinia and French island of Corsica, which had both already been evacuated.

Churchill also launched his own Greek misadventure, sending troops to seize the Italian-controlled islands of the Aegean in mid-September. The Germans counterattacked after the Italians had lost the islands and recaptured them two months later, giving the now two-wheeled Axis command of that sea.

Meanwhile, German troops began to organize their defenses in Italy. Rommel was assigned to pacify the north, recapture Allied prisoners released after Mussolini's arrest, and eliminate any resistance to German occupation. Rommel easily disarmed the roughly 1 million Italian soldiers, few of whom were interested in continuing to fight. Most surrendered and were sent to slave-labor camps in Germany, where many died.

While Rommel outfoxed the Italians in the north, General Albert Kesselring convinced Hitler he could establish a perimeter south of Rome to stop the Allied advance. Kesselring had about 400,000 men under his command and received reinforcements of crack SS units from the eastern front.

Hitler also decided to save Mussolini, sending a group of commandos to free him from the mountain resort of Gran Sasso where he was being held. *Il Duce* was spirited off to Vienna and then to Rastenburg to meet with Hitler, who once again declared his loyalty to his old bumbling friend. Still under the delusion that he was either respected or feared by his people, Mussolini declared a new Italian Social Republic in the north. When he returned to Italy, he controlled little more than the villa he lived in with his mistress Clara Petacci, in the town of Gargagno.

On October 13, 1943, Italy officially joined the Allies and declared war on Germany. Given that few Italian troops remained, the only practical effect of this declaration was to give the Allies free reign in the limited area where the Italians were still sovereign.

Ask the General

The Allies bombed Hitler's major source of oil, the fields in Ploesti, Romania, at the beginning of August. The Germans, however, had intercepted the enemy's radio transmissions and met the Allies with heavy anti-aircraft fire and *Messerschmitt* fighters. The oil facilities were damaged, but reserves made up for the shortfall, so the Germans were not adversely affected. The Allies, however, lost 579 men, and 108 of the 177 bombers were either shot down or badly damaged.

The next several weeks of fighting were difficult, and the Allies made only slow progress. By the beginning of 1944, Eisenhower had left for England to plan for Operation Overlord. Montgomery also went home to command the main ground-invasion force. In an effort to break the stalemate, the Allies planned a new landing, Operation Shingle, closer to Rome.

Operation Shingle

On January 22, 1944, Allied troops under the command of Major General John Lucas landed at Anzio, just 30 miles south of Rome. The Germans were caught by surprise, and more than 36,000 troops quickly landed, with a loss of only 13. Lucas was reluctant to press his immediate advantage until his tanks and heavy artillery had landed, and the chance was lost. After he advanced about 10 miles, the Germans, ordered by Hitler to hold the line in Italy at all costs, stopped Lucas and then counterattacked. Hitler hoped to demonstrate to the Allies and his own citizens that an invasion aimed at Germany would be repulsed.

Arrows indicate Allied drives in Italy. Solid lines indicate front in October. Sawtooth line shows German defense positions between Mt. Massico and the Matese Mountains. (AP/Wide World Photos)

The Germans could not throw the invaders into the sea, however, and the Allied force managed to stay alive, though under siege, for several more months. Most of the Allied troops remained bottled up further south, blocked by the Gustav Line, the German defensive perimeter that traversed Italy's width north of Naples and south of Rome.

One crucial victory for the Allies had been the capture of the airfields near Foggia. These bases allowed the Allies to extend the range of their bombers. They hoped to capture additional airfields north of Rome to further expand their bombing capabilities.

Battle Royale at Cassino

The Allies' road to Rome crossed the Gustav Line and passed the town of Cassino, northwest of Naples. The town was dominated by a Benedictine monastery on the summit of Monte Cassino, a nearly impregnable barrier. On three occasions—in January, February, and March—a massive bombardment was followed by an Allied attack on the fortress, and each time the Germans fought off the attack.

In the middle of May, the Allies tried yet another assault, this time supported by more than 3,000 aircraft. After a week of heavy fighting, the monastery was finally captured. This critical breakthrough allowed all the Allied troops to advance on Rome. Even the beleaguered troops who had been trapped in Anzio since January were able to break out when the Fifth Army joined them from the south.

Less than two weeks later, the troops from the Fifth Army were the first to reach Rome. In a rare act of charity, the Germans had declared it an open city, sparing the Eternal City the ravages of war that had destroyed so many other historic places in Europe. Kesselring's forces retreated to the next most defensible line, roughly 150 miles north of Rome near Pisa.

The Allies would continue to pursue the Germans and fight for almost another full year before gaining control of Italy just five days before Germany surrendered. By June of 1944, however, virtually all the attention of the Allies was focused on the beaches of France.

Ask the General

Just when the Allies were stymied by the Germans, they were thrown for a loop by the Italians. On March 13, 1944, the British and Americans learned that Badoglio had signed an agreement with the Russians in which the Russians offered to recognize the Italian monarchy. Neither the British nor Americans were sure they wanted to move in that direction, but they decided to go along with the Soviets until the Italian people had a chance to determine their own fate (which, in 1946, was to create a democratic republic).

The Least You Need to Know

➤ After Operation Torch bogged down in Tunisia, the Allied forces regrouped and forced the Germans and Italians to evacuate, leaving all of North Africa in Allied hands.

➤ The Allied plan to trap German and Italian troops in Sicily failed, but caused another humiliation of Mussolini, which led him to be replaced.

➤ Eisenhower became Supreme Allied Commander in preparation for the cross-Channel invasion.

➤ The Allies invaded Italy to try to knock it out of the war; Hitler responded by abandoning all offensives on the eastern front in order to occupy northern Italy.

➤ Rome fell to the Allies, and Italy joined the fight against Hitler.

Chapter 17

The Eastern Front Falls Back

In This Chapter

➤ Hitler won't make peace with Russia

➤ Germany is down but not out

➤ The Soviets go on the offense

➤ The Big Three finally meet

➤ The German empire begins to crumble

When Hitler began his war of conquest, he was determined not to repeat the mistakes of the past and yet he did. The most crucial element of his strategy was the avoidance of a two-front war. He had planned to knock the British out of the war and then the Soviets; however, the failure of the Battle of Britain left him fighting an ongoing battle with England as he launched his eastern offensive.

Mussolini had further complicated his plans by forcing him to divert his resources, troops, and energy to other theaters. Finally, the entrance of the United States into the conflict in Europe raised the stakes and the cost of the war, ultimately, beyond what he could bear.

Hitler's Friends Urge Peace

As we saw in the last chapter, Mussolini desperately needed help from Hitler if he hoped to survive. *Il Duce* wanted Hitler to negotiate an end to the war with Russia. This was unlikely even if Hitler would consider abandoning his goals there, because he couldn't risk leaving a strong Red Army to threaten him in the future. Stalin, moreover, wouldn't have given up any of the areas Hitler would have insisted on keeping.

Japan also counseled Hitler to seek peace with Stalin, reasoning, like the Italians, that the Germans would be far better off fighting one front against the British and Americans. This would, of course, also increase the pressure on the United States and, ideally, reduce the resources available to American forces in the Pacific. Hitler saw the situation almost in reverse. He wanted the Japanese to take the pressure off *him* by attacking the Soviets from the rear.

The point had come to where the Axis was virtually down to one wheel. The Japanese did little or nothing to aid the German war effort in Europe, and Mussolini mostly made things worse. Hitler continued to believe, and reassured both the Japanese and Italians, that all was well on the eastern front, and he would soon launch new offensives, but fewer and fewer people believed him.

The Red Army Rolls

Even before the Americans joined the fighting and widened the second front in North Africa, the Germans were in trouble on the eastern front. The hope of the *Blitzkrieg* overrunning the key cities of the Soviet Union and capturing its vital resources had frozen during two long winters of fighting. Hitler still expected to hold the line and launch a new offensive on the Soviet oil fields, but his army was gradually being worn down.

Hitler had promoted General Friedrich von Paulus to the rank of field marshal, hoping that the knowledge that no field marshal had ever been captured would stiffen his resolve. Instead, after enduring a bombardment by the largest concentration of artillery in history, Paulus surrendered the troops he had outside Stalingrad. This surrender was the end of Hitler's high-profile attempt to take the city.

Hitler's Blame Game

The importance Hitler had placed on Stalingrad and the worldwide publicity given to its defense magnified the German defeat. The aura of German invincibility was shattered once and for all. Beyond the humiliation, the Germans lost 150,000 men; another 90,000 were captured, and some 30,000 wounded were evacuated. As always, Hitler did not accept responsibility for the defeat, blaming it instead on the incompetence of his generals. He was now more committed than ever to exerting battlefield control over the troops and replacing the professional officers with more reliable Nazi commanders.

Hitler could also use the excuse that his allies had let him down in the fighting. Armies of Romania, Hungary, and Italy had all been routed. None of these losses sat well with the people back home. The same was true for German citizens who did not care about excuses. They knew things were going badly and were now increasingly absorbing the fury of the Allied bombardment. Still, Hitler retained his iron grip on the country, and no signs of serious dissent from his policies appeared.

Foreshadowing a New Empire

The Allies were certainly pleased by the developments on the eastern front, but they became alarmed by some of Stalin's actions, particularly his announcement in 1943 that all Poles who were on Soviet territory in November 1939 were Soviet citizens. Stalin also ignored the Polish government-in-exile based in London in favor of Polish communists under his control. This ominous development meant the Soviets were unlikely to relinquish power once they marched through Poland on their way to Berlin.

The United States was also angered by Stalin's refusal to allow American planes to use Soviet bases either to bring in Lend-Lease supplies for the Russian troops or to launch attacks on Japanese positions. Instead, the United States flew supplies into Alaska where Soviet pilots picked them up to take home. Meanwhile, the Americans knew from intercepts of Japanese messages that the Soviets were continuing to promise to remain neutral in the Pacific. Thus, the Soviets were allies primarily in their willingness to accept Western aid to defeat the common German enemy. Beyond that, Stalin was disinclined to do anything to help either Britain or the United States achieve their war aims.

Though the United States and Britain tried to reassure Stalin about their intention to see the war through to the unconditional surrender of Germany and to open a second front to relieve the Red Army, Stalin continued to dally with the idea of a separate peace. It is unclear how serious he was, but the Allies knew that the Japanese were trying to facilitate a settlement and the Italians were urging one on Hitler. When Stalin withdrew his ambassadors from London and Washington in June 1943, the Allies' anxiety was heightened. In the end, Britain, the United States, and the Soviet Union were reassured, though still cautious, about their respective intentions.

Words of War

"We shall not settle for less than total victory. That is the determination of every American on the fighting fronts. That must be and will be the determination of every American at home."

—Franklin Roosevelt, fireside chat, July 28, 1943

Still Plenty of Fight in the Germans

As bad as the Germans' deployment seemed, they still had the capacity to launch an effective counteroffensive in February and March. Once again, the town of Kharkov fell, and the Germans regained much of the territory they lost outside the major cities. The battle lines were not much different by the summer of 1943 than they had been the previous summer. The fact that Germany had recovered the initiative and appeared far from beaten alarmed Stalin, who now realized the war, and danger to his regime, was far from over.

Stalin's most trusted military advisor, General Zhukov, suggested that the Red Army wage a war of attrition, holding the line as much as possible to wear down the Germans, while trying to degrade their *panzer* divisions. After the Germans were weakened, the Soviets could bring in fresh reserves to drive the Germans back for good.

Words of War

"The world has never seen greater devotion, determination, and self-sacrifice than have been displayed by the Russian people... under the leadership of Marshal Joseph Stalin. With a nation that in saving itself is thereby helping to save all the world from the Nazi menace, this country of ours should always be glad to be a good neighbor and a sincere friend in the world of the future."

—President Roosevelt, fireside chat, July 28, 1943

By 1943, the Red Army was stronger than ever before. It now had perhaps the best tank in the war, the T-34, the strongest artillery in the world, and the Katyusha rocket launcher. The Soviets also used the lull in fighting in the spring to fortify their defenses, particularly in the area of the Kursk salient.

The *Wehrmacht* had been weakened by the loss of men and equipment, but the army still could put more than 3 million troops in the field. After months of delay, Hitler finally decided on June 12 to put them to the test in one great offensive that he said "will shine like a beacon around the world." Operation Citadel was aimed at eliminating the Red Army at Kursk. Originally, the offensive was to quickly follow the successful recapture of Kharkov, but bad weather, indecision, and distractions on other fronts postponed the attack.

When the Germans were finally ready to go, the Soviets had been given time to prepare. The German attack began on July 5 and moved steadily for four days before stiff resistance stopped it. The Russians counterattacked and began to reverse the German gains. Suddenly, Hitler called off Citadel to divert troops to meet the Allied forces that had just landed in Sicily.

What made the defeat particularly damaging to the German war effort was the loss of equipment. The fight for Kursk involved the largest tank battle in history, a total of 6,000 tanks, and the German loss of approximately 3,000 was devastating because new ones were not manufactured quickly enough to replace them. The air battle was equally fierce, with 4,000 aircraft in combat. Again, the Germans bore the brunt, losing nearly 1,400.

The Russians were not about to give the Germans a break. On August 3, 1943, the Red Army attacked Kursk and overwhelmed the troops that had been on the attack a month earlier. The Germans were on the run once again. Ignoring pleas for reinforcements, Hitler instead ordered the creation of a fortified line, the East Wall—not to give his troops a place to fall back to and hold, but rather to prevent a retreat.

By the end of August, the Russians had retaken Kharkov yet again and were threatening the German Army Group Center. Over the next few weeks, the Red Army continued to push the Germans back, forcing troops in both the north and south to join those in the center in a general retreat. The East Wall had not been built, so there was no barricade to withdraw behind. Instead, the Germans tried to hold positions on the western banks of the Dnieper, Pronya, and Sozh rivers.

As the Germans pulled back, a total of roughly 150 miles from their forward positions across a 650-mile line from north to south, they adopted a scorched-earth policy, razing everything that might be of use to the Russians. Though they succeeded in knocking industrial targets such as factories and railroads out of commission, they could not destroy all the food and consumer goods.

Molotov's Diplomatic Cocktail

At the end of October 1943, the foreign ministers of the Allies met for the first time in Moscow. Anthony Eden represented the British, Cordell Hull the Americans, and Vyacheslav Molotov the Russians. The American objective was to get the Soviets to support the goal of unconditional surrender of the Axis and to recognize China as a major power. The former was readily accepted; however, neither Britain nor the Soviet Union would yield on the China issue. The Soviets were especially concerned that such a move would jeopardize their relationship with Japan. The Soviets also refused to recognize the London-based Polish government-in-exile. The British, meanwhile, wanted the Americans to recognize de Gaulle's French National Committee of Liberation. Reluctantly, Hull agreed to offer some form of recognition.

Words of War

"As Stalin entered the room every Russian froze into silence, and the hunted look in the eyes of the generals showed all too plainly the constant fear in which they lived. It was nauseating to see brave men reduced to such servility."

—General Hastings Ismay, Churchill's military assistant, Moscow, October 1943

Roll Call

By the end of the summer of 1943, the number of German deaths since the start of the war had grown to more than half a million. Nearly 2 million had been wounded, and several hundred thousand were taken prisoner.

An understanding was also reached on the desirability of disarming and denazifying Germany after it was defeated. Another consensus issue was to try war criminals for their atrocities. Warnings were issued throughout the war to discourage German mistreatment of civilians and POWs, with no apparent impact on the killing machine. Beyond that, the ministers could not decide on the future of Germany's borders, other than a return of Austria's independence, or what sort of reparations Germany might be required to pay.

Another American idea was to win the other powers' endorsement of a new world organization, the United Nations, that would act in the interests of world peace and, ideally, transcend international rivalries. Eden and Molotov were amenable to the general concept, but more negotiations would be required before the world body could win their support. From the American perspective, the most important accomplishment of the meeting was securing Stalin's pledge to join the United States against Japan after Germany was defeated. What he did not say was what he would expect in return.

Words of War

"We cannot stand such a drain for long.... [If it continues] we are in danger of slowly bleeding to death in the East."

—Joseph Goebbels on the heavy losses suffered by the *Wehrmacht* in Russia

Here We Snow Again

The Red Army was still on the march when its old ally, winter, again joined the fight. Heading into their third winter campaign, the Germans had finally learned some survival skills and received cold-weather clothes and equipment. In November and early December, however, "General Winter's" offensive had been unusually mild, with more rain and sleet than snow.

In these conditions, the Russians still had an advantage because their trucks and armor performed better in the mud than the Germans' equipment. The Red Army also had fresher troops and higher morale as a result of its recent victories. The last major city still in German hands was Kiev. In early November, the Soviets attacked the German forces controlling the city and threw them back toward the Dnieper line.

The Big Three Finally Meet

Despite their alliance, Stalin had never met with both Roosevelt and Churchill at the same time. Repeated invitations to join talks had been rebuffed. Finally, at the end of November, Stalin agreed to discuss strategy with his counterparts. He had not left the Soviet Union since the revolution in 1917 and insisted that the meeting be held close to Moscow. The Allies agreed to meet in Tehran, the capital of Iran, from November 28 until December 1, 1943.

The main issue on the agenda was the plan to launch the cross-Channel invasion in 1944. Churchill explained that certain conditions had to be met for Operation Overlord to proceed. For example, the number of planes available to the *Luftwaffe* in the west must be reduced, and the Germans must be unable to transfer divisions to defend against the invasion.

Stalin agreed to launch an offensive coordinated with the attack to tie down Hitler's troops, although, believing the British were hedging on their commitment to open a second front, he was suspicious. The British were not being underhanded; they were displaying the same ambivalence they'd demonstrated in prior negotiations with the Americans—the British still wanted to attack from the south. Despite the hesitation regarding Operation Overlord, Stalin repeated his promise to enter the war with Japan after Germany was defeated.

The other important decision was to endorse the concept of the United Nations, which would be dominated by the four major powers (France, Britain, Soviet Union, and the United States). Roosevelt thought the institution could maintain peace and stability, if the powers cooperated. If they could not work together, the organization would fail. So much time was devoted to military strategy that little was left to discuss future border arrangements and the disposition of the currently occupied territories.

Fend for Yourselves, Guys

At the beginning of 1944, the Germans had been expelled from the Northern Caucasus, most of the Ukraine, and were trapped in the Crimea. German troop strength was still 3,000,000, but the Red Army now held nearly a two-to-one advantage with 5,700,000 men and overwhelming superiority in tanks and artillery.

The Soviets could call on still more reserves if necessary, but the Germans had been bled to near exhaustion and were spread thinly across Europe with troops in Scandinavia, the Balkans, western Europe, and the Mediterranean. The one good thing about their defeat in Africa was to eliminate one front on which they had to fight. Hitler could now see that an Allied invasion was coming, and preparations for that attack had to be his highest priority. Thus, he told his generals in the east that they were essentially on their own; nothing could be spared until the danger in the west was eliminated.

Throughout the winter months, the Germans struggled to hold their lines, fighting in mud, sleet, and snow. Part of German Army Group South could not maintain its front and was driven all the way back beyond the 1939 Polish border. The other German armies were barely holding positions behind the Dnieper.

The Germans made it through their third winter, but spring brought a renewed Soviet offensive in Ukraine. The Germans were again in retreat with some of their forces encircled by the onrushing Red Army. Hitler's response was typical: He fired two of his generals. But no change in leadership could prevent the collapse of Army Group South. By May, the Germans were trying to evacuate from the Crimea, losing more than

100,000 troops. On May 9, the Soviets recaptured Sevastopol, taking 30,000 German prisoners. The Red Army had advanced 165 miles and was still on the march.

Hitler still believed his forces could recoup. Albert Speer's drive to mobilize German industry had been quite successful, and Germany was now producing enough weapons to equip new divisions in the west. The *Luftwaffe* had nearly 40 percent more aircraft than it had a year earlier. Oil production reached its peak. Despite the strains of nearly five years of war, Germany was still a very strong nation.

Words of War

"Had I known they had as many tanks as that, I would have thought twice before invading."

—Hitler expressing regret that he had not heeded warnings about Russian productivity

The problem was that the Allies were stronger. The United States alone produced ships, planes, tanks, guns, and every other war material in quantities far beyond those of the Germans. The British added additional industrial capacity. Even the Russians, reliant on American Lend-Lease and British aid to maintain their forces, were outproducing the Germans. In 1944, for example, German tank production reached its peak of 17,800. Soviet output was 29,000.

Stalin's D Day

In Tehran, Stalin promised to launch a major offensive to coincide with the Allied invasion. Operation Overlord went forward on June 6, and Stalin launched his own attack, Operation Bagration (named after a czarist general), on the 22nd, the third anniversary of Hitler's invasion of Russia. The invasion force consisted of 1,700,000 troops supported by 6,000 aircraft, nearly 3,000 tanks, and 24,000 artillery pieces.

GI Jargon

People usually associate the term **D day** with the Allied invasion at Normandy on June 6, 1944, but it is a generic military term for the date and time (or **H hour**) of an attack.

When Stalin's *D day* arrived, only German Army Group Center retained a significant area of Soviet territory, and it came under attack in late June. In less than two weeks, nearly 70 percent of its divisions were destroyed. At about the same time, the Russians pushed northward against the Germans and Finns. Everywhere the Germans were in retreat and the holes in their lines were growing every day.

By the end of July, the Russians were approaching Warsaw. The Poles started an uprising against the Germans still controlling the city, partly because they'd been encouraged to do so by Polish communists who suggested the Red Army would come to their aid. Stalin, however, refused to provide any help and prevented the Allies from flying in arms or supplies. The Germans encircled the city, halting the Russian advance, and, after two months of fighting, suppressed the uprising. The SS then took over and slaughtered roughly 200,000 Poles in subsequent massacres.

Because the Germans were being thrown back and clearly losing the war on the eastern front, it's easy to forget that the cost in Russian lives was enormous. Incredibly, perhaps as much as 90 percent of all Soviet men 18 to 21 years old were killed in the fighting. Despite such losses, the Red Army didn't let up.

By mid-August, the German Army Group Center had been destroyed, and 350,000 soldiers were dead, wounded, or captured. The Soviet offensive had moved the front 300 miles west to the outskirts of Warsaw. By the end of August, the Red Army had overwhelmed Romania's troops. More than 100,000 Germans were killed, and similar number captured. The Romanians opted for peace, but before the armistice was signed on September 12, the Russians seized the Ploesti oilfields. Though it made no practical difference, because the country had been overrun by the Red Army, Romania declared war on Germany. The Russians then entered Bulgaria and achieved the same result, an armistice and declaration of war on Germany.

The Finns, who had earlier missed a golden opportunity to get out of the war largely unscathed, were the next to give in to the Red Army. Thanks to German help, they kept the Russians from overrunning the country, but this time the Finns jumped at the chance for peace. On September 19, 1944, they signed an armistice that was surprisingly generous, restoring the borders to where they had been in March 1940, and removing all Soviet occupation forces. The Finns tried to disarm the German troops still occupying the country, but Hitler ordered them withdrawn. For the next four months, the 200,000 Germans who'd spent the war in Finland marched 500 miles through the Arctic.

The Germans were recalling troops from the Mediterranean and trying to consolidate them to defend Yugoslavia and Hungary. The Red Army continued its steady march, however, capturing Belgrade on October 20 and then launching an attack against Budapest. The Russian advance was slow but inexorable, and Hungary fell just before the end of the year, joining the other Russian-occupied nations in declaring war on Germany.

Churchill met with Stalin in October to discuss strategy and the disposition of the conquered territories after the war. The British prime minister had much experience with the division of war spoils and the negotiation over colonies, so it was not surprising that he proposed divvying up the Eastern European and Balkan countries between the powers. Churchill told Stalin that people feared that Communist domination would replace Nazi domination and that they should be allowed to determine their own political fate. The tenor of the discussion and the reality of the fighting, however, made it clear that the Russians would be making the decisions for the people living in the territories they controlled.

The Least You Need to Know

➤ Hitler's allies realized that Germany couldn't fight the Western powers and Russia at the same time and urged him to make peace, but he wouldn't give up his dream of conquering the Soviet Union.

➤ The Soviet Union made clear it wouldn't support democracy in Poland.

➤ Germany continued to mount offensives, but the Red Army gradually pushed the German troops back and began its inexorable march toward Berlin.

➤ Stalin met with Roosevelt and Churchill for the first time and agreement was reached to demand unconditional surrender, try war criminals, and create the United Nations. Stalin promised to attack Japan after Germany was defeated.

➤ One by one, the countries that had forcibly joined the Axis were overrun by the Soviets, and their governments switched sides.

Pacific Island-Hopping

The Americans fighting in the Pacific learned it was not necessary to capture every island held by the Japanese. Bypassing those with no strategic value saved lives and effectively isolated the Japanese defenders left with no one to fight against. By the end of 1943, the troops under General MacArthur and Admiral Halsey had successfully completed Operation Cartwheel (see Chapter 15 for more information) and converted the former Japanese stronghold of Rabaul to an American base.

The next stage of the campaign became even more difficult as the Americans attempted to hop from island to island in the Central Pacific. These islands were mostly very small and in some cases heavily defended. Isolated as they were, with no hope of evacuation, the Japanese could be expected to fight to the death—as they had on most of the bigger islands. In addition to the anticipated resistance, the Americans were handicapped by the increasingly long supply lines.

China Breaks Free

I haven't said a lot about China to this point, but U.S. policy there played an important role in the conduct of the war. Throughout the war, Roosevelt tried to secure recognition of China as a major power and a prominent place in the nascent United

Nations. The British disagreed with the Americans and did little to bolster the Chinese nationalists under Chiang Kai-Shek, focusing more on their imperial interests in India, which were also being threatened by Japan.

Chiang's Kuomintang government was the legitimate ruler of China, with the largest army in the world (though it could only arm a fraction of its divisions). Chiang's rule was challenged before the war by a communist army led by Mao Zedong. Though they continued to fight each other, the two armies also agreed to attack the Japanese, though Mao's forces allowed Chiang's to do most of the work. The two armies did not coordinate their actions and were hundreds of miles apart: Chiang's in the south and Mao's in the north. Chiang's troops were not enthusiastic about fighting; moreover, he controlled only a fraction of the armed men, many of whom were loyal to local warlords or the communists.

Reopening the Burma Road

In May 1942, the Japanese conquered Burma and closed the main supply route into China, the Burma Road. In October 1943, the Japanese completed a railway connecting Burma and Thailand that was constructed by POWs and Burmese slave laborers. Approximately 16,000 of the 46,000 POWs died working on the project, as did more than 50,000 Burmese.

War Lore

The Burma-Thailand railway connection required the construction of a bridge over the River Kwai, immortalized in the 1957 movie, *The Bridge on the River Kwai*. The film won seven Academy Awards, including Best Picture, Best Actor (Alec Guinness), and Best Director (David Lean). Lean later won another Oscar for *Lawrence of Arabia* and was nominated for *Dr. Zhivago*. The film's score, which also won an Oscar, included the World War I whistling tune (you'd know it if you heard it), the "Colonel Bogey March." The screenplay was credited to Pierre Boulle, on whose novel the movie was based, but it was written by Carl Foreman and Michael Wilson, who were blacklisted in the early 1950s for refusing to cooperate with the House Committee on Un-American Activities. They received their Academy Awards posthumously in 1985. The bridge over the River Kwai was destroyed on June 24, 1945, by British bombers.

Japanese control of the Burma Road forced the United States to try to build a new route to bring supplies into China. General Joseph Stilwell was in charge of the project, as well as trying to organize and train Chinese troops. The distance between the United States and China, lack of enthusiasm of the British and Chinese nationalist forces, and the generally low priority given to the theater restricted Stilwell's ability to accomplish anything.

Moreover, the commander of the Air Force in China, General Claire Chennault, disagreed with Stilwell's idea of opening a land route to bring supplies into China. Chennault preferred to concentrate on creating bases from which to launch air attacks on Japan. The United States originally intended to use bases in China for its air offensive against the Japanese home islands. This plan was also jeopardized by the interruption of the supply route from Burma and later made less important by the capture of the Marianas, which put Japan within the range of the B-29s.

A Chinese soldier guards a line of American P-40 fighter planes, painted with the shark-face emblem of the Flying Tigers at an airfield in China circa 1942. (National Archives Still Pictures Branch)

A compromise was eventually reached, and Stilwell was allowed to lead his Chinese troops against Japanese forces in Burma and succeeded in building a road that joined the old Burma Road. Chennault, meanwhile, was given permission to fly in supplies over the "hump"—a 14,000-foot mountain chain separating India and China—and to prepare to mount the air offensive on Japan.

Japan's inability to resist expanding its Asian empire to China and Burma had a debilitating effect similar to that of the German campaign against Russia: It diverted resources from the main fight against the Allies for Pacific islands. One of Japan's objectives was to capture the Chinese bases designed for American use. In April 1944, the Japanese began an operation to do just that, killing more than 300,000 of Chiang's troops and leaving the Chinese Nationalist Army in disarray. The loss of most of the air bases Chennault had planned to use reduced the American interest in China and reshaped the strategy in the Pacific.

War Lore

The Japanese devised a plan to set the forests of America's Pacific Northwest and Canada ablaze to cause chaos and devastation in those regions. The idea was to launch balloons across the Pacific carrying incendiary materials that would fall in the forests. According to Gerhard Weinberg, 9,000 balloons were released between November 7, 1944, and March 1945, and more than 1,000 hit their targets. The balloons did little damage, but they did remind Americans that they were not beyond the reach of Japanese offensive operations.

The British had greater success beating back a Japanese offensive aimed at India, which began in March 1944. By mid-July, British and Indian troops had repulsed the invaders. The defeat was humiliating and was Japan's costliest defeat to that point.

Merrill's Marauders

Despite being forced to surrender territory and air bases to the Japanese in April 1944, Stilwell remained committed to his plan for a land route for supplies from northern Burma to China and organized a special force to try again. They were called Merrill's Marauders, after their commander Brigadier General Frank Merrill (yes, this story was made into a movie also).

The Marauders were drawn from volunteers who had responded to a presidential request for "a dangerous and hazardous mission." Nearly 3,000 American soldiers came forward. Their main objective was to penetrate enemy lines deep in the Burmese jungle and destroy Japanese communications and supply lines. The unit covered more than 100 miles as it marched through the mud, scaled mountains, and hacked its way through the dense jungle. In addition to disrupting Japanese communications and supplies, the Marauders seized the airfield at Myitkyina, giving the Americans their first base in Burma.

Small Islands, High Human Cost

The initial major objective in the Central Pacific was the capture of the Marshall Islands. These islands could be used to base the new B-29 bombers for attacks on the Philippines and even the Japanese homeland.

War Lore

The B-29 Superfortress was designed in the late 1930s to be the United States's long-range bomber. It was not produced for deployment until 1943, but its introduction gave the United States unprecedented firepower. The new bomber had a 1,500-mile range, double that of existing aircraft, which allowed the United States to greatly extend the range of its air campaign against the Japanese and not be restricted to the use of carrier-based planes. The B-29's top speed was 400 miles per hour, and it could carry a 2,000-pound bomb load. The atomic bombs were dropped from two B-29s.

Admiral Nimitz ordered an attack on two of the Marshall Islands, Kwajalein and Eniwetok. The invasion began January 31, 1944, and Americans used lessons learned in earlier fighting to quickly overcome the resistance and inflict more casualties on the Japanese than at Tarawa, while suffering fewer of their own. Simultaneously, the air force bombed the large naval base at Truk in the Caroline Islands. Though the Japanese fleet had already moved to Palau, any ships, planes, or supplies left behind were destroyed or commandeered.

In April 1944, Operation Persecution was launched. More than 80,000 American troops landed on the northern coast of New Guinea, which was defended by only 15,000 Japanese, most of whom were not combat soldiers. Despite the numerical disadvantage, the Japanese held out for three months. By the end of the fighting, only about 3,000 Japanese had survived; the United States lost 527 men.

On June 14, just a week after the Normandy invasion, the Americans launched their first B-29s against Japan's home islands. Using one of the bases established in China, the bombers attacked the iron and steel works on Honshu. The people of Japan began to realize the war was getting closer to home.

This map shows the Pacific islands and initial gains by the Japanese that were rolled back as American forces made their way toward Japan's home island. (The Illustrated London News Picture Library)

A Turkey Shoot

On June 15, more than 20,000 of an eventual force of nearly 60,000 Americans landed on the island of Saipan. Saipan, along with Guam, were two key targets of the American offensive in the Marianas. Once again the fighting was brutal, with a numerically inferior Japanese force holding out to the last man. This time the battle raged for three weeks. After the Japanese commander committed suicide, another 7,000 of his men followed his example. More than 4,000 Japanese made a final "banzai" charge and almost all of them were killed. Many of the surviving soldiers and civilians jumped off a cliff to their deaths. Japanese fatalities totaled 20,000; the United States lost 3,426.

While the Americans pounded the island, Admiral Jisaburo Ozawa moved his fleet into range to counterattack. Alerted to the Japanese fleet's movements, the American task force commanded by Vice-Admiral Marc Mitscher joined the battle. This battle was one of the first instances where the disparity in shipbuilding became obvious. Now the U.S. force had an advantage of 15 carriers to 9. The U.S. Navy also now had a new fighter plane, the Hellcat, which was faster and more powerful than the Japanese Zero. In what became known as the Great Marianas Turkey Shoot, 243 of 373 Japanese aircraft were downed, and only 29 American planes were lost.

In this Battle of the Philippine Sea, the American surface ships, planes, and submarines also combined to sink three Japanese carriers, including the largest in their fleet, and damaged two others. Of the 27 Japanese submarines sent to the Marianas, 17 were sunk. The Americans suffered only minor losses.

Fighting on the islands of Tinian and Guam was also fierce. The Japanese inflicted heavy casualties on the Americans, but were completely wiped out themselves. Nevertheless, by mid-August, the Marianas were in American hands, opening up the Philippines to MacArthur.

A naval base was created on Guam, which Nimitz used as his headquarters. The most important gains were the six airfields built in the Marianas: three on Guam, two on Tinian, and one on Saipan. On November 24, the first large-scale air attack was launched from these bases. The raid was not very

Roll Call

In 1944, Japanese aircraft production reached its peak, 28,180, which was dwarfed by the American output of 100,752. The disparity was even worse, given that Japan had nothing to compare to the B-29 bombers rolling off the American assembly lines.

Roll Call

When the Japanese captured Guam in December 1941, they lost only one soldier. In the 20-day effort to stop the Americans from retaking the island two and a half years later, 18,500 died. U.S. forces lost 2,124 men.

successful: Only 88 of 111 aircraft were able to drop their bombs, and most missed their targets. Subsequent sorties fared no better during the remaining weeks of the year. It would take a new strategy and a special commander to make the bombing campaign effective in 1945.

Though it may have seemed impossible to those who had fought so far, the war got worse for the Americans when they began their offensive in the Caroline Islands. In mid-September, the Americans suffered the highest casualties of any of their amphibious operations when more than 9,000 men died in the 11 days it took to capture the island of Peleliu. The Japanese lost more than 13,000 men.

MacArthur's Return

The Americans had leapfrogged across the Pacific and wiped out all vestiges of Japanese occupation on all but the handful of islands they purposely bypassed. The time had come to fulfill MacArthur's promise and retrieve their prize Pacific possession and the last major obstacle to large-scale attacks on Japan: the Philippines.

Ask the General

To understand the war in the Pacific, you must appreciate the extent of Japanese brutality. Already mentioned were the Bataan Death March and the bayoneting and beheading of POWs. Another example is the merciless attacks on helpless survivors of torpedoed ships. In February 1944, for example, Japanese submarines torpedoed three British merchant ships, and then machine-gunned the survivors floating in life rafts and clinging to the wreckage.

The prelude to the attack involved a two-day air raid in September on Manila that resulted in the destruction or disabling of 103 Japanese ships and 405 aircraft. Only 15 American planes were lost. A few weeks later, American B-29s carried out a three-day attack on Taiwan to protect the northern flank of the invasion forces and further cripple Japan's air and naval assets. The attacks were devastating, destroying 40 Japanese ships and 500 aircraft; the United States lost only 89 planes.

As these softening-up operations continued, MacArthur steamed toward the Philippines with an armada of 600 ships and 250,000 men. Japan had 270,000 troops in the Philippines, but expecting the Americans to land on Luzon, they had stationed only 16,000 on Leyte, where MacArthur had decided to begin the invasion. On October 20, 1944, in a carefully staged operation, MacArthur stepped ashore on Leyte—with photographers there to capture the moment. "People of the Philippines," he declared, "I have returned."

The Japanese decided to again try to fight a decisive naval battle and sent most of what remained of its fleet to attack MacArthur's invasion force. The idea was to use their carriers to lure Admiral Halsey's fleet away from the beaches so that the Japanese battleships could destroy the American transports and landing craft.

General Douglas MacArthur wades ashore during the initial landings at Leyte, October 1944. (National Archives Still Pictures Branch)

The battle began on October 23, 1944, and initially went according to plan. The news of the Japanese carriers' approach prompted Halsey to go out to meet them. Meanwhile, the Japanese First Attack Force moved into position to challenge the American amphibious vessels, and Japan's Philippines-based aircraft fatally damaged the carrier *Princeton*.

Soon, however, American planes began sinking and damaging Japanese ships so quickly the task force had to withdraw. The commander, Vice-Admiral Takeo Kurita, changed his mind in mid-retreat and decided to return to the original plan and once again headed for Leyte. Before he reached the landing sites, he was met by American warships, which, though outgunned, still managed to force Kurita into another withdrawal.

Halsey, meanwhile, had not yet caught up with the oncoming Japanese carriers and was forced to turn around to aid in the defense of Leyte against the Japanese. His planes had already done plenty of

Ask the General

Japan's greatest fighter ace, Hiroyoshi Nishizawa, was killed when American fighters downed the transport plane that he was flying on. Before his death, Nishizawa had shot down 87 American planes.

damage, however, sinking 36 ships, including 4 carriers, 3 battleships, 6 heavy cruisers, 3 light cruisers, and 10 destroyers. American losses totaled 6 ships. It was the greatest naval battle in history and a victory for the U.S. Navy.

Kamikazes

On the last day of fighting on Leyte, the Japanese introduced a new and terrifying weapon, the *kamikaze*. On October 25, 1944, one *kamikaze* flew into the flight deck of the carrier *St.-Lo,* causing it to explode and sink. During the remaining months of the war, the *kamikazes* would sink another 33 American warships at a cost of 5,000 pilots. The damage caused by the Japanese suicide attacks was serious enough that MacArthur and Nimitz ordered the news of them to be censored to prevent Americans from panicking and the Japanese from learning their effectiveness.

GI Jargon

The word **kamikaze** is Japanese for "divine wind." The Japanese created a special group of suicide pilots known as the kamikazes to purposely crash their planes into American ships.

Although the decisive battle at sea took only three days, the land campaign continued as both sides sent in reinforcements. The Japanese mounted a counterattack to try to capture the main American airfield, but it was repulsed and the remaining resistance slowly suppressed. The 67-day battle had been costly: Roughly 70,000 Japanese and 15,500 Americans lost their lives.

The high casualties were particularly tragic because one of the major objectives of the Leyte operation was not accomplished. The Americans had planned to build airfields to support the upcoming attack on Luzon, but they discovered the topography (notably the swampy ground) of the island made their construction impossible.

Even the elements conspired against the Americans in the Philippines. Two ships were sunk by *kamikazes* on the way to the island of Mindoro in mid-December. The following day, a violent storm packing 90-mile-per-hour winds hit the island and sank three destroyers, drowning 279 men. After the typhoon, the U.S. force secured the island and began to construct and expand airfields needed to support the upcoming invasion of Luzon.

As the Americans began to move through the Philippines, the Japanese again dealt brutally with the prisoners they'd taken. One particularly horrifying example involved 150 American POWs on the island of Palawan who were told to go into air-raid shelters on December 15 because American planes were coming. The Japanese then threw buckets of gas into the shelter and lighted torches. Men ran out screaming, on fire, and were shot or bayoneted. Some dying men were buried alive. Only five survived. Several thousand POWs were shipped from the Philippines to Japan, though many died en route from disease, starvation, and having their prison ships attacked by American warships and torpedo planes.

Japan Doesn't Know the War Is Over

When 1944 ended, the Japanese were in serious trouble. Though still on the offensive in parts of China, they were on the run everywhere else. Thanks to the bases in China and the Marianas, the United States was within B-29 striking distance of the Japanese mainland.

The combined American naval and armed forces had hopscotched from the South Pacific to the North Pacific. The sea battles at Midway and Leyte had almost completely decimated the Japanese navy and its carrier aircraft. U.S. submarines had destroyed nearly half the merchant ships and were reducing the flow of oil and other vital goods bound for Japan to a trickle. The mighty U.S. fleet now had roughly 4,000 vessels commanding the ocean.

The war should have been over, but Japanese leaders, like Hitler, would neither give up nor consider negotiating until they had no choice. With substantial ground forces still on islands in the Pacific, and the home islands still relatively unscathed, neither Tojo nor the emperor were prepared to stop fighting.

The Least You Need to Know

➤ The United States tried to establish a foothold in China from which to attack Japan, but its Chinese allies were of little help.

➤ American forces needed to establish airfields on islands nearer to Japan for basing B-29s. Victories cost many American lives while the Japanese fought to the last man.

➤ MacArthur returned to the Philippines with a successful landing on Leyte. The island proves unsuitable, however, for needed air bases.

➤ The U.S. Navy knocked the Japanese fleet out of the war in the decisive battle at Leyte Gulf.

➤ Japanese *kamikazes* proved an effective and terrifying new weapon.

Part 5
Let Freedom Ring

D day arrives, and the Allies land at Normandy. An assassination plot fails in Germany, but Hitler cannot stop the Allies' inexorable march on Germany. Hitler launches a last-ditch offensive that becomes the Battle of the Bulge. Thousands of soldiers become prisoners of war. American Jewish soldiers are particularly at risk. POWs are also sent to concentration camps, while those in one conventional POW camp stage the "Great Escape."

Still, it is only a matter of time before the Red Army surrounds Berlin, and the Western Allies destroy what remains of the Wehrmacht. Hitler commits suicide at almost the same time Mussolini is murdered by partisans. Germany surrenders.

In the most brutal fighting yet, Americans capture Iwo Jima, Okinawa, and the Philippines. Preparations are made to invade Japan when the Manhattan Project succeeds in building an atomic bomb. When the Japanese refuse to surrender, Truman decides to use the bomb to force them to capitulate. The strategy works, though at a high cost of Japanese lives. The war is over.

Invasion!

The British, the Americans, and the Germans all knew that an invasion was coming in 1944. Hitler did not know when the thrust would come or where it would originate. He knew it was most likely to come across the English Channel, but that did not narrow the battlefield enough to choose the proper place to defend. The Germans were already fighting losing battles on two fronts, though Hitler was by no means ready to concede defeat on either. The eastern front would soon take on a whole new meaning as the Red Army continued its drive west.

In Italy, the Allies were continuing their drive north, and Mussolini, Hitler's only real ally (the Japanese contributed nothing to the war effort beyond diverting American forces to the Pacific), had proven worse than useless in the long run. *Il Duce*'s ill-advised invasions, combined with incompetent, outmanned troops had drawn the Germans into too many unnecessary battles.

The losses on both those fronts had degraded the quality and quantity of his men and equipment, and now he would have to shift significant amounts of both in anticipation of the invasion. The *Wehrmacht* was still a mighty fighting force, but it had little chance divided among three fronts. Moreover, Hitler's gamble that the Russians could be held while his army pushed the British and Americans into the sea was a long shot at best, and insanity at worst.

Hitler's Secret Weapons

One reason for Hitler's continuing optimism in the face of an almost continuous string of defeats was his faith in the secret (and not-so-secret) weapons he had in development. The V-1 and V-2 rockets would soon be available. A second new weapon, an improvement on one of their most effective tools early in the war, was the snorkel submarine. When these U-boats put to sea they would be able to operate longer underwater and cruise at a higher speed. The last surprise Hitler was waiting for was his new jet aircraft. In early January, he told his top advisers that if he could get the jets in time, he could stop the invasion. "If I get a few hundred of them to the front line, it will exorcise the specter of invasion for all time," he said.

Fortunately for the world, neither the submarines nor the jets were ready in time to make any difference in the war. The submarines' utility was limited by the Soviet offensive in the Baltic area where the new subs had to be tested and the crews trained. Allied victories also limited ports available to launch or dock the U-boats. The Germans also did not have the air support needed to make the U-boats effective against the large convoys and improved antisubmarine tactics employed by the British and Americans.

Similarly, by the time the jets were operational, in late spring, the Allies had so depleted the *Luftwaffe* that the handful of new planes faced overwhelmingly superior numbers of Allied planes whenever they got off the ground. The pilots were also unable to spend the time needed for adequate training, and before the year was out, the Germans would be so short on fuel that they had to severely restrict their air operations.

The rockets, as you'll see, did cause great damage and some loss of life and satisfied Hitler's objective of terrorizing the British population. The Allies already were well aware of the rocket program. They'd slowed it down with the raid on Peenemünde in August 1943, and would continue to actively try to knock out German rocket bases.

None of these weapons had the decisive effect upon the outcome of the war that the Americans' truly secret atomic bomb would. Still, Hitler believed the super weapons could sufficiently terrorize the British population and interrupt the Allied supply lifeline to allow him to snatch victory from the jaws of defeat.

Words of War

"To be a successful soldier, you must know history.... What you must know is how man reacts. Weapons change but man who uses them changes not at all. To win battles, you do not beat weapons—you beat the soul of man, of the enemy man."

—George Patton, June 6, 1944

The Atlantic Wall

Preparing for the coming invasion, Hitler ordered the building of the Atlantic Wall, a series of fortifications similar in concept to the Maginot Line (and using materials the Germans took from the French). Hitler's idea was to put mines, barbed wire, and various obstacles on the beaches and build protected concrete positions overlooking the landing areas. *Panzer* divisions would be deployed nearby to prevent the invaders from getting off the beaches before the infantry arrived.

Hitler assigned Rommel the task of building his wall. When the Desert Fox went to the French coast to report on the state of the existing defenses, he was appalled to find how little had been done. He immediately ordered a crash program to lay mines and build barriers on the beaches. Soon the Germans were laying more than one million mines per month, up from 40,000 before Rommel's arrival. By mid-May, more than four million mines were in the Allies' presumed path, along with half a million obstacles.

Rommel knew it would take more than a man-made wall to stop an invasion. Given his experience in Africa, he believed the best chance of stopping the landing force was to deploy his tanks near the beach and prevent the Allies from gaining a foothold. Here he came into conflict with one of the army's other top generals, Gerd von Rundstedt, who maintained it was better to assess the situation after the landing and then counterattack. Rommel argued, correctly, that the Allies' air superiority would allow them to counteract such a strategy.

As usually happened with such a high-level dispute, the decision was left to Hitler, who undermined both strategies. He allowed Rommel only three *panzer* divisions to defend the beaches, only one of which would ultimately be defending Normandy. Von Rundstedt was also given three divisions for a counterattack, but Hitler hamstrung him by requiring that he get approval before sending them into battle.

Roll Call

By 1944, the *Luftwaffe* had only 400 fighter planes in France, most not operational, to defend against the Allies' 12,000. Heavy losses on other fronts continued, largely because the Allies could read their air force codes. In February 1944 alone, nearly 1,300 German planes were shot down, with even more lost in accidents. Germany produced nearly 40,000 planes in 1944, but the United States built more than 96,000, the British another 26,000, and the Soviet Union 40,000.

Even with three *panzer* divisions in reserve, Rommel still faced the dilemma that generals on the other side had faced back at the beginning of the war: How should he disperse his forces? He could not defend everything, but concentrating his troops would only work if he knew where the invasion would be. He could guess, but that would not satisfy Hitler. Fortunately, the Allies decided to make it easier for him.

War Lore

General von Rundstedt fell in and out of favor with Hitler. In 1938, von Rundstedt was in charge of the occupation of the Sudetenland. He retired, but was recalled to command the assault through the Ardennes that outflanked the Allies in 1940. Made a field marshal, von Rundstedt commanded Army Group South in the attack on the Ukraine. In November 1941, he was fired for defying Hitler and ordering a retreat, but Hitler recalled him to prepare for the Allied invasion. In July 1944, he was again fired, but chosen to preside over the trial of the conspirators in the attempted assassination of Hitler. When the Allies advanced on Germany, Hitler brought him back again, and he temporarily stopped their offensive. The British captured von Rundstedt, but decided not to try him because of his ill health. He died in 1953.

Patton's Phantom Army

Operation Overlord's planners knew the key to its success was to trick Hitler into believing the invasion would be mounted far from where the landing would actually come. The place they chose for the fictitious invasion was Pas de Calais. It was convincing because the Channel was narrowest at that point, and that area of France offered the most direct route to Germany. Of course, the Germans knew other landing sites were possible; Hitler mentioned Normandy as the probable invasion point on several occasions prior to D day, but he never redeployed his forces to defend that region against the expected large-scale landing.

To further confuse the Germans about their intentions, the Allies created a phantom invasion force, the First US Army Group (FUSAG), and put General Patton in command. Patton was not too happy about being recalled from Italy to sit around England to give credence to the charade. He was itching to be given command of one of the main invasion forces, but he would have to wait to take charge of the Third Army until the invasion had succeeded. In the meantime, his selection for FUSAG added credibility to the deception, because the Germans were familiar with Patton's reputation and believed he was likely to play a major role in the invasion. The Allies also strung the Germans along by sending fake messages about FUSAG and mentioning it in genuine communiques as well.

War Lore

When Patton was reassigned to command the Third Army, FUSAG remained intact. The new commander was Lieutenant General Leslie McNair, the commanding general of Allied Ground Forces. McNair was killed by an Allied bomb on July 25. He was one of the highest-ranking American officers killed in World War II. Lieutenant General John DeWitt replaced McNair to maintain the deception.

The British had already captured all the Nazi agents in Britain and used those who agreed to work for them as double agents to pass on messages authenticating the intelligence about a landing at Calais. British intercepts indicated the Germans had fallen for the "unit that never was" the way they had earlier accepted "the man who never was." The Allies gained crucial time to establish beachheads and begin their breakout because Hitler remained convinced until the end of July that Normandy was the diversion and that the main invasion was yet to come from Calais.

Why Normandy?

If Calais was the logical place to attack, why did the Allies choose Normandy instead? One reason was that Pas de Calais was so obvious the Germans would almost certainly defend it heavily. Realizing this, the planners evaluated the other possible landing sites.

One condition was that the beaches must be within the range of the Spitfire, the main fighter plane in the Allied arsenal, which would be needed to ensure air superiority over the battleground. This condition narrowed the choice to the area between Calais and Cotentin. Within this band, however, most of the beaches were unacceptable because of the surrounding cliffs, the depth of the inlet, or some other logistical or geographical reason. The only suitable choices were Pas de Calais and Normandy.

GI Jargon

Mulberries refer to the two artificial harbors secretly constructed by the British to unload as much as 7,000 tons of vehicles and supplies per day off the coast of Normandy. These ports were made of approximately six miles of flexible steel roadways that floated on steel or concrete pontoons. Mulberry A was towed across the Channel and set up off Omaha Beach, and Mulberry B was positioned near Gold Beach.

Normandy had a major deficiency, however: the absence of a port. The nearest French ports would surely be watched by the Germans, who believed they could deny the Allies the supplies they would need, so the Anglo-American planners decided to build their own temporary, mobile ports, referred to as *Mulberries*.

The plan was to bombard the coast from the air and sea while several divisions landed. Paratroopers would be dropped to positions where they could provide cover for the seaborne troops and capture critical bridges. Allied bombers would also try to knock out the railroads, bridges, and roads leading to Normandy to prevent the Germans from counterattacking and bringing up reinforcements.

The main features of Operation Overlord were hammered out by the end of January, but D day was still more than four months away. The continuing fighting in Italy, meanwhile, contributed indirectly to the operation. The ongoing Allied offensive, slowly pushing northward, diverted many German troops.

The Battle of Berlin

The area-bombing campaign the British began in November 1943, which became known as the Battle of Berlin, continued through the winter and into the early spring of 1944. In roughly three and a half months, 16 raids were conducted. During the early ones, the citizens of Berlin were relatively unaffected, and the government and industry functioned normally. Because the city was newer than places such as Hamburg and not as densely built up with wood buildings, the attacks did not cause the wanton destruction from firestorms that earlier raids had inflicted on other cities.

The increased intensity of attacks on the city in 1944, however, began to have a profound effect on life in Berlin. Nearly one quarter of the population was urged to leave to escape the bombings. By the end of the campaign, 6,000 people had been killed, and 1.5 million had been made homeless.

Words of War

"Of course the Germans began it, but we do not take the devil as our example."

—Lord Salisbury, expressing discomfort with Allied bombing of German cities

When the Battle of Berlin ended, the air forces of England and the United States were placed under the command of Eisenhower's deputy, Air Chief Marshal Arthur Tedder, who was to use them to prepare for the invasion. The RAF commander, Arthur Harris, was not happy about losing his command to the type of precision bombing he'd argued against when the Americans first joined the war. He believed that bombers were not accurate enough to pinpoint targets; therefore, he preferred to bomb the entire area where the target was located. This strategy was more effective, Harris maintained, but Tedder was put off by the fact that it also led to greater civilian casualties and destruction of property near the military objective.

In the two months leading up to D day, the Allied air forces dropped nearly 60 percent of their bombs, 20,000 tons, on France with the intent of disrupting the railways and infrastructure the Germans would need to move up reinforcements. Germany received the other 40 percent—and by June had lost 90 percent of its synthetic oil production—but the attacks Germany absorbed shrank as those directed at France grew over the summer months.

The strategic bombing was no turkey shoot, however: The Allies lost 2,000 planes and 12,000 men. Many downed airmen were picked up by the French resistance, but others were captured and sent to POW camps or, in a few instances, concentration camps (see Chapter 20).

Massing the Troops

The invasion plan was completed in the spring of 1944. The American First Army was to land on Normandy in the area of Carentan-Isigny. The Fourth Infantry Division was assigned to invade on Utah Beach, and half the First and 29th Infantry Divisions were tasked with securing Omaha Beach. The British assigned the 50th Division to Gold Beach, and the Canadian Third Division was sent to Juno Beach.

Ask the General

One vital resource Germany needed was chrome. Turkey was their main source, much to the Allies' chagrin. Like many neutrals, the Turks hoped to appease Hitler and turn a nice profit. In 1944, as the Allies began to squeeze Germany, they imposed sanctions on Turkey. Turkish leaders saw the advantage of siding with the British and Americans and ceased chrome shipments by the end of April. In August, they formally broke relations with Germany.

All the land forces were to travel across the English Channel in transports and then board amphibious landing craft that would take them onto the beaches in waves. The troops were to be supported by a naval bombardment against German defensive fortifications and an umbrella of fighter planes to repel any *Luftwaffe* challenges.

A flotilla of 6,000 ships would transport and back up the operation. The first wave scheduled to hit Omaha and Utah beaches on D day was composed of 60,000 men and 6,800 vehicles for each location. In the next two days, another 43,500 troops and 6,000 vehicles were scheduled to reach Normandy. Similar numbers of British/Canadian troops were assigned the other landing areas. All together, nearly 3 million men in 47 divisions were deployed for the invasion. Most divisions, 21, were American; the rest were primarily British and Canadian, with some French, Polish, Belgian, Italian, and Czech soldiers thrown in. Air support would be provided by 5,000 fighters.

In early May, Eisenhower decided that June 5 would be D day; however, poor weather conditions the day before forced him to postpone the invasion until the 6th. Some ships had already left port and had to be recalled. The elements were crucial in planning the campaign. Another delay would have meant putting the whole operation off until at least the 19th, the next date when the moon and tides would be optimal.

Ask the General

Operation Overlord's success depended on surprise; preparations were one of the war's most closely guarded secrets. An American officer assigned to the Army Postal Unit in Britain, Sutton Coldfield, made the mistake of discussing the U.S. First Army's objectives with a member of the adjutant general's staff. Coldfield was sentenced to one year of hard labor at the Disciplinary Barracks at Greenhaven, New York, and thrown out of the military.

Words of War

"Soldiers, sailors, and airmen of the Allied Expeditionary Force! You are about to embark upon the Great Crusade, toward which we have striven these many months. The eyes of the world are upon you. The hopes and prayers of liberty-loving people everywhere march with you...."

—Eisenhower, Order of the Day Upon the Invasion of Normandy, June 6, 1944

The Germans were also watching the weather and felt confident no invasion could take place in early June because high seas would make naval operations difficult, if not impossible, and poor visibility would keep aircraft grounded. Von Rundstedt believed the Allies needed four consecutive days of good weather, and his forecasters said this would not happen in early June. Because the Allies could read the German message in which von Rundstedt made this prediction, Eisenhower knew that he could pull off a surprise if he gave the invasion order at the beginning of the month.

Rommel agreed with von Rundstedt's assessment of the likelihood of immediate invasion and left France to celebrate his wife's birthday in Germany. Ironically, he was also going to speak to Hitler about the need for more troops and supplies to prepare for an Allied assault.

D Day

The evening of June 5, the wind was blowing at 15 to 20 knots and six-foot waves were roiling the ships, but the Royal Air Force meteorologist predicted the skies would be clear the next day. Conferring with the other military leaders, Eisenhower got conflicting advice from the army generals, including Bradley and Montgomery, who wanted to go ahead, and the air force and navy generals, who preferred to wait. After a few moments of deliberation, Eisenhower said three words that changed history: "Okay, let's go."

The BBC broadcast a coded message that instructed members of the French resistance to cut railway lines throughout the country. Nearly all of those targeted were successfully severed.

Eisenhower did not plan to go to Normandy with his troops. Instead, he went to Newbury and wished the 23,000 paratroopers luck. He knew many might die that evening, because the British air commander, Trafford Leigh-Mallory, had told him to expect casualties as high as 75 percent. However, Leigh-Mallory proved completely wrong in his estimate.

The attack began with more than 1,000 RAF bombers attacking coastal targets. This attack was followed by 18,000 paratroopers being dropped inland to capture key bridges and roads and cut German communications. The British Sixth Airborne Division suffered few casualties and succeeded in capturing bridges at the Orne River and the Caen Canal.

The Americans had a harder time. Their 101st and 82nd Airborne Divisions missed their drop zone and were scattered. Many men drowned when they landed in the water. The dispersion of the Americans helped confuse the Germans, but it also meant that troops who survived the jump (and many didn't) were isolated and easier to kill or capture. But in the end, they achieved all their objectives and played a major role in the securing of Normandy. Dying was not a danger for the dummy paratroopers—literally dolls dressed up like soldiers—that were also dropped away from Normandy to deceive the Germans as to the location of the attack.

Minesweepers cleared lanes in the English Channel for the transports. The beaches were 60 to 100 miles away when the armada of nearly 7,000 ships left from ports such as Portsmouth, Southampton, Chichester, and Falmouth. Soon that 100 miles would be covered with 59 convoys that included 4,000 landing craft, 7 battleships, 23 cruisers, and 104 destroyers.

German torpedo boats out of the port at Le Havre were the first to encounter the Allied forces, but they were quickly driven off. Having spotted the invasion fleet, German coastal batteries began firing at the approaching ships. At the same time, Allied warships began bombarding the beaches, destroying bunkers, setting off land mines, and destroying obstacles in the path of the landing parties.

Words of War

"We want this war over with. The quickest way to get it over with is to go get the bastards who started it. The quicker they get whipped, the quicker we can go home. The shortest way home is through Berlin and Tokyo. And when we get to Berlin, I am personally going to shoot that paper-hanging son-of-a-bitch Hitler."

—General Patton's speech to the Third Army on June 5, 1944, which George C. Scott recites in front of a giant American flag in the film *Patton*. The actual speech was more moving—and much more vulgar.

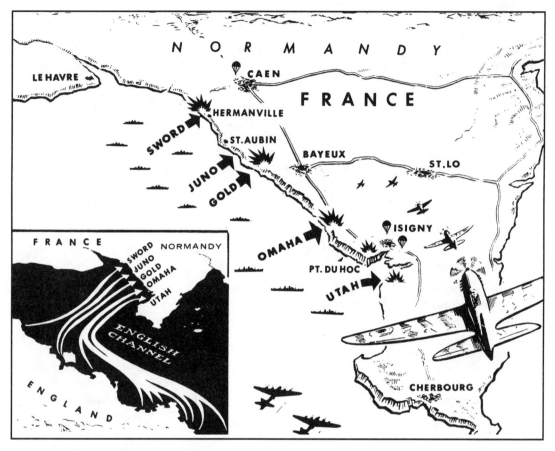

Nearly 200,000 troops stormed the beaches along the 60-mile coastline of Normandy on June 6, 1944. (UPI/Corbis-Bettman)

No Day at the Beach

The first troops hit the beaches about 6:30 a.m., with 23,000 men rushing onto Utah Beach and quickly securing the area against light opposition. Within a few hours, supplies and additional troops were also coming ashore.

Another large American force landed at about the same time on Omaha Beach. This beach was the largest landing area (six miles) and the most vulnerable: 100-foot cliffs overlooked the beach. Also, the defensive force the Americans confronted, an elite German infantry division, was far stronger and better trained than expected. Heavy clouds protected the German defenders from Allied bombers, who dropped their payloads in fields beyond the beachfront, and the poor visibility also prevented offshore guns from initially offering much support. In addition, 27 of the special amphibious Sherman tanks made for the invasion immediately sank upon debarking the transports, taking their crews to the bottom.

In writing, much of the fighting can only be described in a sterile fashion that doesn't capture the horror of combat. Omaha Beach was as hellish as any battle of the war. The first landing parties, seasick from the rough crossing, were literally ripped apart by mines, artillery, and machine-gun crossfire. Many soldiers drowned in deep water before their craft were close enough to the beach or were killed before they could stagger ashore. The beach offered no cover, the only place to go was forward, and the chances of making it across in the early stages were practically zero. Waves of landing craft continued to drift ashore, many exploded by shells or mines, and the numbers of Allied soldiers and casualties piled up.

The landing stalled, and all organization fell apart as soldiers, boats, and bodies jammed the single narrow channel engineers were able to clear among the German mines and obstacles. Trapped behind a low shelf halfway across the beach, under withering German fire from above, isolated groups and individuals with no choice but to get off the beach gradually fought their way forward and eventually took key points at each end of the beach. It took several hours, and heavy navy bombardment, to secure the beachhead, as well as a courageous effort by Army Rangers to scale the surrounding cliffs with rope ladders to take out the guns guarding the coast.

Words of War

"Two kinds of people are staying on this beach: the dead and those who are going to die. Now let's get the hell out of here!"

—Colonel George A. Taylor, Omaha Beach, D day

The British troops landed at 7:20 on Gold Beach, where they also found opposition stiffer than expected. Still, by the end of the day, they had advanced five miles beyond the coast. The Brits who landed at Sword Beach had a similar experience, as did the Canadian contingent on Juno Beach.

By 10:15 a.m., Rommel had learned that the Allies had landed and rushed back to France. Hitler had ordered him to drive the invaders back into the sea, but still had not given him the military resources he needed to do so. One of the strongest *panzer* divisions, equipped with new, state-of-the-art Tiger tanks, was sent to reinforce the defenders at Normandy, but its trip from Toulouse was repeatedly delayed through the sabotage efforts of British agents and French partisans, who turned what should have been a 3-day race to the front into a 17-day crawl.

Ask the General

Steven Spielberg's film *Saving Private Ryan* probably comes the closest of any film to capturing what it was like at Omaha Beach on D day, but even that vivid portrayal cannot fully depict the gore, the fear, the noise, or the smells of that day.

These survivors of an American landing party reached Utah Beach, near Cherbourg, by using a life raft, June 6, 1944. (National Archives Still Pictures Branch)

Another *panzer* division tried to split the British and Canadian forces by shooting through the gap between Sword and Juno. Had it succeeded in reaching the sea, it might have caused serious trouble, but the British were able to neutralize the German force before it could do any serious damage.

In the terrifying first hours making their way under fire from the stormy sea to shore, the Allies suffered surprisingly few casualties. On that first day, roughly 155,000 soldiers had come ashore and approximately 2,500 had been killed. The Americans had suffered the fewest casualties (dead or wounded) on Utah Beach, approximately 300, but also the most, 2,400, on Omaha. In the first two days, the number of men and vehicles the Allies got across the Channel was well below what was planned; still, Eisenhower was happy the deception had worked, and the Germans were unable to stop them on the beaches.

On to Paris!

Monitoring German military messages after the invasion, the British picked up the crucial piece of information that the *Luftwaffe* was dangerously short of aircraft fuel. Knowing this, war planners made Germany's synthetic oil factories their top priority for air strikes as soon as Overlord could spare the planes.

Within a week, American and British forces linked up, clearing the beachheads. With this done, the Seventh Corps, under Major General J. Lawton Collins, moved on Cherbourg and took the city on June 27. This port was meant to receive men and supplies, but it took several weeks for the damage to be sufficiently repaired. The delay was a factor in stalling the later offensive, but once the port was fully operational, it was the entry point for more than half of all American supplies sent to France.

The victory at Cherbourg was important for demoralizing the Germans, particularly after Hitler had ordered the port held at all costs. Afterward, Rommel and von Rundstedt went to see Hitler, to ask again for more troops and equipment, and to find out how he intended to win the war. Hitler's reaction was to deny the requests, sack von Rundstedt, and replace him with Field Marshal Günther Hans von Kluge. (Rommel and von Kluge would later commit suicide after the assassination plot against Hitler, discussed in Chapter 21.)

Germany Gives Britain the Old V-1, 2

Hitler held out the hope that his new rockets could alter the course of the war. In June 1944, he finally found out. On the 13th, while the invasion was in full swing, the British absorbed the first of the V-1 salvos. Four V-1 rockets were fired on England, but only one hit its London target, causing minimal property damage and killing six people. Two days later, 244 rockets were fired. Fewer than 200 made it across the English Channel; 12 were shot down

Ask the General

The combination of sabotage and carpet bombing wrecked the French infrastructure Germany needed to reinforce its troops. In contrast, the English Channel was essentially a wide-open highway for Allied transports to bring men and equipment in with virtually no opposition. This difference was one of the keys to the invasion's success. However, the destroyed roads and bridges hindered the Allies once the drive toward Germany began.

Roll Call

The total casualties suffered during the entire Normandy invasion will never be known. The nations involved had different record-keeping methods and different ideas of the duration of the battle. According to one estimate, the United States suffered a total of 135,000 casualties, including 29,000 killed; the British had 65,000 casualties, with 11,000 killed; and the Germans had 320,000 casualties, including 30,000 killed.

by anti-aircraft guns; another 8 were shot down by fighters. Seventy-five V-1s landed on London and killed 50 people.

Roll Call

Although most supplies were transported across the sea, one of the most crucial supplies, gasoline, was also delivered via PLUTO, a pipeline built under the ocean. More than 1 million gallons of fuel per day were pumped into Normandy without the Germans' knowledge.

Words of War

"This new form of attack imposed upon the people of London was a burden perhaps even heavier than the air raids of 1940 and 1941. Suspense and strain were more prolonged. Dawn brought no relief, and clouds no comfort."

—Winston Churchill

Despite the relatively low death toll, Churchill was so angered by what he considered terror attacks on civilians that he was prepared to use poison gas in retaliation. The Americans talked him out of it. Afterward, the missiles began to rain down on London and other parts of England at a rate of about 100 a day. A V-1 landed near Churchill's home at Blenham, hitting an orphanage and killing 22 children and 5 adults.

The Allies learned that the V-1s were being produced in an underground factory near Nordhausen, where the project had moved after the facilities at Peenemünde were destroyed. Slave laborers from the nearby concentration camp constructed the missiles, and 20,000 died during the project. The U.S. Air Force dropped 36,000 tons of bombs in an effort to destroy the Mittelwerke factory and lost 2,000 airmen, but it never succeeded in stopping production.

The German V-2 rockets were not introduced until September 1944. Over the next six months, 1,200 were fired at England. Unlike the V-1s, which could be shot down, the V-2s flew too high and too fast to interdict. When the German missile attacks finally ended in March 1945, they had killed more than 6,000 people, wounded thousands more, and damaged 1 million buildings. Despite the death and destruction the rockets caused, the results were far short of Hitler's expectations and had little impact on the course of the war.

The Return of de Gaulle

The Allied operation was again complicated by inclement weather, which wreaked havoc on the troops and ships at sea for three days in mid-June. The American Mulberry was destroyed, the British one was damaged, and many vessels were sunk. Another threat to the invasion force was the German torpedo boats that were attacking ships crossing the Channel. The overwhelming superiority of the Allied fleet and its air support helped to quickly eliminate this danger. In one raid on June 14, RAF bombers attacked the torpedo-boat pens at Le Havre and put 15 of 16 boats out of commission.

Three days later, Charles de Gaulle, fresh from the Free French Forces' successful capture of the Italian island of Elba, went to Normandy for his first visit to France in four years. Earlier, on June 2, de Gaulle had declared the Committee of National Liberation to be the provisional government of France. Roosevelt was angered by the unilateral action, but he agreed to recognize the new authority when de Gaulle came to Washington that July.

War Lore

Though generals such as Eisenhower, Bradley, and Patton, reaped much of the glory for the invasion, none of them landed with the troops at Normandy. The only general officer in the first wave on the beaches was a 57-year-old brigadier general named Theodore Roosevelt, Jr. When his men landed a mile south of their assigned place on Utah Beach, he said, "We're going to have to start the war from here." He died of a heart attack on July 13, 1944, and was posthumously awarded the Congressional Medal of Honor. He lies buried at the Omaha Beach cemetery next to his brother Quentin, who was a fighter pilot killed on the western front in 1918.

The Allies also failed to capture one of their major objectives, the city of Caen, where the Germans had a communications center and through which reinforcements were expected to pass. Rommel had wanted to attack the American bridgehead, but he was ordered by Hitler to engage the British at Caen instead. Thus, instead of overrunning Caen on D day, the Allied advance became immediately bogged down in a battle that would last for two months and exacerbate the already tense relationship between General Montgomery, who was leading the attack, and the Americans.

By the end of June, the Allies had put roughly 1,000,000 men, 177,000 vehicles, and 500,000 tons of supplies ashore in France. And more of everything was on its way. The Germans, meanwhile, continued to believe that Normandy was a diversion, and that the major invasion was still to come from Calais. Hitler therefore kept forces that could have reinforced Rommel's troops sitting in anticipation of an attack that would never come. Worse yet, from the German point of view, Allied intelligence knew from its intercepts that this was what the Germans were thinking.

Words of War

"Compared to war, all other forms of human endeavor shrink to insignificance. God, how I love it."
—Patton, August 1944

Looking back, of course, D day is clearly a key, if not *the* key moment in the war. In June 1944, however, it is important to remember that battles were raging not just in Normandy but on five other fronts. The Russians launched their "Bagration" offensive against the retreating German forces on the eastern front, the Allies were gradually pounding their way north through the German defense in Italy, and American and British forces were fighting the Japanese in New Guinea, Burma, and China. The blood of thousands of men from even more nations was being spilled in a war that continued to suck in even more combatants and showed no signs of ending soon.

The Least You Need to Know

➤ Hitler's scientists were developing secret weapons that he expected to change the course of the war; however, the snorkel submarine, jet aircraft, and V–1 and V–2 rockets made little difference in the outcome.

➤ The Germans knew the Allies planned to invade, but they didn't know exactly where or when. Allied deceptions helped fool them.

➤ Rommel tried to build a defensive wall against a cross-Channel invasion, but was hindered by Hitler's unwillingness to give him the troops he needed.

➤ The Allies mounted a series of bombing raids on Berlin that damaged the city and forced the evacuation of a quarter of the population.

➤ The largest amphibious assault in history was launched on D day, June 6, 1944. The Allied force met light resistance on three of the four beaches, but the Americans on Omaha Beach suffered heavy casualties.

For You the War Is Over

Millions of soldiers fought in World War II, and hundreds of thousands were captured during various battles. Some prisoners were summarily executed, but most were sent to prisoner of war (POW) camps. The first American POW in Germany in World War II was captured on April 14, 1942. A total of approximately 93,941 U.S. Army and Air Corps personnel were POWs in more than 50 permanent camps in the European and Mediterranean theaters. Almost 99 percent survived. Of the 1,121 who died, approximately 6 percent were in the little-known camp of Berga, discussed later in this chapter.

It Wasn't *Hogan's Heroes*

The image many of us have of German POW camps, or *Stalags*, comes from the movies, where evil Germans match wits with clever Allies trying to escape, or from the old TV show, *Hogan's Heroes*, in which the prisoners chose not to escape so they could run an espionage ring under the noses of the incompetent Nazi commandant, Colonel Klink, and the bumbling guard, Sergeant Schultz. In truth, most POW camps were run by competent Germans who maintained tight control over prisoner behavior. Generally, the Germans treated the soldiers with a measure of respect, though guards were ruthless in some cases. Many POWs were murdered, but most suffered because of the conditions in the camps: a lack of food, medicine, and hygiene.

War Lore

Two of the actors in *Hogan's Heroes* had real-life war experiences that were very different from their on-screen portrayals. Sergeant Schultz was played by John Banner, an Austrian Jew who fled the country in 1938 after the *Anschluss*. During the war, he posed for U.S. Army recruiting posters. Robert Clary, the French POW LeBeau in the show, spent three years in a concentration camp. For the last several years, he has given lectures and spoken to school groups about the Holocaust.

GI Jargon

The Germans kept most enlisted men in POW camps called **Stalags**, short for *Stammlager*, which roughly translated means "common stock." A **Stalag Luft** (*Luft* meaning air) was for airmen. **Dulag** and **Dulag Luft** camps (abbreviations of *Durchgangs Lager* or entrance camp) were transit stations. An **Oflag** (short for *Offizier Lager* or officers camp) was a permanent camp for officers. One reason most POWs were treated relatively well is that the camps were run by soldiers rather than the SS, which controlled the concentration camps.

The mistreatment of captured soldiers should have come as no surprise to the U.S. government given what they knew of Nazi atrocities committed against civilians. As the U.S. Counsel at Nuremberg, Thomas Dodd, explained, "The transition from the mistreatment of political opponents, of racial and religious groups, to the abuse and the killing of prisoners of war in violation of the rules of warfare was not difficult for the members of the indicted organizations." He was referring to the Nazi Party, which authorized the lynching of Allied airmen by civilians, the military units of the SS, which executed POWs on every battlefield, and the Gestapo and the SD, which carried out Hitler's October 1942 "commando order" to summarily execute Allied commandos and paratroopers.

Soviet prisoners were the most ruthlessly treated. The Germans captured more than 5 million Soviet troops. As mentioned in Chapter 9, Hitler issued the Commissar Order in 1941, which called for the elimination of political representatives and commissars whom the *Führer* considered the "driving forces of Bolshevism."

That July, all Jewish POWs from the eastern front were ordered killed. Many Soviet prisoners were sent to concentration camps. For example, in 1941, 18,000 Soviet POWs were murdered at Sachsenhausen; in 1942, 4,000 Jewish Soviet POWs were sent to Majdanek, only a few survived; and from May 1, 1940, to December 1, 1943, 20,000 Russian POWs were murdered at Auschwitz. All together, an estimated 3,300,000 million Soviets died in Nazi captivity, most as a result of lack of food and adequate shelter, but hundreds of thousands were executed.

"H" Is for Hebrew

Hitler never ordered the murder of Jewish POWs from Britain, France, or the United States. Although Nazi propaganda claimed the Allies did not care about Jews, the Nazis realized those nations would care very much if Jews from their armies became victims. Moreover, the Nazis were concerned that the 370,000 German POWs would be mistreated if the Western nations learned Jewish prisoners were being abused.

American Jewish soldiers, nevertheless, risked mistreatment because of their religion and the ultimate threat of being deported to a concentration camp. The U.S. military increased the probability of captured Jews being identified by stamping their dog tags with an *H* for Hebrew. This stamping was ostensibly done so the correct chaplain could be called if a soldier was wounded or killed. The consequence of this practice was to unnecessarily place at risk 600,000 American Jewish soldiers.

One POW camp where the possibility of deportation to a concentration camp nearly became a reality was in Stalag Luft I, an air force officer camp in Barth, near the Black Sea. After the massive Allied bombing of Dresden in early 1945, Jews in the camp were segregated by the Nazis. Some Jews threw away their dog tags or tried to hide their identity, but the Germans had their own methods of distinguishing prisoners, capriciously choosing those who looked Jewish or whose names sounded Jewish. The absurdity of their actions was clear when the Germans posted a list of names of the Jewish officers in each barracks that included Kellys and O'Briens.

Roll Call

Approximately 600,000 Jews served in the United States armed forces in World War II. More than 35,000 were killed, wounded, captured, or missing. Approximately 8,000 died in combat.

Ask the General

Even today, soldiers have their religion stamped on their dog tags. Technically, it is voluntary, but they are rarely told they have a choice. Instead of an *H*, soldiers now have *Jewish* printed on the tags. This stamping again was potentially dangerous during the Gulf War because of Saddam Hussein's attitude toward Jews. No Jewish soldiers were taken prisoner; however, Bob Simon of CBS, a Jewish journalist, was held by the Iraqis and was very scared of what might be done to him. He suffered some abuse, but he was ultimately released.

While in the camp, the Jews were not mistreated. They even were permitted to conduct religious services, which they did at least initially "to piss the Nazis off," according to a former POW. In the end, the Jews were never transferred from the POW camp, though the deportation order probably would have been carried out if the Germans had won the Battle of the Bulge.

The Soldiers of Berga

During the Battle of the Bulge in December 1944, more than 4,000 American GIs were captured and imprisoned at Stalag IX-B at Bad Orb, approximately 30 miles northwest of Frankfurt-on-Main. One day the commandant ordered all Jews to report to a separate barracks. The non-Jews told their Jewish comrades not to come forward. The commandant then said the Jews would have until six the next morning to identify themselves. The prisoners were told, moreover, that any Jews in the barracks after 24 hours would be shot, as would anyone trying to hide or protect them.

American Jewish soldiers had to decide what to do. All had gone into battle with dog tags bearing an H for Hebrew. Some had disposed of their IDs when they were captured; others decided to do so after the commandant's threat. Approximately 130 Jews ultimately came forward. They were segregated and placed in a special barracks. Some 50 noncommissioned officers from the group were taken out of the camp, along with the non-Jewish NCOs.

The Germans had a quota of 350 for a special detail. All the remaining Jews were taken, along with those they thought were Jewish, prisoners considered troublemakers, and others chosen at random. This group left Bad Orb on February 8. They were placed in trains under conditions similar to those faced by European Jews deported to concentration camps. Five days later, the POWs arrived in Berga, a quaint German town of 7,000 people on the Elster River, whose concentration and labor camps appear on few World War II maps.

Conditions in Stalag IX-B were the worst of any POW camp, but they were recalled fondly by the Americans transferred to Berga, who discovered the main purpose for their imprisonment was to serve as slave laborers. Each day, the men trudged approximately two miles through the snow to a mountainside in which 17 mine shafts were dug 100 feet apart. There, under the direction of brutal civilian overseers, the Americans were required to help the Nazis build an underground armament factory.

The men worked in shafts as deep as 150 feet that were so dusty it was impossible to see more than a few feet. The Germans would blast the slate loose with dynamite, and then, before the dust settled, the prisoners would go down to break up the rock so that it could be shoveled into mining cars.

On April 4, 1945, the commandant received an order to evacuate Berga. This was but the end of one chapter of the Americans' ordeal. The human skeletons who had survived found no cause to rejoice in this flight from hell. They were leaving friends behind and returning to the unknown. Fewer than 300 men survived the 50 days they had spent in Berga. Over the next two-and-a-half weeks, before the survivors were liberated, at least 36 more GIs died on a march to avoid the approaching Allied armies.

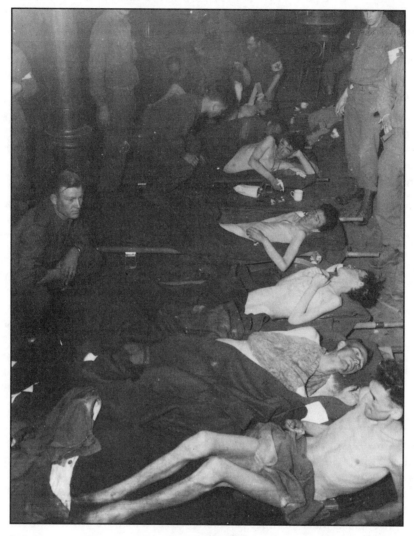

Lying on stretchers are some of the 63 emaciated American POWs liberated in Fuchsmuehl, Germany. (National Archives Still Pictures Branch)

The fatality rate in Berga, including the march, was the highest of any camp where American POWs were held in Europe—nearly 20 percent—and the 70 to 73 men who were killed represented approximately 6 percent of all Americans who perished as POWs in Europe during World War II. The U.S. government never publicly acknowledged that the POWs in Berga were mistreated. One survivor was told he should go to a psychiatrist. Officials at the VA told him he had made up the whole story.

The Horrors of Buchenwald

In April 1945, at the request of General Eisenhower, a congressional committee visited Buchenwald, Nordhausen, and Dachau. They submitted a detailed report of the shocking conditions. "In the first place," the report noted, "the concentration camps for political prisoners must not be confused with prisoner-of-war camps. No prisoners of war are confined in any of these political prisoner camps, and there is no relationship whatever between a concentration camp for political prisoners and a camp for prisoners of war."

There were indeed distinctions between the types of camps, but many POWs were sent to concentration camps—including those visited by the committee—where the prisoners were tortured and killed, and the United States government knew it. Some of the concentration camps where Allied prisoners were sent included Dachau, Sachsenhausen, Flossenbürg, Buchenwald, and Mauthausen.

Six months before the congressional delegation arrived, 168 Allied airmen, including 82 Americans, spent nine weeks in Buchenwald. Most were shot down over France during the summer of 1944, taken in by the resistance, and eventually betrayed.

The Allied airmen captured around Paris were taken to Fresnes Prison in the city, where they were incarcerated with other "criminals." Most of the POWs were not severely mistreated in prison, though some were beaten or placed in solitary confinement. Around midnight on August 15, 1944, all the prisoners in Fresnes were put in old 40-and-8 boxcars (so named because they were designed for 40 men or 8 horses) originally used in World War I to carry troops to the front. The trains carried 1,650 prisoners, including the POWs. About 850 of the passengers were women who were sent to Ravensbrück; some eventually came to Buchenwald as "volunteers" for the brothel. The rest arrived at Buchenwald around noon on August 20, 1944. Fewer than 300 would go home to France.

When the prisoners left the train, they walked through the camp gate and saw naked people coming out of the building to which they were being led. The men were then stripped, and their clothes and personal effects were taken away. The men were given about a two-minute shower. The Germans then issued each man a thin shirt and light denim pants, which were taken from Jewish prisoners who had been exterminated. The shirt had a red triangle with the letter *A* over their hearts to signify they were political prisoners. A black number was stenciled on a piece of white tape stuck to their pants. The POWs' shoes were not returned.

Initially, the men were forced to sleep outside in a yard paved with large granite stones. At first, the weather was relatively warm, but it later rained for nine straight days. This meant the men had to sleep in wet clothes on the damp ground. It was freezing, but the POWs had only one blanket for every five men. They slept belly to butt to keep warm. One guy would say "turn over," and everyone would reverse positions. Because they had no shoes, many men cut their feet, which then became infected. During the last week, it snowed, and the temperature dropped to 5 or 10 degrees above zero. Sometimes the men had to stand outdoors for up to seven hours, barefoot, at attention, while the entire camp was counted during the roll calls.

After about two weeks, the soldiers were moved to an old horse barn that served as a barracks. It had been formerly occupied by 500 gypsy children, ages 2 to 12, who had been exterminated. The barracks had no mattresses, only one thin blanket full of vermin. They also had no heat. Breakfast consisted of about one-third loaf of black bread and one-twentieth of a pound of margarine issued at 5 a.m. For lunch, each man was given one liter of soup made of dehydrated vegetables that were always wormy. The prisoners called this soup the "green death."

Some POWs were beaten, but by and large they were not physically abused by the guards. Many POWs' lives were undoubtedly saved because they managed to avoid working. The Germans wanted the POWs to work breaking up stones in the quarry. They threatened to take the POWs' rations away and later to execute them. But the Allies refused to work, and the Germans never carried out their threats.

The SS may have been reluctant to kill prisoners who were technically the responsibility of the army, but the POWs had no way of knowing this. Most had doubts they would ever get out of Buchenwald. No one knew where they were, and the Germans had already murdered 37 British secret agents who were held at Buchenwald.

The principal threats to the POWs were malnutrition and disease. Allied prisoners had to mingle with sick political prisoners, some of whom had been in the camp for years. Not surprisingly, at least 30 men were sick, the majority with pneumonia and pleurisy. Most of the other men had dysentery. They all lost 10 to 60 pounds.

Ask the General

Although most POWs avoided the hospital, they could not escape Nazi experimentation. None of the men know why, but they all received an inoculation of some "green stuff" in the left breast. The same needle was used until it broke off. At first the POWs thought the shots were for TB, but they began to have doubts when they learned about other experiments. The only immediate reaction was for the area where they were injected to turn black and blue, though some men now say their left breasts became larger afterward.

Two Allied soldiers died in Buchenwald, one British and one American. RAF officer Philip Hemmens died first, around September 14, of rheumatic fever. He had received practically no medical attention for seven days before he was put in the hospital. The next day he died. The American, Lieutenant Levitt Beck, died of pneumonia, perhaps contracted during the first couple of weeks when the soldiers slept outside in the rain.

The senior Allied officer, Phil Lamason, worked with two British spies, Yeo-Thomas and Christopher Burney, and the Communist Underground Committee to smuggle out

Ask the General

When the POWs from Buchenwald arrived at Sagan, Luft III on October 21, 1944, they were surprised to find the Allied officers there took great interest in their experiences. Earlier, 50 of the Sagan prisoners had been murdered following their "Great Escape." This incident, combined with the revelations about the concentration camps, convinced the senior Allied officers that they had to be prepared for anything.

a list of the Allied prisoners through a trusted Russian prisoner who worked at a nearby airfield. The Russian told a *Luftwaffe* officer that Allied airmen were at Buchenwald. Not long afterward, two officers from the *Luftwaffe* came to interrogate the POWs. They said they'd heard a rumor that the Allies were there and had come to verify it. They said that the Allies' transfer to the concentration camp was "all a mistake" and that they had lost track of the POWs after they left Paris.

On October 19, at 4:00 p.m., the soldiers were removed from Buchenwald and taken to the POW camp for airmen at Sagan, Luft III. The POWs would never forget the men who died or what they had seen during their stay in Buchenwald. The fact that so few men died was probably because the soldiers were young and in good shape. Nevertheless, most felt they barely survived two months in a camp where some inmates lived, incredibly, for years. Still, they did not realize how lucky they had been until nearly 40 years after the war. Then they learned their execution was scheduled for October 26. Lamason was the only one who knew.

Murder at Mauthausen

Shortly after the Slovak uprising in August 1944, the Czech Intelligence Service in London learned several British and American flyers recently liberated from German POW camps in Slovakia were at Banska Bystrica and Tri Duby. This area was where a group of Czech partisans were defending a liberated area against enemy troops. The information was forwarded to the Office of Strategic Services (the OSS was the forerunner of the CIA) in London. A decision was made to send teams of agents into Slovakia to evacuate downed airmen, provide supplies to the partisans, and gather intelligence. These teams were to be the first OSS units to operate in central Europe.

Words of War

"I heard rumors that an American jeep and half-tract were at the entrance, and, staggering through the frenzied crowd, I found Sgt. Albert Kosiek. I could only say, 'God bless America,' and hold out my dog tags with a quavering hand."

—Lieutenant Jack Taylor

The OSS arranged for the 15th Air Force to send an evacuation flight on September 17, 1944. Two B-17s with fighter cover landed at a secret air base established at Tri Duby. They stayed on the ground for less than an hour, picking up 17 flyers and dropping two teams of OSS agents.

The operation was a failure. Between November 6 and December 26, 1944, 15 agents were captured along with two American civilians, two British officers and one private, and a Czech officer who had joined the group. They were all taken to Mauthausen. During the next few days, the British and American POWs were tortured. When the Germans were satisfied they had elicited all the information they could, the POWs were shot.

War Lore

Despite the covert nature of the operation, the OSS gave Associated Press correspondent Joseph Morton permission to accompany one of the teams and report on the evacuation of flyers. He sent a message to AP saying he was off to cover the "greatest story of his life." When he arrived in Slovakia, Morton immediately sent back a story with the plane that had carried him there, but the dispatch was snatched up by censors. He was never heard from again. Months later, the OSS learned that Morton had been captured with a group of its agents and murdered at Mauthausen. Morton was the only American reporter murdered in a Nazi death camp.

Meanwhile, the need to obtain information from Austria prompted the OSS to send in a new team of agents. The mission, code-named Dupont, was led by Lieutenant Jack Taylor, an experienced agent who had one of the most outstanding records in the European theater. Once again, the operation did not go as planned. Taylor was arrested on December 1, 1944, and ultimately sent to Mauthausen.

He was assigned to help build a new crematorium. "We dawdled at our work to delay completion of the crematorium," Taylor said, "because we knew that the number of executions would double when cremation facilities were available." One morning, two SS officers informed the *Kapo* overseeing the project that it had to be finished and ready for operation on the following day or the workers would be the first occupants of the new ovens. "Needless to say," recalled Taylor, "we finished the job in the allotted time."

GI Jargon

A *Kapo* is a prisoner in charge of a group of inmates in a Nazi concentration camp.

Taylor's next job was carrying large soup kettles (110 pounds each) about one-half mile within the outer cordon of guard posts and barbed wire to the neighboring Hungarian camp. It was populated by nearly 20,000 Jews, mostly Hungarians, who had been marched to Mauthausen.

Taylor's last job was to dig up the space next to the barracks and plant a garden. By then he was so sick with dysentery and fever he could hardly walk to the dispensary. He had lost more than 50 pounds.

When the Allies finally overran Mauthausen, the liberators wanted to send Taylor to a hospital, but he insisted that valuable testimony and documents were at Mauthausen, and he wanted to return for it. One thing he learned was that he was supposed to be executed on April 28, 1945, but "a friendly Czech" had destroyed the paperwork. Taylor proved to be a key witness in the subsequent trial of Nazis responsible for Mauthausen.

Massacre at Malmédy

Combat during World War II was horrible enough, but soldiers sometimes went to extremes that resulted in mass murder. Chapter 6 mentioned the Soviet massacre of Polish officers in the Katyn Forest. Another such atrocity occurred on the second day of the Battle of the Bulge, December 17, 1944, when SS troops herded a group of Americans from the 285th Field Artillery Observation Battalion into a field near the Belgian town of Malmédy. The POWs were lined up, and then the Germans suddenly opened fire on them.

As the German soldiers and tanks left the area, they shot Americans who showed signs of life and pumped more bullets into those already dead. The exact number killed was never determined with certainty, but it was between 90 and 130. Several men somehow escaped, but some were found hiding in a nearby cafe. The Germans set the building on fire and then shot the men as they ran out. A handful of other GIs eluded the Germans and got out the word that the Germans were shooting POWs. News of the atrocity was widely reported and helped stimulate the Allies to fight even harder.

The Great Escape

Thousands of Allied airmen who were captured during the war were sent to Stalag Luft III in Sagan, about 100 miles southeast of Berlin in what is now the Polish town of Zagan. Many of the those imprisoned in March 1942 to 1944 had escaped from other camps, and a group of them formed a committee to plan attempts from Sagan.

It was the duty of captured prisoners to try to escape. In most cases, however, it didn't make sense to risk being recaptured or shot. The POW camps were located far from Allied lines (until the very end of the war), so it was highly unlikely an escapee could make his way across miles and miles of enemy territory to safety. Also, after weeks, months, or even years of malnutrition and disease in the camps, many prisoners would not have been physically able to make a run for it. The men in Sagan, however, were in good shape and determined to escape. They figured that, at worst, they would force the Germans to divert scarce resources to pursuing them even if they didn't make it to freedom.

War Lore

The 1963 film *The Great Escape* was an accurate portrayal of the actual events, though most of the characters, including Steve McQueen's Cooler King, were composites. One of the most memorable scenes, when McQueen tries to escape by jumping a motorcycle over a barbed-wire fence, was a Hollywood invention. The film was based on a book by former POW Paul Brickhill and written by James Clavell, better known for his novel *Shogun*. Clavell was in a Japanese POW camp during World War II, and his novel based on that experience was made into the movie *King Rat*. You can find an excellent Web site on the Great Escape at http://www.foobar.co.uk/~elsham/gt_esc.html.

The leader of the group was Roger Bushell, who was shot down in May 1940, during the Battle of France. Bushell put together a group of tailors, forgers, and engineers with the goal of getting 250 men out of the camp. The team was remarkably resourceful in making uniforms, compasses, fake IDs, and other materials needed to escape and avoid capture.

Wally Floody, the "Tunnel King," was a mining engineer before the war and was the man responsible for the construction of three tunnels, which were named Tom, Dick, and Harry. The entrances to the first two tunnels were hidden under stoves; the third was hidden under a drain in the shower room. Digging the tunnels under the noses of the Germans was no easy feat. Prisoners filled long thin bags with sand and carried them in their pants while they walked outside, sprinkling the sand as they went. The insides of the tunnels were held together by 4,000 bed boards.

When the Germans suddenly cleared the trees outside the gate and built a new compound, the POWs had to abandon Dick, but they used the tunnel for storage. In the summer of 1943, just before the tunnel was completed, the Germans discovered and destroyed Tom.

All efforts were then focused on "Harry," which was 28 feet below the ground and extended 336 feet from the barracks, and out beyond the camp fence. The POWs discovered, however, that it had not gone as far as they intended, and stopped short of the forest, which meant they'd have to make a run for the trees in the open.

On March 24, 1944, 200 men prepared to go into the tunnel. The men who spoke German, the experienced escape artists, and those who'd worked the most on the

project were given forged documents and civilian clothes and allowed to be the first ones into the tunnel. When the men began to crawl out, problems arose, and the operation went more slowly than planned. After 76 men had escaped, the next one in line was waiting for the all clear signal when a German guard strolled right past the tunnel exit. Thinking he'd gotten the signal to come out, the POW emerged and was immediately spotted. The barracks were quickly raided, and the tunnel destroyed.

A nationwide alert was issued, and Hitler personally ordered that all of the men who were recaptured be shot. He later amended the decree and said more than half should be killed. The POWs were soon caught and driven to remote locations where they were shot, according to the reports, "while trying to escape."

In all, 50 men, including Bushell, were murdered by the Gestapo. Another 17 were taken back to Sagan, 4 were sent to Sachsenhausen, and 2 to Colditz Castle. Only 3 men made it to safety. Two Norwegians, Per Bergstrand and Jens Muller, reached England via Sweden, and Dutchman Bram van der Stok made it to England through Spain.

Special Treatment

The most dangerous time for any soldier was immediately following their capture, particularly after Hitler began to encourage the lynching of airmen and other summary executions of the enemy. The fate of a GI often depended on who captured him and how disciplined they were. Generally, when prisoners were taken by the regular German military, they were not mistreated. If the Gestapo got hold of them, however, they could be killed or sent to a concentration camp.

Angered by the death and destruction caused by Allied bombers, Hitler declared in May 1944 that enemy airmen who were shot down should be executed without court martial if they had attacked downed German airmen, public-transport trains, or civilians. Under the decree, essentially everyone in the Allied air forces became a *Terrorflieger* (terror flyer). German civilians were also encouraged to lynch captured pilots. Those airmen who were turned over to the authorities were subject to "special treatment" at the hands of the SD (the intelligence service of the SS)—that is, they were killed. Hitler's order was enforced haphazardly. Nazi fanatics and local police carried out sporadic lynchings, but the *Luftwaffe* did not pass the order down the chain of command.

Prisoners in the Pacific

Approximately 26,000 Americans became POWs in the Pacific theater. Roughly 40 percent died in captivity. As described in Chapter 12, as many as 5,200 Americans died on the Bataan Death March in the Philippines, and hundreds more died in the POW camp the survivors were sent to. Other prisoners were executed brutally with bayonets or beheaded.

This picture, captured from the Japanese, shows American prisoners using improvised litters to carry those of their comrades who, from the lack of food or water on the march from Bataan, fell along the road, May 1942. (National Archives Still Pictures Branch)

German POWs in the United States

While Americans were in many cases being starved, beaten, and worked to death in German POW camps, Germans imprisoned in the United States probably felt more like they were in summer camp. Most of them, for example, were much better fed than they had been under war conditions. Some were allowed to travel, even getting tours of places like George Washington's home at Mount Vernon and the colonial town of Williamsburg, Virginia. Other prisoners were allowed to study English or work in private industry. The United States maintained 155 POW camps in 47 states—every state except Montana. During the war, nearly 700,000 Germans spent some time in one of these camps.

War Lore

On August 9, 1945, Kurt Rossmeisl escaped from Camp Butner in North Carolina. He managed to get to Chicago and evaded capture for 14 years. After living under an assumed name and making a life for himself, he decided one day to turn himself in to the FBI.

The Ones Left Behind

One of the worst aspects of captivity was that the POWs knew their families were suffering. The military often had no idea where they were and, worse, would sometimes provide incorrect information to families about the fate of their loved ones.

Mrs. Robert Chalot, for example, received a letter on March 30, 1944, from the Eighth Fighter Command saying that her son John had died. Four months later, the War Department informed her that her son was missing. On December 3, almost nine months after being told her son was dead, Mrs. Chalot received a telegram saying he was a POW, but that was not the end of the correspondence. A chaplain wrote on March 6, 1945, almost exactly a year after he had first been reported missing, reaffirming that John was a POW and assuring her that he'd been treated well. No official ever told the Chalots that their son had been in Buchenwald.

The American Red Cross, meanwhile, adopted the attitude that it should not do anything to upset families; therefore, its *Prisoner of War Bulletin* was filled with glowing reports of POW camps, letters from cheerful prisoners, and photos of happy Americans. The U.S. government took a similar line and did not allow war correspondents to report on the treatment of POWs until very late in the war, usually after they were liberated.

Toward the end of the war, the United States formally denounced the Germans' "deliberate neglect and shocking treatment" of American POWs and vowed that the perpetrators of these "heinous crimes will be brought to justice." In reporting this, the *New York Times* correspondent said the State and War Departments "had taken off the kid gloves in dealing with a topic heretofore handled with extreme delicacy."

Though many American POWs suffered terribly, and most were caught through no fault of their own, they felt ashamed when they returned home. There was a largely unspoken feeling that prisoners were cowards who had been caught fleeing battle, though this was very rarely the case. Thus, the POWs shared with Holocaust survivors the desire to put their war experiences behind them and get on with their lives. Those who survived concentration camps such as Berga, Buchenwald, and Mauthausen were usually reluctant to discuss their tribulations because they found no one believed them.

War Lore

Writer Kurt Vonnegut, Jr. was a POW in Dresden at the time of the bombing. The title of his book *Slaughterhouse Five* comes from the cellar under a cattle slaughterhouse where he was held.

Though many ex-POWs participated in various military unit reunions, most of the men who lived through the worst experiences, slave labor or concentration camps, did not even tell their families what had happened for 40 or more years. Some still carry physical scars from their ordeals, and all of them bear psychological scars from what they saw, did, and had done to them.

The Least You Need to Know

➤ Nearly 100,000 Americans were held prisoner in Europe. Most were treated reasonably well, and fewer than 1,200 died in captivity.

➤ Jewish soldiers could be identified by the *H* on their dog tags. They were singled out in only a handful of cases. In at least two POW camps, Jews were segregated from other prisoners.

➤ One group of Jewish soldiers was sent from a POW camp to a slave labor camp at Berga that had the highest fatality rate of any camp where Americans were held in Europe.

➤ In several instances, soldiers were sent to concentration camps such as Flossenbürg and Mauthausen. The largest number was probably sent to Buchenwald, but 166 out of 168 sent at one time survived and were transferred to a POW camp.

➤ Nearly 400,000 Germans were in POW camps in the United States. They were treated very well.

➤ Families faced terrible strains wondering what happened to their loved ones. The Allied governments concealed what they knew about the mistreatment of POWs, and most survivors did not want to talk about their experiences when they returned home.

Chapter 21

Hitler Cheats Death

In This Chapter

➤ The Allies achieve a breakthrough in France

➤ A bomb blows up on Hitler's opponents

➤ Roosevelt is reelected

➤ An epic Battle of the Bulge

➤ The Axis begins to crumble

The Red Army kept marching west after driving the Germans out of Russia and was steadily making its way across the conquered lands of Europe with an eye toward Berlin. By the end of 1944, the only question was whether it would beat the British and Americans to the prize.

The Mark of Caen

The beachheads at Normandy were secured during June 1944, but Allied efforts to break out into the French interior were stymied by stiff German resistance. The initial focus of the fighting inland was Caen, where a series of offensives led by Montgomery's troops failed. By D+43 (the 43rd day after the invasion), the Allies had only reached the point they were expected to have captured on D+17.

By this time, the Americans had grown increasingly impatient with the British general. Montgomery was a cult hero at home, largely on the strength of his early victories in Africa when Britain was taking it on the chin everywhere else. From the introduction of American troops in the theater and their initially poor performance, he had developed a low opinion of their fighting ability and the leadership of their generals. His imperious personality, meanwhile, rubbed Americans the wrong way.

The relationship began to seriously sour during the fighting in Italy when Montgomery's caution, viewed by some as timidity and by others as petulance over not being given a greater role in Operation Overlord, resulted in his failure to capitalize on opportunities to make greater advances in Italy. The situation only got worse as disagreements over strategy increased during the push toward Berlin.

Words of War

"The troops are everywhere fighting heroically, but the unequal struggle is approaching its end."

—Field Marshal Rommel in a letter to Hitler pleading for more troops

Ask the General

One of the many unfortunate aspects of every war is casualties caused by "friendly fire," that is, when soldiers accidentally kill their own men. Numerous incidents occurred during World War II, including an instance where American bombers did not hear that a planned attack near St.-Lo had been postponed and dropped 700 tons of bombs on their own troops.

In the early weeks of the invasion, however, Montgomery was focused on Caen and launched a new offensive in July. The main effect was to allow American forces to take advantage of German armor being locked in battle with Monty and make a break toward Brittany with the intention of encircling the Germans in Normandy.

General Omar Bradley commanded the American First Army fighting the "battle of the hedgerows" (natural fortifications composed of earth, roots, and hedge). Using these obstacles for defense, and benefiting from rains that prevented the Allies from supporting the attack with air cover, the Germans fought ferociously, inflicting 40,000 casualties on Bradley's troops by the time the Americans captured the town of St.-Lo. The Americans were now in position to move into Brittany to the west and to turn east and head for Paris.

Montgomery's troops finally penetrated Caen in the middle of July after massive bombing of the German defenders left many shell-shocked. He made it only another six miles, however, before again being stopped on the road to Falaise.

On July 17, 1944, in the midst of the battle, Rommel was disabled when his staff car was strafed by a British fighter and forced into a ditch. The general suffered a concussion and was sent to the hospital. While he recuperated, Kluge, who'd taken over for von Rundstedt, was also given Rommel's command.

Meanwhile, in Britain, the prospect of more German missiles raining down prompted a mass evacuation from London. More than 2,700 bombs had fallen on Britain, and they had killed about one person per bomb. By the date of Rommel's accident, more than half a million civilians had left the capital, and a similar number would leave in the coming weeks.

American howitzers shell German forces retreating near Carentan, France, July 11, 1944. (National Archives Still Pictures Branch)

The Assassins' Plot Explodes

After the Allied invasion, however, and the collapse of the eastern front, a handful of military officers felt the time was right to spare Germany total defeat and stage a coup. On July 16, 1944, while the battle for Caen raged, Colonel Caesar von Hofacker met with Colonel Claus von Stauffenberg and decided to go forward with a plan they'd hatched to assassinate Hitler.

Four days later, von Stauffenberg attended a meeting with Hitler in his Rastenburg headquarters. The colonel left his briefcase under the table and left. At 12:42 p.m., as Hitler and his generals leaned over the table studying maps, a bomb exploded. Von Stauffenberg saw the room blow up and believed Hitler was dead. He rushed to the airport and flew back to Berlin.

War Lore

In July 1998, newly released British documents showed that British agents closely monitored Hitler's diet, activities, and surroundings with the intention of assassinating him. SOE agents came up with a variety of ideas for killing Hitler, including shooting him during his daily morning walk at Berchtesgaden, blowing up his train *Amerika*, or injecting him with a biological agent such as anthrax with a fake fountain pen. The plots apparently began around the time of the Normandy invasion and remained under active consideration until April 1945, when the project was canceled just before Hitler committed suicide.

When von Stauffenberg got to Berlin four hours later, he discovered that four men had died in the explosion, but Hitler wasn't one of them. He had escaped with only minor bruises, probably because another general had inadvertently kicked the briefcase further away from the *Führer*. Von Stauffenberg gambled anyway on implementing the operation.

One of the conspirators, General von Hase, the Berlin commander, ordered troops to surround the government offices. Before carrying out the order, however, Major Otto Ernst Remer received a call from Goebbels telling him the *Führer* was still alive. Remer talked to Hitler and declared his continued loyalty, essentially cutting off the narrow limb the conspirators were clinging to. For this, Hitler later awarded Remer the Knight's Cross.

Over the next several months Hitler tracked down all the conspirators, would-be conspirators, and suspected conspirators and had them executed. The same day as the assassination attempt, von Stauffenberg was shot. Many of the plotters committed suicide before they were caught or executed.

Probably the greatest impact the attempted assassination had on the war was Germany's loss of Rommel to lead its defense. Although Rommel was at home recovering from the wounds he suffered in France, Hitler was convinced the general had been a part of the plot against him and sent two generals to see him at his home in Herrlingen. Because of his stature, Rommel was given the choice of a public trial and hanging or committing suicide. He chose to take the cyanide capsule the generals had brought for him. He was accorded a state funeral afterward, with no public mention of his suspected treason.

The man who had replaced Rommel, General Kluge, also was implicated in the bomb plot. Hitler relieved him of command and ordered him to return to Berlin. Fearing he would be tried and executed, Kluge committed suicide on August 19.

For Hitler, surviving yet another attempt on his life reinforced his belief that he was destined to lead Germany to greatness. The consequence of the plotters' failure was to put him more firmly in control than ever and to give Himmler's SS an excuse to tighten its control on the internal security of Germany.

The Allies Take Offense

On August 1, 1944, Patton finally got his chance to rejoin the war, leaving behind his fictional command to lead the Third Army. He immediately began a drive around the German flank with the aim of meeting up with the First Army and Montgomery's troops, which finally made it past Caen. The Allies hoped their pincer movement would encircle the German forces that had tried to stop the invasion. The Germans' only chance of escape was to try to shoot through a gap between the converging Allied forces.

The Battle of the Falaise Gap was an epic tank battle, with 10 divisions on each side battling for two weeks over an 800-square-mile area. When it was over, the Germans had broken through the 15-mile gap between the Allied forces and were able to retreat and regroup at the Seine. Roughly 300,000 Germans got away with 25,000 vehicles, but little else. Still, they were luckier than the 50,000 Germans who died and the 200,000 who were captured.

The day before D day, Allied forces captured Rome, freeing up troops for a second invasion planned for the south of France. On August 15, while the tank battle was raging in the north, Allied troops landed in Operation Anvil (also code-named Dragoon) between Cannes and Toulon. Anvil had been a cause of tension within the Alliance because Churchill had preferred to devote the energy and resources to additional operations in the Mediterranean. Eisenhower insisted, however, that Anvil was important to the success of Overlord because it would pin down German forces in southern France and provide an additional port through which supplies could pass.

The invasion went as smoothly as could have been hoped, with more than 80,000 men landing without meeting serious resistance. The troops overcame stiffer opposition in Toulon and Marseille. By the end of the month, the Anvil forces were moving north and linked up with the Overlord troops in mid-September near Dijon.

About the only good news for Hitler was that his troops had fulfilled his directive to hold on to the Channel ports of Le Havre, Calais, Dunkirk, and Boulogne. The Allies had chosen not to attack them immediately, preferring instead to advance on Paris and beyond. Though Hitler could claim success in keeping these ports out of Allied hands, thereby denying them important ports for resupplying their troops, he also tied down troops in static positions that could otherwise have joined in the defense elsewhere.

War Lore

In late August, Churchill finally agreed to a long-standing request to allow Jewish soldiers, mainly from Palestine, to serve in their own special unit. He even agreed that the Jewish Brigade Group could carry their own flag, the Star of David on a white background with two light blue bars, which later became the flag of Israel. One reason for Churchill's reluctance earlier was the often brutal fighting between British soldiers and Jewish paramilitary squads in Palestine. The Jews of Palestine saw the British as an obstacle to their independence, but recognized Hitler was a greater menace to the Jews. Thus, Palestinian Jews were willing to fight with the British to defeat the Nazis and, not coincidentally, gain valuable experience in combat for future use against the British.

American officer and French partisan crouch behind a car during a street fight in a French city, circa 1944. (National Archives Still Pictures Branch)

The Liberation of Paris

By mid-August, Patton's troops, as well as others, were crossing the Seine. Eisenhower then had to decide whether to try to liberate Paris or to bypass it and move on toward Germany. Hitler had said the city would be held to the last man and threatened to leave the city in ruins. Eisenhower and his generals preferred to avoid the almost certain house-to-house fighting that capturing the city would require, as well as the attendant destruction. It wasn't simply a military decision, however; politics dictated that Paris be captured to allow de Gaulle to establish his new government and to provide a final victory to the French resistance.

The decision was made for Eisenhower when resistance forces staged an uprising on August 19. Ignoring Hitler, the German commander, Dietrich von Choltitz, decided he did not have the resources to suppress the rebellion with the Allied forces on his doorstep. He was also unwilling to raze the city. Instead, the Germans laid down their arms and surrendered after a combined French-American force entered the city. The next day, August 26, General de Gaulle triumphantly marched down the Champs Élysées.

"We couldn't stick around long though. The Jerries were on the run and we wanted to keep them that way. The Tricolor from the Arc de Triomphe looked pretty good as we went through," American tank in Paris, August 1944. (National Archives Still Pictures Branch)

Words of War

"I had thought that for me there could never again be elation in war. But I had reckoned without the liberation of Paris—I had reckoned without remembering that I might be a part of this richly historic day. We are in Paris—on the first day—one of the great days of all time."

—Ernie Pyle, August 28, 1944

On October 23, 1944, the United States, Britain, and the Soviet Union granted diplomatic recognition to the provisional French government under de Gaulle. From that point on, he would insist that France be treated as an equal with its Allies.

The liberation of Paris and capture of most of France by the Allies prompted not only a German withdrawal, but a Vichy one as well. Pétain and Laval both joined the retreat in the hope of establishing a government-in-exile in Germany.

The Offensive Runs Out of Gas

The next stage of the offensive involved sending Montgomery's 21st Army Group north of the Ardennes into the Ruhr to capture Germany's coal mines, factories, and remaining industry, as well as the port of Antwerp. Montgomery was also tasked with destroying the many rocket launching sites in Belgium. Bradley's 12th Army Group was assigned the route south of the Ardennes into the Saar to destroy German industry there.

The Allies quickly ran into a somewhat unexpected problem: Rather than being stopped by German resistance, they were halted by a lack of supplies. As the Germans were forced to retreat, they at least had the benefit of shortening supply lines. The rapid Allied advance, however, put many of the troops too far ahead of the supply trucks and ever greater distances from the debarkation ports, not to mention the factories in the United States. It could take, for example, four months for equipment to reach France from the United States.

Because the Allies had destroyed the French railways to prevent the Germans from bringing in supplies, they now had to repair the tracks that were creating the same problem for them. One partial solution was the use of thousands of trucks, which came to be known as the Red Ball Express, to bring supplies up to forward depots. Still, for five days at the end of August, Patton's army was forced to stop because it had literally run out of gas.

While one general ran out of gas, another ran out of patience. On September 1, 1944, Eisenhower took command of the Allied land forces, pushing Montgomery aside. One practical reason for the change was the fact that most of the troops were Americans. The other was the aforementioned personality conflicts between Montgomery and just about everyone else, including Eisenhower. Montgomery remained in charge of his immediate army and captured Brussels two days after losing the larger command. The following day he took Antwerp. Still, German attacks helped prevent the British from opening the port until early November.

War Lore

Germany was forced to find more able- and not so able-bodied men to defend the Fatherland. A new militia, the *Volkssturm,* was created, with all men 16 to 60 now required to serve. Many were World War I veterans, some with infirmities, sent to guard prison camps or to perform other non-combat roles. Younger men were often shipped to a front. Despite all the defeats, Hitler still had 10 million men in uniform. In October, Hitler finally allowed women to take a more active military role, assigning some to anti-aircraft batteries.

No Picnics at Market-Garden

After years of resisting his generals' pleas for strategic retreats, Hitler finally saw an advantage to falling back to the Siegfried Line. This line of defense was a series of concrete pillboxes, troop shelters, and other fortifications arranged as much as three miles deep that stretched from Switzerland to the border where the Rhine enters the Netherlands. Hitler hoped to make his stand there long enough to send in reinforcements.

The Allies guessed Hitler's strategy (and also knew much of what the Germans were doing from messages they decrypted) and planned to outflank it by landing paratroopers behind the Siegfried Line. Operation Market-Garden was the largest airborne operation of the war, with three divisions parachuting on September 17 near Eindhoven, Arnhem, and Nijmegan.

Words of War

"Maybe there are 5,000, maybe 10,000 Nazi bastards in their concrete foxholes before the Third Army. Now if Ike stops holding Monty's hand and gives me some supplies, I'll go through the Siegfried Line like shit through a goose."

—General George Patton

The idea was for the paratroopers to open up enough of a gap for the ground troops to break through and then outflank the Germans in the Netherlands. The British airborne division at Arnhem, however, ran into stiff resistance, and the ground troops could not get through to support the attack. The 2,000 survivors of the air drop had to retreat back across the river after the other 7,000 men were killed or taken prisoner.

Roll Call

The once frightful German U-boat fleet had been so depleted that only one small merchant ship was sunk in October 1944. The new snorkel subs Hitler counted on were delivered in June 1944, and by February 1945, the Germans had the largest number of boats, 400, of the war. However, the new U-boats didn't sink any Allied ships, and the sub-building program diverted resources from production of other weapons.

Words of War

"[Roosevelt] lied us into war because he did not have the political courage to lead us into it."

—Congresswoman Claire Boothe Luce during the 1944 campaign

The failure of Market-Garden reflected the general stalemate that persisted in the fall. Not until mid-November did the Allies mount a major offensive. This time the full weight of Allied air power was brought to bear, with more than 4,000 aircraft dropping more than 10,000 tons of bombs on the Germans near Aachen. Even with all that firepower, however, the ground troops could make little headway and the Allies remained largely stalled west of the Siegfried Line.

The Politics of War

While the future governments of European nations were being determined by bullets, Americans were preparing to choose theirs by ballot. In November 1944, Roosevelt was running for a fourth term after already serving for an unprecedented three. He was opposed by the popular liberal Republican governor of New York, Thomas Dewey.

The physical contrast was stark between the youthful, 42-year-old Dewey and the increasingly frail incumbent. Dewey also had on his side the American penchant for change—and one was long overdue, after having the same president for 12 years. On the other hand, Americans are not apt to change their commander-in-chief during wartime, especially after Roosevelt had brought the nation out of the Depression and appeared to be leading it to victory against America's enemies.

Roosevelt won by more than 3 million votes and an overwhelming majority of electoral votes (432 to 99). The result was expected, but more surprising was the fact that Roosevelt had dumped Vice President Henry Wallace before the election in favor of a little-known senator from Missouri named Harry Truman.

The Battle of the Bulge

The Germans had one last great offensive in them, or so Hitler thought. Hoping that history would repeat itself, he planned to throw the weight of his remaining western forces into the Ardennes, where he had launched the attack that crushed the Allies four years earlier and allowed him to capture most of Western Europe. The operation, code-named Autumn Mist but now known as the *Battle of the Bulge,* was launched on December 16, 1944.

Unbelievably, the Allies had played into Hitler's hands by dividing their forces to the north and south of the Ardennes rather than concentrating a force where Hitler successfully attacked four years earlier. Worse, the 80,000 troops in the area were either battle weary or fresh off the boat.

When Hitler's *panzers* pounced on the Ardennes with a force of roughly 250,000 battle-tested soldiers, they caught their prey unprepared, undermanned, and ill-equipped. The Germans encircled the inexperienced 106th Division near St. Vith, capturing two-thirds of the men, but were stopped from taking the town by reserves rushed in by General Bradley.

With Bradley's forces rushing in from the south and Montgomery's from the north, the Allies were able to halt the German advance. Throughout the Battle of the Bulge, the weather limited the ability of the Allies to use their air superiority, but when the weather cleared, the bombers decimated the attacking forces.

A race was taking place meanwhile to get to the town of Bastogne. A German *panzer* army had crossed into Luxembourg and was trying to cross the Meuse River. The Allies had few men to defend the town and were rushing in reserves. Before they arrived, however, the Germans surrounded the town and gave the Americans one chance to surrender. The American commander, Brigadier General Anthony McAuliffe, gave a famous one-word response, "Nuts!"

Clearing skies allowed Allied aircraft to drop supplies into the town, and the day after Christmas Patton's Third Army arrived and relieved the pressure on Bastogne. Fighting continued for another week, but the German gambit had failed. Eisenhower wanted Montgomery to counterattack, but he proved once again too cautious to seize the advantage, allowing a significant number of German troops to escape to fight another day.

In the four weeks of fighting at the Bulge, the Allies, almost entirely American, suffered 19,000 casualties and had more than 15,000 men taken prisoner—9,000 in the battle at Schnee Eifel, the largest surrender in U.S. history after Bataan. The early success of the

GI Jargon

The **Battle of the Bulge** took its name from the fact that a bulge 70 miles wide and 50 miles deep was created in the Allied lines when the Germans moved into the Ardennes and split the American and British forces.

Ask the General

The same day the Battle of the Bulge started, the Germans fired a V-2 rocket into Antwerp, Belgium, where it hit a movie theater and killed 567 people, including nearly 300 Allied soldiers. About a week later, the first German jet aircraft bombed the railway providing supplies to the Allied troops in the Bulge. This was the first jet bomber raid in history.

offensive as the *panzers* drove 30 miles into Belgium and Luxembourg gave the Germans renewed hope and justified Hitler's unreal optimism about winning the war. Like dictators even to this day, Hitler totally misunderstood the United States and failed to appreciate either the commitment of the nation or its tremendous resources.

On June 6, 1944, Allied landings on the north coast of France plus the drive in Italy and potential new offensives on the Russian front confronted Germany with pressure from three sides. Shaded arrows and figures indicate strategic distances—from LeHavre to Berlin, from Rome to Berlin, and from Lwow to Berlin. (AP/Wide World Photos)

The British and Americans, meanwhile, were forced to reevaluate the prospects for an early victory and acknowledge the Germans still had plenty of fight left in them. Still, it should have been clear that the defeat in the Ardennes was one of the last battles the Germans would be able to fight. The Germans, after all, had lost 100,000 men, 1,000 aircraft, and 800 tanks from their already exhausted supplies. Neither the men nor the machines could be replaced in the foreseeable future. On the other hand, the Americans would soon pour tens of thousands more men into the theater over the coming weeks.

War Lore

Although he eventually reaped the glory for the Normandy invasion, Eisenhower wasn't promoted to general until December 1944. After the war, Eisenhower commanded the occupation in Germany and served as Army Chief of Staff as the United States demobilized. When he retired in 1948, he resisted appeals from both parties to run for president and became president of Columbia University. In 1950, President Truman named him commander of the newly formed North Atlantic Treaty Organization (NATO) forces. Two years later, dismayed by the direction the country was going, Eisenhower agreed to head the Republican ticket and was elected the 34th president of the United States. He served two terms and then retired to his farm in Gettysburg, Pennsylvania. He died in 1969 at the age of 78.

Hungry for Hungary

While the Allies were slowly fighting toward victory, the Germans were still using an iron fist in the territories they retained. The killing of Jews not only went on unabated, but was accelerated, to the detriment of the war effort (for example, trucks and trains that could have been used for supplies were instead ferrying Jews to their deaths).

In October 1944, the Hungarians began to flirt with the idea of making peace with the Soviets. When the Germans found out, they arrested the regent, Admiral Miklós Horthy (he was ultimately freed by the U.S. army and lived out his life in Portugal); seized the capital; and installed a new leader, Ferenc Szálasi, to ensure Hungary stayed in line. Szálasi, the leader of a fanatical group called the Hungarian Arrow Cross, almost immediately began deporting the three quarters of a million Hungarian Jews—the only large population of Jews still alive in Europe—who had been protected by Horthy.

Also, in October, the Germans withdrew from Greece. The British entered, but they soon became embroiled in a civil war between left-wing and anti-Communist Greek partisans. The British subsequently helped broker an agreement to end the fighting that was signed in February 1945.

As 1944 ended, Germany's defeat was clear to everyone but Hitler, who was determined to fight on. Nothing was left of the German empire. On the last day of the year,

Hungary joined Romania and Bulgaria in abandoning the Axis after Budapest was encircled by the Soviets. The noose was tightening around Germany, but it would take almost five more months to close.

The Least You Need to Know

➤ After overcoming heavy resistance, the Allies broke through German defenses and advanced through the heart of France, liberating Paris at the end of August 1944.

➤ A plot to assassinate Hitler failed, and the conspirators were caught and executed.

➤ Roosevelt's stewardship of the war effort was rewarded when he was elected to a fourth term. His decision to replace his vice president with Harry Truman proved to have historic consequences.

➤ Hitler gambled he could stop the Allies with a last great offensive. The Battle of the Bulge followed and was ultimately won by the Allies.

➤ The last of Germany's allies began to desert Hitler as the Red Army rolled across Eastern Europe.

Chapter 22

Victory in Europe

In This Chapter

➤ The "Big Three" meet at Yalta

➤ Firestorm at Dresden

➤ British and American troops in Germany

➤ The Red Army lays siege to Berlin

➤ Hitler kills himself

➤ Mussolini is murdered

➤ The Allies divvy up Berlin

Hitler's offensive had failed in its main objective—to destroy Montgomery's army—and, in the end, gained no ground at all. In addition to the direct cost at that front, the campaign was even more damaging to the remaining chance of stopping the Red Army's advance from the east. In addition, once the Allies opened the port at Antwerp at the end of November, they could bring in most of their supplies that way, and Hitler's effort to hold onto French ports to block them was also thwarted.

No Happy New Year for Germany

The Germans were losing the Battle of the Bulge, but the danger was far greater in the east, where the Red Army had 6 million men under arms and another 5.5 million in reserve facing 3 million German soldiers with just 2.5 million left in reserve. The more than two-to-one disadvantage the Germans suffered in troops was still better than the

Roll Call

In mid-January 1945, the United States and Britain announced the number of war dead since the start of the war. The figures for the United States were 138,393 dead and another 73,594 missing and presumed dead. The British lost 199,497 men in just over five years of fighting. The toll for other Commonwealth nations included 28,040 Canadians, 18,015 Australians, 17,415 Indians, 8,919 New Zealanders, and 5,783 South Africans.

disparities in planes and tanks. The Soviets had more than 15,000 aircraft; the Germans had fewer than 2,000; the Soviets had nearly 13,000 tanks; the Germans had 4,000.

In January 1945, Hitler tried to counterattack the Russians flooding into Hungary, but failed. The Red Army captured Budapest on February 13 and continued a steady march that took them across the border of Austria at the end of March and led to the capture of Vienna on April 13.

On New Year's Day, Hitler ordered the last major air strike on Allied airfields, sending 1,000 German planes out to try to cripple the enemy air force. The *Luftwaffe* lost the battle, however, destroying and damaging fewer than 300 planes while losing 277 of its own dwindling supply of aircraft.

On the ground, the Allies were steadily advancing, forcing the Germans to retreat to the Roer River. The last vestiges of the bulge in the Allied lines were gone. Now a dispute broke out between Bradley and Montgomery over whether to attack south on the Roer River or north. Eisenhower sided with Montgomery and transferred some of Bradley's troops to Montgomery's command. Faced with stiff resistance, the northern assault took heavy casualties and moved slowly. The remaining troops in the south, however, moved quickly toward the Rhine before linking up with their comrades in early March. By this time, the Americans were already in Cologne.

Yalta Sets the Agenda

The big three decided it was necessary to meet again to discuss the final strategy for defeating Germany and Japan and make postwar arrangements. Stalin was reluctant, and only agreed to meet at a location close to Moscow. Yalta, a city in southern Ukraine on the Black Sea, was the site chosen and the meeting held in Livadiya Palace, February 4 to 11, 1945.

Many of the contentious issues had already been settled either at the Tehran Conference or in the interim between the meetings. The Soviet occupation of much of eastern Europe, for example, presented the British and Americans with a fait accompli with regard to the independence of Poland, which was now under Moscow's control. The Allies still feared this would be viewed as a sellout by the Poles (which had the fourth largest number of men among the Allied forces after Russia, the United States, and Britain) fighting with them and would effect their willingness to fight.

Conference of the Big Three at Yalta makes final plans for the defeat of Germany.
Prime Minister Winston Churchill (left), President Franklin D. Roosevelt (center), and
Premier Josef Stalin (right) sit on the patio. (National Archives Still Pictures Branch)

War Lore

On February 19, without Hitler's knowledge, Heinrich Himmler met with a Swedish Red Cross official to discuss beginning negotiations with the Western Allies. Count Folke Bernadotte asked Himmler to first transfer control of the concentration camps to the Red Cross, but Himmler agreed only to allow prisoners, except Jews and Slavs, to receive Red Cross packages. They agreed to have further talks, but nothing came of the contacts. Bernadotte would later play a role as a mediator in the Palestine dispute between the Jews and Arabs. He was murdered by Jewish extremists from the Stern Gang in 1948.

With the expected conquest of Berlin, the powers decided to divide the city into occupation zones. The British and Americans lobbied on France's behalf for a share of the pie as part of their effort to ensure the French an important role in the postwar world. Stalin agreed only after Churchill and Roosevelt said they would carve France's zone out of their own. (After the meeting, de Gaulle refused to meet with Roosevelt, who had wanted him replaced, worsening the already testy Franco-American relationship.)

A major focus of discussion had to do with procedures at the proposed United Nations organization. Stalin agreed to an American proposal that the major powers not be allowed vetoes of procedural issues. This concession was offset by his demand that each of the Soviet Republics be given a seat in the planned General Assembly. This effectively ensured 16 votes for any position Moscow took. The Americans and British went along with a pared-down proposal for three Soviet seats.

The United States insisted that the founding conference be held in San Francisco, in part to ensure the United States was as deeply involved in the organization as possible and avoid a repetition of the failures of the League of Nations. The big three also agreed that France and China would join them in holding permanent seats on the Security Council.

Words of War

"We have learned that we cannot live alone, at peace; that our own well-being is dependent on the well-being of other nations, far away. We have learned that we must live as men, and not as ostriches, nor as dogs in the manger. We have learned to be citizens of the world, members of the human community."

—President Roosevelt, Fourth Inaugural Address, January 20, 1945

With regard to the conduct of the final phases of the war, the Soviet Union was no more willing to cooperate or coordinate its activities than it had been for most of the war. The Americans' main objective was to win reassurance of Soviet involvement in the war against Japan after Germany was defeated. Stalin, however, made a number of territorial demands as a condition, including recognition of Mongolia as a Soviet satellite, Soviet control over the Kurile Islands, and the return of territories captured by Japan in the Russo-Japanese War of 1904 and 1905. As distasteful as the decision was to make, Roosevelt believed conceding these issues, as well as Polish independence, was necessary to ensure victory in the Pacific. The Soviets also requested air support to prevent the transfer of German troops from the west to the east and to further disrupt communications. The Allies agreed to help.

Dresden Goes Up in Flames

After Yalta, the few remaining "neutral" countries began to align themselves with the Allies, in part because they could see the likely outcome of the war and because the great powers had made this alliance a prerequisite to admission to the new United Nations. Thus, countries such as Argentina and Turkey joined the Allies and declared war on Germany, and Sweden and Spain reduced or halted their cooperation with the Axis.

Meanwhile, to fulfill their commitment to Stalin at Yalta, the Allies continued their strategic bombing campaign against German cities. On February 13, the most destructive attack of all was launched against the city of Dresden. More than 1,200 Allied bombers took part in the two-day raid, with the loss of only eight bombers.

Dresden was crowded with refugees and virtually defenseless after its anti-aircraft guns were sent to the western front. The firestorm that followed the raid caused blazes that burned for a week and turned the city center to ashes. No one knows exactly how many died in Dresden. Thousands were believed buried under the rubble of shattered buildings or incinerated by the fires. The "official" death toll is nearly 40,000. Afterward, the Germans forced Allied POWs (one of whom was Kurt Vonnegut) to dig out the bodies at Dresden.

Roll Call

The Allies' strategic bombing campaign was murder on civilians. In addition to the people who died in Dresden, at least 50,000 people died in Hamburg and Berlin, 20,000 in Cologne, 15,000 in Magdeburg, 4,000 in Würzberg, and 87,000 in the towns of the Ruhr. Altogether, 600,000 civilians, many of whom were women and children, were killed, and 800,000 were injured.

Hitler's Last Stand

On the ground, Montgomery had reached the Rhine and was making preparations to cross. No army had crossed the Rhine into Germany since Napoleon 140 years earlier. South of Montgomery's forces, one of the American armored divisions also reached the Rhine and was surprised to find the Germans had left a bridge at Remagen intact (the Germans had tried unsuccessfully to blow it up). The Americans rushed across and established a foothold on the other side.

Hitler again shuffled his commanders in hopes of finding someone who could win the victory he knew was Germany's destiny. In this case, he fired von Rundstedt (again) and replaced him with Field Marshal Albert Kesselring, who'd been brought up from Italy. At the end of March, with Churchill and Eisenhower as witnesses, Montgomery made his move and crossed the Rhine on pontoon bridges. The Germans now had no hope of stopping the advance on Berlin.

Eisenhower decided, much to the chagrin of the British, to have the Allied troops crush the remaining German forces in the west rather than race to beat the Soviets to Berlin. Eisenhower's reasoning was that Churchill and Roosevelt had already conceded an occupation zone in Berlin to Stalin, so beating the Red Army would not affect control of the city. Given that political reality, he preferred to let the Russians bear the brunt of the fighting—and the casualties—in capturing Berlin.

Words of War

"Better enjoy the war; the peace will be terrible."

—German joke as the end of the war drew near

In March alone, the Allies had dropped nearly 250,000 tons of bombs, flying as many as 11,000 sorties in a single day. Virtually nothing was left of the *Luftwaffe* or its airfields. The German army still had about 26 divisions facing 85 in the west alone (4 million men).

The Allied forces moved quickly through Germany and soon surrounded the German troops in the Ruhr, taking 300,000 prisoners. The Germans had held out 18 days against overwhelming odds. After the defeat, the German commander, Field Marshal Walther Model, the man Hitler had sent to different fronts whenever his other generals had failed him, committed suicide to avoid capture.

By now, Churchill was convinced that Stalin could not be trusted to keep any of his promises—he'd already lied about his intentions in Poland—and urged Eisenhower to "shake hands with the Russians as far to the East as possible." Despite this, Churchill and Roosevelt both continued to send staggering amounts of aid to the Soviets. Under a new agreement signed at the beginning of April, this assistance included more than 3,000 aircraft and tanks, 40,000 trucks, and 16,000 weapon carriers.

With everything collapsing around him, Hitler on March 19 ordered a scorched-earth policy for his own country, hoping to destroy Germany's assets before they fell into Allied hands. This was one of the few orders that his subordinates disobeyed. The man who had helped build the new Germany, Albert Speer, did what he could to sabotage the plan.

The Germans launched a brief offensive in a futile effort to open a road for one of the German divisions to break out of the Harz Mountains and join in the defense of Berlin. The Americans referred to the attack as Operation Kaput and easily stifled the attack.

Roll Call

In April, the British updated their casualty lists and revealed that more than 216,000 soldiers had died since the start of the war, along with 30,000 merchant seamen and nearly 60,000 civilians.

Words of War

"[President Roosevelt] died in harness, and we may well say in battle harness, like his soldiers, sailors, and airmen who died side by side with ours and carrying out their tasks to the end all over the world. What an enviable death was his."

—Winston Churchill, April 17, 1945

FDR's Death Stuns the World

On April 12, Roosevelt died without having ever traveled to the battlefield or witnessing any of the war's destruction. The following day he was scheduled to give a speech that concisely stated the Allied war objective, "More than an end to war, we want an end to the beginnings of all wars." Roosevelt's death came as a shock and was a blow to the morale of the Allied forces, particularly the Americans. It was a cause of brief joy and optimism for the Germans, but both feelings soon passed.

The Siege of Berlin

On April 16, 1945, the Soviets began to bombard Berlin. Hitler ordered anyone who ordered a retreat to be shot, but there was no longer anywhere to escape. Nearly half a million Russian soldiers, led by General Zhukov, soon ringed Berlin.

Most high-ranking Nazis, including Göring, Jodl, Keitel, and Dönitz (who Hitler had designated as his successor), had already left the capital. Several, such as Himmler, Göring, and Speer, had been expelled from the Nazi Party for their real and imagined acts of disloyalty (Göring, for example, had sent a telegram to Hitler saying that if he didn't hear back, he would assume control of Germany). Hitler insisted on remaining in his bunker below the Chancellery.

Even at this late date, with Germany about to fall, Hitler refused requests to move the remaining troops in Italy north to join in the final defense of the Fatherland. Meanwhile, Allied bombers hit the remaining *Luftwaffe* air bases and destroyed virtually all of the planes that were still operational. The Americans also shot down 22 of the new jets that Hitler had placed so much faith in.

Various Germans had begun to sound out the Allies regarding surrender terms. Himmler, for example, offered to surrender to the western Allies on April 22, but not to the Russians. Himmler was told there could be no separate arrangements; Germany must surrender unconditionally on all fronts.

Words of War

"The Germans should have thought of some of these things before they began the war, particularly before attacking the Russians."

—General Montgomery's reaction to one German's request to surrender only to the British and Americans

Bunker Pill

The war was rapidly coming to a conclusion now. On April 25, an American lieutenant crossed the Elbe near the village of Leckwitz and bumped into a Soviet soldier. They soon realized the two armies had linked up.

On April 29, 1945, just nine days after his 56th birthday, Hitler married his longtime mistress Eva Braun and dictated a final, rambling political testament that repeated the ravings that brought his country to the brink of destruction. "Above all I charge the leaders of the nation and those under them to the scrupulous observance of the laws of race and to merciless opposition to the universal poisoner of all peoples, international Jewry." To the last, Hitler remained obsessed with the extermination of the Jews.

Roll Call

Roughly 125,000 Germans died in the siege of Berlin. The casualty toll for the Red Army was more than 300,000. Thousands more Russians died in remaining skirmishes, including 60,000 casualties in the siege of Breslau, which didn't end until May 6.

The next day Hitler took cyanide and shot himself through the mouth with a pistol. Eva Braun, who had told friends, "A Germany without Adolf Hitler would not be fit to live in," also committed suicide. Their bodies were carried into the garden of the Reich Chancellery and burned. The next day, Goebbels poisoned his six children, and then he and his wife killed themselves. The Nazi terror was finally over.

Roll Call

Allied casualties in Sicily and Italy alone totaled more than 320,000. More than 1 million more were suffered in the campaigns in Africa. After D day, the Germans suffered 263,000 dead and more than 8 million captured in the west alone. The Allies lost nearly 187,000 men, plus many of the 110,000 declared missing, and had more than half a million wounded.

Il Duce's Reward

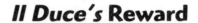

The Allied forces in Italy fought their way north throughout April, smashing what remained of the German army. On April 28, Mussolini and his mistress, Clara Petacci, were captured by partisans while trying to escape to Switzerland. They were both shot. The next morning—the same day Hitler took his own life—their bodies were taken to Milan and hanged upside down.

Mussolini was buried in Milan, but his body was stolen in 1946. His remains were found and reburied near Milan. In 1957, *Il Duce* was moved one last time to a cemetery in Predappio where he had originally requested to be buried and where his son had also been laid to rest.

On April 29, the German commander in Italy agreed to surrender unconditionally. The agreement went into effect three days later and hostilities came to an end. Almost 1 million German soldiers gave up, ending the war in the Mediterranean.

Germany Surrenders

On May 2, 1945, Zhukov accepted the surrender of Berlin. In the days immediately before and afterward, the Soviets took approximately 2,000 prisoners.

Churchill continued to be concerned with Soviet moves in the east. He was particularly concerned about the fate of Czechoslovakia and pleaded with the Americans to get to Prague before the Russians, but Truman refused to interfere with the decisions of his military commanders. As Churchill feared, Czechoslovakia fell into Stalin's hands and became dominated by the Communist Party.

Words of War

"Personally and aside from all logistic, tactical, or strategical considerations, I would be loath to hazard American lives for purely political purposes."

—Chief of Staff George Marshall to Eisenhower regarding Churchill's request to beat the Soviets to Prague

On May 3, the German forces in Denmark, Holland, and North Germany surrendered. On the 5th, a German representative went to Eisenhower's headquarters to discuss surrender and again tried to do so only with the western Allies. A message to this effect was sent to Dönitz, who then sent Jodl to continue the negotiations. Eisenhower warned the German general that he would seal the front and prevent any further westward movement of Germans if they did not quickly surrender to all the Allies. Jodl contacted Dönitz and requested permission to sign the unconditional surrender. This was done at 2:41 a.m. on May 7, 1945.

V-E Day (Victory in Europe Day) was celebrated on May 8, but several other nations and territories remained occupied by German forces. Norway, for example, was liberated on May 8. The remaining areas under German occupation all surrendered, with the final peace coming on May 11.

Because Dönitz and the remaining Nazi officials were all arrested, Germany had no functioning government. On June 5, the Allies formally assumed power, which was to be exercised by the Allied Control Council.

Words of War

"You have completed your mission with the greatest victory in the history of warfare. You have commanded with outstanding success the most powerful military force that has ever been assembled. You have been selfless in your actions, always sound and tolerant in your judgments, and altogether admirable in the courage and wisdom of your military decisions."

—General Marshall's cable congratulating Eisenhower on the victory in Europe

Field Marshall Wilhelm Keitel, signing the ratified surrender terms for the German Army at Russian Headquarters in Berlin on May 7, 1945. (National Archives Still Pictures Branch)

Dividing the Spoils at Potsdam

The Big Three met at Potsdam on July 17, 1945, to discuss the postwar arrangements for Europe and defeating the Japanese. During the meeting, the world learned the shocking results of the British election held on July 5. This was the first British election in a decade and was meant to end the coalition arrangement that had ruled for five years. Churchill, who had not been defeated in war, was beaten in the political battle by Labor Party leader Clement Atlee.

Churchill had led the nation through its darkest hours, inspiring the people, lifting their spirits, and prodding them to sacrifice for the good of all. Now at the moment of his greatest triumph, the victory over Nazi tyranny, he was cast aside. Why? Perhaps because the British had grown tired of Churchill's party and needed a change after a decade of Conservative rule. Many Britons believed Churchill was the right man to prosecute the war, but would not be the best person to direct the government in the postwar world. Whatever the reasons, the consequence was that Atlee took over for Churchill for the remainder of the talks.

Truman's objective, like Roosevelt's at Yalta, was to get Stalin's commitment to join the war in the Pacific as soon as possible. He was not interested in a declaration after the battle was decided, as many neutral nations had done on the eve of Germany's defeat. What the United States needed from the Soviet Union was a promise to attack Japan and tie down its forces in Manchuria and China. When Stalin announced he would enter the war on August 15, Truman was ecstatic.

The three leaders also had to decide on what to do about Germany. They agreed that the Allied Control Council would administer the country. If no agreement could be reached, which was the likeliest scenario, the commanders in each zone could act independently. Within a few weeks of the German surrender, it was already clear the four nations were planning to run their zones in their own way, with the Soviets already beginning the first small steps that would ultimately lead to the country's partition and the Communist domination of what would become East Germany.

The Soviets were also demanding huge amounts of reparations, some $10 billion. Ultimately a compromise was reached by which Stalin got what he wanted in terms of the revision of the Polish border, transferring the territory east of the Oder and western Neisse to the Poles and reserving the decision on the final border for a peace conference. The German population was also to be resettled within the borders of Germany. Stalin promised to allow free elections, but these were never held.

In exchange, Stalin agreed that Soviet reparations would be extracted from the Soviet Union's occupation zone in addition to receiving some of the industrial facilities from the other zones that were not needed to rebuild the German economy. The Americans, in particular, wanted to prevent the Soviets from confiscating the entire productive capacity of Germany and thereby ensuring it could never recover. Stalin also agreed to provide some necessities, notably food and coal, to the German zones that lacked them.

General Dwight Eisenhower, accompanied by General Omar Bradley, and Lieutenant General George Patton, Jr., inspect art treasures stolen by the Germans and hidden in a salt mine in Germany, April 12, 1945. (National Archives Still Pictures Branch)

During the talks, Truman learned that the atomic bomb had been successfully tested in New Mexico. Though Truman knew that Soviet agents had already passed on information about the progress of the Manhattan Project to Stalin, he decided to inform the Russian dictator that the United States now had a weapon capable of mass destruction.

Before the end of the conference, a warning was issued to Japan that it must surrender or face "the utter devastation of the Japanese homeland." The Allies laid out the terms of surrender, which included complete disarmament, respect for human rights, and guarantees of freedom of speech and religion. Japan, the Allies said, would be allowed to retain control over its four home islands, and perhaps some smaller ones, and would be allowed to keep "such industries as will sustain her economy." The Japanese rejected the call to surrender. The war would continue at great cost to all the participants—and the nuclear genie would be let out of the bottle.

The Least You Need to Know

➤ Roosevelt, Churchill, and Stalin, meeting in Yalta, agreed on the strategy to defeat Germany and Japan. The United States got what it wanted, a Soviet commitment to attack Japan.

➤ The Allied bombing campaign intensified and left Dresden in flames.

➤ The British and American armies had an opportunity to beat the Soviets to Berlin, but Eisenhower decided it wasn't worth the cost and chose instead to destroy what remained of the *Wehrmacht* as the Soviets surrounded and bombarded Berlin.

➤ Hitler committed suicide, and his reign of terror ended by his own hand.

➤ Italian partisans murdered Mussolini.

➤ Germany surrendered, and the powers divided Berlin between them at Potsdam. Truman learned that his secret weapon worked.

Chapter 23

The Red Sun Sets

In This Chapter

➤ The Philippines return to U.S. control

➤ The flag is raised over Iwo Jima

➤ One last battle before going to Japan

➤ Roosevelt okays the Manhattan Project

➤ Truman drops the bomb

➤ Japan surrenders to end World War II

When 1945 began, Hitler was on the ropes in Europe, and the Americans were advancing on the Japanese home islands. MacArthur had returned, as promised, to the Philippines, but those islands were not yet secured by his troops. Those Pacific islands that were in American hands, however, could now be used as bases for bombing raids on the citizens of Japan, who, to this point, had largely been spared the horrors of the war. The mighty Japanese fleet was no more, but the fanaticism of the remaining soldiers, which included the *kamikazes*, guaranteed that as long as Japan continued to fight, the war would be very costly for both sides.

Unfinished Business in the Philippines

After the tremendous sea and land battles for Leyte, the United States still did not control the Philippines. To accomplish that goal, they would have to vanquish the 250,000 Japanese on Luzon.

Roll Call

The Americans suffered approximately 38,000 casualties, including 8,000 killed, just on Luzon. The Japanese lost more than 170,000 men.

Words of War

"As soon as I got all the casualties off, I sat down on a rock and burst out crying. I couldn't stop myself and didn't even want to. I had seen more than a man could stand and still stay normal."

—Captain Bill McLain, a battalion surgeon on Corregidor

With only 150 aircraft left, the Japanese had little choice but to resort again to the *kamikaze* tactics they had employed in the last months of 1944. Starting on January 4, all the remaining planes attacked the American invasion fleet, sinking 17 ships and damaging 50 more. This attack did not stop the landing craft from depositing nearly 70,000 men on the shore.

After nearly a month of fighting, the Americans reached the outskirts of Manila. Meanwhile, in the southern part of the city, Japanese troops raped and massacred Filipinos in a small-scale repeat of the Rape of Nanking. It took yet another month to finally capture the city, with the Americans having to fight the 20,000 defenders virtually house by house. The remaining Japanese defenders withdrew into the mountains and held out until Japan surrendered on August 14. The island, however, was effectively under American control by March.

The Americans captured Corregidor Island on February 26, after a two-week battle that ended after the Japanese blew up the largest ammunition dump on the island and killed 52 Americans.

Uncommon Valor

After the American troops leapfrogged across most of the Pacific in 1944, the next major objectives were the capture of the tiny island of Iwo Jima and then the large island of Okinawa. Bases on these islands would put American forces within 400 miles of the southernmost Japanese island of Kyushu.

Iwo Jima was needed as a base for damaged bombers, many of which were being lost because they could not make the long trips back to their bases (a round trip of 2,700 miles that took 16 hours). Located midway between Japan and the bomber bases in the Marianas, Iwo Jima was ideally located for this purpose.

The Japanese commander on the island, General Kuribayashi Tadamichi, believed the Americans would think twice about invading Japan, as indeed they did, if he could inflict enough casualties on them. He spent weeks preparing elaborate defenses, much of it consisting of tunnels underground.

Though the Americans had a foretaste of what Japanese resistance would be like in previous battles, nothing compared with what the marines faced when they landed February 19, 1945. The navy had bombarded the island for three days, but the Japanese were well dug in, with 35-foot deep tunnels honeycombed throughout the island and heavy artillery guarding the beaches. The airfield the Americans wanted was in the center of the island, overlooked by the 546-foot Mount Suribachi.

After the marines made it ashore without much resistance, the guns on Mount Suribachi opened fire; the marines were trapped in the open. Many wounded soldiers were hit again before they could be evacuated. After about nine hours of fierce combat, the Americans landed enough men and supplies to hold the beach. On February 23, 1945, the marines captured Mount Suribachi, and Associated Press photographer Joe Rosenthal took one of the most famous photographs in history, the raising of the American flag by six marines.

Words of War

"Among the Americans serving on Iwo island, uncommon valor was a common virtue."

—Admiral Chester A. Nimitz

Flag raising on Iwo Jima, February 23, 1945. (National Archives Still Pictures Branch)

War Lore

Rosenthal's picture was the second one taken on Mount Suribachi. Earlier a dozen men had raised a flag and were photographed by Marine Sergeant Louis Lowery, but his picture took a month to reach the States. Rosenthal's photo was relayed almost immediately and, in the words of the editors of *US Camera Magazine*, "recorded the soul of a nation." When Roosevelt saw the photo, he ordered all six flag-raisers to come home. Three of the six men, Mike Strank (26), Harlon Block (21), and Franklin Sousley (19), had already died in action. Ira Hayes, John Bradley, and Rene Gagnon reluctantly returned home to help sell war bonds. Rosenthal won the Pulitzer Prize for the photo, which became the model for the Marine Corps Memorial in Virginia, designed by sculptor Felix W. de Weldon. John Wayne received his first Oscar nomination for his role as a marine sergeant in *The Sands of Iwo Jima* in 1949. The three surviving flag-raisers appeared in the film.

Roughly 100,000 men fought one of the most intense battles of the war in an area only five miles by two-and-a-half miles. The island was finally secured on March 16. Even before that date, however, the first B-29 made an emergency landing there; roughly 2,400 others would do the same before the war ended.

The battle on Iwo Jima took 25 days. The American casualties were 6,821 men killed and 20,000 wounded. It was the bloodiest battle in Marine Corps history, and the only time American casualties exceeded those of the Japanese. More than one-fourth of all Medals of Honor awarded during World War II went to men who fought at Iwo Jima. Nearly 800 sailors also died when their ship, the *Bismarck Sea*, was sunk by a *kamikaze*. As was the case on other islands, virtually every Japanese soldier was killed or committed suicide, including General Kuribayahsi. In this instance, only 216 out of 21,000 Japanese soldiers surrendered.

The Last Battle

Next stop for the Americans was Okinawa, an island 80 miles long and no more than 18 miles wide, which was to serve as a staging ground for the attack on Japan. After the horrors of Iwo Jima, the U.S. Navy decided to bombard the island of Okinawa with both barrels—and then some. The shelling lasted for a week before the 50,000 men aboard the 1,300-ship invasion force hit the beach on April 1 (nearly 200,000 more joined the fight later). As in many of the battles, the roughly 120,000 Japanese defenders decided not to try to prevent the landing, but instead to draw the Americans inland and engage them in a bloody war of attrition.

War Lore

Desmond Doss was a medical orderly who, as a Seventh Day Adventist, refused to carry a weapon even in the hellish conditions on Okinawa. He found himself on a ridge surrounded by wounded men. Under heavy fire, he carried 50 wounded men one at a time to the cliff edge and then lowered each by rope to safety. For his heroism, Doss received the Congressional Medal of Honor.

Fierce resistance again slowed the American advance, and it took two months to break through the main Japanese line. Even then, fighting continued for nearly one more month, ceasing finally on June 21. In the middle of the battle over Okinawa, the British secured their greatest victory in Asia, finally recapturing Burma on May 3 after the Japanese hastily evacuated Rangoon.

In the 82 days of combat on and around Okinawa, *kamikazes* sank or damaged 245 ships, including the carrier *Franklin,* which lost 724 men. The Navy's losses, more than 5,000 men, were the largest in the war other than at Pearl Harbor. Total U.S. casualties were approximately 75,000.

The Japanese lost 16 ships at Okinawa, including the largest battleship in the world, the *Yamato,* and a total of 3,000 men in naval battles. The Americans shot down 5,900 aircraft while losing 763 of their own. The Japanese lost more than 1,000 planes in *kamikaze* attacks. Roughly 120,000 Japanese and perhaps as many as 150,000 Okinawan civilians were killed.

Firestorm!

While the last battles were continuing on the islands, the U.S. Air Force, under its aggressive new commander Curtis LeMay, undertook new large-scale raids on the Japanese home islands in the hope that the people would now understand the costs of war and force their leaders to surrender. Taking a page out of the British strategic bombing play book, LeMay was determined to set cities on fire with incendiary bombs. On March 9, 1945, just three weeks after the raid on Dresden, the Americans carried out perhaps the most devastating air raid of the war, bombing Tokyo and causing fires that burned nearly 16 square miles of the city, destroyed 267,000 buildings, killed more than 80,000 people, and injured 40,000 more.

Over the next five months, LeMay's bombers would hit more than 60 other cities, leaving many only slightly less devastated than Tokyo. By mid-June, raids on Japan's five other large industrial centers—Nagoya, Kobe, Yokohama, Osaka, and Kawasaki—left 260,000 people dead, 2 million buildings destroyed, and as many as 13 million people homeless. LeMay's forces suffered the deaths of 243 airmen and only minor losses of aircraft.

Olympic and Coronet

By the time the Americans secured Okinawa, the war in Europe was over, and it was now possible to transfer at least 60 U.S. and 60 British divisions to the Pacific. In addition, the Soviets were expected to contribute troops to the war against Japan.

American military planners were preparing for a final assault on Japan, starting with an invasion of Kyushu in November 1945, code-named Olympic. The following March, the Allies would land on Honshu in Operation Coronet. The success of these operations was thought to depend on Stalin's keeping his promise to attack Japanese positions in Manchuria and China to prevent them from sending reinforcements to the home islands. During the military planning, the Americans could not be sure they could count on the Soviet dictator.

Even with all the firepower available to the Allies, the U.S. military was concerned about the invasion. They had no doubt about the outcome, but they knew the cost would be very high. According to one estimate, for example, nearly 270,000 of the 767,000 men assigned to Olympic were expected to be killed. That total would equal all the battle deaths U.S. forces had faced on all fronts during the war. American strategic planners also talked about the possibility of far higher losses, frequently referring to the possibility of as many as 1 million casualties or even that number of dead.

Truman agreed with his military advisers that Olympic should go forward despite the risks. American preparations began in July while the Japanese, anticipating an attack, readied their defenses. The Japanese had no defense, however, for the new weapon the Americans had developed to bring them to their knees.

The Power of a Particle

In 1938, two German physicists discovered that a neutron could split the nucleus of a uranium atom, a process called fission. This event releases tremendous amounts of energy. By causing a chain reaction that created multiple instances of fission, the energy released would grow exponentially and produce extreme heat and an intense explosion. Scientists also believed that a uranium isotope called plutonium, discovered by American scientists in 1941, might be an even more effective explosive than uranium. (The discoveries that led to the first atomic bomb were, of course, more complex, but this information gives you a general idea of what was going on.)

In 1939, the Nobel Prize-winning physicist Albert Einstein, a German Jew who had stayed in the United States where he was teaching in 1933 after Hitler came to power, wrote to President Roosevelt and told him about the potential for creating a weapon based on the recent discoveries. Einstein also warned Roosevelt that Germany might try to develop such a weapon for use against the Allies.

The president wrote a brief reply thanking the professor and promising to appoint a board to investigate the matter. Einstein and the other expatriate scientists were worried that Germany was already on its way to making a bomb. Einstein's letter also mentioned that Germany had stopped the sale of uranium from the Czechoslovakian mines it had taken over and that the son of the German under-secretary of state worked at the *Kaiser-Wilhelm-Institut* in Berlin where some of the American work on uranium was being replicated.

About six weeks after Einstein sent his letter to Roosevelt, a group of German scientists met in Berlin to discuss how the energy from nuclear fission could be harnessed. The German War Office agreed to pay the cost of the research.

Words of War

"...[T]he element uranium may be turned into a new and important source of energy in the immediate future.... This new phenomenon would also lead to the construction of bombs... extremely powerful bombs of a new type... [which] carried by boat and exploded in a port might very well destroy the whole port together with some of the surrounding territory."

—Letter from Einstein to Roosevelt, August 2, 1939

Dr. Robert Oppenheimer (right), Director of the Institute for Advance Study at Princeton, listens intently as Dr. Albert Einstein tells of his newest attempts to explain matter in terms of space, circa 1948. (National Archives Still Pictures Branch)

The Manhattan Project

Not until December 6, 1941—the day before Pearl Harbor—did a new government committee meet to determine within six months if it was feasible to produce an atomic bomb. When the committee determined the answer was yes, the United States began a crash program to develop an atomic bomb, trying two different approaches, one using uranium and another plutonium.

On June 17, 1942, Roosevelt decided to pursue the development of the bomb. The U.S. Army Corps of Engineers was given responsibility for the program, code-named Manhattan Project (after the location of the initial headquarters). The British were also included in the overall effort, and they conducted parallel research in London.

War Lore

Women from the WAACs also participated in the Manhattan Project. Major Sergeant Elizabeth Wilson ran the cyclotron at Los Alamos, which was used for fission experiments, Jane Heydorn was involved in the construction of electronic equipment used in the development and testing of the bomb, and a group of WAACs at Oak Ridge maintained the top secret files for the project.

Major General Leslie Groves was assigned command of the project. Most of the key researchers on the project were refugees, many of them Jewish, who had escaped from Germany or the occupied territories. These researchers included Enrico Fermi (who, because his wife was Jewish, picked up his Nobel Prize in Stockholm in 1938 and went on to the United States and Columbia University rather than risk returning to Mussolini's Italy) and Leo Szilard, the men Einstein referred to in his letter to Roosevelt. Other researchers included Edward Teller (later to become known as the father of the hydrogen bomb), Neils Bohr, and Eugene Wigner. Einstein was never involved in the Manhattan Project (and became a proponent of disarmament after the war).

Work on the bomb was conducted primarily in three cities: Hanford, Washington; Oak Ridge, Tennessee; and Los Alamos, New Mexico. Facilities were built at Oak Ridge to separate the necessary uranium-235 from the much more common uranium-238, Hanford reactors produced the plutonium for use in the bomb, and Los Alamos was where the bomb components were put together and was the headquarters for the principal research under the direction of J. Robert Oppenheimer. By 1945, 120,000 people were working on the Manhattan Project.

Many of the new discoveries in physics were published, as they usually are, in academic journals and elsewhere. The British and Americans, however, realized the implications of the research and decided to stop making their findings public to ensure that they would not fall into German hands. Few people knew, therefore, that Fermi had made a major breakthrough in 1942 at the University of Chicago when he produced the first self-sustaining nuclear chain reaction, the process that would make an atomic bomb explode.

While Fermi, Szilard, and their counterparts in England tried to solve the various problems associated with creating a bomb, another scientist was devoted to passing on news of their progress to the Soviets. Klaus Fuchs was a German refugee who had gone to Britain in 1933 and joined the English team working on the bomb. In November 1943, 15 British scientists, including Fuchs, went to the United States to join the American team. Another spy, this one an American named David Greenglass, later stole blueprints for the bomb and sold them to the Soviets.

The principal motivation for the Manhattan Project was the fear the Germans might develop a bomb first and, in all likelihood, use it against Britain. Even after the Allies concluded the Germans had given up on their project, they remained committed to building a bomb. By the time this conclusion was reached, the Allies no longer expected to use the bomb against Germany, but they thought it might make it possible to end the war with Japan sooner.

One key to making a bomb was finding a way to slow down the fission process, so the uranium would not destroy itself. The American team used graphite to control the chain reaction needed to produce a bomb. The Germans working on the project had made some mistakes in their research and concluded that graphite would not work, so they concentrated on the use of "heavy water" or deuterium oxide.

Ask the General

When J. Robert Oppenheimer was selected to head the design team of the Manhattan Project, he was less distinguished than the men working for him. He was only 39 and, unlike Neils Bohr and Enrico Fermi, had not won a Nobel Prize. Oppenheimer came under suspicion from FBI Director J. Edgar Hoover and others who believed Oppenheimer's views were too left-wing. Groves ignored the criticism because he was convinced he had the right man for the job.

Ask the General

Scientists in many parts of the world were involved in what later became nuclear physics, but a combination of luck and superior talent gave the United States the edge in the race to build a bomb. The Japanese were also interested in developing nuclear weapons, but they did not have the resources to build them and did not believe anyone else could do so in as little time as the Americans did.

When the Germans took over Norway, they captured the only factory in the world producing large quantities of heavy water, which subsequently became a frequent target of Allied sabotage and air raids. The Germans' mistake about graphite contributed to their failure to ever produce a bomb, though heavy water was later used by the Canadians to generate nuclear power.

Interestingly, Roosevelt was adamantly opposed to the use of biological or chemical agents in the war, unless the enemy did first, but he did not appear to have any reservations about developing and using weapons with potentially far more destructive power.

Keeping the Weapon Secret

Roosevelt was reluctant to share any information about the atomic bomb research with his allies. In a private meeting at Roosevelt's home in Hyde Park in 1943, Roosevelt and Churchill agreed that they would not keep secrets from each other regarding the bomb project and would never use the weapon against each other. They also decided not to use it against a third party or communicate information about the project, except by mutual consent.

Churchill also agreed with Roosevelt's desire that the United States benefit from any postwar commercial or industrial use of the research. This agreement cleared the way for the two countries to closely work on the project code-named Tube Alloys (for the joint part of the project). In the true spirit of capitalism, Roosevelt hoped the United States would reap whatever benefits might come from the power of the atom after the war was over. This was only fair, he thought, given the multibillion dollar investment the United States had made in the project.

Words of War

"The object of the project is to produce a practical military weapon in the form of a bomb in which the energy is released by a fast neutron chain reaction in one or more of the materials known to show nuclear fission."

—Nuclear scientist Robert Serber, to a secret group of chemists and physicists at Los Alamos, April 1943

When the two men met again in September 1944, they were advised that an atomic bomb would probably be ready by August 1945. They agreed that consideration should be given to using it against Japan.

The same day, nearly 3,000 miles away, Oppenheimer was briefing Colonel Paul Tibbets on the danger of the mission he was assigned: dropping the first atomic bomb. Oppenheimer told him the shock waves from the explosion might destroy the plane and that he could not give any assurance that anyone on the flight would survive.

The British were kept informed because they were also contributing to the research, but Roosevelt feared that Soviet spies had penetrated Churchill's government and were passing the information to Stalin. They were. The Soviet leader was not told any of the specifics, only about the existence of a powerful new weapon after it was successfully tested while Roosevelt was at Yalta. The Americans also suspected the Soviets had their own bomb project (which they also began in 1942), and Stalin never shared any information about that (or much of anything else for that matter) with Roosevelt or Churchill.

The Gadget Becomes a Reality

The plans for dropping the bomb were ready, but one technicality remained: Finding out if the *gadget* would work. No one knew if the bomb would explode, nor were they sure exactly what would happen if it did. They were reasonably confident that it would "go bang" and cause extensive damage, but they didn't *know*.

A test was scheduled for July in the Jornado del Muerto desert in Alamogordo, New Mexico. Oppenheimer called the site Trinity, after a John Donne poem he'd been reading:

> *Batter my heart, three-person'd God; for, You*
> *As yet but knock, breathe, shine, and seek to*
> *mend.*

The components were produced by July 13 and assembled at Trinity. The gadget was hoisted to the top of a 100-foot tower, where it would be detonated.

Doctors were sent to nearby populated areas to evacuate the people if the yield was greater than expected. The consensus was the size of the explosion would be relatively small, though Fermi was taking bets that the bomb would incinerate the state, and Groves warned the governor of New Mexico that the entire state might have to be evacuated.

GI Jargon

When Oppenheimer's assistant Robert Serber gave a series of lectures outlining progress on the Manhattan Project, a group of workmen was nearby finishing construction of the building. Serber was told to use the word **gadget** instead of *bomb* in case his lectures were overheard. From then on, the device was referred to as a gadget.

GI Jargon

Ground Zero is the point where a nuclear device is detonated.

At 5:30 a.m. on July 15, the bomb exploded with the force of 21,000 tons of TNT, instantly vaporizing the tower that held it. The temperature at *Ground Zero* was three times hotter than the interior of the sun. Within a mile of the detonation, no living thing remained. The explosion could be heard for 50 miles, and the flash was visible for 250.

"The war is over," Groves' deputy, General Thomas Farrell, said after the test. "Yes," Groves said, "just as soon as we drop one or two of these things on Japan." The Manhattan Project was an incredible success, rapidly accomplishing a difficult scientific and

Words of War

"The whole country was lighted by a searing light with the intensity many times that of the midday sun. Seconds after the explosion came first the air blast pressing hard against the people, to be followed almost immediately by the strong, sustained, awesome roar that warned of doomsday and made us feel we puny things were blasphemous to dare tamper with the forces heretofore reserved for the Almighty."

—General Thomas Farrell after the first atomic-bomb test

Words of War

"To quell the Japanese resistance man by man and conquer the country yard by yard might well require the loss of a million American lives and half that number of British.... I thought immediately of how the Japanese people, whose courage I had always admired, might find in the apparition of this almost supernatural weapon an excuse which would save their honor and release them from their obligation of being killed to the last fighting man."

—Churchill upon learning the atomic bomb test was successful

military objective. It had taken only 2 years, 3 months, and 16 days to produce the first nuclear weapon.

In May, the Americans had begun to evaluate possible targets for dropping the atomic bomb. They narrowed the list to four cities: Hiroshima, Kyoto, Yokohama, and Kokura (Kyoto was later ruled out because it was a cultural and religious shrine, and Yokohama was replaced by another city). After the successful test of the bomb, President Truman was sure he would have to use it, but he was committed to dropping it only on a military target. In July he wrote in his diary, "The target will be a purely military one and we will issue a warning statement asking the Japs to surrender and save lives. I'm sure they will not do that, but we will have given them the chance. It is certainly a good thing for the world that Hitler's crowd or Stalin's did not discover this atomic bomb. It seems to be the most terrible thing ever discovered, but it can be made the most useful."

The Final Countdown

Emperor Hirohito was now in control of the Japanese government. Tojo's militaristic cabinet had fallen in July 1944, as did its successor after the invasion of Okinawa. Though Hirohito ordered his new cabinet to end the war, many Japanese leaders still hoped to have a final confrontation with the Americans.

The Japanese would not negotiate with the Americans and, instead, tried to use the Soviet Union as an intermediary. Because the United States could read all the coded messages the Japanese sent about the discussions, Truman knew they were unprepared to surrender unconditionally.

On July 26, the Allies issued their demand from Potsdam that Japan surrender or suffer "the utter destruction of the Japanese homeland." Even before receiving a formal answer, since he knew from American intelligence the Japanese would not give up, Truman ordered the commander of the Strategic Air Forces, General Carl Spaatz, to "deliver its first special bomb as soon as weather will permit visual bombing after about August 3, 1945, on one of the targets: Hiroshima, Kokura, Niigata, and Nagasaki."

About the time Truman issued his order, the components for the atomic bomb were delivered by the cruiser *Indianapolis* to the island of Tinian. A few days after receiving Truman's order, Spaatz informed his superiors that Hiroshima was the only city on the target list that did not have any POW camps holding Allied soldiers.

War Lore

Just after midnight on July 30, 1945, four days after delivering the bomb components, the *Indianapolis* was sunk by a Japanese submarine. The captain was not able to send out a distress call, and it took four days for rescuers to find the survivors. By then, only 318 men were still alive; 350 had died in the explosion or gone down with the ship, and 484 were either drowned or killed by sharks. It was the greatest loss at sea in U.S. Navy history, and the *Indianapolis* was the last major warship lost in World War II. (Many people know this story from the film *Jaws,* when the shark hunter played by Robert Shaw tells Richard Dreyfuss's character that his tattoo is from the *Indianapolis,* and then relates the real-life tragedy.)

Before going forward with the use of the atomic bomb, the Americans continued to closely monitor the diplomatic messages traveling to and from Tokyo. They knew that the Japanese ambassador in Moscow considered the effort to enlist Soviet mediation a waste of time and urged his government to accept the Allies' terms. It was clear, however, that this was not the prevailing view in the government. On the other hand, intelligence did suggest that the key to Japanese capitulation would be the disposition of the emperor, which led Truman to offer the carrot of allowing the monarchy to survive after the surrender.

The Japanese still would not bend. It became increasingly clear to Truman that the only way to force the Japanese to quit and to save hundreds of thousands, perhaps millions, of American casualties—he feared "an Okinawa from one end of Japan to the other"—was to drop the atomic bomb.

The decision was made to drop two bombs a few days apart in early August. No warning was to be given. Truman hoped the Japanese would think the United States had an arsenal of atomic weapons when, in fact, two was all they had. A third bomb was almost ready, and it would only be a matter of time before more were available, but the expectation was that two would be enough to end the war.

Ground Zero

On August 6, a specially modified B-29 named the *Enola Gay* took off from Tinian Island. On board was the 15-kiloton atomic bomb nicknamed Little Boy. Written on the side was the message, "Greetings to the emperor from the men of the *Indianapolis*."

At 8:15 a.m. Japanese time, the plane piloted by Colonel Tibbets dropped the first atomic bomb on Hiroshima. In a little over a minute, it exploded about 1,800 feet over the city. "My God, look at that son-of-a-bitch go," Captain Robert Lewis said as the bomb exploded.

In an instant, 80,000 people died, and more than 35,000 were injured. Many people were incinerated immediately by the 7,000-degree heat at Ground Zero, others died within a few months, and still more died years later from the effects of the radiation released by the bomb. The total death toll will never be known, but it could be as high as 200,000.

Words of War

"Sixteen hours ago an American airplane dropped one bomb on Hiroshima.... The force from which the sun draws its power has been loosed against those who brought war to the Far East."

—Truman's announcement that the atomic bomb was dropped, August 6, 1945

In addition to death, the bomb caused the total devastation of the city. Two-thirds of all the buildings were destroyed, including 52 of the 55 hospitals and clinics. Much of the destruction was caused by the incredible winds generated by the explosion, 980 miles per hour where the bomb exploded and as much as 190 miles per hour a mile away.

The White House called on Japan to surrender or "expect a rain of ruin from the air." The Japanese did not respond, and the order was given to prepare for a second attack. In the meantime, Japan's last hope for Soviet intervention ended on August 8, when Stalin declared war and launched attacks on Japanese positions in Manchuria, Korea, and Sakhalin. Even before details of this new assault reached Tokyo, the Americans dropped a 20-kiloton bomb (nicknamed Fat Man) on Nagasaki. Though the bomb was more powerful, the death toll was lower, about 40,000, because of the geography of the city.

A dense column of smoke rises more than 60,000 feet into the air over the industrial center of the Japanese port of Nagasaki, the result of the second atomic bomb ever used in warfare, dropped from the B-29 Bock's Car on August 8, 1945. (National Archives Still Pictures Branch)

War Lore

The *Enola Gay* became well-known for dropping the first atomic bomb, but few people know the name of the B-29 that bombed Nagasaki. It was *Bock's Car*, named after the plane's usual commander, Frederick Bock. For this mission, the pilot was Major Charles Sweeney. The original target was Kokura, but that city was spared because Sweeney had been ordered to attack a clear target and Kokura was obscured that day by haze.

Japan Surrenders

The atomic bombs had not killed as many people as the earlier American raid on Tokyo, but the difference was the huge number of casualties in Hiroshima and Nagasaki had been inflicted by just two planes dropping only two bombs, as opposed to hundreds of aircraft dropping thousands of bombs. The Japanese Imperial Council met the night of August 9 and deadlocked 3-3 on the question of whether to continue the war. The emperor voted for surrender, the first time an emperor had intervened this way in half a century. The Japanese offer of surrender contained the condition, however, that the imperial system be retained.

This was not the unconditional surrender the Allies demanded. There was strong opposition within and without the American government to making this concession. Truman, seeing the chance to end four years of war, decided to offer a compromise that accepted the imperial system, but made the emperor's authority subordinate to the supreme commander of the Allied powers. The more important point for him was that the Japanese people would be allowed to choose their own form of government in the future. To encourage a positive response to this gesture, Truman ordered the continuation of conventional bombing attacks on Japan.

The anti-surrender camp in Japan tried to stage a coup to prevent any agreement, but the attempt failed, and the emperor assented to the terms Truman had proposed. On August 14, MacArthur was appointed supreme commander and plans were immediately made for the occupation of Japan. A typhoon forced the postponement of the American landing, but it finally took place on August 30.

Fighting in Manchuria did not end until August 21, and it took until October 24 before all the major Japanese troops were disarmed. By the end, the Americans had taken more than 7 million Japanese soldiers and sailors prisoner.

War Lore

On January 1, 1946, an American soldier on Corregidor was shocked to see 20 Japanese soldiers coming toward him waving white pieces of cloth as if to surrender. It turned out the men had been living in tunnels and didn't know the war had ended until one of them went out to look for water and saw a newspaper mentioning the Japanese surrender.

The formal surrender ceremony was held on September 2 on the battleship *Missouri* anchored in Tokyo Bay. MacArthur signed the document for the Allies, and Foreign

Minister Mamoru Shigemitsu and Chief of Staff of the Army General Yoshijiro Umezu signed for Japan. World War II was over, but the final reckoning was just beginning.

The Least You Need to Know

➤ The fighting was drawn out for months, but the United States recaptured the Philippines.

➤ U.S. forces suffered heavy casualties in battles for Iwo Jima and Okinawa. The "uncommon valor" of the marines raising the flag on Iwo Jima inspired Americans then and continues to do so today.

➤ American bombers launched the most destructive raid of the war against Tokyo while a ground invasion of Japan was planned.

➤ Roosevelt launched the Manhattan Project, a crash program to develop an atomic bomb.

➤ The *Indianapolis* sank, and the U.S. Navy suffered its worst loss ever. The incident was particularly gruesome because many of the victims were eaten by sharks while waiting to be rescued.

➤ Truman decided to drop atom bombs on Hiroshima and Nagasaki. The atomic age began.

➤ The Japanese surrendered, sparing themselves further atomic bomb attacks and saving the Americans from what was expected to be a horrific battle to occupy Japan. World War II was over.

Part 6
The Smoke Clears, and the Reckoning Begins

In addition to the horrors of the battlefield, World War II is also marked by atrocities against civilians. The Nazis murder approximately 12 million people. The Jews are singled out for extermination, and 6 million are killed in the Holocaust. After the war, many war criminals are convicted, but many receive lenient sentences or evade justice altogether.

The book concludes with a look at the human and material cost of the war. The United States emerges stronger than ever and uses its economic power to aid in the recovery of Europe and Japan. The Soviet Union, however, drops an "Iron Curtain" across Eastern Europe and seeks to spread Communism around the world. The ensuing Cold War between two superpowers now armed with increasingly lethal nuclear weapons threatens the well-being of the planet.

The United Nations is created in the hope that future wars can be averted through international mediation and diplomacy. A third world war does not appear on the horizon before the end of the century, but will the lessons of the first and second be learned?

Night and Fog

The first 23 chapters of this book have described the causes of World War II and attempted to relate some of the horrors associated with that war. Throughout, however, I have only touched on one of the defining aspects of this conflict: the Nazi campaign to exterminate the Jewish people. As many or more books have been written about the Holocaust, or *Shoah*, as the war itself, so one chapter cannot possibly give more than a cursory overview. But the war cannot be understood, nor can events since, without a discussion of Hitler's "Final Solution."

The Nuremberg Laws

As noted in Chapter 3, anti-Semitism featured prominently in Hitler's ideology from an early age. His obsession with the Jews was evident in his rise to power and all the years that followed. Hitler's agenda was never a secret; he publicly stated over and over that his goal was the destruction of the Jews.

The killing did not start immediately. Hitler began with a series of measures to isolate and humiliate the Jews. Prior to Hitler, Germany was one of Europe's most cultured, sophisticated societies, and all German Jews, regardless of whether they were religious, considered themselves integral to that society. They were among the elite of German society: prominent doctors, lawyers, professors, and industrialists. Many were assimilated and were not practicing Jews; some had even converted.

GI Jargon

Shoah is the Hebrew word for catastrophe. It is often used to describe the destruction of European Jewry during World War II. This is the term most commonly used in Israel, which commemorates the Holocaust each year with a special day called **Yom ha-Shoah.**

Words of War

"The end of German Jewry has arrived."

—Rabbi Leo Baeck, shortly after Hitler took power

Through the skillful use of propaganda and terror, the *Führer* succeeded in marginalizing and dehumanizing the Jews to the point where ordinary citizens were capable of participating in the persecution, and later murder, of Jews—or at least capable of standing by and watching. Regardless of whether one believes the controversial hypothesis Daniel Goldhagen put forward in *Hitler's Willing Executioners*—that Germans were essentially predisposed to anti-Semitism—the reality was that few people were prepared to raise any objections to Hitler's genocidal policies. Those not inclined to actively hate or persecute the Jews were at least convinced that there was little to be gained in Hitler's Germany by defending them.

The official persecution of the Jews began in April 1933, when the Nazis initiated a boycott of Jewish businesses throughout Germany. Signs and graffiti warned Germans not to buy from the Jews. This boycott was followed by the first of 400 separate pieces of legislation that, over the next six years, prevented Jews from working, going to school, or otherwise taking part in German society. These laws robbed them of their possessions and demonized their religion.

In 1935, German Jews were stripped of their citizenship, and Jews were barred from marrying Aryans. These laws were part of Hitler's notion of racial purity and the superiority of the Aryan race. Because the new laws were announced at a Nazi rally at Nuremberg, they became known as the Nuremberg Laws.

The situation for Jews continued to deteriorate. They were treated worse than blacks in the American South, prevented from staying in hotels, going to restaurants, theaters, or shops, or even sitting on Aryan park benches. By the middle of 1938, most Jewish businesses had been taken over by the Germans. Still, many Jews simply could not conceive of anything permanently altering their status—let alone conceive of the proportions of Hitler's ultimate plan. It was this disbelief, even as the persecution against them went from bad to worse, that led so many to stay in their homes rather than flee. By the time those who remained realized what Hitler intended—and the willingness of their fellow Germans to go along—it was too late to escape.

In December 1939, Hitler issued the "Night and Fog" decree, which authorized the arrest of anyone endangering German security. Those who were seized were to "vanish without a trace into the night and fog." Some voices of dissent were heard, but they were either muted or quickly silenced by bullets or incarceration. The Reverend Martin Niemöller, for example, led a group of churchmen who opposed the Nazis. "No more are we ready to keep silent at man's behest when God commands us to speak," Niemöller said in his last sermon. "We must obey God rather than man." He was arrested and sent to Dachau.

Nowhere to Run

On November 9, 1938, Nazi-inspired violence broke out throughout Germany in what came to be known as *Kristallnacht* (see Chapter 5). The authorities' clear role in the attacks convinced more Jews the time had come to flee. The problem, for those with the courage and the means to leave their homes and all they knew, was where to go.

Just four months earlier, a conference with delegates from 32 countries had met at Evian, France, to discuss what to do about the growing number of refugees trying to flee Europe. The United States, which had initially proposed the conference, showed so little interest in solving the problem that other countries felt no need to open their doors to fleeing Jews. In the end, the Dominican Republic was the only country that welcomed Jews.

War Lore

In 1938, when no other nation would welcome Jewish refugees, Rafael Trujillo, the Dominican Republic strongman, offered to take in 100,000. Approximately 5,000 visas were ultimately issued that allowed Jews to escape from Hitler. Only 645 went to the island. They settled in a special community Trujillo planned called Sosua. Today, about 30 of the original families remain in Sosua.

From 1933 to 1945, 132,000 refugees found refuge in the United States—the largest number accepted by any country, but still a paltry total given the magnitude of the problem and the danger the Jews faced. The reasons for the failure to accept more of the people fleeing persecution were concerns about the economy, anti-Semitism, and xenophobia.

By the time the war started, the United States was just coming out of the Great Depression, and Americans were concerned that a flood of refugees would threaten the recovery and be a drag on the economy. The nation also had a strong undercurrent of anti-Semitism, which increased the reluctance of the government to offer specific aid to Jews. This undercurrent was further exacerbated by a general distrust of foreigners, feelings that persisted even in this great nation of immigrants.

War Lore

On May 13, 1939, 936 people (all but six were Jews) boarded the *SS St. Louis* for Cuba in Hamburg, Germany. The ship reached Havana on May 27, but Cuban authorities refused to honor the passengers' visas and demanded a ransom of as much as $1 million to allow the passengers to land. The Cubans eventually said they'd accept just under half that, but the money could not be raised. The ship sailed up the Florida coast while appeals were made to the U.S. government to allow the ship to land. They were denied, and Coast Guard ships ensured no one tried to jump off and swim to shore. The *St. Louis* was forced to turn back. Almost one month after leaving Germany, the ship returned to Europe, debarking its passengers in Antwerp. Some European nations accepted the refugees, but most were overrun when the war started. Besides the 288 who made it to England, few others survived. The story was told in the book, *The Voyage of the Damned*, which was later made into a movie with an all-star cast that included James Mason, the actor who twice played Rommel in films.

Though the average Jew had little chance of reaching the United States, "persons of exceptional merit" were sought out by rescuers led by Varian Fry. Through Fry's efforts, and that of others, some of the greatest Jewish artists, scientists, and writers escaped. Some of them later contributed to the Manhattan Project; others founded the New School for Social Research in New York City.

The Nazi Euthanasia Program

The first people that Hitler systematically began to murder were not Jews. In September 1939, he gave an order authorizing doctors to grant "the incurably ill a merciful death." The program was based in Berlin at No. 4 Tiergartenstrasse and became known afterward as the T-4 program.

This program was one of the most diabolical of Hitler's schemes. For example, babies born with disabilities were killed under this program to prevent mothers from developing bonds with them. Patients from hospitals all over the *Reich* who were considered senile, insane, or in some way "mentally defective" were marked for death. Initially people were killed by starvation, then injections of lethal doses of sedatives, and ultimately gas. The gas chambers, disguised as showers, were first developed for use in the T-4 program, and corpses were cremated as Jews would later be in the camps.

Some institutions refused to surrender their patients, and eventually public protests were heard. The most notable was Bishop Clemens August von Galen of Münster, who denounced the program in August 1941. Afterward, the program continued secretly and on a smaller scale.

Roll Call

Between September 1939 and August 1941, roughly 4,000 people a month were killed under the T-4 program. A total of 80,000 mental patients and 10,000 concentration camp prisoners were among the first victims of Hitler's murder machine.

The Final Solution

Hitler's extermination campaign was already nearly three years old when Reinhard Heydrich, head of the SS *Reich* Security Main Office, arranged for a conference in the Berlin suburb of Wannsee on January 20, 1942. The objective was to find all 11 million Jews in Europe and coordinate "a final solution to the Jewish problem." During the meeting the participants discussed their "practical experience" in dealing with the Jewish problem, which included the *Einsatzgruppen*, the use of mobile gas vans, and experiments with gas chambers. The only "favor" the representative of the General Government, Dr. Joseph Bouhler, asked for was a solution to the Jewish question "as rapidly as possible."

Building Walls Around the Jews

Jews made up a significant proportion of the population of many cities in Eastern Europe, particularly those in Poland. Before Hitler decided upon the most efficient way to murder thousands of people at once, the Jews of Poland and the German-occupied areas of the Soviet Union were herded into ghettos. The first *ghetto* was established in 1940, and soon the Jews in places such as Warsaw, Vilna, Lublin, and Krakow were isolated.

Before the war, Jews made up roughly 30 percent of Warsaw's population. The 375,000 Jews living there made it the second largest concentration of Jews after New York City.

In November 1940, approximately one half million Polish Jews were crowded into an area in Warsaw that had previously housed half that many people. Surrounded by an 11-mile wall, the Jews were starved and worked to death. Almost 45,000 Jews died in the Warsaw ghetto in 1941 alone.

GI Jargon

The word **ghetto** comes from the Italian word for foundry. The Jewish quarter in Venice was on the site of a cannon foundry and referred to as a ghetto.

The ghettos were governed by Jewish councils (*Judenrat*) appointed by the Nazis to maintain order and to apportion food, jobs, and most other necessities. As time wore on, their jobs became increasingly difficult because they were forced to collaborate in the deportations from the ghettos to the camps. The lack of food and sanitation in the ghettos led to starvation and disease. The Jews tried to live as normally as possible under the conditions, but the worsening conditions in the ghettos made survival a daily struggle. In 1942, Hitler decided to liquidate the ghettos and, within 18 months, had the more than 2 million Jews who'd survived the ghettos deported to death camps.

Words of War

"For the first time since the occupation, we saw Germans clinging to walls, crawling on the ground, running for cover, hesitating before taking a step in the fear of being hit by a Jewish bullet."

—Tuvia Borzykowski recalling the Warsaw ghetto uprising

The Germans ordered the Jewish "police" in the Warsaw ghetto to round up people for deportation. Hundreds of thousands of men, women, and children were packed in cattle cars and transported to the Treblinka death camp where they were murdered. In April 1943, the Jews learned the Germans planned to deport all the people who remained in the Warsaw ghetto to Treblinka. A group led by Mordecai Anielewicz shocked the Nazis by revolting on April 19. The 1,200 ghetto fighters had a handful of pistols, 17 rifles, and Molotov cocktails against more than 2,000 German troops supported by tanks and flame throwers.

After several days without quelling the uprising, the German commander, General Jürgen Stroop, ordered the ghetto burned to the ground. Still, the Jews held out against the overwhelming force for more than a month before the ghetto was liquidated. Approximately 300 Germans and 7,000 Jews were killed, and another 7,000 Jews were deported to Treblinka. The outcome was preordained, but the dramatic act of resistance helped raise the morale of Jews everywhere, if only briefly.

The Model Ghetto

Thousands of Jews on the way to Auschwitz were sent to Theresienstadt, a camp built in 1941, 40 miles from Prague. In 1943, 456 Danes who had failed to escape to Sweden were sent to Theresienstadt. The Danes demanded they be accounted for, and the Germans reluctantly agreed to allow the Red Cross to visit the camp.

Seeing this event as a propaganda opportunity that would allow them to refute allegations about the mistreatment of Jews in camps, the Germans spent the weeks before the visit turning the ghetto into a model city. When the people from the Red Cross arrived, they were greeted by the head of the Jewish Council in a suit and top hat and band music. Everywhere they looked, they saw happy people playing soccer, reading books, or sitting in a cafe.

The visitors were completely fooled and, as the Nazis had hoped, reported that Jews were being treated well. But, of course, it was all an act. As soon as the delegation left, the deportations to Auschwitz resumed, and many of the "actors" were killed immediately to ensure their silence.

The *Einsatzgruppen*

When Germany invaded the Soviet Union, Hitler was suddenly confronted with the problem of having hundreds of thousands more Jews to exterminate. To hasten the process, mobile killing squads, *Einsatzgruppen*, were created to mop up the Jews after the army overran an area. The killers didn't do anything fancy; they simply rounded up all the Jews, marched them to an isolated spot, shot them, and buried them in a mass grave.

The most notorious of the *Einsatzgruppen* actions, known as Babi Yar, occurred on September 19, 1941, when the Germans captured the city of Kiev. All the Jews were marched to a ravine and ordered to strip. They were then machine-gunned, and their bodies fell into the ravine. More than 33,000 Jews were murdered. Two years later, as the Red Army advanced, the *Einsatzgruppen* commander, Paul Blobel, brought a group of concentration

Words of War

"If Auschwitz was hell, Theresienstadt was the anteroom."

—A Jewish Holocaust survivor

Ask the General

Some Germans did protest the murder of civilians. One general was incensed that the SS men were "demonstrating their courage against defenseless civilians" instead of on the front. Despite the implied threat of punishment for failing to carry out orders, some Germans refused without suffering serious consequences. When Major General Friedrich Mieth, Chief of Staff of the German First Army, for example, said the mass executions besmirched the honor of the army, he was simply dismissed. The notion that Germans had to kill or be killed is untrue.

camp prisoners to the site and had them help dig up the bodies so they could be burned to destroy the evidence of the massacre. Afterward, the prisoners were shot, but a handful escaped and lived to tell the tale of Babi Yar.

At the same time the *Einsatzgruppen* were conducting their murder spree, the Germans were experimenting with less violent means of killing Jews. At the Chelmno death camp, mobile gas vans were used to asphyxiate their passengers. The problem was that this method took a long time, and the capacity of the vans was too small. The solution was to create gas chambers in the concentration camps, which could handle hundreds of people at one time.

The Camps

The first concentration camp was built long before the war. Dachau was erected in 1933 to house political prisoners. It was followed by the construction of Sachsenhausen, Buchenwald, Mauthausen, Flossenbürg, and the women's camp Ravensbrück.

The Germans later built camps specifically for murdering Jews. These camps were all built near the main railroad line in Poland to facilitate transportation from the ghettos. The six death camps were Chelmno, Treblinka, Sobibor, Belzec, Majdanek, and Auschwitz/Birkenau. These camps killed millions of Jews, Gypsies, and others. In Auschwitz alone, more than 1,000,000 people were murdered, most in gas chambers.

Of course, the Jews were killed in all the concentration camps, but most of the other camps did not execute their victims immediately. With the exception of Majdanek and Auschwitz, which also had slave-labor camps, most of the prisoners were killed upon arrival in the death camps.

When prisoners arrived at the camps, they were immediately subject to "selection." An SS officer would direct people to the left or right. One direction meant life in the camp—at least for a while. The other meant death. The most notorious of these SS officers was Dr. Josef Mengele, the "Angel of Death," who also performed gruesome medical experiments on prisoners.

Women, children, the elderly, and the sick were immediately directed to a place where they were told to undress. Then they entered a room labeled "showers." The door was closed behind them. A few moments later, instead of water, poison gas rained down on their heads. After experimenting with different poisons, the Nazis discovered that the insecticide Zyklon B could kill 2,000

Words of War

"In Germany they came first for the communists, and I didn't speak up because I wasn't a communist. Then they came for the Jews, and I didn't speak up because I wasn't a Jew. Then they came for the trade unionists, and I didn't speak up because I wasn't a trade unionist. Then they came for the Catholics, and I didn't speak up because I was a Protestant. Then they came for me, and by that time no one was left to speak up."

—Reverend Martin Niemöller

people in less than 30 minutes and that became the preferred "showering" agent.

Those who were not immediately killed were segregated by sex, their personal possessions were taken away, and their heads were shaved. They were issued prison uniforms and had numbers tattooed on their arms.

The numbers of bodies being buried eventually grew so large that the mass graves were overflowing. Ovens were installed in some camps to cremate the dead. After the Jews were killed, camp inmates were forced to extract gold from the teeth of the corpses, as well as to confiscate money, jewelry, and anything else of value, which was then delivered to the German *Reichsbank*. Other personal items such as clocks, wallets, and clothes were cleaned and delivered to German troops. The best of the loot was reserved for SS officers.

Ask the General

Concentration camp prisoners were not just killed by gas. Some of the other methods of murder included: shooting, hanging, clubbing, heart injections, starvation, burying them alive, kicking them in the genitals, putting a red-hot poker down their throats, forcing them into an electric fence, locking them in a building and setting it on fire, and many more too grisly to mention.

Another feature of the camp system was forced labor. At the entrance to camps such as Auschwitz, a sign read, *Arbeit Macht Frei*, "Labor wins freedom." Thousands of prisoners died working in German industrial factories owned by large companies such as IG Farben (which produced synthetic rubber and fuel) and Krupp (which produced fuses).

Bones of anti-Nazi German women are still in the crematoriums in the German concentration camp at Weimar, Germany, April 14, 1945. (National Archives Still Pictures Branch)

The Jews are sometimes said to have gone into the gas chambers like sheep to slaughter, but as Chapter 20 suggested, even battle-trained soldiers taken prisoner stood little chance of escaping the camps or resisting the Germans. What chance did starving, disease-ridden, unarmed civilians have?

War Lore

Auschwitz was the only place where prisoners were given tattoos. The practice began in 1941 when Soviet POWs were stamped on the upper left breast. The Nazis found the device they used was impractical, so they adopted a different method to tattoo the left forearm of prisoners. Jews started receiving tattoos in 1942, and all other prisoners, except prisoners from the *Reich* (Germans), ethnic Germans, and police prisoners, began to get them shortly thereafter.

Still, many examples of resistance can be found. In addition to the Warsaw Ghetto uprising, Jews fought with partisan groups. At several concentration camps, groups of prisoners fought back against all odds. For example, prisoners attacked the guards at Treblinka, and about 200 escaped, half of whom evaded capture. At Birkenau, a group of inmates assigned to empty the gas chambers and stoke the ovens blew up one of the four crematoria.

Probably the most dramatic camp revolt was at Sobibor where a Soviet Jewish prisoner and the leader of the camp underground planned a daring escape. Two SS guards were lured into an ambush and killed. The prisoners took their weapons and set the camp on fire. The guards were overpowered (11 were killed), and 300 fled the camp into the forest. Most were later recaptured and shot, but approximately 50 survived (look for the 1987 movie *Escape From Sobibor* with Alan Arkin and Rutger Hauer).

Medical Experiments

Because the Germans believed the Jews were inferior and essentially subhuman, they felt no hesitation about using them for cruel experiments. Some of these experiments are so heinous that it is difficult to write about them.

At Auschwitz, the Germans experimented with sterilization techniques. If Jews couldn't breed, after all, they would die out without the Germans having to kill them. "Doctors" would bombard the testicles of men and ovaries of women with X rays to see the impact of different doses. At Birkenau, one of the subcamps of Auschwitz (the largest and deadliest of all the concentration camps, where 1.1 million people were murdered), Dr. Mengele was the chief physician. He was interested in proving the superiority of the Nordic race and conducted gruesome experiments on Gypsy children, twins, dwarfs, and people with various abnormalities. The subjects of the research were killed, and then autopsies were conducted to analyze their bodies. Interesting anatomical findings were often preserved for additional analysis.

At other camps, the Nazis broke bones over and over again to see how many times it could be done before the bone would no longer heal. They hit people's heads with hammers to see what their skulls could withstand. Prisoners were exposed to extreme heat and cold to determine the maximum and minimum temperatures at which people could survive. At the special request of a *Luftwaffe* surgeon, experiments were conducted to determine the effects of atmospheric pressure on the body. Prisoners were also injected with different drugs and infected with diseases to test poisons and new drugs. Limbs were amputated and muscles cut for transplantation experiments.

Many of the results of the Nazi experiments were used by doctors, though no medically valuable research came from any of them. Today, reference to or use of the Nazi research is considered unethical, and a controversy recently arose over the widespread use of a textbook on anatomy that contains drawings made using the corpses of political prisoners.

Gypsies, Gays, and Jehovah's Witnesses

Jews were the primary targets of Hitler's genocidal policies, but they were not the only ones. Gypsies (also called Roma), a nomadic people living in Europe since the 15th century, had long been persecuted in Germany. In 1942, Nazis determined that Gypsies were threats to the "purity of the race" and therefore subject to the Final Solution. No one knows how many Gypsies were killed, but it is estimated that as many as half of the European population died at the hands of the Nazis.

Homosexuality was against the law in Germany, as it was elsewhere in Europe, but gays had a relatively open lifestyle, and many were in positions of power, including Ernst Röhm, the head of Hitler's storm troopers (who was murdered on Hitler's orders because of a power struggle within the Nazi Party). After becoming *Führer*, Hitler almost immediately began to crack down on organizations associated with homosexuals (such as gay bars) and sent those individuals who were caught to concentration camps.

The tiny population of Jehovah's Witnesses in Germany also became subject to persecution, not so much because of their religion as their unwillingness to conform to the demands of Nazi discipline. They would not participate in the army, refused to give the *"Heil Hitler"* salute, and continued their proselytizing activities despite being ordered to stop. Hitler had them sent to concentration camps, where many perished. Unlike every other group in the camps, the Witnesses had the opportunity to leave—if they renounced their beliefs. Few did.

War Lore

In the concentration camps, prisoners wore different badges or arm bands to identify what category they fell under. Jews, for example, wore yellow Stars of David. Gypsies wore brown triangles, criminals wore green ones, and Jehovah's Witnesses wore purple ones. Homosexuals were given pink triangles, which is now a symbol of the gay rights movement. Initially, however, they wore yellow bands with a letter *A* for *Arschficker.* The 76,000 Jews still living in Berlin in September 1941 were also required to wear yellow stars.

These were three of the major non-Jewish categories of people who were sent to camps to be murdered. Others included freemasons, socialists, criminals, and anyone deemed an enemy of the *Reich.*

Words of War

"That's the difficulty of these times: ideals, dreams, and cherished hopes rise within us, only to meet the horrible truth and be shattered. It's really a wonder that I haven't dropped all my ideals because they seem so absurd and impossible to carry out. Yet I keep them, because in spite of everything, I still believe that people are really good at heart. I simply can't build up my hopes on a foundation consisting of confusion, misery, and death."

—From the diary of Anne Frank, July 15, 1944

Anne Frank

Anne Frank was born in Germany. After Hitler came to power, her family fled to the Netherlands. After that country was overrun, the persecution of Jews began, and orders were given to report to the Westerbork "work" camp. To avoid deportation, Jews had to find hiding places with non-Jews. Such hideaways were hard to find, but Anne's family found shelter in the annex of the building that housed her father Otto's business.

On July 6, 1942, the family went into the attic. Even though Anne first saw hiding as an exciting adventure, the tiny room soon became too small for her restless spirit. For more than two years she wrote in a diary about her daily life in hiding.

On August 4, 1944, the Security Police raided the building. Anne Frank and the seven others in hiding were arrested and transported to Auschwitz. After a month at Auschwitz, Anne and her sister Margot were sent to Bergen-Belsen where they both contracted typhus and died in March 1945. Anne was just shy of her 16th birthday when she died. Of all those in hiding, only Otto Frank survived the camps.

Otto later retrieved Anne's diary, in which she had written of her desire to publish a book entitled *The Annex* after the war. Otto published the diary in 1947. It has since sold roughly 20 million copies. The stage play based on the book won the Pulitzer Prize, and two films were also made about the Franks' life in the attic. The Anne Frank House is now a museum in the Netherlands (it also has a web site at http://www.annefrank.nl/).

Americans Also Died in Camps

Hundreds, perhaps thousands, of Americans were in every major concentration camp: Auschwitz, Mauthausen, Dachau, Buchenwald. Americans were even in the Warsaw ghetto. More than 5,000 Americans were imprisoned in internment camps. The total number who died in Nazi camps is uncertain, but it definitely was in the hundreds.

American Jews were subject to the same anti-Semitic regulations and dangers as any other Jews who came under the control of the Nazis. Hundreds, perhaps thousands, of lives could have been saved had the United States government taken action to rescue people claiming American citizenship. Often it did just the opposite, creating obstacles that impeded Americans from obtaining the necessary documents to escape from the Nazis.

In 1939, more than 80,000 American citizens were believed to be living abroad. State Department officials held that citizens who had no apparent intention of returning to the United States could not expect their government to feel any obligation to protect them. An even deeper prejudice lay behind this viewpoint: the belief that citizens returning from abroad would become welfare cases. Initially, U.S. officials thought American Jews were safe. In 1941, Secretary of State Cordell Hull said he expected Americans to be exempt from anti-Jewish laws. A few months later, he was explicitly told the Germans would make no distinctions based on nationality.

In places such as France and Hungary, American property was confiscated. As early as January 1942, the State Department learned that Americans were being arrested. In one case, a group of 35 American Jews was threatened with deportation from Slovakia, and another 70 Americans sought repatriation. The department refused to help them because it believed Slovak authorities were trying to use the Americans to pressure the United States to recognize Slovakia.

Once that decision was made, the State Department was forced to cover up its failure to act out of

Words of War

"It is the perpetrators who tell us of their own voluntarism in the slaughter, of their routine brutalities against helpless Jewish victims, of their degrading and mocking of the Jews. It is they who tell us of their boasting, celebrations, and memorializations of their deeds, not the least of which are the many photographs which they took, passed around, put in their albums, and sent home to loved ones."

—Daniel Goldhagen

331

fear of public reaction. A top official admitted that "if the Axis propaganda mill should give publicity to the proposed ill treatment of American citizens of Jewish race in Slovakia there may be considerable criticism of the department by Jewish circles in the United States." This is perhaps the clearest statement that the State Department was aware of the seriousness of the plight of Jews in Eastern Europe, was sensitive to public opinion, and still was unwilling to act.

Americans in the occupied territories could not travel and communicate freely; they needed special permits to leave, and those were rarely given. The situation was exacerbated when the Germans closed U.S. offices in Germany and the occupied territories. One State Department official suggested that the Passport Division provide a list of passports issued in Europe during 1941, as well as a list of Americans whose passports were validated in 1940 or 1941 for continued stays in Europe, so the Department could check for Americans in Europe who might be entitled to repatriation. The idea was vetoed. Swiss officials in charge of American affairs were left to identify U.S. citizens, but, contrary to the usual practice, were refused access to American files.

Officials planned to decide whom they wanted to allow to return to the United States. The official responsible for helping U.S. citizens overseas, Breckinridge Long, said in June 1942 that Americans in Germany awaiting repatriation "ought to be examined and *only those we want* should be accepted (emphasis in the original)."

Even less attention was paid to whether Americans were in concentration camps. When the issue was raised, the government denied any Americans were in the camps, but the U.S. government knew Americans were in concentration camps. For example, the State Department had reliable information that about 200 people claiming U.S. citizenship were in Bergen-Belsen in July 1944.

In January 1940, President Roosevelt sent a list of 200 names to the State Department with instructions that they be given emergency visas. Had he given the same type of special assistance to all U.S. citizens throughout the war, thousands would have been spared needless suffering, and hundreds would have been saved from execution.

What's Different About the Jews?

Hitler killed approximately 12 million people. People sometimes ask, therefore, why special attention should be given to only half the victims, the Jews. The eminent Jewish philosopher, Emil Fackenheim, offers a concise outline of the distinguishing characteristics of the Holocaust in his book, *To Mend the World:*

➤ The Final Solution was designed to exterminate every single Jewish man, woman, and child. The only Jews who would have conceivably survived had Hitler been victorious were those who somehow escaped discovery by the Nazis.

➤ Jewish birth (actually mere evidence of "Jewish blood") was sufficient to warrant the punishment of death. Fackenheim notes that this feature distinguished Jews from Poles and Russians who were killed because there were too many of them and from "Aryans" who were not singled out unless they chose to single themselves out. With the possible exception of Gypsies, Jews were the only people killed for the "crime" of existing.

➤ The extermination of the Jews had no political or economic justification. It was not a means to any end; it was an end in itself. The killing of Jews was not considered just a part of the war effort, but equal to it; thus, resources that could have been used in the war were diverted instead to the program of extermination.

➤ The people who carried out the "Final Solution" were primarily average citizens. Fackenheim calls them "ordinary job holders with an extraordinary job." They were not perverts or sadists. "The tone-setters," he says, "were ordinary idealists, except that their ideals were torture and murder."

Other examples of mass murder exist in human history, such as the atrocities committed by Pol Pot in Cambodia and the Turkish annihilation of the Armenians during World War I. But none of those other catastrophes, Fackenheim argues, contain more than one of these characteristics.

The Least You Need to Know

➤ Hitler never made any secret of his intention to exterminate the Jews. As soon as he came to power, Hitler institutionalized anti-Semitism.

➤ Escape from the Nazis became increasingly difficult as the years went by, but even before the war, all but a handful of nations refused to allow Jewish refugees to enter.

➤ The Nazis began their campaign of mass murder with the euthanasia program directed against the old, the disabled, and the mentally ill.

➤ Special mobile killing squads, the *Einsatzgruppen*, engaged in mass murders. The numbers they killed became so large, more efficient methods were needed. Gas vans and chambers were created to accelerate the "Final Solution."

➤ Concentration camps were established for political prisoners. Later, death camps were built specifically to exterminate the Jews.

➤ In addition to Jews, homosexuals, Gypsies, and Jehovah's Witnesses were persecuted and murdered. Even some Americans ended up in concentration camps.

➤ Though Jews comprised only half of all the people murdered by Hitler, the systematic way in which they were singled out for extermination makes the Holocaust unique.

Chapter 25

Liberators, Rescuers, and Avengers

In This Chapter

➤ Liberators discover the horrors of the camps

➤ The Allies won't bomb Auschwitz

➤ True heroes

➤ What we knew and when

➤ Some Nazi criminals are brought to justice

By the end of the war, most people had some idea about what the Nazis had done to the Jews and others. Until they saw the pictures from the concentration camps, however, no one fully understood the magnitude of the atrocities that had been committed. Even battle-hardened soldiers who'd seen the horrors of war were unprepared for the sights, sounds, and smells they found when they entered the camps. Once the truth was known, no one questioned the need to bring the perpetrators of history's greatest crime against humanity to justice.

Liberation

As the Allies approached, some of the concentration camps were dismantled, and the prisoners were taken on forced marches for miles in the cold and snow. Many were so weak from their time in the camp that they died on the road. Those who fell or were too slow were usually shot.

The images most people have of the Holocaust are those from the pictures taken after liberation: the emaciated bodies of the living, half-burned corpses, ashes in crematoria ovens, stacks of naked bodies, and mountains of hair, glasses, and shoes. Photographs, however, cannot capture the sounds of suffering or the smell of death.

The Polish death camp Majdanek was the first to be liberated. Soviet soldiers entered the camp on July 23, 1944. Few prisoners were found alive, but they did find 800,000 pairs of shoes. Shortly thereafter the Red Army overran several other killing centers. In January 1945, Auschwitz was liberated.

The Allies did not liberate their first camps until April 1945, when the British entered Bergen-Belsen and the Americans found Buchenwald. The headline of one Army journalist's story may have expressed the liberators' feelings best, "Dachau Gives Answer To Why We Fought."

Even after the Allies arrived, many prisoners were beyond help. In Bergen-Belsen, for example, 300 former prisoners died each day for a week. Nearly 2,500 of the 33,000 survivors of Dachau died within six weeks of liberation. Disease, malnourishment, and mistreatment had worn them down too much.

After the camps were liberated, prisoners sometimes took justice into their own hands and turned on their guards. In a few instances, the liberators themselves were so horrified by what they saw that they summarily executed the Nazis they captured.

These men are slave laborers in the Buchenwald concentration camp. Many prisoners had died of malnutrition when U.S. troops of the 80th Division entered the camp, April 16, 1945. (National Archives Still Pictures Branch)

Flying Around Auschwitz

One of the long-standing controversies about World War II involves the question of whether the Allies could have and should have bombed Auschwitz. In his seminal work, *The Abandonment of the Jews*, David Wyman argued that the failure to bomb the camp was a result of the Allies' indifference to the fate of the Jews rather than the practical impossibility of the operation.

Some critics argue the Allies did not know about the Final Solution early enough to make plans to bomb the camps, and they didn't have reliable intelligence about their location. In fact, the Allies had information about the Nazi plan to exterminate the Jews by 1942. As early as June 1944, the United States had detailed information about the layout of Auschwitz, and bombing the camp would have been no more complex than other missions.

Other defenders of the Allied policy argue Auschwitz should not have been bombed even if it were possible because many prisoners would have been killed. The counter to this is that prisoners would surely have died in any raid, but the emphasis should be on the number of Jews who might have been saved by the bombing.

Yet another argument for not bombing the camps is that it would have made no difference. Without the extermination facilities, however, the SS undoubtedly would have been forced to slow or altogether halt the deportations (which in the spring/summer of 1944 amounted to 70,000 to 80,000 Hungarian Jews a week) while they resorted to other, less efficient means of killing and body disposal.

The argument made by military officials at the time was that bombing Auschwitz would have required a diversion of aircraft needed for other military operations. If Churchill or Roosevelt had ordered an attack, however, it would not have been considered a diversion. With the kind of political will and moral courage the Allies exhibited in other missions throughout the war, it is plain that the failure to bomb Auschwitz, the site of humanity's greatest abomination, was a missed opportunity of monumental proportions.

Words of War

"As I approached them, I could see that they had sunken cheeks, distended bellies, and swollen ankles. Their complexion was sallow. In each row a sick woman was supported or dragged along by her fellow detainees. The young SS woman supervisor with a police dog on a leash led the column, followed by two girls who incessantly hurled abuse at the poor women."

—A Red Cross official present as 17,000 women were marched out of Ravensbrück

Words of War

"You were our liberators, but we, the diseased, emaciated, barely human survivors were your teachers. We taught you to understand the Kingdom of Night."

—Elie Wiesel, concentration camp survivor and Nobel Laureate

337

U.S. Army Air Force aerial reconnaissance photo of Auschwitz I, August 25, 1944, enlarged from the original negative and captioned in 1978 by the CIA. (National Archives Still Pictures Branch)

The focus on bombing Auschwitz may be misplaced, however, because that was just one of hundreds of concentration camps (albeit perhaps the worst). Many Jews could have been saved by bombing other camps. The Allies did bomb Buchenwald, for example, but not for the purpose of saving Jews.

The Danish Rescue

Once Germany overran a country, whatever officials Hitler left in control were expected to cooperate with the Final Solution. Many, including Vichy France, Croatia, and Slovakia, enthusiastically deported their Jews to concentration camps. In a handful of places, such as Finland, Bulgaria, Greece, Yugoslavia, and the unoccupied parts of France, efforts were made to shelter Jews.

Hitler was particularly infuriated by the fact that Mussolini would not be more cooperative. Though Mussolini made his share of anti-Semitic remarks and imposed his own racial laws in 1938 after Germany introduced the Nuremberg Laws, he was more of an opportunist than an anti-Semite. In fact, many of the early leaders of the Fascists were Jews. Mussolini never understood Hitler's obsession with the Jews and did not share it. The Italian racial laws were not nearly as broad or severe as Germany's, and the Italians were far less zealous in their application. Moreover, it was not until after the Allies had invaded Italy and Mussolini was deposed that Germans occupying the country could implement Hitler's program.

In Hungary, Admiral Horthy ordered an end to deportations after a series of Allied bombing raids on Budapest, including one that dropped leaflets warning that those responsible for the persecution of Jews would be punished. By then, nearly half a million Hungarian Jews had been deported. Hitler's response was to arrest Horthy two months later and replace him with Ferenc Szàlasi, who happily resumed the deportations. By this time, October 1944, the Soviets were rapidly approaching. The Hungarian Jews were forced to dig anti-tank trenches, and thousands were shot.

War Lore

A small town near Lyon in Vichy-controlled France was a haven for 5,000 Jews. The Protestant pastor of Le Chambon-sur-Lignon helped organize the people in the town to hide Jews in homes, farmhouses, monasteries, and convents. An even smaller town, Nieuwlande, in the northeast Netherlands, was another example of a place where townspeople risked their lives for their fellow man. Hundreds of Jews were rescued by the 250 residents of that town.

The most dramatic effort to save Jews was in Denmark, which had a tiny Jewish community of 7,000. One of the Jews, physicist Niels Bohr, escaped with his wife to Sweden on September 29, 1943, and pleaded with the government to help. The day before the Danish Jews were scheduled to be deported, nearly all 7,000 were smuggled by Danish fisherman across the water to Sweden, which shielded them for the duration of the war. Meanwhile, Bohr went on to the United States, joined the Manhattan Project, and helped end the war.

Righteous Persons

The Yad Vashem Holocaust Memorial Museum in Israel honors people who risked their own lives to save Jews during World War II. These individuals are referred to as Righteous Persons (or Gentiles). Though the vast majority of Germans and other nationals in territories occupied by the Nazis were either perpetrators or bystanders, more than 14,000 people have been recognized for their courage and morality. Most of these people were in Poland (where anyone aiding Jews was automatically subject to the death penalty), the Netherlands, and France.

Given the difficulty and peril involved, perhaps it is remarkable even this many people acted as they did. Most of these heroes are little-known or anonymous, but one man in particular has become a symbol of what one man can do in the face of tyranny. That man was Raoul Wallenberg.

Wallenberg was a Swedish aristocrat who was sent to Hungary in July 1944 to save the remaining Jews. In the two months before he arrived, more than 400,000 Jews had been deported to Auschwitz. A temporary suspension was in progress when Wallenberg reached Budapest, but he knew the Nazis were agitating for a resumption of the deportations. Wallenberg began issuing Swedish passports to Jews. When the Nazis ordered a new roundup of Jews, Wallenberg handed out passports to every Jew he could find. Whenever the Germans tried to stop him, he ignored or intimidated them and went ahead with his work.

War Lore

In July 1941, after a Pole escaped from Auschwitz, the commandant ordered 10 men from his block to be starved to death. A Polish Catholic priest, Father Maximilian Kolbe, came forward and asked to take the place of one of the men who was selected. Kolbe said, "I am alone in this world. That man, Francis Gajowniczek, has a family to live for." The commandant accepted the offer, and Kolbe was taken away. At Kolbe's beatification 30 years later, Francis Gajowniczek and his wife were in the audience.

When the Soviets overran Hungary, Wallenberg went to meet with them to discuss the future of the remaining Hungarian Jews. He was last seen on January 17, 1945. For years, the Soviets denied he had been taken prisoner. When they finally admitted it, they claimed he died in 1947. Some people continue to believe that he may be alive.

Wallenberg is credited with saving roughly 100,000 Jews. The street in front of the U.S. Holocaust Memorial Museum is named after Wallenberg who, in 1981, became one of only two people to ever receive honorary U.S. citizenship (the other was Churchill).

A man whose motives were less pure, at least initially, but who has become famous because of Steven Spielberg's Oscar-winning 1993 film *Schindler's List* (which was based on Thomas Keneally's 1982 book) was Oskar Schindler. For those who haven't seen the movie—and everyone should—it is the true story of a German profiteer who established an enamel works in Zablocie, outside Krakow, in which he employed mainly Jewish workers, thereby protecting them from deportations. When the liquidation of the Krakow ghetto began in early 1943, many Jews were sent to the Plaszow labor camp, whose commandant, Amon Goeth, had a reputation for exceptional cruelty. Schindler carefully cultivated relations with high German officials to obtain permission for about 900 Jews from Plaszow to work in his factory.

As the Red Army grew nearer, Schindler moved to Brunnlitz, Czechoslovakia, and started an armaments factory. He prepared a list of Jewish workers to bring with him from Zablocie, which the Nazi authorities approved. Roughly 1,200 Jews ultimately came to work for him. Throughout the time he employed Jews, Schindler provided them with food and medical care and humane working conditions unknown in other companies employing slave labor.

When the Allied armies were about to overrun the area, the people Schindler saved, the *Schindlerjuden*, gave him a letter in Hebrew explaining what he'd done for them. They also gave him a ring made from gold fillings extracted from one of the grateful Jews. The ring was inscribed with the Talmudic verse, "He who saves one life, it is as if he saved the entire world." Schindler had little success in business after the war and died a poor man in Frankfurt in 1974 at the age of 66. His true worth, however, is best reflected in the 6,000 Jewish descendants of the *Schindlerjuden*. Schindler is buried in Israel.

War Lore

Many movies have been made about the Holocaust. Some of the best non-documentary films include *The Diary of Anne Frank; Europa, Europa; Shoah; Music Box;* and *QB VII.* For a list of web sites related to the Holocaust, see http://www.us-israel.org/jsource/bibliow.html.

Perhaps an even more unlikely savior of the Jews was a member of the Axis. Polish refugees in Lithuania discovered that Curacao and Dutch Guiana (now known as Suriname) did not require formal entrance visas. To get to these islands, the refugees needed to pass through the Soviet Union. The Soviet consul agreed to let them pass if they obtained a visa from the Japanese, because they would have to pass through Japan on their way to the islands. The lives of the Poles depended then on the willingness of Japan's Consul-General, Chiune Sugihara, to help them.

Sugihara tried unsuccessfully three times to get permission from his government to issue visas (incidentally, the Japanese did not persecute Jews). Despite the risk to his career, Sugihara ignored the negative replies and spent every day from July 31 to August 28, 1940, writing and signing visas. Jews were standing outside the consulate day and night. Soon they began scaling the walls, and he had to reassure them that he would help everyone. On September 1, Sugihara boarded a train for Berlin. As it pulled away, he was still handing visas out his window. As many as 6,000 refugees made their way to Japan, China, and other countries in the following months; their lives were saved by the courageous actions of a Japanese diplomat.

We Closed Our Eyes

The Allies knew about the persecution of Jews from the beginning. It is sometimes claimed that no one knew what was going on in the concentration camps until late in the war, but this isn't true. Given Hitler's public statements, there should have been no doubt as to what would happen to people in his prisons. By 1942, the Allies were well aware of the extermination campaign. Recently released intelligence reports suggest the British might have known even earlier.

In December 1942, the "Big Three" issued a declaration specifically mentioning the transportation of Jews, the liquidation of the ghettos, and mass executions. "The number of victims of these bloody cruelties is reckoned in many hundreds of thousands of entirely innocent men, women, and children." The statement went on to denounce the German atrocities, but no actions were taken then or later. The Allies believed that winning the war was the best strategy for saving the Jews; unfortunately, millions of Jews could not wait that long.

The press and public found out about the atrocities being committed at almost the same time as the government. The press did a horrible job of covering the story, and the reports that were printed usually were buried in the depths of the paper, which seems inconceivable now given some of the headlines and their accompanying stories:

➤ "25,000 Jews Seized in Southern France" (*New York Times*, August 28, 1942)

➤ "Jewish Children Interned by Vichy" (*Chicago Sun*, August 31, 1942)

➤ "35,000 Jews Executed in Five Polish Towns" (*New York Herald Tribune*, March 21, 1943)

➤ "50,000 Jews Put in Nazi Prison 'Die Like Flies'" (*Washington Times Herald*, September 3, 1943)

➤ "50,000 Jews Dying in Nazi Fortress" (*New York Times*, September 3, 1943)

➤ "Nazi Slayings Near 250,000" (*Baltimore Sun*, September 22, 1943)

➤ "Poles Report Nazis Slay 10,000 Daily" (*Washington Post*, March 22, 1944)

➤ "1,000,000 Hungarian Jews Face Massacre, Hull Says" (*Chicago Sun*, July 15, 1944)

Even with this information there was an air of disbelief. Given the exaggerations during World War I about atrocities, some of which were invented, people in and out of government were reluctant to accept that these events were occurring or that killing could be done on such a large scale.

Remembrance

Approximately 1 million Jewish children under 15 were killed during the Holocaust. How many of them would have grown up to be another Chagall or Einstein or Freud? Today, more than 50 years after the Holocaust, it is important to document the facts. People still claim it never happened; their ads appear in student newspapers at colleges around the country. We owe it to the 6 million to remember them so that nothing like the Holocaust can ever happen again.

In 1980, Congress voted unanimously to create the United States Holocaust Memorial Museum adjacent to the National Mall in Washington, D.C. The museum is the United States's national institution for the documentation, study, and interpretation of Holocaust history and serves as the national memorial to the victims of the Holocaust.

War Lore

Today, most major American cities have their own Holocaust memorials, and many have built museums. Yad Vashem (http://www.yad-vashem.org.il/) in Jerusalem, Israel, is recognized as the primary institution for the remembrance of the Holocaust.

The museum's primary mission is to advance and disseminate knowledge about the Holocaust, to preserve the memory of those who suffered, and to encourage visitors to reflect upon the moral and spiritual questions raised by the events of the Holocaust as well as their own responsibilities as citizens of a democracy. Everything about the museum is powerful; even the architecture was intentionally designed to give visitors a sense of life under the Nazis. The stark brick and limestone exterior is supposed to remind people of a German factory. Inside, James Freed's design seems flawed: Rooms do not always have right angles, the windows are different sizes, the floor is fractured, and the interior brick walls are uneven in shape and color, as were the bricks used in the crematoria. Freed intentionally wanted to convey the sense of a world gone awry.

When it first opened, some wondered how many people would want to see such a depressing museum when the fun and interesting Smithsonian Institution is down the street. In April 1998, five years after its dedication, the museum welcomed its 10 millionth visitor. It is now considered the second most popular Washington tourist

Words of War

"What makes this inquest significant is that these prisoners... are the living symbols of racial hatreds, of terrorism and violence, and of the arrogance and cruelty of power.... Civilization can afford no compromise with the social forces which would gain renewed strength if we deal ambiguously or indecisively with the men in whom those forces now precariously survive."

—From the opening statement of Justice Robert Jackson, lead U.S. prosecutor at the Nuremberg Trial

attraction after the Air & Space Museum. You can visit the Museum's web site at http://www.ushmm.org/.

"I Was Just Following Orders"

During the war, a decision was made not to pursue war criminals until after an Allied victory for fear of provoking reprisals against POWs. Instead, officials were secretly to gather evidence of war crimes for use after the war.

Many Nazis fled after the war. Some were helped by the Director of the German Church in Rome. Argentina proved to be one of the most popular havens for war criminals, many of whom were aided by ODESSA, an organization of SS men set up to aid them.

As many as 10,000 Nazis may have entered the United States. Some were helped by intelligence agencies interested in soliciting their help in the new war against communism. Operation Paper Clip was a deliberate program by the U.S. military that brought approximately 1,600 scientists to the United States to work on various projects.

War Lore

Arthur Rudolph became the director of the *Saturn V* moon rocket program. During World War II, he had used slave laborers from the Dora concentration camp to work on the V–2 rocket.

In the end, most Nazis who might have been tried for war crimes either evaded capture, were purposely allowed to come to the United States (and other countries), or were simply not prosecuted. Others who were caught or about to be captured (including Goebbels and Himmler) committed suicide before they could be tried or executed.

Looking down on the defendants' dock at the Nuremberg Trial, circa 1945 to 1946. (National Archives Still Pictures Branch)

Many war crimes trials were held at Nuremberg (ironically, the site of Hitler's largest Nazi rallies), but when one speaks of "The Nuremberg Trial," the reference is usually to the trial of 21 of the top surviving Nazi officials (22 were indicted, but Robert Ley, who headed the Reich Labor Front, hanged himself in his cell before the trial). They were charged with crimes against peace, war crimes, and crimes against humanity.

Of the 21 Nazis tried at Nuremberg, 14 were sentenced to hang; the remainder were given prison sentences. Göring committed suicide before he could be executed. The bodies of the men who were killed were taken to Dachau and cremated in the ovens. Their ashes were dropped into a river. Perhaps the most important long-term outcome of the trial was the rejection of the defense argument that "just following orders" was an excuse for committing war crimes.

The Other Nuremberg Trials

Twelve other trials were held in Nuremberg to prosecute groups of Nazis who had the chief responsibility for a variety of crimes. These trials included the "Medical Case," the "I.G. Farben Case," and the "*Einsatzgruppen* Case." The trial dealing with the mistreatment of POWs was the "High Command Case."

The head of the POW department of the High Command, Herman Reinecke, and 13 others were charged with "murder and ill-treatment, denial of rights and status, and employment under inhumane conditions and prohibited circumstances" of enemy belligerents and POWs. The evidence was almost entirely focused on the mistreatment of Soviet POWs. Reinecke was found to have been responsible for the segregation and liquidation of POWs and sentenced to life imprisonment.

The "Bitch of Buchenwald"

Trials were also held for the Germans responsible for individual concentration and POW camps. William Denson, the chief prosecutor of the major concentration camp trials—Buchenwald, Flossenbürg, Mauthausen, and Dachau—tried 177 criminals in the four cases.

The Buchenwald concentration camp case was tried from April 11 to August 14, 1947. The prosecution established that the Germans at Buchenwald and its 100 sub-camps participated in the torture and abuse of the inmates by starvation, beating, and killing. The death rate reached a high of 5,000 a month toward the end of the war. The defense denied the charges and attempted to justify and explain the large number of deaths by attributing them to natural causes, legal executions, and superior orders. The evidence of atrocities was sufficient for the court to convict all 31 of the accused for violations of the laws and usages of war.

The man who commanded the camp until early 1942, Colonel Karl Koch, was executed by the Nazis for the embezzlement of SS funds and for the murder of someone with whom he had personal difficulties. Colonel Koch's successor, Herman Pister, was sentenced by the Allied tribunal to hang, but he died in prison.

Koch's wife was sentenced at Nuremberg to life imprisonment, though this sentence was subsequently reduced to four years because reviewers said there was no convincing evidence that she selected inmates for extermination to secure tattooed skin or that she possessed any articles made of human skin. When Americans learned the "Bitch of Buchenwald" had been let off the hook, it caused a major furor in the United States that ultimately led to a congressional investigation. In 1951, she was retried in Germany and sentenced to life imprisonment. Koch committed suicide in prison 16 years later.

Taylor's Revenge

In the Mauthausen trial, one of the star witnesses was Lieutenant Jack Taylor, the OSS officer. He may have been the only American citizen to testify at a concentration camp trial. In his closing argument, prosecutor Denson observed: "There was no other camp under the German *Reich* where the conditions were as terrible, where beatings were more severe, where the prisoners received less food, than at Mauthausen."

Words of War

"There is no doubt that this is probably the greatest and the most horrible crime ever committed in the whole history of the world, and it has been done by scientific machinery by nominally civilized men in the name of a great State and one of the leading races in Europe. It is quite clear that all concerned in this crime who may fall into our hands, including the people who only obeyed orders by carrying out the butcheries, should be put to death after their association with the murders has been proved."

—Churchill after learning details about Auschwitz in July 1944

The court found "it was impossible for a governmental, military or civil official, a guard or a civilian employee, of the concentration camp Mauthausen… [not to have] acquired a definite knowledge of the criminal practices and activities therein existing." Most of the Mauthausen defendants were hanged.

Quisling and Quislings

Besides the major trials that were held primarily in Nuremberg and Dachau, other countries tried Nazis and collaborators for crimes against their citizens. For example:

➤ Jürgen Stroop, the SS commander who suppressed the Warsaw Ghetto uprising, was extradited to Poland where he was executed (after already being sentenced to death by the Americans for murdering pilots in Greece).

➤ Pierre Laval, the Vichy Prime Minister, was convicted of treason and shot.

➤ Henri Pétain, the head of the Vichy regime, was convicted of treason and sentenced to life in prison, where he died. He was already nearly 90 when he was convicted.

➤ Vidkun Quisling was found guilty of criminal collaboration and executed in Oslo.

The Japanese Face the Music

An International Military Tribunal for the Far East was set up in Tokyo in May 1946 to try Japanese officials and military personnel who committed war crimes. A total of 25 men were indicted; two men died during the trial, and a third was considered mentally unfit to be tried. The best-known defendant was Hideki Tojo, who had led Japan throughout the war. All of the men were found guilty, and seven, including Tojo, were sentenced to death and hung. Sixteen others received life sentences, and two men who'd served for short periods as Foreign Minister received prison terms. One, Mamoru Shigemitsu, returned to politics and served again as Japan's foreign minister.

In 1947, the Americans shifted the remaining trials to the Philippines. A tribunal there convicted General Masaharu Homma for his responsibility for the Bataan Death March. Another general, Tomoyuki Yamashita, was also executed for crimes against Americans and Filipinos. The U.S. Navy also held trials on Kwajalein in the Marshall Islands for crimes committed in the Pacific. These trials exposed more atrocities, including medical experiments conducted on Americans at Truk.

Additional trials were conducted in Yokohama, Japan. The British tried criminals who'd mistreated civilians and soldiers in places such as Borneo, Singapore, and Burma. In one of these trials, the two Japanese officers responsible for the brutality associated with building the bridge over the River Kwai were hung. China, Australia, France, and Russia also held trials.

Emperor Hirohito was never tried despite widespread demands that he be held accountable for the war. This was largely a political decision based on the promise to retain the imperial system as part of the terms of surrender, and the fear that prosecuting him would destabilize the country.

Roll Call

According to the UN War Crimes Commission, as of October 31, 1946, 1,108 accused war criminals were tried in Europe, 413 were sentenced to death, 485 imprisoned, and 210 acquitted. The United States held approximately 900 trials with 3,000 defendants. Of those tried in Germany, 1,380 were convicted, and 241 were acquitted. A total of 421 death sentences were handed down, but many were commuted. Trials were also held at Dachau for conventional war crimes. Of 1,672 tried, 426 were sentenced to death, but most sentences were never carried out.

Roll Call

Roughly 5,600 Japanese were tried for war crimes in 2,200 trials. More than 4,400 were convicted, and 1,000 were executed.

"Justice" for the Victims of Berga

Two men responsible for the mistreatment of Americans at the Berga concentration camp, company commander Ludwig Merz and commandant Erwin Metz, were tried at Dachau in 1946, a year-and-a-half after the survivors of Berga were liberated. Both defendants were present for the trial, but not one former POW attended. The court found Ludwig Merz and Erwin Metz guilty on all charges and sentenced both men to hang.

After a series of appeals, General Lucius Clay commuted the sentence of Erwin Metz to life imprisonment. He also reduced Merz's sentence to five years. Three years later, almost exactly six years after his conviction, Metz's sentence was reduced again, this time to 15 years. The chief of the War Crimes Branch, Colonel W.H. Peters, Jr., said, however, the sentence should be commuted to the time served from June 19, 1945. Instead of being hanged, the two men responsible for tormenting American POWs and killing more than any other Nazi camp officials were freed after serving only about six years.

John J. McCloy, the United States High Commissioner for Germany, came under tremendous pressure from the Pope, the German government, and others to grant clemency to convicted war criminals. Also, by the time many of the trials were held, and sentences were reviewed, the Cold War had begun, and the United States did not want to provoke the German people, whose support would be needed in the confrontation with Moscow. Interest in the trials waned, and subsequently, McCloy commuted the sentence of Ernst von Weizsacker, a Nazi foreign office official convicted of complicity in the deaths of 6,000 Jews transferred from France to Poland, and commuted or reduced the sentences of all convicted concentration camp doctors, 20 of the 25 SS officers convicted of serving in the *Einsatzgruppen,* and the Nazi industrialist Alfried Krupp. In 1951, McCloy issued a general amnesty.

Ask the General

In July 1946, 74 former SS men were tried for their role in the Malmédy Massacre. All were found guilty. Forty-three were condemned to death, 22 were sentenced to life imprisonment, and the remainder received long jail terms.

Still Hunting Nazis

Some people seeking justice or vengeance, such as renowned Nazi hunter Simon Wiesenthal, continue to look for Nazi war criminals. For some time, there were doubts as to whether certain high officials such as Martin Bormann or even Hitler had died. Those two were dead, but many others, such as Josef Mengele, lived comfortably with different identities (and sometimes in the open) in places such as Argentina, Paraguay, and Syria.

One man who was found alive was Adolf Eichmann, the SS official responsible for the deportation of Jews. Israeli secret agents tracked him down to his home on Garibaldi Street in Buenos Aires and spirited him away to Jerusalem, where he was tried, convicted, and hung in 1962. To this day, he is the only person ever to be executed in Israel.

The United States set up an Office of Special Investigation in 1979 to track down Nazis who entered the country illegally. It continues to locate these criminals and usually seeks to strip them of their American citizenship and to deport them to the countries where they committed their crimes. Other countries, such as France and Italy, have reluctantly tried former officials in recent years, which forced them to confront their roles in the Holocaust. Though the surviving Nazi war criminals are all very old and usually in ill health, they still must be held accountable for their actions.

Words of War

"The fact that an individual got away so long didn't diminish or mitigate his crimes. If, 40 years from now, the perpetrator of some horrible crime was found, no one would say, 'Don't prosecute.'"

—Neal Sher, former director of the Office of Special Investigation, when asked why it was still important to pursue Nazis

Countries that helped the Nazis must be held accountable, too. Though the Swiss would insist for 50 years that they remained neutral in the war, new revelations have come to light detailing the extent to which Switzerland collaborated with the Germans, particularly in the laundering of Nazi gold. According to a U.S. State Department report released in 1997, Swiss banks dealt in $400 million of Nazi gold, $300 million of which was looted from European banks. The Swiss also accepted gold taken from Jews in concentration camps and kept money from bank accounts belonging to Jews murdered in the Holocaust.

After the war, the Swiss refused to cooperate with Allied efforts to retrieve and redistribute looted gold. Recently, Switzerland agreed to set up a fund to compensate Holocaust survivors, and negotiations continue on how much money should be returned and how it should be distributed. Investigations into Switzerland's wartime activities are ongoing and continue to reveal shocking examples of Swiss cooperation with Germany.

The Least You Need to Know

➤ The Allies liberated the concentration camps and were shocked by the horrors they discovered.

➤ Despite numerous excuses, the Allies could have bombed Auschwitz and other concentration camps to stop or at least slow down the killing.

➤ Despite the risks, thousands of people did save Jews. The country of Denmark saved its entire community. Individuals such as Raoul Wallenberg, Oskar Schindler, and Chiune Sugihara saved thousands of lives.

➤ The Allies knew early on that the Germans were exterminating the Jews, but they did little or nothing to save them.

➤ Many Nazi war criminals were tried and most were convicted; however, the United States conspired to reduce many of the sentences.

➤ A large number of Nazis escaped and lived out their lives in relative peace and comfort. Nazi hunters continue to look for those who remain fugitives from justice.

Chapter 26

Freedom's Heavy Price

In This Chapter

➤ The staggering human cost of war

➤ Every death was meaningful

➤ The United States helps rebuild the shattered economies of Europe

➤ Refugees seek homes

➤ The tools of war grow more lethal

➤ The United States and the Soviet Union begin an arms race

➤ Can the United Nations stop wars?

What did nearly six years of global warfare accomplish? Millions of lives were lost, millions more lives were disrupted, economies were destroyed, and property was damaged, often beyond repair. The costs were staggering.

And the benefits? The aggressive designs of maniacs and tyrants were stopped. Other than that, one of the few good things to come out of the war was a realization that a repetition of such a global conflict could mean the end of the human race. Fear of this possibility has helped stave off World War III, at least, it appears, for the rest of this century.

Casualties of War

The appendixes provide some of the figures on war casualties. Here are a few lowlights from the war:

➤ Just under 300,000 American soldiers were killed, and only a handful of civilians died.

➤ Roughly 326,000 military deaths were recorded by the British. Their civilian deaths were just over 60,000.

➤ Of the 60,000 British civilians who were killed, 85 percent died in bombing raids. Of the rest, 6,184 died from V-1 rockets, 2,754 from V-2s, and 148 from artillery fire.

➤ Japan suffered 1.5 million military and 300,000 civilian deaths. The latter figure, according to some estimates, is closer to 1 million.

➤ The British lost 5 aircraft carriers, 5 auxiliary aircraft carriers, 4 battleships, 2 battle cruisers, 33 cruisers, 154 submarines, 138 light warships, and 1,326 other vessels.

➤ The United states lost 5 aircraft carriers, 6 escort carriers, 71 destroyers, 10 cruisers, 4 battleships, and 52 submarines. Nearly 200 Americans died at sea from "friendly fire."

➤ The Allies lost more than 5,000 merchant ships and more than 21 million tons of supplies. Nearly 80 percent of these losses occurred from 1940 to 1942.

➤ The Allies sank 785 German U-boats. In 1939, they sank only 9, but the number grew as high as 242 in 1944. More than 25,000 Germans died on submarines, which was more than 60 percent of those who served. The Germans also lost more than 2,000 warships.

➤ The Japanese navy lost 20 carriers, 38 cruisers, 10 battleships, 115 destroyers, and 119 submarines.

➤ The Germans suffered more than 4 million combat-related deaths. Nearly 600,000 civilians died in Allied bombing attacks.

➤ More than 2,000 members of the South African Air Force were shot down and killed.

➤ At least 10 million Soviet soldiers died in combat and more than 3 million more died as POWs. Well over 7 million civilians in the Soviet Union were killed.

One of the most controversial statistics is the number of Japanese civilians that died, in large part because of the uncertainty regarding the number killed by the atomic bombs. Japanese officials revised the figures upward over the years as they attributed more deaths after the war to radiation-related illnesses. Thus, the 300,000 civilian deaths cited may be a third or a fourth of the true number.

Silhouetted in a Pacific sunrise, crosses mark the graves of American boys who gave their lives to win a small atoll on the road to the Philippines. A Coast Guardsman stands in silent reverence beside the resting place of a comrade, 1944. (National Archives Still Pictures Branch)

Almost all the Japanese civilians died during American bombing raids. After eschewing the area bombing strategy in Europe, one might ask why the Americans decided to implement it in the Pacific. Contrary to some claims that this, like the use of the atomic bomb, was evidence of American racism, the more likely explanation was that little sympathy was given to the Japanese given the casualties they were inflicting in the Pacific and the "cowardly" attack on Pearl Harbor. The Americans could also afford to be more particular about their targets in Germany because the British were already bombing the cities. Also, Japanese industry was spread throughout populated areas, so it was impossible to attack without killing civilians as well. Finally, remember that the atomic bombs were developed initially for use against white people, the Germans, and were only employed against the Japanese when they refused to surrender.

The People Behind the Statistics

Throughout the book, I have given figures for the cost in human lives of this world-wide conflagration. I realized when citing them that I was not doing justice to the memories of those who died. Dry recitation of statistics is common in any history book, but something is wrong whenever the word *only* appears before a list of dead and wounded. Comparatively speaking, of course, some battles resulted in higher numbers of casualties than others, but even in a case where a single individual was killed, that person was a victim of war.

War Lore

Many men who died in battle and POW or concentration camps were buried close to where they fell. After the war, some, but not all, were disinterred and brought home to family plots or military burial grounds such as Arlington National Cemetery. Most of the men who died at Normandy were buried nearby or in mass graves. After the war, the bodies of 9,000 Americans who were not repatriated were reburied at Saint-Laurent near Omaha Beach.

Statistics also fail to capture the ripple effect of each death. As I noted in speaking about the murder of children in the Holocaust, we can never know how many would have grown up to be doctors, lawyers, scientists, politicians, and athletes. The same is true for the civilian and military casualties of the war. Many of the soldiers were young men in their teens and early twenties who had not even begun a career or a family. All those who died left behind mothers, fathers, siblings, and spouses who had to live with the tragedy of losing a loved one. In the recent movie *Saving Private Ryan*, we see the grief of a fictional mother who learned three of her sons had perished. Imagine the pain of the real-life mother of the five Sullivan brothers who died when the *Juneau* was sunk in 1942.

In addition, it is hard to gauge the psychological impact of the war on those in combat and the effects that lasted after they came home. In one famous incident, General Patton slapped an enlisted man whose nerves were shot from fighting and called him a coward. In 1944, however, Eisenhower distributed a report from the Surgeon General to all his commanders that said combat was hazardous to one's mental as well as physical health. "The danger of being killed or maimed imposes a strain so great that it causes men to break down," the report stated. It added that one could never get used to combat.

Economies in Shambles

Beyond the lives that were shattered by war, the economies of nations were also in shambles. With the exception of the United States, every country involved in the fighting had to spend every dime it had, and many did not have to produce what was needed for the war. The other Allies depended heavily on the United States for assistance, which was generously supplied through the Lend-Lease program.

A handful of countries profited from the war, notably Switzerland. Revelations of recent years have shown that the Swiss knowingly laundered gold for the Nazis and played a crucial role in financing Hitler's war effort. After the war, Swiss banks kept the money—perhaps billions of dollars—left behind by Jews murdered in the Holocaust and only now are giving in to international pressure to return what's left to the rightful heirs. In August 1998, Switzerland's two largest commercial banks agreed, after months of negotiations with attorneys and Jewish groups representing survivors, to pay $1.25 billion over a three-year period to settle all Holocaust-era claims against Swiss interests, except insurance firms. Other nations, such as Turkey and Sweden, were happy to sell vital resources to Hitler and did not stop their profiteering until the war had clearly turned in the Allies favor and it was in their interest to join the winning side.

Roll Call

From 1940 to 1945, the U.S. defense budget increased from $1.9 billion to $59.8 billion.

Beyond damaged currencies and industries, the amount of property destroyed was overwhelming. Hiroshima and Nagasaki, of course, were almost completely razed by the atomic bombs, but even cities that absorbed conventional bombing, such as Hamburg, Dresden, and Cologne were left in rubble. Many cultural and historical landmarks were destroyed; what is amazing is that any survived. Cities such as Rome, Florence, Athens, and Paris emerged with their architectural jewels intact. Despite the German blitzes, Britain's historic cities also emerged largely unscathed.

Words of War

"In War: Resolution. In Defeat: Defiance. In Victory: Magnanimity. In Peace: Good Will."

—Winston Churchill, from *The Second World War: Moral of the Work, vol. I, The Gathering Storm*

Most of the world's art treasures also survived. The British, for example, concealed theirs in caves in Wales. Much of the art in the territories occupied by the Germans was stolen rather than destroyed, and the Allies discovered much of it hidden in salt mines and in the personal collections of high Nazi officials. Some of the art was never returned to its original owners and is hanging in art museums or the homes of private collectors. Only recently has an effort been initiated to trace the origins of potentially stolen artworks so that they might be returned to their rightful owners.

The Marshall Plan

Looking at the world today, it is hard to imagine the chaos of the late 1940s. After all, in recent years two of the world's leading economic powers have been Germany and Japan. The recovery of Europe and the United States's former enemies is largely attributable to Truman's decision to provide massive amounts of aid to reconstruct their economies.

Ask the General

After the war, the United States had amassed a tremendous quantity of arms that it no longer needed. In 1946, at the initiative of Senator J. William Fulbright, the American government decided to sell its surplus weapons and use the profits to create an international scholarship program. The Fulbright Scholarships allowed the United States to create educational exchanges with more than 60 countries, a program that continues today.

The Marshall Plan, named after General George Marshall, head of the Joint Chiefs during the war and Secretary of State afterward, was a program designed to provide economic assistance to Europe. After overcoming initial Congressional reluctance to spend more money to help others, the Marshall Plan was approved. On June 5, 1947, all the former combatants were offered assistance. The Soviet Union refused the offer of aid, however, and prevented the Communist bloc nations from accepting any U.S. help.

From 1945 to 1954, the United States provided more than $35 billion in aid to Europe (mostly to Britain, France, Italy, and West Germany) and nearly $9 billion to Asian and Pacific nations. Soon most of these countries were exceeding their prewar levels of economic growth, and some, such as Japan, began several decades of exceptional prosperity. Germany's recovery was further assisted by agreements reached on resolving its World War I reparation debts. By agreeing to take token payments, the Allies showed they were willing to provide the loans Germany needed to rebuild its economy.

Emerging from the Rubble

The Eastern European countries of Poland, Romania, Bulgaria, Czechoslovakia, and Albania emerged from the war under the "protective" umbrella of the Soviet Union. Yugoslavia also chose the path of communism, but it succeeded in winning independence from Moscow. The Soviet Union also annexed the Baltic states of Estonia, Latvia, and Lithuania, which did not regain their independence until 1990.

When Japan surrendered, the Vietnamese Communist guerrilla leader, Ho Chi-Minh, seized power in northern Indochina, prompting the French to intervene in what would escalate into the Vietnam war and eventually ensnare the United States.

Italy never fully emerged from the chaos of the war. The economy recovered, but it never became an economic powerhouse like some of its neighbors. It also adopted a democratic system, but one that proved so unstable that more than 50 different governments have held power since the war.

Though France also made a successful recovery from the ravages of the war, it never could regain its status as a major power. De Gaulle's effort to win recognition as such was successful at the United Nations and some other forums, but the nation's military would never become as strong as the United States, the Soviet Union, or even Great Britain.

China, which the United States had fought to protect, also fell to the communists. The United States's ally, Chiang Kai-Shek, was forced to set up shop on the island of Formosa, which China reclaimed from Japan. A half century of controversy has followed as the Chinese government has insisted on the unification of what is now called Taiwan and the mainland. Taiwan, meanwhile, has evolved into a prosperous democracy with powerful American friends. The overwhelming desire to do business with the world's most populous nation, however, has led recent American presidents to minimize the U.S. commitment to the small island's freedom.

People Without a Country

The Second World War caused the greatest displacement of people in history. Millions were left homeless, many were unable to return to their native countries, and still others had no desire to go home but were not allowed to go elsewhere. These people were crowded into displaced persons (DP) camps and had to wait sometimes for months before they could find new homes.

The remnant of European Jewry that survived the Holocaust was in perhaps the most precarious position. Most did not want to return to the countries that had abandoned them or collaborated in their destruction. Some who did return found that it was still not safe for them. In Poland, for example, anti-Semitic riots in Kielce on July 4, 1946, killed 42 and wounded 50 of the 150 Jews who tried to return to their homes. Before the war, 24,000 Jews had lived in the town.

The United States remained reluctant, as it had been throughout the war, to welcome large numbers of refugees, though many eventually settled there. Many Jews wished to go to Palestine, which was then controlled by the British. The British had also locked the gates to most Jews who tried to escape Hitler and even after the war did not wish

Words of War

"As matters now stand, we appear to be treating the Jews as the Nazis treated them except that we do not exterminate them. They are in concentration camps in large numbers under our military guard instead of SS troops. One is led to wonder whether the German people, seeing this, are not supposing that we are following or at least condoning Nazi policy."

—Earl Harrison, reporting to President Truman on the treatment of Jews in the American zone

to upset the Arabs or their colonial interests in the Middle East by opening the door to large numbers of Jews who hoped that the British government's promise to create a state in Palestine would be fulfilled.

These Jewish children are on their way to Palestine after having been released from the Buchenwald concentration camp. The girl on the left is from Poland, the boy in the center from Latvia, and the girl on the right from Hungary, June 5, 1945. (National Archives Still Pictures Branch)

Ultimately, the Jews, through their own efforts in diplomacy and war, created a Jewish state whose *raison d'etre* was to provide a haven for any Jew in need of shelter. If there had been an Israel in 1939, there probably could not have been a Holocaust, and so long as Israel survives, there can never be another. In 1952, four years after the establishment of Israel, the West German government agreed to pay reparations to the Israeli government and to several Jewish organizations to compensate the Jews for their mistreatment at the hands of the Nazis. East Germany refused to make any such payments, and none were made on its behalf after reunification.

Besides the Jews, other large population transfers also occurred. In particular, the German population east of the Elbe was reduced from 17 million to maybe 100,000.

Tools of War

One consequence of the war was the development of new weapons and improvement of old ones. The V-1 and V-2 rockets had the beneficial impact of helping eventually put men on the moon, but the less benevolent impact of heralding the age of ballistic missiles. Another development that cut both ways was radar, which has made a considerable difference in various aspects of warfare, but also has peaceful applications in, for example, commercial aviation.

Airplanes were already old hat by the time the war started, but the needs of the war stimulated lots of improvements in the materials used to build aircraft, aircraft weapons, the size of aircraft, aircraft speed, and maneuverability. By the end of the war, jets were introduced that would eventually revolutionize both civilian and military aviation.

Yet another wartime invention that has had enormous consequences for both military and civilian life was the computer. The initial devices were large, slow, and primitive, but extremely valuable to the Allied code-breaking efforts that ultimately played a major role in the outcome of the war.

Of course, the weapon that made the most profound impact, in every sense of the word, was the atomic bomb. Since the first bomb was created, scientists have developed hydrogen bombs, which are far more destructive than those used on Japan, and neutron bombs, which are supposed to kill people without destroying buildings. "Nukes" now come in different sizes—some small enough to fit in a backpack—and can be launched from planes, missiles, and submarines. On the positive side, research in nuclear physics has produced all sorts of discoveries and peaceful applications such as power generation (albeit with serious complications related to radiation fallout) used for spacecraft, aircraft carriers and submarines, and electricity.

World War II also produced certain changes in the way wars are fought, such as the use of airborne troops, air support, and aircraft carriers. Though air power was a major factor in the Allied victory, the war proved that superiority in the air could not, by itself, be decisive.

A New Cold War Begins

The prospects for a peaceful future dimmed quickly as the Soviet Union began to impose its will on the countries it occupied after the war. A wall went up to divide Berlin and eventually create a new communist country that would deprive its citizens of the freedoms the Western Allies had fought so hard to preserve. The nations of Eastern Europe were drawn behind the "iron curtain" and became subject to Soviet domination.

The term "new world order" took on a very different meaning after the war. Instead of the Third *Reich* ruling the globe, the world broke down into two political and military blocs. On one side was the Soviet Union and its satellites, which composed the Warsaw Pact. On the other side were the democracies of Western Europe, led by the United States, which created the North Atlantic Treaty Organization (NATO) in 1949 to protect the nations beyond the iron curtain from the communists. NATO was largely a success, and today, after the collapse of the Soviet Union, many Warsaw Pact nations are applying for membership in the alliance. Russia may one day even become a member.

The Nuclear Arms Race

The United States knew the Soviets were carrying on their own nuclear research program; nevertheless, it was a shock when they quickly succeeded in building their own bomb. From that point on, the two countries would be viewed as superpower rivals, determined to achieve military superiority over the other.

Once two nations on opposite sides possessed nuclear weapons, the world held its breath to see whether a war would break out that would irradiate the planet. After amassing thousands of nuclear warheads deliverable by bombers, missiles, and submarines, the two countries began to realize it was in their mutual interest to draw down their stockpiles. Starting in the 1970s, agreements were reached to limit the arsenals on each side, and negotiations toward reducing the number of nuclear weapons continue to this day.

Even as the two superpowers tortuously negotiate reductions in their supply of nuclear weapons, other nations are striving to build their own bombs or increase their arsenals. As the number of nuclear powers has grown—in 1998, Pakistan joined the "club"—the danger that the next war will "go nuclear" has increased.

The recognition of the likely outcome of a nuclear war discouraged the superpowers from going to war; however, the fear today is that radical states seeking a nuclear capability, such as Iran, Iraq, or Libya, might not feel such restraint or that a war between rival powers such as India and Pakistan could escalate to the nuclear level. In addition, even after the fall of the Soviet Union, many nuclear weapons remain in Russia and the newly independent nations and pose a potential long-term threat to the United States and other nations.

The Disunited Nations

The hope for a better future was reflected in the creation of the United Nations. Like the League of Nations before it, the idea was that an international body could resolve disputes through discussion and diplomacy to avert or stop wars.

The Allies had endorsed the concept in 1943 and met at Dumbarton Oaks in Washington from August 21 to October 9, 1944, to hammer out details of how it would operate, such as the creation of a large legislative body called the General Assembly and a smaller executive committee known as the Security Council. The latter would have a rotating membership, except for five permanent members—Britain, the United States, the Soviet Union, China, and France—each of whom would have the right to veto resolutions affecting their security and sovereignty (which turned out to be everything). The Allies also helped encourage other nations to join the war effort against Germany by making this a prerequisite for initial U.N. membership.

The formal charter of the United Nations was adopted at the San Francisco Conference that convened on April 25, 1945. Although Woodrow Wilson was unable to win support for U.S. participation in the League of Nations, Roosevelt and Truman were more successful in convincing the public that the war that had just been fought made membership in the new body vital to the United States's interest in peace and stability. By this time Americans were more willing to participate in world affairs and to see that isolationism could not protect the country and was, in fact, dangerous to its interests.

The headquarters of the United Nations in New York. (National Archives Still Pictures Branch)

Unfortunately, the optimism was misplaced. The United Nations was set up to fail because of the insistence on giving the major powers permanent seats on the Security Council and the option of vetoing resolutions. Throughout the Cold War, this setup ensured that any resolution aimed at either superpower or its allies would be quashed by a veto. In addition, the Soviet Union refused to support any resolution that would authorize the United Nations to create a peacekeeping force, meaning the institution had no real means of backing up its paper resolutions.

War Lore

Kurt Waldheim began working with the United Nations when his native Austria became a member in 1958. In 1971, he was elected to a five-year term as secretary general, succeeding the retiring Myanmar diplomat U Thant. He was reelected in 1976. Seeking an unprecedented third term in 1981, Waldheim was vetoed by China during 16 rounds of balloting before he withdrew. In 1986, Waldheim was elected president of Austria despite revelations that he was implicated in Nazi war crimes while he was a lieutenant in the German army during World War II. He had, for example, written intelligence reports describing the activities and murder of partisans in Greece. As a result of this discovery, Waldheim was banned from entering the United States. He also did not seek another presidential term.

For all its failings as a bloated bureaucracy and a haven for anti-Semites, the United Nations has at times played a constructive role in the resolution of disputes. Its greatest success, however, has been in providing humanitarian aid. Immediately after the war, for example, the U.N. Relief and Rehabilitation Administration (UNRRA) was established to provide assistance to the nations devastated by war. The United Nations International Children's Emergency Fund (UNICEF) was also created specifically to help the mothers and children who were in need as a result of the war.

Telling the Story of World War II

Students today are taught little about the war, and what they find in textbooks is usually so cursory as to be useless. The previous chapter noted how Holocaust revisionism has become a growing problem as the witnesses to that tragedy pass away.

Much of what kids know today they get from TV and movies, and many TV shows and movies have been made about the war. In an interview to promote *Saving Private Ryan*, Steven Spielberg mentioned 85 movies on the war, but the number is probably much higher. Many of these movies, including Spielberg's latest, are very good. Several have won Academy Awards (*The Bridge on the River Kwai, Patton, Schindler's List*). As I noted throughout the text, movies have been made about many of the battles, personalities, and incidents, such as *Midway, The Desert Fox, Merrill's Marauders, Tora, Tora, Tora,* and *The Great Escape*. Many others, such as the *Dirty Dozen* and the classic *Casablanca* are fictional or loosely based on actual events.

One interesting aspect of war movies is how they have changed over the years. During the war, movies were blatantly propagandistic, designed to paint the Allies as unambiguous heroes and the Germans or Japanese as evil incarnate. They were aimed at supporting the war effort and boosting morale. Most glorified war. Even many of the movies made afterward had a similar rah-rah quality and made war seem relatively sterile. Bullet wounds were small little holes that didn't bleed much. Heroes ran through a fusillade of machine-gun fire without ever being touched.

Gradually more realism crept into the movies, particularly after the Vietnam War. Remember, censors did not allow Americans to see pictures of dead GIs in World War II, and there were no television reports from the battlefield. After Vietnam, this was no longer the case. Still, for sheer realism, no film has been as powerful or graphic as *Saving Private Ryan*. Since it opened as the number one film in the United States, people apparently were not put off by the violence. Perhaps after seeing how bloody war really is, even if only through a movie, people will seek other ways to resolve their disputes.

The military is sometimes ridiculed for its desire to amass ever greater quantities of weapons and to spend trillions of dollars on new weapons systems, and then be reluctant to fight the nation's enemies. The fact is, soldiers have seen what these weapons can do and, therefore, hesitate before using them.

Will World Wars End at Two?

Despite people's wishes, movies aren't going to end war. The war after the war to end all wars did not curb the human appetite for conquest or bloodshed. Within a decade of V-E and V-J days, the United States was embroiled in a new war in Korea, Jews and Arabs had fought the first of six wars, the French would become entangled in a war in Southeast Asia that would eventually enmesh the United States, and on and on. Even a half century after World War II, war continues in different parts of the world.

The good news is that the prospect of world war seems more remote today than at any time in the century. This is partly attributable to the fear of a nuclear holocaust, but it is mostly a consequence of a change in the relations of the major powers. Despite their constant quarrels, the nations of Europe get along reasonably well today and are part of a common market that will soon have a single currency.

Words of War

"As long as there are sovereign nations possessing great power, war is inevitable."

—Albert Einstein on the atomic bomb

Though neo-Nazi and other right-wing fanatics cause disturbances now and again, Germany has remained peaceful and a good neighbor. In the more than 40 years since the resumption of conscription there, not a single German soldier has been killed in combat. Japan is forbidden by its constitution from using force under any circumstances. Ironically, the United States urged both countries toward slightly more militaristic positions when they desired backing for military action in Iraq.

The greatest change in international relations, of course, was the fall of the Soviet Union, which eliminated the greatest threat to world peace and the most likely cause of a nuclear exchange. Even before the fall, the Soviets had, until the war in Afghanistan, fought their wars primarily by proxy.

Still, one can never know what spark might light a new global conflagration. The assassination of an Austrian archduke, after all, does not in retrospect seem to have justified the world war that followed. But today there are hot spots, such as the former Yugoslavia and the India-Pakistan border, that could start a skirmish that could escalate to a wider war. One can only hope this never occurs and that the lessons of the Second World War are never forgotten.

The Least You Need to Know

➤ More than 57 million people were killed in World War II. More than half of these casualties were civilians, many of whom were women and children.

➤ Every death had an incalculable effect on the surviving families and on history.

➤ The United States emerged from the war the most powerful nation in history. It provided aid through the Marshall Plan to help resuscitate the economies of both its friends and enemies.

➤ Millions of refugees from the fighting had no place to go. The survivors of the Holocaust, in particular, were people without a country until the establishment of Israel.

➤ The Soviet Union refused American aid and dropped an "iron curtain" across Eastern Europe that would spark a four-decade cold war and a nuclear arms race that threatened the world with annihilation.

➤ The United Nations was a symbol of hope for a better future. Though it has made a contribution to world peace, it has fallen far short of the goal of resolving all disputes through discussion rather than war.

➤ World War II was seen as a heroic struggle while it was being fought. Only later was the war portrayed in more realistic terms to capture its full horror.

➤ Despite the Cold War and a growing nuclear power club, a third world war has been avoided.

Roll Call

The numbers in the following table are estimates of the civilian and military deaths during World War II. The true figures will never be known. Many people died without any record of their death, particularly in some of the massacres committed by different armies. It was also difficult for records to be kept in many instances where the battle-field situation was confused, such as Normandy during the invasion. In addition, many of the statistics are being revised, particularly since the archives of the former Soviet Union became available. Much of that wartime material is still being analyzed. If anything, these numbers are probably on the low side for what was the most lethal conflict in human history.

Country	Military Deaths	Civilian Deaths	Total
Soviet Union	13,600,000	7,700,000	21,300,000
China	1,324,000	10,000,000	11,324,000
Germany	3,250,000	3,810,000	7,060,000
Poland	850,000	6,000,000	6,850,000
Japan	1,506,000	300,000	1,806,000
Yugoslavia	300,000	1,400,000	1,700,000
Rumania	520,000	465,000	985,000
France	340,000	470,000	810,000
Hungary			750,000
Austria	380,000	145,000	525,000
Greece			520,000
Italy	330,000	80,000	410,000
Czechoslovakia			400,000
Great Britain	326,000	62,000	388,000
USA	295,000		295,000
Netherlands	14,000	236,000	250,000

continues

continued

Country	Military Deaths	Civilian Deaths	Total
Belgium	10,000	75,000	85,000
Finland	79,000		79,000
Canada	39,000		39,000
India	36,000		36,000
Australia	29,000		29,000
Spain	12,000	10,000	22,000
Bulgaria	19,000	2,000	21,000
New Zealand	12,000		12,000
South Africa	9,000		9,000
Norway	5,000		5,000
Denmark	4,000		4,000

Victims of the Holocaust

As is the case of the total deaths during the war, the figures here for the number of Jews killed by the Germans and their allies is only an estimate. The Nazis kept meticulous records, but many deaths still went unaccounted for, particularly in the case of mass murders by the *Einsatzgruppen*. If you add up the following numbers, you will see that they come out to a little less than the 6 million figure typically used to describe the number of Jews murdered in the Holocaust. Over the years, scholars have debated the numbers, but 6 million is still the commonly accepted total. This table does not include the 6 million non-Jews murdered by the Nazis. This omission is not to diminish these deaths, but to distinguish them from the systematic murder of Jews under Hitler's Final Solution. For more details, see Chapters 24 and 25.

Estimated Number of Jews Killed in The Final Solution

Country	Estimated Pre-Final Solution Population	Estimated Jewish Population Annihilated	
		Number	*Percent*
Poland	3,300,000	3,000,000	90
Baltic countries	253,000	228,000	90
Germany/Austria	240,000	210,000	90
Protectorate	90,000	80,000	89
Slovakia	90,000	75,000	83
Greece	70,000	54,000	77
Netherlands	140,000	105,000	75
Hungary	650,000	450,000	70
SSR White Russia	375,000	245,000	65
SSR Ukraine*	1,500,000	900,000	60
Belgium	65,000	40,000	60

continues

continued

Country	Estimated Pre-Final Solution Population	Estimated Jewish Population Annihilated	
		Number	*Percent*
Yugoslavia	43,000	26,000	60
Romania	600,000	300,000	50
Norway	1,800	900	50
France	350,000	90,000	26
Bulgaria	64,000	14,000	22
Italy	40,000	8,000	20
Luxembourg	5,000	1,000	20
Russia (RSFSR)*	975,000	107,000	11
Denmark**	8,000	--	--
Finland**	2,000	--	--
Total	8,861,800	5,933,900	67

* The Germans did not occupy all the territory of this province.

** Virtually all of the Jews in these countries survived.

Source: Holocaust Denial: A Pocket Guide. *Anti-Defamation League, 1997.*

GI Jargon

Barbarossa   The invasion of Russia was originally called Operation Fritz. Hitler changed the name to Barbarossa, after Frederick Barbarossa, the Holy Roman Emperor who had set out to conquer the Holy Land in 1190.

Battle of the Bulge   Military campaign that took its name from the fact that a bulge 70 miles wide and 50 miles deep was created in the Allied lines when the Germans moved into the Ardennes and split the American and British forces.

D day   People usually associate the term *D day* with the Allied invasion at Normandy on June 6, 1944, but it is a generic military term for the date and time of an attack.

Dulag/Dulag Luft   Abbreviation of *Durchgangs Lager* or entrance camp; these were transit stations for prisoners of war.

Fascism   From the Italian word meaning group, the term came to be applied to right-wing advocates of totalitarianism and extreme nationalism. Fascism emphasizes the importance of the state rather than the individual, like communism, but it does not call for state ownership of property.

gadget   When Oppenheimer's assistant Robert Serber gave a series of lectures outlining progress on the Manhattan Project, a group of workmen was nearby finishing construction of the building. Serber was told to use the word *gadget* instead of *bomb* in case his lectures were overheard. From then on, the bomb was referred to as a gadget.

Geneva Convention   This term refers to a series of international agreements aimed at ensuring the humane treatment of prisoners, civilians, and wounded soldiers in war. Sixteen countries agreed in the first convention to respect the neutrality of civilians and of medical personnel and hospital ships identified with the Red Cross insignia and to treat the war wounded humanely. It was signed in Geneva, Switzerland, in August 1864. Subsequent conventions added additional guidelines for behavior during wartime. Hitler routinely violated the conventions.

ghetto   The word *ghetto* comes from the Italian word for foundry. The Jewish quarter in Venice was on the site of a cannon foundry and was referred to as a ghetto.

Ground Zero   The point where a nuclear device is detonated.

Huff-Duff   Nickname for High-Frequency Direction Finders (HF/DF). In the summer of 1942, the Allies began using these direction finders, which allowed them to locate German submarines by their radio transmissions.

kamikaze   Japanese for "divine wind." The Japanese created a special group of suicide pilots to purposely crash their planes into American ships that was known as the *kamikazes*.

Kapo   A prisoner in charge of a group of inmates in a Nazi concentration camp.

Kristallnacht   German for "The Night of Broken Glass," this term refers to the windows and storefronts shattered when the Nazis attacked Jews throughout Germany, Austria, and Sudetenland on November 9–10, 1938. The cost of the broken window glass was roughly $2 million. *Kristallnacht* also represented the destruction of Jewish life under the Nazis, which thousands saw as a message to flee before it was too late. Millions more did not read the message correctly.

Lebensraum   A German word that means "living space." Friedrich Ratzel, a German geographer and ethnologist, developed the idea, which Hitler later used to suggest Germans needed room for expansion, a convenient rationalization for his territorial ambitions.

Low Countries   Belgium, Luxembourg, and the Netherlands. The term refers to their location near sea level on the North Sea.

Molotov cocktails   The Finnish soldiers effectively used a new type of weapon against the Soviet tanks, a bottle filled with gasoline that had a rag stuffed inside that could be lit. The lit bottle was then thrown like a grenade. These bombs became known as Molotov cocktails in honor of the Soviet foreign minister.

Mulberries   The two artificial harbors secretly constructed by the British to unload as much as 7,000 tons of vehicles and supplies per day off the coast of Normandy for the D day invasion. These ports were made of approximately six miles of flexible steel roadways that floated on steel or concrete pontoons. Mulberry A was towed across the Channel and set up off Omaha Beach, and Mulberry B was positioned near Gold Beach.

Nazi   Abbreviation for the National Socialist German Workers' Party (*Nationalsozialistische Deutsche Arbeiterpartei*, or NSDAP). The original abbreviation of National Socialist was *Nasos*. Nazi was a term of derision first applied to the group by journalist Konrad Heiden.

Oflag   Short for *Offizier Lager* or officers camp, this was a permanent prisoner of war camp for officers.

OSS   The acronym for the Office of Strategic Services, which was the forerunner of the Central Intelligence Agency. It was established on June 13, 1942, to collect and analyze information for the Joint Chiefs of Staff and was run by William Donovan. One of its principal activities was to conduct secret missions behind enemy lines.

partisans Irregular troops engaged in guerilla warfare, often behind enemy lines. During World War II, the term was applied to resistance fighters in Nazi-occupied countries.

quisling Before invading Norway, Hitler had conferred with the leader of the Norwegian Nazi Party, Vidkun Quisling, who encouraged the Germans to attack quickly and subsequently provided intelligence to aid in the Nazi takeover. When the fighting ended, Quisling was made the head of a puppet government. His treasonous behavior gave rise to the term *quisling* to describe someone who betrays their country by aiding an invading enemy. Ironically, 15 days after Quisling came to power, Hitler replaced him with a German Nazi Party official.

Shoah Hebrew word for "catastrophe." It is often used to describe the catastrophic destruction of European Jewry during World War II. This is the term most commonly used in Israel, which commemorates the Holocaust each year with a special day called *Yom ha-Shoah.*

Stalag Luft A *Stalag Luft* (*Luft* meaning air) was a prisoner of war camp for airmen.

Stalags The Germans kept most enlisted men in prisoner of war camps called *Stalags*, short for *Stammlager*, which roughly translated means "common stock." One reason most prisoners of war were relatively well treated is that the camps were run by soldiers rather than the SS, which controlled the concentration camps. Also, there were large numbers of Germans in Allied POW camps.

Third *Reich* The Nazis identified their rule as the successor to the Holy Roman Empire and the German Empire of 1871 to 1918. They called their regime the Third *Reich.*

U-boat A German submarine was also known as a U-boat, short for the German *Unterseeboot.*

USO The acronym for the United Service Organizations, which was created in 1941 to provide a variety of services to American soldiers, such as recreation centers, care packages, and celebrity shows. There are approximately 175 USO centers around the world, staffed mainly by volunteers, meeting the educational, social, and religious needs of American military personnel. Between 1941 and 1947, more than 7,000 "soldiers in greasepaint" performed 428,521 USO shows.

Recommended Reading

Thousands of books have been written on World War II, and the following selections represent a tiny fraction of the available material. Books related to the Holocaust alone number in the hundreds, if not thousands. This book was designed to give an overview of the war, but many excellent books go into far greater detail about specific campaigns and aspects of the war, such as Stephen Ambrose's book on D day. Martin Gilbert, who was Winston Churchill's official biographer, has written a number of Holocaust-related books, and his history of World War II offers a nearly day-by-day report on all aspects of the war. John Keegan's work focuses more on the nuts and bolts of the battles, an approach I eschewed, and is good for people who want to know about armaments and which division fought where.

For some interesting tidbits you won't find in other books, take a look at Mike Wright's book, *What They Didn't Teach You About World War II*. A recent bestseller and highly controversial analysis of the Holocaust is *Hitler's Willing Executioners* by Daniel Goldhagen. I'd be remiss if I didn't recommend my own study of the shocking story of what happened to American civilians and POWs captured by the Nazis during the war, *Forgotten Victims: The Abandonment of Americans in Hitler's Camps*.

Abzug, Robert H. *Inside the Vicious Heart: Americans and the Liberation of the Nazi Concentration Camps*. NY: Oxford University Press, 1987.

Adelsberger, Lucie. *Auschwitz: A Doctor's Story*. MA: Northeastern University Press, 1995.

Adelson, Alan and Robert Lapides, editors. *Lodz Ghetto: Inside a Community Under Siege*. NY: Penguin, 1991.

Aharoni, Zvi, et al. *Operation Eichmann: The Truth About the Pursuit, Capture and Trial*. NY: John Wiley & Sons, 1997.

Allen, William Sheridan. *The Nazi Seizure of Power: The Experience of a Single German Town, 1922–1945*. NY: Franklin Watts, 1984.

Ambrose, Stephen E. *Citizen Soldiers: The U.S. Army from the Normandy Beaches to the Bulge to the Surrender of Germany, June 7, 1944–May 7, 1945*. NY: Simon & Schuster, 1997.

——. *D-Day, June 6, 1944*. NY: Simon & Schuster, 1994.

——. *Pegasus Bridge, June 6, 1944*. NY: Touchstone Books, 1988.

Anger, Per. *With Raoul Wallenberg in Budapest: Memories of the War Years in Hungary.* Holocaust Library, 1996.

Arad, Yitzhak. *Belzec, Sobibor, Treblinka—The Operation Reinhard Death Camps*. IN: Indiana University Press, 1987.

——, editor. *The Pictoral History of the Holocaust*. NY: Macmillan, 1991.

Arad, Yitzhak, Shmuel Krakowski, and Shmuel Spector, editors. *The Einsatzgruppen Reports*. DC: U.S. Holocaust Memorial Museum Shop Memorial Council, 1990.

Arendt, Hannah. *Eichmann in Jerusalem: A Report on the Banality of Evil*. NY: Penguin, 1994 (originally published in 1965).

Bailey, Thomas & David Kennedy. *The American Pageant*. MA: DC Heath and Co., 1987.

Bard, Mitchell G. *Forgotten Victims: The Abandonment of Americans in Hitler's Camps.* CO: Westview Press, 1994.

Barker, A.J. *Behind Barbed Wire*. London: B.T. Batsford Ltd., 1974.

Barnett, Corelli, editor. *Hitler's Generals*. NY: Quill, 1991.

Bauer, Yehuda. *A History of the Holocaust*. NY: Franklin Watts, 1982.

——. *American Jewry and the Holocaust: The American Jewish Joint Distribution Committee 1939–1945*. MI: Wayne State University Press, 1981.

——. *Jewish Reactions to the Holocaust*. VT: Jewish Lights Publishing, 1997.

——. *Jews for Sale?: Nazi-Jewish Negotiations, 1933–1945*. Yale University Press, 1995.

——. *They Chose Life: Jewish Resistance in the Holocaust*. NY: American Jewish Committee, Institute of Human Relations, 1973.

Berenbaum, Michael, editor. *Witness to the Holocaust*. NY: HarperCollins, 1997.

——. *The World Must Know: The History of the Holocaust as Told in the United States Holocaust Memorial Museum*. MA: Little, Brown and Co., 1993.

Blumenson, Martin. *Patton: The Man Behind the Legend, 1885–1945*. Quill, 1994.

Breitman, Richard and Allen Kraut. *American Refugee Policy and European Jewry, 1933–1945*. IN: Indiana University Press, 1987.

Browning, Christopher. *Ordinary Men: Reserve Police Battalion 101 and the Final Solution in Poland*. NY: HarperCollins, 1992.

Bullock, Alan. *Hitler, a Study in Tyranny*. NY: HarperCollins, 1994.

Carter, Kit. *Army Air Forces in World War 2 Combat Cronology 1941–1945*. Ayer Co Pub., 1979.

Carter, Kit and Robert Mueller, editors. *The Army Air Forces in World War II*. Office of Air Force History, 1973.

Conot, Robert. *Justice at Nuremberg*. NY: Carroll & Graf, 1984.

D'este, Carlo. *Decision in Normandy*. NY: Harperperennial Library, 1994.

——. *Patton: A Genius for War*. NY: Harperperennial Library, 1996.

Dawidowicz, Lucy S. *The War Against the Jews, 1933–1945*. Bantam Doubleday Dell, 1991.

Durand, Arthur. *Stalag Luft III: The Secret Story*. LA: Louisiana State University Press, 1988.

Eisenhower, David. *Eisenhower at War, 1943–1945*. NY: Random House, 1986.

Eisenhower, Dwight D. *Crusade in Europe*. Garden City, NY: Doubleday, 1948.

Eliach, Yaffa and Brana Gurewitsch, editors. *The Liberators: Eyewitness Accounts of the Liberation of Concentration Camps: Volume I: Liberation Day: Oral History Testimonies of American Liberators from the Archives of the Center for Holocaust Studies*. Brooklyn, NY: Center for Holocaust Studies Documentation & Research, 1981.

Feingold, Henry. *The Politics of Rescue: The Roosevelt Administration and the Holocaust, 1938–1945*. NJ: Rutgers University Press, 1970.

Foot, MRD. *SOE In France*. MD: University Publications of America, 1984.

Foot, MRD. *SOE: The Special Operations Executive 1940–46*. CT: Greenwood Publishing Group, 1984.

Foy, David. *For You The War Is Over*. NY: Stein and Day, 1984.

Frank, Anne. *Anne Frank: Diary of a Young Girl*. Amereon Ltd., 1967.

Friedlander, Saul. *Nazi Germany and the Jews: The Years of Persecution, 1933–1939 (Vol 1)*. NY: HarperCollins, 1997.

Friedman, Saul S. *No Haven for the Oppressed: United States Policy Toward Jewish Refugees, 1938–1945*. MI: Wayne State University Press, 1973.

Gelb, Norman. *Ike and Monty: Generals at War*. NY: Quill, 1995.

Genizi, Haim. *American Apathy: The Plight of Christian Refugees from Nazism*. Ramat-Gan, Israel: Bar-Ilan University Press, 1983.

Gilbert, Martin. *Auschwitz And the Allies*. NY: Holt Rinehart Winston, 1981.

——. *The Boys: The Untold Story of 732 Young Concentration Camp Survivors*. NY: Henry Holt & Company, 1997.

——. *The Day the War Ended: May 8, 1945: Victory in Europe*. NY: Holt, 1996.

——. *The Holocaust: A History of the Jews of Europe During the Second World War*. NY: Henry Holt And Co., 1987.

——. *The Second World War*. NY: Henry Holt And Co., 1989.

——. *Holocaust Journey : Travelling in Search of the Past*. NY: Columbia University Press, 1997.

Goldhagen, Daniel Jonah. *Hitler's Willing Executioners: Ordinary Germans and the Holocaust*. NY: Alfred A. Knopf, 1996.

Gun, Nerin E. *The Day of the Americans*. NY: Fleet Publishing, 1966.

375

Gutman, Israel, editor. *Encyclopedia of the Holocaust. Vols. 1–4*. NY: Macmillan, 1995.

——. *Resistance: The Warsaw Ghetto Uprising*. VT: Chapters Publishing Ltd., 1998.

Isser, Harel. *The House on Garibaldi Street*. NY: Frank Cass & Co., 1997.

Hamerow, Theodore S. *On the Road to the Wolf's Lair: German Resistance to Hitler*. Belknap Press, 1997.

Hastings, Max. *Victory in Europe: D-Day to V-E Day*. MA: Little, Brown, 1992.

Heger, Heinz. *The Men With the Pink Triangle*. MA: Alyson Publishing Co., 1994.

Heimler, Eugene. *Night of the Mist*. NY: Gefen Books, 1997.

Hilberg, Raul. *The Destruction of the European Jews*. NY: Holmes & Meier, 1985.

——. *Perpetrators Victims Bystanders: The Jewish Catastrophe 1933–1945*. NY: Harper Perennial Library, 1993.

International Military Tribunal. *Trial of the Major War Criminals*. Nuremberg, 1947.

Kater, Michael. *The Nazi Party: A Social Profile of Members and Leaders, 1919–1945*. MA: Harvard University Press, 1983.

Keegan, John, editor. *The Second World War*. NY: Penguin Books, 1989.

Keneally, Thomas. *Schindler's List*. NY: Simon & Schuster, 1994.

Kennan, George. *Memoirs: 1925–1950*. MA: Little Brown, 1967.

Kenrick, Donald. *The Destiny of Europe's Gypsies*. NY: Basic Books, 1973.

Kershaw, Ian. *The Nazi Dictatorship: Problems and Perspectives of Interpretation*, 2nd ed. London and NY: E. Arnold, 1993.

Kimball, Warren F. *Forged in War: Roosevelt, Churchill, and the Second World War*. NY: William Morrow & Company, 1997.

Kogon, Eugene. *The Theory And Practice Of Hell*. NY: Berkley Publishing Group, 1998.

Koonz, Claudia. *Mothers in the Fatherland: Women, the Family, and Nazi Politics*. NY: St. Martin's, 1988.

Lanzmann, Claude. *Shoah: The Complete Text of the Acclaimed Holocaust Film*. Da Capo Press, 1995.

Laska, Vera, editor. *Women in the Resistance and in the Holocaust: The Voices of Eyewitnesses*. CT: Greenwood Press, 1983.

Le Chene, Evelyn. *Mauthausen*. London: Methuen and Co., Ltd., 1971.

Lengyel, Olga. *Five Chimneys: A Woman's True Story of Auschwitz*. IL: Academy Chicago Pub., 1995.

Levi, Primo. *Survival in Auschwitz: The Nazi Assault on Humanity*. NY: Collier Books, 1995.

Levine, Hillel. *In Search of Sugihara: The Elusive Japanese Diplomat Who Risked His Life to Rescue 10,000 Jews from the Holocaust*. NY: Free Press, 1996.

Lifton, Robert J. *The Nazi Doctors: Medical Killings and the Psychology of Genocide.* NY: Basic Books, 1986.

Lipstadt, Deborah. *Beyond Belief.* NY: Free Press, 1993.

Lipstadt, Deborah. *Denying the Holocaust: The Growing Assault on Truth and Memory.* NY: Free Press, 1993.

Mark, Ber. *Uprising in the Warsaw Ghetto.* NY: Schocken Books, 1975.

Marrus, Michael R. *The Nuremberg War Crimes Trial of 1945–46: A Documentary History.* Bedford Books, 1997.

——. *Vichy France and the Jews.* CA: Stanford University Press, 1995.

Mason, Tim. *Nazism, Fascism and the Working Class.* Edited by Jane Caplan. Cambridge: Cambridge University Press, 1995.

Meltzer, Milton. *Rescue: The Story of How Gentiles Saved Jews in the Holocaust.* NY: HarperCollins, 1991.

Mitcham, Samuel W. Jr. *The Desert Fox in Normandy: Rommel's Defense of Fortress Europe.* NY: Praeger, 1997.

Morse, Arthur. *While Six Million Died: A Chronicle of American Apathy.* NY: Random House, 1967.

Nazi Conspiracy and Aggression, Vol. IV. DC: Government Printing Office, 1946.

Newton, Verne E., editor. *FDR and the Holocaust.* NY: St. Martin's Press, 1996.

Orlow, Dietrich. *The History of the Nazi Party.* Harpercrest, 1969.

——. *The History of the Nazi Party,* Vol. 2. PA: University of Pittsburgh Press, 1973.

Overy, Richard J. *War and Economy in the Third Reich.* Oxford: University Press, 1995.

——. *Why the Allies Won.* NY: W.W. Norton & Company, 1997.

——. *The Origins of the Second World War.* Longman Publishing Group, 1998.

Petropoulos, Jonathan. *Art as Politics in the Third Reich.* NC: University of North Carolina Press, 1996.

Richarz, William, et al, editors. *The 390th Bomb Group Anthology,* Vol. 1. AZ: 390th Memorial Museum Foundation. Inc.

Roy, Morris. *Behind Barbed Wire.* NY: Richard R. Smith, 1946.

Ryan, Cornelius. *The Longest Day.* NY: Touchstone Books, 1994.

Sainsbury, Keith. *Churchill and Roosevelt at War: The War They Fought and the Peace They Hoped to Make.* NY: New York University Press, 1994.

Shennan, Andrew. *De Gaulle.* MA: Addison-Wesley, 1993.

Spiegelman, Art. *Maus: A Survivor's Tale,* Vols. 1 and 2. NY: Pantheon Books, 1986, 1992.

Stephenson, Jill. *Nazi Organization of Women.* London: Barnes & Noble Books, 1980.

Stewart, Barbara McDonald. *United States Government Policy on Refugees from Nazism 1933–1940*. NY: Garland, 1982.

Taylor, A.J.P. *The Origins of the Second World War*. NY: Atheneum, 1961.

Taylor, Telford. *The Anatomy of the Nuremberg Trials*. NY: Little Brown & Co, 1993.

Trevor-Roper, Hugh. *The Last Days of Hitler*. University of Chicago Press, 1992.

——. *Trials of War Criminals*. DC: Government Printing Office, 1950.

Turner, Henry A. *German Big Business and the Rise of Hitler*. NY: Oxford University Press, 1985.

Tusa, Ann and John. *The Nuremberg Trial*. NY: McGraw-Hill, 1985.

United States. 79th Congress, first session, May 15, 1945. Senate Document No. 47: Report of the Committee requested by Gen. Dwight D. Eisenhower through the Chief of Staff. Gen. George C. Marshall to the Congress of the United States Relative to Atrocities and Other Conditions in Concentration Camps in Germany.

Vietor, John. *Time Out: American Airmen at Stalag Luft I*. Aero Pub., 1985.

Weinberg, Gerhard L. *The Foreign Policy of Hitler's Germany : Diplomatic Revolution in Europe 1933–36*, Vol. 2. NJ: Humanities Press, 1994.

——. *The Foreign Policy of Hitler's Germany: Starting World War II 1937–1939*, Vol. 2. NJ: Humanities Press, 1994.

——. *A World At Arms*. NY: Cambridge University Press, 1994.

Whiting, Charles. *The Hunt for Martin Bormann: The Truth*. NY: Combined Books, 1996.

——. *Massacre At Malmédy*. NY: Combined Books, 1996.

——. *Werewolf: The Story of the Nazi Resistance Movement 1944–1945*. NY: Combined Books, 1996.

Wiesenthal, Simon. *Justice Not Vengeance*. NY: Grove, 1990.

——. *The Murderers Among Us: The Simon Wiesenthal Memoirs*. NY: McGraw-Hill, 1967.

Wistrich, Robert S. *Who's Who in Nazi Germany*. NY: Routledge, 1995.

Wright, Mike. *What They Didn't Teach You About World War II*. CA: Presidio Press, 1998.

Wyman, David S. *The Abandonment Of The Jews*. New Press, 1998.

Yahil, Leni. *The Holocaust: The Fate of European Jewry, 1932–1945*. NY: Oxford University Press, 1991.

Index

H

N

Q-R

X-Z

About the Author

Mitchell Bard is the executive director of the nonprofit American-Israeli Cooperative Enterprise (AICE) and a foreign-policy analyst who lectures frequently on U.S. Middle East policy. Dr. Bard is a member of the United Jewish Appeal Speakers Bureau. For three years he was the editor of the *Near East Report*, the American Israel Public Affairs Committee's (AIPAC) weekly newsletter on U.S. Middle East policy.

Prior to working at AIPAC, Dr. Bard was a postdoctoral fellow at the University of California at Irvine, where he collaborated on a book examining the politics behind the rescue of Ethiopian Jews. He also served as a senior analyst in the polling division of the 1988 Bush campaign.

Dr. Bard's work has appeared in academic journals, magazines, and major newspapers. Recent articles include profiles of William Kristol, editor of *The Standard*, for *B'nai B'rith Jewish Monthly*; Pulitzer-prize winning columnist Charles Krauthammer and Ambassador Stuart Eizenstat for *Lifestyles*; Librarian of Congress James Billington for *The World & I*; and *Washington Post* reporter Bob Woodward and sportswriter John Feinstein for *Writer's Digest*.

He is the author of *The Water's Edge and Beyond: Defining the Limits to Domestic Influence on U.S. Middle East Policy; Partners for Change: How U.S.-Israel Cooperation Can Benefit America; U.S.-Israel Relations: Looking to the Year 2000;* and coauthor of *Myths and Facts: A Concise Record of the Arab-Israeli Conflict.* His most recent works are *Forgotten Victims: The Abandonment of Americans in Hitler's Camps,* and *Building Bridges: Lessons for America from Novel Israeli Approaches to Promote Coexistence.*

Bard holds a Ph.D. in political science from UCLA and a master's degree in public policy from Berkeley. He received his B.A. in economics from the University of California at Santa Barbara. He lives in Maryland with his wife Marcela and sons Ariel and Daniel.